To my NAFUSA colleague
Steve Easton, with professional respect
and best personal regards —

John E. Clark

The Fall of the Duke of Duval

A Prosecutor's Journal

By

John E. Clark

EAKIN PRESS 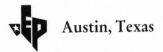 Austin, Texas

To Carolyn
"True love is a durable fire."
— Sir Walter Raleigh

FIRST EDITION

Published in the United States of America
By Eakin Press
An Imprint of Sunbelt Media, Inc.
P.O. Drawer 90159   ★   Austin, TX 78709-0159

2   3   4   5   6   7   8   9

ISBN 1-57168-049-7

Library of Congress Cataloging-in-Publication Data

Clark, John E., 1933–
    The fall of the Duke of Duval : a prosecutor's journal / by John E. Clark.
        p.   cm.
    Includes index.
    ISBN 1-57168-049-7
    1. Parr, George Berham, d. 1975 — Trials, litigation, etc. 2. Trials (tax evasion) — Texas — Duval County.   I. Parr, George Berham, d. 1975.
    KF224.P39C55   1996
    345.73'0233--dc20
    [347.305233]   95-40801
                                                                          CIP

Contents

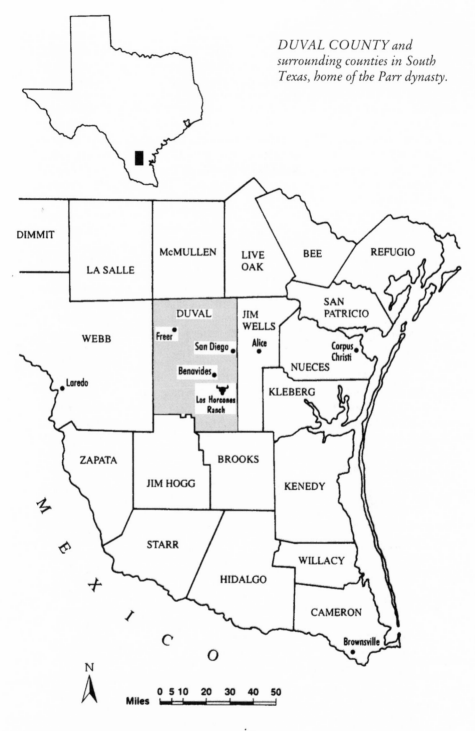

DUVAL COUNTY and surrounding counties in South Texas, home of the Parr dynasty.

DIMMIT

LA SALLE

McMULLEN

LIVE OAK

BEE

REFUGIO

SAN PATRICIO

WEBB

DUVAL

JIM WELLS

Freer

San Diego

Alice

Corpus Christi

Benavides

NUECES

Laredo

Los Horcones Ranch

KLEBERG

ZAPATA

BROOKS

JIM HOGG

KENEDY

M E X I C O

STARR

WILLACY

HIDALGO

CAMERON

Brownsville

N

0 5 10   20   30   40   50

Miles

Foreword

One of the greatest ironies in this true story of the collapse of the infamous Parr empire is the belief its rulers professed to hold about the genesis of the investigation that brought it down. From the start, George Parr and his henchmen insisted that the investigation was politically inspired. They had to put up with this kind of harassment every time the Republicans controlled the White House, they said (ignoring the fact that George was prosecuted for income tax evasion in 1934, during FDR's first term). This latest investigation, they told anyone who would listen, was just like all the others that preceded it: a calculated, partisan effort by a vengeful Republican president who had ordered the Internal Revenue Service and the Department of Justice to ruin them. The investigation had been inevitable, they said, once Richard Nixon won the 1968 presidential election.

The truth, though, as John Clark documents in these pages, is that the investigation resulted from sheer happenstance. The consequences that flowed from that improbable beginning are, if anything, even more intriguing for that reason.

I first met John Clark early in the fall of 1969, when both of us reported to Washington to join the Justice Department's Criminal Division. Assistant Attorney General Will Wilson had given me the assignment of forming and heading the Government Operations Section. In that volatile era of social and political unrest I was to oversee the enforcement of federal criminal laws governing three sensitive subjects: selective service, pornography, and election fraud and campaign contributions. Clark became a member of the section and was assigned to the enforcement of election fraud and campaign finance laws. His performance in that role over the next two years led me to invite him to return with me to San Antonio in August

1971, when I was appointed U.S. attorney for the Western District of Texas. There, John served as first assistant U.S. attorney for more than three years, until my appointment to the United States District Court.

Although we were unaware of it at the time, events occurring in Austin in the autumn of 1971, near the time when we arrived in San Antonio, would soon involve us in a monumental struggle to penetrate the cocoon of secrecy in which the Parrs had wrapped Duval County to conceal from the outside world their abuse of that rural fiefdom.

Wherever it finds a breeding ground, corruption weakens and ultimately rots the fabric of every human endeavor it touches. Where corruption gains a foothold in government it undermines and, if not rooted out, destroys the very foundation upon which our system of representative self-government is built. When elected officials corruptly serve private masters — and themselves — to the detriment of those who entrust them with public office, the democratic process is made a mockery and democracy dies.

Perhaps nowhere else in Texas did the forces of corruption ever rule so completely and so long as in luckless Duval County. There, the domination continued for decades, from generation to generation, while those who profited from the system grew ever more powerful and ever more arrogant in their defilement of the public trust, and ordinary citizens resigned themselves to their inability to change things for the better. As democracy shriveled and died in Duval County a feudal system took its place, with first Archie Parr and later his son, George, as lord of the manor.

Duval County seems at first glance a doubtful setting for an exploitative political dynasty to acquire wealth and power. Its population has always been small and predominantly poor. The arid landscape is inhospitable to most vegetation except mesquite and cactus without the addition of copious quantities of water, a scarce commodity. But Archie Parr saw the county's potential as his own political stronghold early in this century when the shotgun murder of John Cleary, the county tax collector and Democratic Party chairman, gave him the opportunity to take control of both the party and the county. Over the next two decades Archie became the first Duke of Duval, creating a ruthlessly effective political machine and a personal economic empire. Archie made county government his private domain and its public treasury his own bank account.

George, succeeding his father as the second Duke, refined Archie's system, tightening his political grip and creating still more public entities with treasuries full of tax revenue, much of it paid by absentee landowners such as oil and utility companies, to loot. George's legendary ability to control the votes cast and the returns reported in every election in the county extended his political influence far beyond Duval's modest borders to the highest levels of government in Austin and the District of Columbia.

When IRS District Director Bob Phinney invited me to Austin in January 1972, to discuss the results of an Austin architect's income tax audit, John Clark accompanied me. By the time the meeting ended, the Sessions and Clark Duval Expedition was about to begin. In May, with the appearance of the first witness before a grand jury in San Antonio, the investigation was under way in earnest. Many months would go by, many witnesses would testify, and much would be learned about Duval County and its rulers by the time it ended.

The investigation had its comical aspects, to be sure, but in a larger sense it exposed a tragic and outrageous state of affairs that had existed for sixty years in twentieth-century Texas. It was clear that the population and resources of an entire county had been subverted through corruption for decades to the personal exploitation of one powerful man — the Duke of Duval — and the handful of accomplices through whom he ruled.

The Fifth Amendment to the Constitution of the United States is best known for its guarantee that no person shall be compelled in any criminal case to be a witness against himself. We are seldom reminded, however, that the Fifth Amendment begins with the promise that "No person shall be held to answer for a capital, or otherwise infamous crime, *unless on a presentment or indictment of a Grand Jury.*" Too few of us, lawyers included, have ever pondered the significance of that guarantee. Those twenty-four words call into play the grand jury system — a citizen arm of the judicial branch of government, charged with the responsibility of determining whether there is "probable cause" to accuse someone of a serious crime. Its beginnings can be traced back to the signing of Magna Charta at Runnymede in 1215. Today it is part of our constitutional system of checks and balances, designed to protect us all from misuse of the prosecutive power of the executive branch.

For many years the grand jury as an institution of both state and federal governments has been under attack from some quarters as anachronistic and unnecessary. Most of the advocates of abolishing grand juries begin with the argument that they are mere "rubber stamps" for the prosecution and serve no useful purpose. Even those who would feel comfortable giving prosecutors the sole, unbridled authority to initiate felony criminal charges, however, should realize that the grand jury's other historic function, the investigation of suspected crimes, is irreplaceable and nondelegable. The successful investigation of many sophisticated, complex, well-concealed crimes can be accomplished only through the powers of the grand jury, backed up by the enforcement authority of a court. These awesome powers are best exercised as they are today, by grand juries comprising a cross-section of the community. They are too important to be delegated to anyone else.

Without the investigative powers of the federal grand jury in San Antonio and its members' collective commitment to learn the truth about people and events in Duval County, our investigation could not have succeeded. The twenty-three people who assembled for the first time on May 9, 1972, to hear the first of many witnesses were no rubber stamps. They quickly developed a sense of what they wanted to know and never wavered in their determination to find it out. In their long journey of discovery with Clark and me and the indefatigable agents of the Internal Revenue Service, each obstacle we encountered, from willfully forgetful witnesses and perjured testimony to destroyed records, only strengthened their resolve. Their successful search for the truth that could help make Duval County free was in the finest tradition of the grand jury system. It is a story every American can stand up and cheer.

WILLIAM S. SESSIONS
Former Chief United States District Judge and
Former Director, Federal Bureau of Investigation

Preface

George Parr inherited from his father in the 1930s a political empire founded on feudalistic concepts and sustained for the previous two decades by corruption and violence. Over the next twenty years — an era stained by the murders of political dissidents and by a brazen election theft that changed the course of American history — George accumulated power until he ruled as absolutely as any monarch.

A short-lived resistance movement challenged his authority briefly in the early 1950s when combat veterans returning home after liberating Europe and Asia in World War II had the audacity to think Duval County should be free as well. Parr's excesses in crushing that political uprising, coupled with the fetid stench of corruption that hung persistently over the Duval County Courthouse, led to criminal investigations in the 1950s that threatened his very liberty. In the end, Parr sustained a few battle scars but preserved his liberty and his empire for another twenty years into the mid-1970s. He did it by maintaining discipline in the ranks of his followers, calling in political chits in high places, besting his enemies in appellate courts, and outlasting the naive reformers who aspired to change things in a land where most people either weren't interested in reform or believed the effort was futile.

After the dust settled in the 1950s the Duke of Duval reigned with the same iron grip as before over the county he still owned, until another criminal investigation, this one triggered by chance and blessed by fate, began in 1972.

When the investigation became the province of a federal grand jury in San Antonio, George Parr placed one obstacle after another in the grand jury's path, just as he and his father before him had done for decades whenever they were threatened by investigations

ix

they couldn't control. The Duke engaged the federal forces in a prolonged game of wits in which the grand jury's power to seize evidence and compel testimony was matched against his power to conceal evidence and control witnesses. The investigation broadened to include Parr's key confederates and moved to Corpus Christi; federal prosecutions ensued and the state of Texas followed with prosecutions of its own. This time, the empire crumbled.

Only rarely does testimony before a federal grand jury become public. The testimony recorded in this grand jury investigation did, however, in the course of six federal prosecutions for income tax offenses and two for perjury; scores of state prosecutions for related offenses in the nature of misappropriation of public funds, public property, and the services of public employees; and the impeachment and conviction of a state judge. Those public disclosures have allowed me to draw freely from grand jury transcripts in telling the story of the investigation from the inside, as I lived it.

Acknowledgments

The real heroes of this story are the federal grand jurors and the Internal Revenue Service agents about whom I have written in this book. The wily Duke of Duval used every trick at his command to stall this investigation and keep it from uncovering the truth, but the grand jurors never lost confidence in themselves or in us, and their resolve to see it through never wavered. The IRS agents confronted deceit, obstructionism, and hostility at every turn in Duval County. They responded with determination, ingenuity, and dedication to the successful completion of the task at hand.

In eight years as a federal prosecutor, I never worked with a more professional or a more capable team of investigators than those whose names appear in these pages. The four with whom I worked most closely — I. A. Filer, Jerry Culver, Ed Watts, and the late Charlie Volz — proved to be the finest I've ever known.

William S. Sessions, the U.S. attorney for the Western District of Texas from 1971 through 1974, deserves great credit for his leadership in the entire effort. By participating personally in the investigation and in two of the trials that followed, he conveyed to Department of Justice and IRS officials, grand jurors, investigators, assistant U.S. attorneys, trial jurors, and judges the importance the U.S. attorney himself attached to removing the yoke of corruption that had oppressed Duval County for sixty years. Ray Jahn, another of Sessions' assistants in San Antonio, contributed substantially to the success of the grand jury investigation. Ed McDonough, George Kelt, and John Smith, assistant U.S. attorneys for the Southern District of Texas at the time, distinguished themselves in some of the most important trials to result from the investigation.

Those who urged me for years to put this colorful chapter of Texas history in writing spoke in many voices, but all sounded a similar theme: It's too important a story to be left untold. The prosecutors and investigative agents who fought these battles with me gave freely of their time, not only to ensure the accuracy of the events described but also to help me gather records, notes, photographs, correspondence, and memorabilia to make the story complete. My former secretary, Audrey Pridgen, who provided outstanding logistical support throughout the investigative and trial stages, later guided me to the recovery of historical records in the federal archives. Dan Moody, Jr., graciously made available Governor Moody's litigation file on the infamous Box 13 election theft. Pamela Findlay combined contagious enthusiasm with patient mentoring in her role as my personal editor until her untimely death. My colleague in the practice of law, the late John W. Goode, Jr. — who fought a few battles of his own for causes he believed in — thought it important that I write this book and never let me forget it. Most of all, though, it was the loving encouragement and unflagging support of my wife, Carolyn, that brought about the completion of the manuscript, and to her I shall always be grateful.

Chapter 1

Manhunt

What other dungeon is so dark as one's own heart! What jailer so inexorable as one's self!

— Nathaniel Hawthorne

April 1, 1975 — 10:30 A.M.
Corpus Christi International Airport

THE THREE MEN BOARDING the DPS helicopter had spent a long Tuesday morning waiting for the fog to lift so they could get on with their mission. All three were law enforcement officers: FBI Special Agent Ruben Martinez, of Corpus Christi; Maj. Kent Odom, commander of the Texas Department of Public Safety's Corpus Christi District; and Lt. Weldon Elliott, a DPS helicopter pilot from nearby Portland. Odom and Elliott were in uniform. All three men were armed.

Thick fog had covered the South Texas coastal plain at daybreak, making driving risky and low-altitude flying impossible. Unable to get under way at first light, as planned, they had waited impatiently for the fog to burn away. By midmorning the South Texas sun won out, and at 10:30, with its rotary wings *whop-whop-whopping* the thinning mist, the helicopter lifted off. A few hundred feet off the ground Elliott swung the craft's nose around in a smooth, banked arc. The flat, green cotton and milo fields of Nueces County began slipping away beneath them as they headed west toward the rolling brush country of Duval County.

Elliott, Odom, and the helicopter were the state's contribution to a multi-agency manhunt for a federal fugitive. The state's enthusiasm for intergovernmental cooperation was enhanced by the iden-

1

tity of the fugitive: seventy-four-year-old George Parr, the legendary political boss of Duval County. Parr's name was synonymous with the most notorious stolen election in American history, the 1948 "Box 13" fraud that put Lyndon Johnson in the United States Senate by eighty-seven votes. Parr had fascinated and frustrated law enforcement officials from Austin to the District of Columbia for forty years. There were few law enforcement officers in Texas — and probably no politicians — who didn't know his name and his reputation.

Before vanishing the previous afternoon, Parr had armed himself with a semiautomatic rifle and a .45-caliber pistol, with plenty of ammunition for both. Moreover, his emotional stability was suspect. The circumstances of Parr's disappearance suggested strongly that he intended to use the guns to avoid going to prison.

While Martinez, Odom, and Elliott had waited, fogbound, at the airport, four FBI agents and three deputy U.S. marshals departed Corpus Christi in automobiles to grope their way through the fog to Duval County. Three of the FBI agents were scheduled to rendezvous with the helicopter at a site outside the town of Benavides, near Parr's ranch. All of the officers were armed.

The April Fool's Day manhunt was triggered by Parr's failure to show up for a required appearance in federal court on the afternoon of March 31. Nearly a year earlier, U.S. District Judge Owen Cox, of Corpus Christi, had sentenced Parr to prison after a jury found him guilty of income tax evasion. Cox allowed Parr to remain free on a $75,000 cash bond posted by another colorful Duval Countian, Clinton Manges, while Parr's lawyers appealed the conviction. On Monday, March 24, 1975, Parr's luck ran out: The New Orleans-based U.S. Court of Appeals for the Fifth Circuit affirmed his conviction, and Parr was a giant step closer to a federal prison cell.

Parr still had the right to ask the U.S. Supreme Court to review his case, but that was a slim hope at best. Unlike the intermediate-level Court of Appeals, which is required to review a defendant's conviction on request, the Supreme Court's jurisdiction is discretionary. It receives thousands of applications — petitions for writ of certiorari — every year, but grants only the relative handful it perceives as presenting issues of unusual significance. The Supreme Court had negated a prison sentence for Parr and a gaggle of his cronies in 1960 by reversing their convictions for mail fraud, but the chances of Parr's current conviction being reviewed by the high court were essentially nil. Although he didn't practice law for a living, Parr was a lawyer. Both he and his defense team knew the Fifth Circuit almost certainly would have the last word this time.

The federal grand jury investigation that resulted in Parr's indictment was conducted in the Western District of Texas, the district in which his tax returns were filed. Once Parr was indicted, however, he exercised his statutory right to be tried in his home district, the Southern District of Texas. I had been the assistant U.S. attorney principally in charge of the grand jury investigation in San Antonio; when the case was moved to Corpus Christi for trial, I became a member of a three-attorney team to prepare and present the government's case to a jury in Judge Cox's court. The other two were assistant U.S. attorneys for the Southern District of Texas: Ed McDonough, who headed the criminal division of that office and later served as U.S. attorney, and George Kelt, a former IRS agent turned prosecutor.

Although Parr's appeal was being handled by highly competent lawyers, we were confident the Fifth Circuit would affirm the conviction. The case against him was solid, and the trial was free of the kinds of procedural and substantive mistakes that lead to reversals on appeal.

But even though we expected the conviction to be affirmed, all of us doubted that Parr would go quietly to prison when his appeals were exhausted. He was wealthy; he was still powerful; he spoke Spanish like a native of Mexico; and he lived less than a hundred miles from the Mexican border. We had long thought he might make a run for it, perhaps as soon as the Fifth Circuit ruled on his appeal. Lately, our concern had been heightened by reports from Duval County that Parr was becoming increasingly belligerent and unpredictable. We knew he had an extensive gun collection in his fortress-like Mediterranean villa in San Diego, the county seat. We began to fear that if he really was becoming unstable he might decide, instead of fleeing the country, to hole up at home with his own private arsenal and shoot it out with whoever was sent to take him into custody.

Parr had spent a few months in federal prison nearly forty years earlier, and he was said to have vowed never to be taken there again. After his current conviction, though, he told a reporter he wasn't worried about the possibility of returning. "I've been before," he told Spencer Pearson of the *Corpus Christi Times*. "You know, it's just like a kid. You put him in jail one time and he's scared to death. The next time, he says, 'I'll take my lunch with me because I know what's going to happen.'"

Because we thought the folklore about Parr's earlier vow reflected his true feelings about going back to prison, we anticipated having to move quickly to get him in custody when the Court of Appeals affirmed his conviction.

McDonough arranged for the court clerk in New Orleans to call immediately when the court announced its decision. Upon getting the good news from the clerk, McDonough called me in San Antonio. "We've got to revoke George's bond and get him in custody," McDonough said. "He's been saying he's going to kill the Carrillos, and he shot at somebody in San Diego the other day. When he finds out he's lost the appeal, he'll probably either boogie to Mexico or lock himself in that big old house of his and tell us to come and get him."

The IRS agents who helped develop the case against Parr were confident they could obtain affidavits about his recent behavior that would convince Judge Cox that Parr was dangerous to himself and others. McDonough assigned George Kelt to prepare a motion to revoke Parr's bond.

A convicted defendant who is permitted to remain free on bail while appealing to the intermediate-level federal circuit court can also be allowed to remain at liberty after losing that appellate round, while he petitions the U.S. Supreme Court to review his conviction. But freedom on bail while appeals are pending is a privilege, not a right, and the trial court can revoke bail at any time to prevent a defendant from fleeing, or from endangering himself or others.

Friday afternoon, March 28, 1975
United States Courthouse, Corpus Christi

George Kelt filed the government's motion with the clerk of the court and delivered a copy to Judge Cox's office. IRS Special Agents I. A. Filer, Jerry Culver, and Buddy Adams had obtained the accompanying affidavits of five Duval County residents documenting Parr's oral threats to kill his former political ally, County Commissioner Ramiro Carrillo, and reporting also that Parr was carrying a concealed weapon. Three more affidavits, these by Texas Rangers, told of Parr's threats to other persons at gunpoint. All eight affidavits were submitted to Judge Cox with the government's motion to revoke Parr's cash bond and hold him in custody while he pursued any further appeals. Kelt sent a copy of the motion to Parr's San Diego attorney and longtime associate, Nago Alaniz, as required by federal procedural rules. It was no surprise to Alaniz, however; news that IRS agents and Texas Rangers were gathering affidavits about Parr's recent activities had reached Parr before the interviews were concluded, and he and Alaniz both guessed the significance of the government's actions.

Monday, March 31, 1975 — 8:30 A.M.
United States Courthouse, Corpus Christi

After reading the government's motion and affidavits, Judge Cox signed an order reciting that the United States attorney had made "a showing sufficient to cause this Court to believe that Defendant George B. Parr may pose a danger to other persons and to the community in which he lives, [and] that . . . George B. Parr should be brought before this Court for a hearing on such matter."

Cox's written order commanded the United States marshal to "produce instanter before this Court George B. Parr, and to keep him in custody until the matter of the revocation of his present bond is determined." Cox concluded by ordering "that George B. Parr be required to appear at a show-cause hearing as to whether his appeal bond should be continued," and scheduled the hearing for 4:00 that afternoon. Given a copy of the order to serve on Alaniz, Deputy U.S. Marshal Laurence Allen Wenzel was able to perform his duty almost immediately; Alaniz was in the federal courthouse that morning on other business, and he had a copy of the order in his hands before 9:00 A.M.

Alaniz quickly sought out Judge Cox and urged him to give Parr a chance to turn himself in without being summarily arrested by the marshal. Cox consented and orally modified the order: Parr would be allowed to comply by showing up in court on his own at 4:00 that afternoon.

Alaniz immediately called Parr and arranged to meet him at noon at the office of Douglas Tinker, the Corpus Christi lawyer who had been lead counsel for Parr in the tax evasion trial. Tinker and Alaniz, planning their strategy for the show-cause hearing, thought it might help to have some character witnesses on hand. Alaniz put out the word to the faithful to assemble in the courtroom at the appointed hour. The news that Parr had been ordered to report to Judge Cox that afternoon spread with astonishing speed, by telephone and by word of mouth, to every corner of Duval County. It also made the *Corpus Christi Times*, the afternoon newspaper on which Duval and other rural counties in the area depended for news in print.

March 31, 1975 — 12:05 P.M.
Corpus Christi

Parr arrived at Tinker's law office. Although he held no public office, he was driven there from his San Diego home as a matter of course by a Duval County deputy sheriff, Rene Martinez. Alaniz, Tinker, and Parr talked for about an hour, discussing how to combat the government's case, while Martinez thumbed through magazines in Tinker's waiting room. As Parr walked out of the office, Tinker reminded him not to be late.

"Don't you worry," Parr replied. "I'll be there."

The deputy sheriff and the most powerful man in South Texas drove away in the deputy's Cadillac. Before leaving Corpus Christi, Parr had Martinez stop at an H.E.B. grocery store. Martinez tagged along while Parr bought orange juice, bananas, and cantaloupes. Back on the highway to San Diego, they were flagged down for a roadside visit by an old friend of Parr's, LULAC Executive Director Tony Bonilla. Continuing their journey a few minutes later, they were rear-ended on State Highway 44 near Robstown when Martinez slowed his car to allow the motorist in front of him to turn left. No one was injured, and Martinez's car was not damaged. After a brief delay the two men drove on to San Diego.

As they entered the town, Parr directed Martinez to stop at Nago Alaniz's law office. Parr got out of the car, walked briskly into the office, and returned shortly, appearing agitated. In his hand was a black, semiautomatic .45-caliber pistol. Alaniz kept other pistols in his office, between the books on the shelves of his law library, gun handles sticking out for ready access in an emergency, but this .45 was different. George Parr had given it to him. Alaniz kept it in his desk, and Parr knew exactly where it was. Parr resumed his seat in the car and told Martinez to take him home. As they drove, Parr talked with increasing animation, waving the pistol in Martinez's direction. Alarmed by his passenger's demeanor and disconcerted by having to look into the muzzle of the .45, Martinez asked Parr, "Do you want to kill me with it?" Parr put down the gun and grew quieter, telling Martinez he "would rather die at the ranch than die in jail." When Martinez pulled into Parr's driveway, the Duke exited the car and dismissed the deputy. "You go on home, now," he told Martinez. "You'll find me in the morning."

Martinez, an eighth-grade dropout who had been one of Parr's faithful minions for thirty years, gave a written statement later to investigating Texas Ranger Gene Powell. Parr never said he was going to kill himself that day, Martinez told Powell, "but I knew what he meant."

March 31, 1975 — 2:00 P.M.
San Diego, Texas

By Martinez's estimate, he dropped Parr at home between 2:00 and 3:00 P.M. on that Monday. Riddled with worry about Parr's intentions, though, the deputy couldn't quite bring himself to carry out the Duke's instructions to go home. Minutes after driving away he turned his car around and drove anxiously back to the big house. Disregarding any order from Parr was out of character for Martinez, but "it rang a bell, everything that was going on," he testified later. "George and the Carrillos and everybody was in a feud there as to political deals, and it worried me he would hurt somebody." At Parr's house, Martinez's fears were confirmed when Parr's wife, Eva, told him that Parr had just left with a rifle. She said he "laughed real loud and said they wouldn't take him to jail, and that he was probably going to hurt somebody," Martinez recalled.

Distressed, but unsure how to head off the disaster he knew was coming, Martinez headed for the Duval County Courthouse. On the way there he spotted his boss, Sheriff Raul Serna, arriving at Nago Alaniz's law office, and Martinez pulled in to report. Alaniz had called Serna a few minutes earlier, upon learning from his secretary that Parr had taken the black .45. Acutely worried about his client's intentions, Alaniz also called the U.S. marshal and the FBI.

After a hurried discussion at Alaniz's office, Serna mustered his deputies and sent them off to find Parr.

Wilma Villegas was a lifelong resident of Benavides (population a little under 2,000), the third largest town in Duval County, fifteen miles south of San Diego. She was also a friend of the Carrillo family, longtime political allies of convenience with the Parrs. The Carrillos had seen their power in the county grow, with George's blessing, until they were true partners in the power structure, second only to the Parrs in political prominence and influence. The Carrillo family included Oscar, a former state representative; O. P., the local district judge; and Ramiro, a county commissioner. The patriarch of the family was their father, shrewd old D. C. Chapa, president of the board of directors of the Duval County Conservation and Reclamation District — a grandly named governmental entity that had nothing to do with conserving or reclaiming anything.

The alliance between the Parrs and the Carrillos had begun to come apart in 1974, when it became apparent that George's problems with the federal government weren't going to go away. And as the unbelievable — that George Parr might go to prison — became believable, even probable, the Carrillos began preparing for their own succession to his power. The effect on Parr was predictable: He was outraged. "Don't raise crows," George railed. "They'll grow up and peck your eyes out."

By March 1975, the county was no longer big enough for both families, and a High Noon showdown was building. District Judge O. P. Carrillo removed County Judge Archer Parr, George's nephew, from office after Archer's conviction in San Antonio for lying to the grand jury that investigated George. Archer defiantly formed a rival commissioners court while George vented his rage in death threats against first one of the Carrillos and then another, meanwhile accusing Clinton Manges of maneuvering behind the scene to seize power for himself. Dedicated political partisans lined up nervously behind their posturing chiefs while the rest of the populace, like saloon patrons watching two gunslingers face off, tried to look neutral and stay out of the way.

March 31, 1975 — 3:30 P.M.
Benavides, Texas

On the afternoon of March 31 Wilma Villegas stopped in front of Oscar Carrillo's house to pick up her sister, who was visiting the family. She first saw George Parr a little before 3:30, driving past Oscar Carrillo's house. That surprised her; like so many others in gossip-loving Duval County that day, Mrs. Villegas had heard the news that Parr was supposed to be in a Corpus Christi courtroom at 4:00 P.M., and Corpus Christi was more than an hour away. While sitting behind the wheel of her car, she testified later, she observed him at close range, "passing by real slow, and mumbling something."

Mrs. Villegas was alarmed by the anger she saw in Parr's red face. "I had seen him mad, but I had never seen him that mad," she said. As soon as Parr turned the corner, she scurried to the front door of the house to warn Oscar and her sister not to come out. Carrillo took her advice and remained inside the glass-enclosed front porch, peering anxiously up and down the street, while Mrs. Villegas and her sister returned to the car. The two women watched as Parr drove slowly about the quiet streets, turning corners and circling blocks, disappearing behind an intervening house or one of the few, small commercial buildings, then emerging again.

Parr interrupted his curious excursion by pulling into the town's Texaco service station to buy gasoline. Attendant David Leal pumped $8.40 worth into the big Chrysler Imperial's tank to fill it. Parr didn't want the windshield wiped or the oil checked; when the pump clicked off he paid in cash and left without comment, still unaware that he had attracted the attention of Mrs. Villegas and her sister.

Because the terrain was flat and few other cars were on the streets, the two women were able to keep Parr in sight from their parked car in front of Oscar Carrillo's house. When they saw Parr drive away from the service station, they decided to follow him. They trailed him first to D. C. Chapa's house, where he slowed his car to a crawl and peered intently at the old man's residence. When no one appeared, Parr retraced his route to Benavides and the Texaco station and then turned in the direction of Oscar Carrillo's house again.

At that point Mrs. Villegas demonstrated an investigative agent's instinct for surveillance operations. Aware that Parr knew her, she told her sister, "Let's go change cars, because he might recognize us and he might know we've been following him." After making a quick switch the two sisters spotted Parr again. This time he was "going straight, like he was going to the ranch," Mrs. Villegas reported. (By "the ranch," Mrs. Villegas was referring to Los Horcones, the 14,000-acre ranch a few miles south of Benavides that was owned by Hilda Parr, widow of George's brother, Atlee. Although Hilda owned the place and lived in the sprawling ranch house off the Benavides highway, the ranch was identified with George. The extent of his dominion over it, in fact, had been one of the keys to the government's tax evasion prosecution in Owen Cox's court.)

Still puzzled by Parr's behavior but having lost sight of his car, the two women decided to return to Oscar Carrillo's house. As they neared the residence they saw several county automobiles parked nearby; deputy sheriffs were gathering close to Oscar's house, Mrs. Villegas observed, "and then when we were going to stop, the deputies took off, and we followed the deputies." Realizing "something was going on, because the deputies were looking for Mr. Parr too," the women soon abandoned the chase and turned back to tell Oscar Carrillo everything they had seen.

March 31, 1975 — 4:00 P.M.
United States District Court, Corpus Christi

A crowd of Parr's friends and associates had gathered in the second-floor courtroom of Corpus Christi's federal courthouse to witness the drama to be played out that afternoon. These were the home folks, Parr's own. George was the boss, *El Patrón*, the man who ran everything and knew everything and had all the answers. Now he seemed to be up against a power greater than his own, and the people who had accepted him as their temporal lord and protector for so many years were confused and worried. In their experience, Parr didn't *have* problems; instead, he *caused* problems for anyone who crossed him.

Some of those present had been prepared by attorneys Tinker and Alaniz to make a little speech in Parr's behalf, to help convince Judge Cox not to revoke his bond. The crowd was a cross-section of Duval County; mostly male, it included ranchers, small-business owners, sheriff's deputies, elected officials, and assorted Parr loyalists from the payrolls of every governmental entity in the county.

Tight-fitting law enforcement uniforms mixed with the bleached khakis and faded jeans of men who spent their days working in the merciless South Texas sun, and the shiny, doubleknit slacks and occasional wide, polyester ties of courthouse officials and hangers-on. Some were genuinely fond of Parr; some were opportunists who joined his team for personal gain; and some were simply afraid to say no to anything that was asked of them in Parr's name.

A couple of minutes after 4:00 the subdued buzz of conversation was interrupted by three sharp raps from the back side of the judge's door to the courtroom, behind the bench. Judge Cox was announced by the bailiff in a loud voice. The judge strode purposefully into the room, took his seat, and looked expectantly at the lawyers before him.

At sixty-five, Owen Cox was in his fifth year on the federal bench. He was born in Missouri, educated at the University of Kansas, and moved to Texas to practice law. His unabashed Republicanism had made him a rarity among South Texas lawyers in the 1950s and 1960s. Most lawyers in the region were Democrats, because the party was dominant and all of the elected judges in whose courts they practiced were Democrats. Only a handful, like Cox, took leadership roles in the Republican Party and the perennially unsuccessful campaigns of its candidates as the party struggled to establish a political beachhead in hostile territory. In 1970 Cox became the first federal judge ever appointed from Corpus Christi when U.S. Senator John Tower recommended him for the job to President Richard Nixon.

Cox was tall and slender, a distinguished figure in his long, black judicial robe. His features were sharp, though not unfriendly, and his sparse gray hair was cropped close to his head in a bristling crewcut. His piercing blue eyes were framed by bifocals with dark plastic upper rims. Smile- and sun-wrinkles radiated from the corners of his eyes. Cox was soft-spoken and unfailingly courteous to lawyers and litigants who appeared before him, but he could be severe when his anger was aroused. As he surveyed the courtroom on this occasion, his expression was appropriately somber. Visible at the neck of his robe was Cox's sartorial trademark — a crisp, white shirt collar and a conservatively patterned, tie-it-yourself bow tie.

To Parr's anxious supporters, ill at ease in the hushed formality of a federal courtroom and uncertain about what they were going to be involved in, the stern-visaged judge looked like an avenging eagle ready to swoop down on his prey. Alaniz and Tinker, tense and apprehensive, took their seats at one of the two counsel tables inside the low rail that separates the spectators' benches from the trial arena. At the other counsel table a few feet away sat Assistant U.S. Attorney George Kelt, wearing his most serious courtroom face. A copy of the government's motion to revoke Parr's bail lay atop the manila file folder in front of him. The agents who had gathered the affidavits chronicling Parr's recent behavior were in the courthouse, prepared to testify. Kelt was ready for battle.

The clerk solemnly announced the case: "Criminal Action No. 73-C-141, United States of America versus George B. Parr."

Judge Cox leaned forward and began: "This court entered an order this morning that the Defendant, George B. Parr, appear and show cause, if any there may be, as to whether his appeal bond should be continued. And the hearing, as set by the court, was at four o'clock this afternoon of this date, the 31st day of March, 1975. Mr. Parr is not in the courtroom. Where may he be, either Mr. Tinker or Mr. Alaniz?"

Parr's attorneys were hesitant to answer the judge's question fully, in the hearing of the spectators. Tinker and Alaniz knew considerably more about the afternoon's events and the seriousness of the situation than did Parr's friends and neighbors in the courtroom, and the two lawyers weren't eager to disclose the facts except on a need-to-know basis. Nevertheless, because every lawyer is an officer of the court, they had a duty to answer truthfully.

Tinker got to his feet and spoke first, guardedly: "Your Honor, he was in my office between 12:30 and 1:30 today, I don't know exactly. And as he left the office, he said he would be here. And other than that, I don't know his whereabouts."

Judge Cox turned to Alaniz. "Mr. Alaniz, do you?"

Alaniz stood, shifted from one foot to the other, and chose his words carefully. "May it please the court, that is about the extent of what my knowledge is. In other words, I called and asked him to be here, that we would meet at Mr. Tinker's office, which is where we met. And then he said, 'What time am I scheduled in court?' and of course, Mr. Tinker showed him the order. And he said 'All right, I'll be there at four o'clock.'"

When Alaniz paused, Tinker spoke again. "Your honor, may we approach the bench just a moment?"

The judge nodded. Both defense lawyers came forward, as did

Assistant U.S. Attorney George Kelt, and all three pressed close to the front of the bench. Alice Morrison, Judge Cox's court reporter, stationed herself between the prosecution and the defense, steno-type machine at the ready, to record the conversation. The judge turned off the microphone that ordinarily amplified his voice for the benefit of everyone in the courtroom.

Tinker leaned forward anxiously and spoke in a near-whisper, as if there were a jury in the box, to ensure that the spectators could not hear him.

"Your Honor, I wanted to do this at the bench because there are a lot of people from Duval County here. We did receive a call, and Nago actually talked to his secretary, indicating that Mr. Parr had been back in Duval County, in San Diego. That was around one o'clock. We tried to call the marshal's office, and the recording machine was on, and we stated to please call us. And then we called the FBI to let them know, because of some things we learned, that maybe he won't be here, so they could make whatever effort, or they could be here to assure his presence. And there are some other things. I don't know whether the court wants this to go into the record or not, but there is something else."

Judge Cox instructed Tinker to continue. Tinker deferred to Alaniz for a firsthand account of the telephone conversations.

"Your Honor," Alaniz began nervously, "we conveyed this to the FBI immediately. My secretary told me that Mr. Parr had been in my office and picked up a gun that he had given to me previously. Now, she didn't know what to think about that. And we just mulled it over a minute or two and called the marshal's office, because I got to thinking, why would he pick up that gun in my office? He had given it to me, and he has a number of rifles and guns at his home. And that's why we called the FBI immediately, and we left a message for the marshal's office."

Tinker interrupted to correct his earlier estimate of time. It had been about 3:00, he said, not 1:00, when Alaniz's secretary called her boss at Tinker's office.

Alaniz had more to say about his client's recent behavior.

"Your Honor, he has been somewhat, I won't say despondent, but quite concerned about his wife, who has been quite ill. And I believe I speak for most of the people over there, that they will tell you that he has not been quite the same. Being perfectly candid with the court, I have been afraid that he might do away with his wife and his child. This I say in all sincerity, Your Honor."

Judge Cox disclosed that the U.S. marshal had notified him shortly before 4:00 P.M. that Parr might not show up for the hearing. Alaniz hastened to assure the judge that he and Tinker had done their best to find their client.

"Your Honor, we called the sheriff's office and the marshal's office and alerted them. We didn't know what could happen. He could hurt himself or hurt someone. Douglas and I talked about it, and we are officers of the court, and we are responsible and all, but —"

Judge Cox interrupted. "There's nothing that you-all could have done that you didn't do, as far as the court is concerned. I am not in any way trying to fault either Mr. Tinker or you, Mr. Alaniz. But I did want to state that I knew, maybe ten or fifteen minutes before four o'clock, that there was likely to be some problem about it. And I have directed the marshals to go get him, and if the FBI is needed, for them to go along, and to get him and bring him in. And I am going to recess until five o'clock, and if he's here by then, we'll go ahead. If he is not, I am going to recess until nine o'clock in the morning, and during this period of time, the FBI and the marshals are going to be hunting for him."

"I think that's appropriate, Your Honor," Tinker said, "and I appreciate you delaying it as long as you have. Would you announce the delay until five o'clock in open court? We have witnesses who were going to be here and —"

Alaniz jumped in to express his and Tinker's concern about the consequences of disclosing to anyone else the information they had felt obligated to reveal to law enforcement authorities and the judge. "We have some character witnesses here," he said, indicating the crowd in the courtroom, "and if it got out that we related all this information, it could be that some of his friends might not like it, you know."

The lawyers returned to their seats at the counsel tables, and the court reporter resumed her regular station. Judge Cox turned on his microphone again.

"The court is going to recess this hearing, which was supposed to start at four P.M., and we will again come on the bench at five o'clock this afternoon. Whatever the court decides will be at that time."

March 31, 1975 — 5:00 P.M.
United States District Court, Corpus Christi

When 5:00 P.M. arrived, Judge Cox waited in his chambers a few extra minutes. At eight minutes past the hour, satisfied that Parr was not going to show up, he resumed the bench.

"The court again calls Criminal Action No. 73-C-141, the United States of America versus George B. Parr. Mr. Parr does not appear to be in the courtroom at this time. Mr. Tinker, has he appeared at the courthouse since the last —"

"I have not seen him and have had no contact with him."

"Have you seen him, Mr. Alaniz?"

"No, Your Honor."

George Kelt rose to address the court. "Your Honor, at this time the government would request a bond forfeiture and that a bench warrant be issued for the arrest of Mr. Parr, and that he be held without bond pending the disposition of his appeal."

Tinker was on his feet again, asking Judge Cox to wait until tomorrow. "I feel like there must be some explanation for his absence," he told the judge. "I would request that you wait, and give us this evening, and the marshals this evening, to find him."

Alaniz added his own plea for more time. "I think Your Honor knows, this is so unlike Mr. Parr, Your Honor, there's got to be some sort of an explanation."

Judge Cox had anticipated their reaction. "I appreciate what you have said, Mr. Tinker, and also Mr. Alaniz," he told the two lawyers, "but before I came out I gave this matter some considerable thought. And I came out here intending, if he was not present, to forfeit his bond, and I am going to order the forfeiture of his bond. And because he knew of the court's order, his violation of it alone is sufficient for me to consider him subject to being taken into custody, and I now order and direct the issuance of a bench warrant for his arrest. I do not have to fix the amount of the bond at this time, and I'm not going to, but I am going to recess this hearing until two o'clock tomorrow afternoon. At that time, Mr. Parr will have an opportunity, if he shows up, to explain whatever he wishes to explain. I am not making any commitment, one way or the other, as to what will happen at the session tomorrow afternoon if he shows up."

"Your Honor, I sorta feel the only reason he won't show up is because he is dead or something," Alaniz said morosely. "That's how strongly I feel about it."

Cox's expression was unusually somber. "Well, of course, we don't know about that," he said softly.

The Corpus Christi FBI office had been thrust into a state of readiness in midafternoon when Nago Alaniz called to report that Parr had picked up Alaniz's pistol. Alaniz told the FBI at that time, "I don't know what's going on, but I feel obligated to tell you that Mr. Parr has a weapon, and I don't know what he's going to do. I don't know if he's going to appear in court or not."

Protecting federal judges is the responsibility of the United States Marshals Service, but George Parr was no ordinary defendant and this was no ordinary situation. A few minutes later FBI Agents Ruben Martinez, George Small, Frank Chidichimo, and John Newton were at the federal courthouse, armed, awaiting developments. Also present were three deputy U.S. marshals: George Wagner and Rudy Hardy, both of Houston, and Laurence Allen Wenzel, the senior deputy in Corpus Christi. U.S. Attorney Ed McDonough, Assistant U.S. Attorney George Kelt, and IRS Special Agents I. A. Filer and Jerry Culver had been at the courthouse since early afternoon, preparing for the bond revocation hearing.

Parr's failure to appear in court, coupled with the dramatic developments revealed by his lawyers to Judge Cox in the hushed bench conference and the judge's issuance of a warrant for Parr's arrest, immediately shifted the focus of attention back to Duval County. Within minutes after Cox declared a recess, the four FBI agents and three deputy marshals were on their way to Duval County in three government cars. McDonough, Kelt, and the IRS agents remained at the courthouse, ready to go forward with the hearing if Parr showed up. The hunt had begun in earnest.

March 31, 1975 — shortly after 5:00 P.M.
San Diego, Texas

Upon arriving in San Diego, FBI Agent Ruben Martinez spoke first with Nago Alaniz, then interviewed Eva Parr. Another FBI-deputy marshal team drove farther west to Freer to interview Clinton Manges and Parr's former helicopter pilot, James Dula. The third team headed for Benavides, where Parr had last been seen.

At the Parr home, Ruben Martinez questioned Eva about the events of the preceding few hours. "We asked about the weapon that he had, whether he had any ammunition and how much ammunition," Martinez said. "We wanted to make certain about the description of the vehicle, his clothing description, what type attitude he had when he left, and whether he made any direct statements to her about his intentions. Just general information that would be of benefit toward our investigation."

The limited information Eva was able to supply only increased their concern. Martinez knew already that Parr was carrying Nago Alaniz's .45. Having covered Duval County for several years for the FBI, he knew also that Parr owned an AR-15, the deadly assault rifle that had been the standard American infantry weapon since the Department of Defense adopted it for that purpose (as the M16) during the Vietnam War. Fast, powerful, and accurate, the AR-15 was designed specifically to kill men in combat. It can be fired automatically, and its high-velocity, 5.66mm ammunition is supplied in clips of twenty and thirty rounds. In the hands of a good shot, as Parr was, the AR-15 is a devastating weapon. Parr enjoyed shooting deer with it illegally, from a helicopter.

Eva confirmed that George had picked up a rifle, and she was able to show the officers the type of ammunition he had taken with him. Martinez recognized it as ammunition for the AR-15, "so we knew he had a very powerful weapon, and we knew he had that .45 semiautomatic weapon also." Martinez was satisfied after questioning Eva that her husband hadn't told her where he was going or what he intended to do.

Because the prosecutors and the IRS agents believed Parr might try to flee to Mexico, Martinez called the nearby border stations and gave U.S. Customs officials a description of Parr, the clothes he was wearing when he left home, and the Chrysler he was driving. Then Martinez left San Diego and drove south to Benavides. From Wilma Villegas, David Leal, and Oscar Carrillo he elicited details about Parr muttering, red-faced, in his drive-by inspections of the Carrillo residences, the late-afternoon fill-up of the dark blue Imperial at the Texaco station, and Parr's disappearance in the direction of the ranch he loved.

March 31, 1975 — 7:00 P.M.
A few miles south of Benavides, Texas

As evening approached, Duval County Sheriff Raul Serna stationed several deputies near the entrance to Los Horcones and detailed others to keep an eye on Oscar Carrillo's residence in Benavides. Deputy U.S. marshals staked out Parr's home in San Diego.

"We made a search of the area," Ruben Martinez explained, "and in our mind we were certain Mr. Parr was not still in Benavides. It was getting quite late in the evening. The impression we had was possibly that he was at his ranch."

Although nearly all the officers believed Parr was somewhere on the ranch, no one was eager to conduct a nighttime search for a heavily armed man on his own territory. "We were aware that Mr. Parr had a rifle, he had a .45 semiautomatic weapon, and we didn't feel we were in a position at this time to go looking for Mr. Parr on the ranch," Martinez testified later. "We decided we would wait until the following day."

Martinez asked Sheriff Serna who Parr might be willing to talk to if they found him alive, and which of his deputies was most familiar with Los Horcones. "You want Israel," Serna replied, identifying his chief deputy, Israel Saenz. "He'd talk to Israel or me, either one, but Israel knows the ranch best."

By 11:00 P.M., except for those on surveillance duty at Parr's house, all the federal officers had returned to Corpus Christi. Before leaving, however, Martinez had arranged for help from a sister law enforcement agency — the Texas Department of Public Safety — in the form of a helicopter and pilot, to be available at daybreak the next morning.

April 1, 1975 — 11:00 A.M.
South of Benavides, Texas

The DPS helicopter bearing Maj. Kent Odom, FBI Special Agent Martinez, and Lt. Weldon Elliott reached the western edge of Nueces County, continued across the southern leg of neighboring Jim Wells County, and entered the sagebrush duchy of Duval County, heading for a rendezvous point five miles south of Benavides on State Highway 339. Most of the fog had burned away. Deer hunkered under sparse cover as the aircraft passed over scrub-brush ranches at low altitude, its rotary wings flailing the air noisily; here and there, cattle glanced up to see what was causing the disturbance.

In a field across the highway from the entrance to Los Horcones a cluster of men, some in uniform, waited for the helicopter to appear. They were certain now that Parr was somewhere on the ranch, and they knew the aircraft was the key to finding him. Talking quietly among themselves were Sheriff Raul Serna and his chief deputy, Israel Saenz, along with several other deputies; Texas Ranger Gene Powell; IRS Special Agent Buddy Adams, of Corpus Christi; and other federal and local law enforcement officers who had been pressed into service in the search. Also on hand were two local reporters, Joe Coudert of the *Corpus Christi Caller* and Gary Garrison of Associated Press. Elliott set the helicopter down, and Saenz climbed in.

With Saenz aboard as a guide (and as a communicator if Parr were found alive), Elliott lifted off to begin the aerial search of the ranch. The rest of the men waited near the ranch gate, their two-way radios crackling occasionally with terse, static messages. Ruben Martinez, recalling the search later, testified that Saenz "was born and raised in that area, just like Mr. Parr, and was very familiar with it, and he thought of some areas that Mr. Parr had fond memories of, and we started going in those areas."

It took them about ten minutes to find Parr's automobile. In one of the "favorite spots" identified by Israel Saenz, an area known as the Julian Pasture in the southeast corner of the ranch, the sun glinted off the windshield of the big Chrysler. The car was parked in a fenced clearing, near a windmill and a concrete water tank. Mesquite trees lent a lacy, open shade to the periphery of the enclosure, which sat atop a low rise commanding a view of much of the ranch.

"We're going around," Elliott said. "Watch for the artillery."

All eyes were trained on the automobile, alert for any motion inside. Keeping a respectful distance, Elliott began circling.

FBI Special Agent Ruben Martinez described the scene later, in testimony before Judge Cox: "We circled the car, I would say, at least ten to twelve times. We were a little concerned about Mr. Parr having that AR-15 rifle and the fact that he might attempt to shoot down a helicopter. We got in close enough with the helicopter where we could see something on the front seat. We knew he had a brown shirt. We could see something brown laying on the front seat. I decided then we should put the helicopter down and I would go forward to investigate."

Elliott landed seventy-five yards away, still wary. Alighting from the helicopter alone, Martinez ducked into a half-crouch, trotted clear of the chopper's slowing blades, and took the safest route he could to the car, service revolver in hand. There was no movement.

Martinez described what he found: "I walked up to the car. The car engine was running. I went to the passenger's side, looked in, and I could see Mr. Parr slumped to his right side. There was a bullet hole to the right side of his head with an exit wound on the left side. I walked over, shut off the engine, went back to the helicopter to alert the other agents and the other county officials that we had found Mr. Parr and to give them some possible directions on how to locate us. On the front seat of the vehicle was the AR-15. In addition, about eight magazines of loaded ammunition. The .45 was on Mr. Parr's lap. One spent round was found on the floorboard, I believe, of the vehicle."

Parr's dentures were on the floor, also, dislodged by the impact of the .45 bullet that had slammed into his head. Martinez didn't see Parr's glasses. The AR-15 hadn't been fired.

April 1, 1975 — 11:25 A.M.
At the Los Horcones gate

The radio message to the officers waiting at the gate touched off a high-speed dash by a convoy of law enforcement cars. Trailing a billowing plume of white caliche dust, they bounced and twisted over nine miles of winding ranch roads to reach the pasture where Parr's car and the DPS helicopter sat, both engines silent. When a locked gate brought the column to a stop at the entrance to an intervening pasture, Sheriff Serna hurriedly broke the lock and the procession resumed its urgent pace. It was nearly noon when they arrived at the right place. Reporters Garrison and Coudert were allowed to go only as far as the last gate, ten yards short of the car, while law enforcement officers peered into and walked around Parr's vehicle.

IRS Agent Buddy Adams was in one of the first cars to reach the site. He recalled Parr as "just looking kind of peaceful," but he was nonetheless convinced that George "intended to take somebody with him" when he drove out to the ranch, "because of the way he'd been behaving, and because you don't need an AR-15 and all that ammunition just to shoot yourself." Texas Ranger Gene Powell gave the two newsmen an unofficial estimate that Parr had been dead at least three or four hours.

Justice of the Peace Luis Elizondo of Benavides, and San Diego mortician Mike Rios, Jr., were summoned to attend to the formalities. Elizondo inspected the scene so he could make an official report of the cause of death. Rios carefully covered Parr's body with a white sheet and wrapped it in a royal blue blanket as the sheriff's deputies removed it from the front seat of the car and placed it on a collapsible gurney. Silently, Sheriff Serna and his deputies loaded the gurney into the waiting hearse, secured it, and closed the rear door.

At 2:00 P.M., Tinker and Alaniz were back in Judge Cox's court to advise him officially what had happened. "I thought I knew the man," Alaniz told the judge. "I now know that I did."

George Berham Parr, second Duke of Duval, lay dead by his own hand. A long chain of events set in motion by sheer chance three years earlier, in Austin, had ended on a soft April morning in a South Texas cow pasture with the death not only of a man, but also of a political and economic empire unique in Texas history.

Chapter 2

The Dukedom

duke (dook, dyook) n. **1.** a nobleman with the highest
hereditary rank; especially, in Great Britain, a man of the
highest grade of the peerage. **2.** A prince who rules an
independent duchy.

IN RUNNING DUVAL COUNTY as if he owned it, George Parr
was merely managing his inheritance. Archer, George's father and
the original Duke of Duval, had owned the county first. Just like
European nobility, the father had instructed the son in the privileges
and responsibilities of the hereditary estate.

Archer ("Archie") Parr didn't invent the *patrón* system in
South Texas, but from the early 1900s until the mid-1930s he was
one of its most successful practitioners. His principal mentor in the
art was the regional godfather, James Wells, a ruthless Brownsville
lawyer whose power base was Cameron County in the lower Rio
Grande Valley. Other political bosses, contemporaries of Archie,
gained and held power in nearby counties: Rancher Manuel Guerra
ruled Starr County, while John Closner, first as sheriff and later as
county treasurer, kept Hidalgo County under his heel with the support and occasional intervention of Wells. A. Y. Baker had succeeded Closner.

These men, the "establishment" Democrats of their places and
times, maintained a loose but effective alliance for many years
against periodic incursions by "progressive" Democrats, Republicans of every stripe, angry governors, the Texas Rangers, and, occasionally, local dissidents who clung stubbornly to the dream of

22

someday throwing the rascals out. Besides their own counties — Duval, Cameron, Starr, and Hidalgo — Archie and his principal allies had a powerful influence on the politics of nearly every Texas county west and south of Corpus Christi.

As unlikely as it may seem in light of the state's political history since the New Deal era, Duval and other South Texas counties were hotly contested by both Republicans and reform Democrats from the late 1800s until the early 1920s. Nevertheless, the political machines so carefully constructed and so assiduously oiled by Parr, Wells, Guerra, Closner, and Baker enabled the bosses to mobilize their followers whenever it really mattered. During those years they managed to turn back nearly every challenge — political and legal — that threatened their control.

The South Texas formula for successful boss rule was simple and effective: (1) control the election of every local public official; (2) use local government to provide jobs and handouts for your friends and to punish your enemies; (3) help yourself to as much tax money as you wish.

These guiding principles have a couple of important corollaries. First, controlling elections may require intimidation, violence, bribery, fraud, forgery, and worse crimes, so it is not an activity for the squeamish. Second, the right to engage in graft should not be reserved solely to the boss; if key officeholders and other allies are given limited graft rights of their own, they will have a vested interest in perpetuating the system for the benefit of all participants.

South Texas machine politics as practiced by Parr and his friends embodied no novel ideas. Similar techniques had been employed before, notably by the big-city machines of the East and Midwest, to further similar objectives and with similar results. Like most of his urban counterparts, Archie Parr was far more concerned with profit than with ideology. The overriding goal of his machine was simply to endure.

By controlling local government and using its resources to provide financial benefits for the faithful, political bosses like Parr traditionally have ensured their political power, as well as their ability to go on lining their own pockets with public funds. One major advantage South Texas bosses have always enjoyed, however, is the insulation Texas counties enjoy against law enforcement from any outside source except the federal government.

That insulation is provided by the Texas Constitution, written in 1875, adopted the following year, and still the supreme law of the state. By decentralizing state government to ensure a weak executive branch, the post-Reconstruction authors of the Texas Constitution unwittingly created a fertile garden in which the weeds of local political bossism could sprout and flourish. Every potentially powerful office in the executive branch of Texas government is filled by election, independent of every other office, so there is no chain of command. The governor has no cabinet to carry out policies and programs. The only major political appointee in the executive branch is the secretary of state, whose primary functions are to administer the election laws and issue corporate charters. Moreover, every judicial office from justice of the peace to chief justice of the state's supreme court is an elected position. Although the Texas governor does fill some judicial vacancies by appointment, the appointments last only until the next general election.

In law enforcement, the weakness of the decentralized executive branch is especially noticeable and particularly easy to exploit. Decentralization makes every county an island in the Texas criminal justice stream. Because the state attorney general has no independent authority to act as a prosecutor, the power and discretion to enforce the law rests with locally elected prosecutors and judges, county by county. If local officials fail to enforce the law or, even worse, flout it themselves, the citizens of that county have no recourse to a higher authority.

The state attorney general can order the Texas Rangers to investigate crimes, but he has no authority to go into a county to prosecute anyone without a specific invitation from the locally elected district attorney. Therefore, a political boss who controls the elected officials in his home county is virtually immune from prosecution under the laws of Texas. So long as he violates no federal laws, he is free to do whatever his political machine is strong enough to let him get away with.

Thirteen years after the Republic of Texas joined the Union, the state legislature in 1858 drew the boundaries of Duval County on the South Texas map, naming it for two heroes of the Texian war for independence, Capt. Burr H. Duval and his brother, John C. As a disarmed prisoner of war, Burr Duval had the misfortune to be executed at Goliad on Santa Anna's orders in 1836, but his brother, one of the few escapees from that infamous Palm Sunday massacre, lived on to fight for the United States in the Mexican and Civil

Wars, to serve as a Texas Ranger, and to write a book about fellow Texas Ranger Bigfoot Wallace that was much admired by Texas historian J. Frank Dobie. The naming of the county for the gallant Duval brothers probably marked the first and last time reverence for law enforcement played any part in the county's history.

The few residents of the area didn't get around to actually organizing the new county until 1876, after sporadic Indian raids had ceased. In 1879 the railroad stretched westward through the arid grasslands from Corpus Christi to reach the county seat, San Diego. First sheep, then cattle, brought a measure of prosperity to the region and the railroad pushed on to Laredo, linking Duval County's ranchers and businessmen with the Mexican border to the west and the important Texas port of Corpus Christi to the east. Oil was discovered in the county in 1903, a year after Archer Parr's son George was born, but would not be an important factor in the county economy for two decades.

At the turn of the century most of Duval County's non-Hispanic ("Anglo") minority, mostly of English and European ancestry, was concentrated in San Diego, dominating business and politics. A two-party political system existed, complete with spirited competition within and between both parties, although the leaders and the candidates of both the Democrats and the Republicans were almost exclusively Anglos.

Most of Duval's much larger Hispanic population, desperately poor and speaking little or no English, was scattered across the county on ranches and farms and in a handful of tiny rural communities such as Realitos and Concepcion. Citizens of Mexican ancestry in early twentieth-century South Texas weren't known as "Hispanics" or "Mexican-Americans." They constituted more than ninety percent of the county's population, but regardless of their citizenship, and no matter how long they had lived north of the Rio Grande, they called themselves, and were called by others, "Mexicans." Thousands of these Texas citizens sweated their lives away for a bare existence, trapped in an anachronistic North American feudal system. On the South Texas ranches of Anglo landowners, Mexicans were little more than serfs.

With nothing but their physical labor to sell in a perpetual buyer's market, theirs was a struggle merely to survive. Participation in the rites of citizenship of this new country was, like its alien language, important to their masters but irrelevant to their own wretched lives. They thought of themselves simply as Mexicans, and when they went through the motions of voting it was because it was at least an implied condition of their employment, and they had no power to question it. On those occasions they were given poll tax receipts and taken to the polls, where their ballots were marked precisely as their *patróns* wished.

The most important political figure of Duval County's first quarter-century was an English immigrant who served in the Confederate army before locating in South Texas. James Luby, rancher, lawyer, and postmaster, served as Duval's first county judge. Initially a Democrat, Luby switched his allegiance to the GOP in 1884 and was appointed by President Chester A. Arthur to the powerful patronage post of U.S. customs collector for the Port of Brownsville. In 1886, returning from Brownsville to San Diego during Grover Cleveland's administration, the nimble Luby switched parties again and was reelected county judge, this time as a Democrat.

Among the Anglo newcomers to this rough-and-tumble, immature South Texas county in the early 1880s was young Archer Parr, the future Duke of Duval. His arrival was hardly noticed, but his stay would never be forgotten.

Archie Parr's beginnings were quite modest. Born on Christmas Day 1860 on Matagorda Island, fifty or so miles up the coast from Corpus Christi, the boy found hard work an early and constant companion. His father died when he was an infant and at age eleven Archie was already a school dropout, working to help support the family. Using the only marketable skill he had, he found work as a cowboy. At fourteen, young Archie was a respected ranch hand with the big Coleman-Fulton Pasture Company in nearby San Patricio County on the coastlands of the Gulf of Mexico. Later, he graduated to the bone-wearying, but better-paying, job of driving cattle from San Antonio to Abilene, Kansas, on the Chisholm Trail.

Upon arriving in Duval County, Archie hired on as foreman of the Lott and Nielson Pasture Company's Sweden Ranch, south of the new, almost entirely Hispanic, town of Benavides. In 1891 he married Elizabeth Allen, newly graduated from the state teacher's college at Huntsville. The hard-working and ambitious young man had saved enough money by that time to buy a modest spread of his own, and the couple settled in Benavides to raise cattle and six children. Of Archie and Elizabeth's three sons, Givens, George, and

Atlee, only George would inherit Archie's flair for politics. In the strong Mexican culture of the area, it would have been considered inappropriate for any of the three Parr daughters to show an interest in politics.

Archie became fluent in Spanish and demonstrated a respect for the Mexican culture that earned him a far greater measure of acceptance in the little community than most Anglos could ever hope to attain. As time passed and Archie matured, he came to be viewed as the *patrón* by his ranch hands and by most of the other Hispanics in the Benavides community. When Archie began to show an interest in local politics, he found an immediate reservoir of support among both Anglos and Hispanics.

Archie was elected county commissioner from the Benavides area in 1898 as a Democrat, and was reelected in 1900 with strong support from his pleased constituency. Politics and the role of *patrón* came naturally to him. He was usually pleasant, though occasionally short-tempered, and nearly always politically astute. Only a few years after getting into politics, Archie was an important man in the county.

In 1907 the assassination of the county's most powerful Democrat, Tax Collector John Cleary, gave Archie an opportunity to grab the reins of real power. Cleary's shotgun murder took place in the middle of the day in a San Diego restaurant. No one was ever tried for the crime, but the following day Texas Rangers arrested a prominent Republican, T. J. Lawson, as a suspect. Arrested with Lawson were his son, Jeff, and a former deputy sheriff, Candelario Saenz. Lawson was thought to have two possible motives for killing Cleary. It was known around town that Lawson and Cleary claimed competing interests in the Piedras Pintas, the first oil field in Duval County, because they had clashed in public over their business differences. But the two men were also political rivals, and in volatile Duval County, that alone might have been motive enough.

Regardless whether Lawson killed Cleary or whether he might have been driven by business or politics to do it, only Saenz was indicted by the grand jury. Saenz was not entirely luckless, though. Before he could be brought to trial, both of the prosecution's eyewitnesses died, apparently of natural causes, and the case against Saenz was dismissed.

Not a man to waste time worrying over unsolved murders, Archie Parr saw his chance to take over the entire county, and he acted. Cleary had encouraged Hispanics to become active in the party and even to seek the party's nominations — a radical idea at that time — recognizing that harnessing the strength of their numbers would allow the Democrats to overwhelm the GOP. Parr was sufficiently astute and sufficiently unprincipled to see county government and the county's large, mostly dirt-poor Hispanic population as perfect tools for building a personally profitable political empire. With absolute control over the men he allowed to hold office, Archie knew he would have total control over the county's contracts, its finances, and its treasury.

Under Archie's leadership Duval County became the provider of jobs, both real and imaginary, for the unemployed. Contracts were let for inflated prices, with payoffs for Archie figured in. County road and bridge crews swelled, at least on paper. Many on the county payroll were employees in name only, but Parr saw to it that all were paid, and that all were grateful. In return, each man was expected to have a poll tax receipt, the essential little document that qualified the holder to vote. There was never any doubt that anyone would vote as Archie wished.

Nevertheless, elections were too important to allow their outcomes to hinge on mere gratitude. As early as 1906, when the Democrats under Cleary's leadership swept every county office, Duval County Republicans had gone to court unsuccessfully with charges of election fraud. Under Archie's rule, nothing was left to chance. To ensure that the maximum number of voters were on the county's registration rolls, county employees were required to pay their poll taxes.

Parr himself, using money he stole from the county, paid hundreds of poll taxes in the names of others to inflate the number of votes at his disposal. As reminders of his power, he stationed armed deputy sheriffs at the polls to discourage independent-minded voting. Illiterate voters were given marked ballots to drop into the ballot box, or their ballots were marked for them by election officials. Failing all else, Parr simply directed election officials to alter the returns to reflect the results he wanted.

Archie Parr's political power had a three-cornered foundation. Paternalism was one part. A loyal subject down on his luck and in need of a little cash for groceries or doctor bills or funeral expenses could always count on Archie for help. The second base, corruption, went hand in hand with paternalism. Archie could well afford to be generous; he stole the money from the county and it required nothing more than a word from him to put anyone's name on the county payroll or to prompt the county treasurer to hand over without question cash or a check to anyone in any amount Archie directed. The third foundation stone underlying Archie's power was fear: His power depended on elections, and "voting right" was taken seriously once Archie sent the message that a particular race was important to him.

Election procedures in the county made a mockery of the secret ballot. Voting in Archie's day — and for many years thereafter — took place at the courthouse, where the voter was handed a numbered paper ballot and ushered to a bare table a few feet away, in full view of Archie's eagle-eyed election judge, to mark it. Even strong-minded voters felt naked as they sat, pencil in hand, considering whether voting contrary to *El Patrón's* wishes was worth the trouble that was sure to follow. Whether Archie was really responsible for the acts of retributive violence ascribed to him in local folklore didn't matter; his subjects believed he was capable of anything, and most of them behaved accordingly.

On a Saturday morning in May 1912, political infighting involving Parr erupted into a shootout that left three men dead on a San Diego sidewalk. Archie had proposed to incorporate the city of San Diego, mainly to create another tax-collecting government entity whose treasury he could loot. Strong opposition to the plan was led by C. M. Robinson, the county chairman of the Democratic Party, who viewed Archie's corrupt leadership as a potential liability for the party and therefore struggled with him for control. San Diego, home to most of the county's Anglos and Republicans, was not Archie's stronghold. Robinson's opposition to incorporation had split the Democrats, and feelings were running high.

A referendum on the incorporation issue was in progress that warm Saturday morning when Robinson and three other men encountered three Hispanic county officials who, as Parr loyalists, favored incorporation. Words passed between the two groups, arguments grew more heated, and suddenly there was gunfire. All three Hispanic officials were killed; their assailants were uninjured. Fearing a race riot would explode when the county's Hispanic population heard the news, Archie loaded his family on the train and transported them to safety in Corpus Christi, a little more than fifty miles east, then returned to urge Hispanic leaders to contain their rage and avoid further bloodshed. No charges were filed against Robinson, who was unarmed, but his three companions were arrested and charged with murder.

Archie's incorporation referendum failed that day, depriving him of another public treasury to pilfer, but he succeeded in averting a bloodbath when the county's Hispanic leaders took his advice. Grimly, they buried their dead and trudged home, reconciled to letting the law settle accounts for them. Archie's successful intervention headed off a bloody feud in which the county's Hispanics would doubtless have suffered terrible losses. His reputation among them as their friend and advocate, if not founded on that one incident, was greatly enhanced by it.

Presidential politics touched Duval County that same year when reform Democrats backing Woodrow Wilson blocked the seating of Parr's hand-picked anti-Wilson delegation at the state convention. Archie's disdain for reform was at least as fervid as the Wilsonites' disdain for corruption, but the Wilsonites had him outnumbered. After suffering the indignity of exclusion from the Democrats' national convention, Parr sought out a friendly judge back home in San Diego and retaliated with lawsuits that kept Robinson and his supporters off the primary election ballot and gave Archie control of the party. By the end of the year Parr's machine and the Democratic Party were indistinguishable. He was the undisputed political boss of all he surveyed.

Two years went by before the three defendants who had been charged with the 1912 killings in San Diego faced a jury. They were tried in Richmond, Texas, near Houston, after the court granted a change of venue to ensure a fair trial. All three were acquitted.

Being the political boss of a South Texas county required constant vigilance against the disruptive efforts of dissidents, even for those as strongly entrenched as Archie Parr and Manuel Guerra. Both were bedeviled from time to time by Ed Lasater, a wealthy rancher with extensive land holdings in Starr and Duval counties who also happened to be a Republican. Lasater worked doggedly against Parr and Guerra from 1906 to 1911, trying to convince the legislature to carve up several existing South Texas counties and create a new one that would include his sprawling ranch. Parr and Guerra were dead set against giving Lasater a chance to organize a new, Republican-dominated county on their borders.

For one thing, although he had never enjoyed much success in trying to beat them at their own games, Lasater was not above using some of Parr's and Guerra's own dirty tricks to manipulate elections. Furthermore, both Parr and Guerra realized that if Lasater's ranch were placed in a new county, they both would lose the right to tax his land and cattle.

When Lasater's persistence finally resulted in the creation of Brooks County in the 1911 legislative session, however, Archie decided there was something to be said for creating new counties. Taking a page from his adversary's book, Archie used his growing political clout to pull off a stunning political surprise in 1913, by getting a special legislative session to slice Duval County in two, from east to west, just a few miles south of San Diego. The maneuver was calculated to give him a second county to call his own, and Archie planned for Benavides, his home base, to become the county seat. Thus was Dunn County born, its name a tribute to the vanity of the legislator (Patrick F. Dunn) who carried the bill for Archie in the Texas House of Representatives.

Legal battles over the creation of Parr's second county began almost immediately and ended the following year with an adjudication that Representative Dunn's statute violated an obscure provision of the Texas Constitution. Thus was short-lived Dunn County laid to rest, with almost no one but Parr (and, presumably, Dunn) mourning its passing.

For Archie Parr there was both good news and bad news in 1914. The good news was his election to the state senate. The bad news was a serious investigation of corruption in Duval County government.

Archie saw the door to broader horizons of power open for him in 1914, when John Willacy, the longtime South Texas senator whose district included Duval County, decided to run for governor. With the help of his mentor and friend James Wells, Parr won the primary. The Republicans didn't waste their time or their money opposing him in November.

Despite his walk-in election to the senate in the fall, 1914 was a year full of trouble for Parr. His Republican nemesis Ed Lasater and the party-switching former county judge, James Luby, who most recently had been a Democrat, joined forces in another legal offensive that threatened not only Parr's power but also his personal liberty. Lasater and Luby, alleging that county officials were misusing public funds, went to court to demand an audit of Duval County's

accounts. It would be the first audit in more than a decade, even
though state law required one annually. Lasater imported a CPA
from Houston and put him to work in the courthouse, sifting
through the county's public records. By the time Parr's county commissioners realized the threat was serious and sought an injunction
to keep the accountant away from their records, it was too late; he
had already seen convincing evidence that Archie and his cronies
were stealing public funds.

Duval County was part of Judge W. B. Hopkins' district, and it
was he who had granted the injunctions in 1912 that froze C. M.
Robinson off the primary election ballot and solidified Archie's
control of the Democratic Party. But Hopkins didn't live in Duval
County, and this time he didn't feel compelled to do Parr's bidding.
After hearing Lasater's man testify about the irregularities he had
actually seen in the county's financial records, Hopkins refused to
enjoin him from completing the job he was hired to do.

This was a troubling setback for Parr's containment strategy,
and the county commissioners quickly appealed the decision; however, Judge Hopkins had proved to be unreliable, and the appellate
court in San Antonio couldn't be counted on to help. Archie decided it was safer to leave nothing to chance: In the early morning
hours of August 11, 1914, while the appeal was pending, the old
wooden Duval County Courthouse burned to the ground.

From Parr's standpoint it was a successful fire, destroying most
of the records that reflected his guilt and the guilt of the other county officials who were part of his team. Burning down the courthouse, though, is not to be undertaken lightly or often, and Archie
realized as well as anyone that it would not have been necessary if
Judge Hopkins had simply put an end to Ed Lasater's audacious investigation.

Archie had demonstrated earlier that he knew how to use the
legal system to his advantage. Now, however, he was dealing with a
district judge who suddenly seemed more interested in doing what
he thought was right than in doing what was best for Archie. One
way to solve that problem, Parr realized, was to get the legislature to
create a new judicial district for Duval County, and then to sway the
governor to appoint a more sympathetic judge. Being a state senator
would make that task much easier to accomplish, and when the legislature convened in January he would hold that high position.

Before Archie could take office, however, Judge Hopkins

caused more trouble for him by empaneling in December 1914 an independent grand jury. Previous Duval County grand juries had been selected with great care by grand jury commissioners stead-fastly loyal to the Parr machine. The politically reliable grand jurors they chose could be depended on not to indict the wrong persons, regardless of the facts. A majority of this new grand jury, though, was not burdened by loyalty to Parr. Relying on the limited records that survived the courthouse fire, the jurors shocked South Texas by indicting Parr and nearly a dozen other county officials for stealing money from the county.

In Austin, Senator Parr quickly succeeded in getting his new judicial district, complete with a new judge. The governor's appointee, Volney Taylor, was not Parr's first choice for the position, but he was acceptable. Parr was more concerned about the new district attorney, J. E. Leslie, but he need not have been. The prosecution's corruption case against all of the defendants was weak, because most of the county records had gone up in smoke, and the case against Parr was especially thin. After reviewing the evidence available to him, Leslie dismissed most of the charges against Parr. When the defendants sought a change of venue, Judge Taylor obliged by shifting the trial to Hidalgo County, in the heart of James Wells' friendly sphere of influence. Trial day was anticlimactic: Most of the state's witnesses simply failed to show up, and the remaining charges against all of the defendants were dismissed.

At that point, Ed Lasater realized that state law enforcement authorities had neither the tools nor the will to take on Parr, but Lasater wasn't ready to give up. Woodrow Wilson had cast himself as a reform Democrat in his successful 1912 election campaign, and Wilson's attorney general, Thomas Watt Gregory, was a Texan. In 1915 Lasater persuaded Gregory to let a federal grand jury look into the unresolved vote fraud allegations that had clouded the 1912 primary elections in Duval County. The grand jury met in Corpus Christi and found plenty of evidence of election fraud, but no evidence that it had affected any race for federal office. When the Department of Justice declined to take any further action, the first federal threat to Archie's power dissipated as quickly and as harmlessly as a spring thunderstorm.

Lasater was nothing if not persistent. When the county commissioners approved a $100,000 bond issue to replace the courthouse Parr had torched, Lasater found fatal legal defects in their plan and got an injunction to keep them from issuing the bonds. Undaunted, the commissioners built their new courthouse anyway, paying for it with warrants instead of bonds. The dissidents complained of fat overcharges and of kickbacks by the prime contractor, a friend of James Wells. Despite strong indications that they were correct, the dissidents were unable to prove their charges.

Archie's oldest son, Givens, was serving as Duval County judge in 1916 when Lasater and others asked Judge Volney Taylor to remove the county judge and all four county commissioners for misconduct in office. The suit charged the defendants with a multitude of improprieties, such as failing to have the county's books audited; failing to collect debts owed to the county by county officials; paying extra fees to county officials in addition to their salaries for performing their official duties; and using an insolvent bank as the county's depository. One of the more flagrant abuses revealed by the plaintiffs was the county's blatantly illegal payment of fees to Archie, a state senator at the time, for serving simultaneously as a county road supervisor. Taylor did suspend the commissioners temporarily, but he prudently left Givens Parr alone. The suit eventually died a quiet death and no one was removed from office.

Parr's survival instincts were put on full alert in 1917 by the impeachment and removal of Governor James Ferguson on charges that included perjury and misuse of public funds. Parr had been a strong Ferguson supporter and in return Ferguson had usually acceded to Parr's preferences when making patronage appointments that affected Duval County. Senator Archie stuck with the embattled governor to the end, voting against conviction on each of the twenty-one articles of impeachment. Only three other senators were so stalwart in Ferguson's defense.

When the smoke of the impeachment battle cleared from the senate floor, Governor Ferguson was out and the first-term lieutenant governor, William Hobby, was in. Hobby's strong suit was a reputation for honesty, a character trait that would earn him neither admiration nor friends in Duval County's ruling circle. Because it is the Texas lieutenant governor's statutory responsibility to preside over the state senate, Parr and the new governor already knew and disliked each other.

Hobby's antipathy toward Parr resulted in one of the fiercest political brawls of the decade when Parr sought reelection to the senate in 1918. Although the governor had his own battle to fight in the same primary, against the comeback effort of his disgraced predecessor, Jim Ferguson, he joined forces with reform-minded Democrats in South Texas to back D. W. Glasscock against Archie. James Wells backed his old friend Archie for the senate nomination, but supported Hobby for governor. The Hobby-Ferguson contest was one of the few elections ever to divide Parr and Wells, but neither man took it personally. (Another notable exception to the usual Parr-Wells unity occurred in the 1916 Democratic primary contest for the U.S. Senate nomination. Parr supported former governor Oscar Colquitt against the incumbent senator, Charles Culberson. Wells backed Culberson, giving him suspiciously large majorities over Colquitt in Cameron and Hidalgo counties. Colquitt ran poorly in some other South Texas counties, too, but in Duval County Archie arranged for him to trounce Culberson by a margin of 802 to 1.)

The forces arrayed against Archie in his 1918 renomination bid were formidable. They included Governor Hobby, the most powerful leaders of the state Democratic Party, local reformers scattered throughout the senatorial district, and the Hobby-controlled Texas Rangers. A new factor in the election was the women's vote. The cause of women's suffrage was on the march in 1918; the Nineteenth Amendment was nearing ratification by enough states to make it part of the U.S. Constitution, and many states had already amended their own laws in anticipation of its eventual success. Texas had joined the movement halfheartedly: Women would be allowed to vote in primary elections only, beginning in 1918. Parr and his backers were worried about the women's vote; their political instincts told them that Archie's repeated anti-prohibition votes in the senate, his defiant support of Jim Ferguson, and the worsening stench of corruption emanating from Duval County would not sit well with this new segment of the electorate.

Wells did his corrupt best for Parr in the southern part of the district, but Hobby, the Rangers, the women's vote, and the Ferguson stigma were too much even for Wells to overcome, and Glasscock carried Cameron County by 500 votes. With all except Duval County's results reported, it appeared Glasscock had won; he was 1,200 votes ahead of Archie, and Duval County had fewer than 1,000 eligible voters. Glasscock supporters were understandably thunderstruck, therefore, when Duval County reported 1,303 votes for Parr and 23 for Glasscock, giving Parr the nomination by 118 votes.

Political warfare split the party and erupted into rival district conventions, each sending its own slate of delegates to the Democratic state convention. Hobby had defeated Ferguson soundly, and Hobby's supporters were in control of the state convention. The credentials committee seated the Glasscock delegation, and the convention certified Glasscock as the party's nominee for Parr's senate seat.

Once again Archie was back in court, this time to contest his loss of the nomination, and once again fortune smiled on him while the legal system was manipulated for his benefit. Some cynical horse-trading behind closed doors resulted in a swap between Judge Volney Taylor and a jurist from a neighboring district, Judge R. G. Chambliss, to benefit both Parr and Chambliss.

Judge Chambliss happened to be the plaintiff in a similar lawsuit, having lost his own bid for renomination that year. Like Archie, he needed a sympathetic forum in which he could win back what he had lost at the ballot box, and so it had been arranged: Judge Chambliss would preside at the trial of Archie's case in James Wells' backyard, Hidalgo County, and Judge Taylor would preside at the trial of Chambliss' case in San Patricio County. The cards were stacked against Glasscock in any event, but to make matters worse, the attorney representing him also represented Judge Chambliss' opponent in the San Patricio County suit. Few observers were surprised that the winners of the two lawsuits were Archie Parr and Judge Chambliss.

The struggle for Parr's senate seat continued into the fall, as Glasscock's supporters waged a write-in campaign for him in the general election. Governor Hobby, assured of his own election, continued the battle against Archie by mobilizing the Rangers to help Glasscock again. On the governor's orders the Rangers supported Glasscock openly, and on election day their mere presence intimidated many Hispanic voters and election officials at polling places where Parr expected to roll up huge votes from controlled Hispanic populations. When it was all over Archie had won, but not by much. In Duval County, where the 1,300 votes cast in the primary had exceeded the number of eligible voters by nearly 400, only a little more than 200 votes were cast in the general election.

When Archie went to Austin in January 1919 to take the oath of office, he found Glasscock blocking the way again. The Texas Senate is the final judge of the qualifications of its members, and

Glasscock was there to contest Parr's right to be seated. The full senate, excluding Archie, sat for a month as the Committee on Elections and Privileges to hear evidence on the conduct (or, more accurately, the misconduct) of the November election. By the time the hearing was over, the senate had heard evidence of blatant, wholesale election fraud in the counties controlled by Parr and his supporters. Voting by ineligible people had been commonplace; illiterate voters were illegally "assisted" by overly helpful Parr election officials in marking their ballots; and Archie's election judges had thrown out hundreds of Glasscock ballots for spurious reasons. The evidence showed that the election was everything that had come to be associated with Duval County elections: It was rotten to the core.

Unfortunately for Glasscock, the testimony revealed that his supporters had done some cheating, too, and that in some areas the Glasscock campaign had exploited the poor and illiterate Hispanic voters almost as shamelessly as Parr's. In the eyes of many senators those revelations leveled the playing field and gave them an excuse to support the man who was already their colleague, even though the sins of the Glasscock campaign were much less extensive and generally less outrageous than the highly organized election fraud orchestrated by Parr. When the two contestants' attorneys finished presenting the evidence, and all the senators had made their final speeches for the record, the senate voted 16 to 14 to seat Senator Parr again.

Among the many witnesses who testified during the senate's lengthy investigation was James Wells. Responding to suggestions that he was a ruthless political boss who delivered controlled votes, Wells told the senate modestly, "If I exercise any influence among [Hispanic voters], it's because in the forty-one years I have lived among them I have tried to so conduct myself as to show them that I was their friend and they could trust me." Years later Archie's son and successor, George, was fond of saying in response to similar charges, "I don't have influence; I just have friends."

Four years later Archie squeaked by again, and he continued to win, largely on the strength of manufactured majorities from Duval County.

By the early 1920s many of those who had hoped and struggled for decent government in Duval began to leave, seeing no realistic possibility of breaking Parr's stranglehold on the county. It was clear that Archie could stay in control as long as he chose, and his legendary ability to produce lopsided margins for any candidate he favored had made him a powerful figure in state Democratic politics as well. A pilgrimage to San Diego became obligatory for any Democrat seeking statewide office who hoped to reap the bountiful vote harvest Archie could produce.

Archie's sons were a diverse trio. Givens, the oldest, was educated at Yale. He served as county judge twice, but only because Archie needed him there at the time, not because he coveted a political career. His real interest was in business and finance. Atlee, the youngest, made it plain to his father at an early age that he had no interest in college or in politics. He wanted only to be a rancher. George, the middle son, bounced fitfully from one college to another for several years without accomplishing anything. In 1922 he married a Corpus Christi girl and former high school classmate, Thelma Duckworth, and was admitted to the University of Texas School of Law. Although he never acquired a law degree, he did pass the state bar examination. When Givens decided in 1926 to resign as county judge to take a seat on the Dallas Cotton Exchange, Archie called George home from Corpus Christi, where he was selling real estate, to take Givens' place as the titular head of Duval County government.

Although George had displayed no particular talent for anything in his first twenty-five years, it was soon apparent that he was going to be the right man to succeed his father as the Duke of Duval. George had grown up in the world of politics, often serving as Archie's driver as the senator made his rounds and kept his political fences mended. As the aging senator gradually transferred increasing authority to the young county judge, it seemed an entirely natural order of things, a seamless transition of power and position from father to son.

George was careful to do nothing in the process to unsettle the Old Party, as Archie's political machine was known. In time his steady, self-assured performance won the confidence and respect both of its leaders and its followers. Without a power struggle, George progressed from being Archie's right hand to being *de facto* chief executive, while Archie relaxed by degrees into the role of sovereign emeritus.

But while he transferred operational control over county government to George, Archie hung on to his senate seat until 1934. The Duke, then seventy-three, was beginning to show his age as the primary campaign got under way, and James Neal, a lawyer from

Laredo, was no token opponent. And then there were the problems both Archie and George had been having with the Internal Revenue Service — highly visible problems that gave Neal a big stick to use against Archie, at least in the other counties in the district.

The IRS problems had to do with kickbacks, traditionally required of outsiders who wanted to do business with the county. This covert practice popped into public view in 1932, when a federal grand jury indicted young George for income tax violations after he neglected to report and pay taxes on a $25,000 payoff from highway contractor W. L. Pearson of Houston. The following year the government filed a civil tax suit against Archie, alleging that he, too, had accepted money from Pearson and failed to report it. The $25,000 George received was a substantial sum by anyone's standard in depression-wracked South Texas; Archie's take was four times as much, reflecting the market value of his residual power in Duval County and his seniority in the state senate.

George was able to delay the day of reckoning on his criminal charges for two years before pleading guilty in May 1934. Under his plea bargain agreement with the government, George resigned as county judge and received a two-year suspended sentence, with supervised probation on conditions that required him to be a law-abiding citizen. He also paid a $5,000 fine.

The government's civil suit against Archie became an albatross around the old politician's neck in the senate campaign. Here at last were specific charges of corruption, spelled out in black and white and filed in federal court by a Democratic administration's United States attorney, for all the world to see. There was no hiding this wart from the press or from Archie's political enemies. Neal trumpeted the government's allegations from one end of the district to the other as proof of the Duke's corruption. George's criminal conviction for taking a payoff from the same contractor lent credibility to Neal's charge.

In earlier campaigns Archie had turned to James Wells for help when the going got tough. But by 1934 Wells was dead, and the growing influx of sun-seeking snowbirds from the predominantly Republican Midwest into the Rio Grande Valley had eroded his old machine's ability to deliver the overwhelming numbers Archie needed in Cameron and Hidalgo counties. Duval County's population was still almost exclusively homegrown, and Archie's Old Party did about as well as usual for him there, but it wasn't enough.

Neal won the election, Archie retired from active politics, and George, still in control though not in public office, became the unquestioned boss in the county. The transition was complete. George was the new Duke.

The 1934 election also gave George a grudge to nurse against the Kleberg family, owners of the enormous King Ranch in neighboring Kleberg County. Searching for a popular issue to save his election, Archie wanted to champion the construction of a new trans-South Texas highway to speed travel between the cities of the lower Rio Grande Valley and Corpus Christi, but the only feasible route lay across the King Ranch.

Archie had long enjoyed cordial relations with the Klebergs; as a state senator he had been responsive to their needs, and as a fellow rancher — although on a vastly more modest scale — he understood their love for the land that comprised their historic empire. Archie and Robert Kleberg, the head of the family, if not friends were at least friendly. Now the old Duke and his son came calling, badly needing a favor, asking Kleberg to consent to a state highway across the ranch he loved.

Robert Kleberg was torn between his political instincts and his rancher's heart. He sensed what was at stake and agonized over the decision, reluctant to make enemies of the Parrs, but unwilling to allow his family's beloved ranch to be invaded and divided by a busy concrete river of commerce. In the end he declined Archie's request, but he worried about the political consequences.

A combination of factors, not the least of which was the exposure of his own corruption, brought about Archie's defeat that year, but George blamed his father's loss on Kleberg's refusal to accommodate them on the highway proposal. He vowed to get even. Ten years later George was to have an opportunity to settle that score and one of his own with Robert Kleberg's son, Congressman Richard Kleberg.

George's reign as the new Duke was interrupted in 1936, only days before his two-year federal probation term would have ended, when the United States attorney moved to revoke his bond and send him off to prison for an assortment of probation violations. The roster of charges included physically assaulting State Representative J. T. Canales of Brownsville at the Duval County Courthouse; fraudulently altering and recording an oil and gas lease to defraud the lessee; owning a majority interest in a company that distributed liquor illegally; taking payoffs from gamblers who operated in the county; and failing to report regularly to his probation officer. On June 3, 1936, U.S. District Judge Robert J. McMillan revoked his probation and remanded him to the custody of the attorney general to serve his two-year sentence. George spent the next ten months in the federal correctional institution at El Reno, Oklahoma.

So strong was the machine Archie had created, though, and so strong was the new Duke's control, that George's temporary absence made no difference. When he was paroled in April 1937, the young Duke resumed the throne as if nothing had happened.

Chapter 3

Box 13

As long as I count the votes, what are you going to do about it?
— William Marcy Tweed (Boss Tweed)

GEORGE PARR'S 1934 TAX fraud conviction resulted in the automatic forfeiture of his right to vote and to hold public office, but that was a largely theoretical inconvenience for him. He had shown little enthusiasm for holding office anyway ("A political office-holder is nothing but an office boy," George once said), and with the power he continued to accrue from his father, he controlled every aspect of voting in the county. No election judge in Duval County would have refused him a ballot or reported his illegal vote. Indeed, without George Parr's approval no election judge held that insider's position of trust and received the election-day compensation that went with it.

But other legal disqualifications associated with his federal felony conviction may have vexed him more. As a convicted felon, Parr was barred by federal law from doing two things that were important to him: using firearms and owning federally insured banks. George had an extensive gun collection and a great fondness for shooting the deer that abounded on the ranches in the area. He was accustomed to exercising his royal prerogative to shoot game anywhere and anytime he pleased, regardless of hunting seasons, property lines, or county lines.

George's tendency to ignore boundaries when shooting deer

Box 13   43

lasted a lifetime. A member of a prominent South Texas ranching family saw the Duke in action at close range many years later:

> I was on our ranch, which is well inside of Webb County, and I saw a helicopter flying low and I heard shots, and then the helicopter landed not far from me, but I don't think the two guys in it ever saw me. When I started over toward them, I could see they had landed to pick up a deer they had shot, and that made me mad, because they were on my ranch. So I was going to go over and find out what the hell they thought they were doing shooting deer on my ranch. But when I got closer I could see it was George Parr, and I could see the arsenal he had in that helicopter, and I decided right then that if George Parr wanted to shoot a deer on my ranch, that was all right with me.

Parr's conviction didn't actually deter him from shooting deer, because he viewed the risk of detection and prosecution as minimal, but so long as he remained a felon he was committing another federal violation every time he handled a firearm.

More important, though, federal bank regulators took seriously the federal laws that bar convicted felons from controlling federally insured banks. With millions of dollars of tax revenue at his disposal, Parr needed absolute control over banks to put the money in. The few banks that existed in rural South Texas counties were power centers for both business and political interests. With tight control of a small bank, Parr could staff it from the board of directors to the janitor's closet with unquestioning loyalists who would do exactly what they were told to do and keep their mouths shut.

Huge amounts of tax revenue could be deposited month after month, year after year, in accounts that paid no interest, enabling the bank to earn handsome profits for Parr at the taxpayers' expense; funds in any amount could be withdrawn from those accounts at Parr's whim, for whatever personal or political purpose pleased him, and nothing would be said. Control of banks was essential to his system. With tax money to be stolen, profits to be made, friends to reward, enemies to punish, and a political machine to sustain, George Parr would have to resort to bank ownership by subterfuge, and that could be risky. The federal law enforcement establishment had already demonstrated once to George that it was no respecter of his power and would enforce the law against him if violations came to its attention.

The legal stigma of a federal felony conviction can be removed only by the president of the United States, as an act of executive clemency. In 1943, after nine years of legal disability and disenfranchisement, George applied for a presidential pardon and the restoration of all his rights of citizenship.

Because the decision to grant or refuse a pardon is entirely discretionary with the president, applicants for those important and politically sensitive favors often prevail on influential friends — especially public officeholders of the president's own political party — to endorse their requests, in hopes of improving their chance of success. The Parrs had never been particularly close to their congressional representative, the King Ranch's Richard Kleberg, but they had coexisted more or less cordially with the Klebergs for years and had usually supported "Mr. Dick" in his campaigns.

Their peaceful relationship with Dick Kleberg was in large part a reflection of Archie's longstanding compatibility with the congressman's father, Robert Kleberg, which ended in disappointment only when Robert refused to help salvage Archie's 1934 reelection campaign. George had bitterly resented Robert Kleberg's decision not to acquiesce in Archie's highway plan. Overlooking the serious problems Archie had created for himself with his indictable lapses of ethics, George Parr still blamed Kleberg for Archie's loss that year.

Although George had taken no direct action in response to Kleberg's snub, he had neither forgiven the Klebergs nor forgotten the incident. Now it was his turn to seek help from the same family; he needed Congressman Dick Kleberg's active endorsement of his pardon application, and finally, reluctantly, he brought himself to ask for it. Knowing his Duval County neighbor for what he was, though, Kleberg declined to lend his name in George's behalf.

How important Congressman Kleberg's views on the subject were to Franklin Roosevelt is questionable, but Roosevelt denied the pardon. George was furious. Correctly or not, he believed he had lost because of Kleberg, and he was determined to make him pay for his treachery. The old slight to Archie had been hard for George to take, but this latest betrayal was even more intensely personal. It was insult added to injury, salt in an old wound that had never healed.

After pondering an appropriate revenge, George made one of his characteristically canny decisions. He would settle accounts in the way he knew best: politically. Thus when Dick Kleberg ran again

Box 13   45

for Congress in 1944, he learned the price of offending his powerful neighbor. To repay the Klebergs, father and son, for humiliating first Archie and then him, George picked a war hero to challenge Dick Kleberg in the Democratic primary.

Former state representative John E. Lyle, Jr., had been elected to the legislature with Parr's help before the war. In 1944, when George needed him again, he was an officer in the United States Army, on active duty in Europe. Lyle's military record was unexceptional, and he could do nothing to campaign for public office in wartime from an overseas duty station, but he *was* one of "Our Boys in Uniform," and that, together with the Duke's backing, was enough to defeat even a popular incumbent. Lyle outpolled Kleberg by a lopsided margin in the Democratic primary, which in one-party Texas was the only election that mattered. The general election in November was a mere formality.

When Congress reconvened in January, John Lyle took the oath of office, and Parr quickly applied again to the president for a pardon. He left nothing to chance this time, securing the backing of not only his appropriately grateful new congressman but also a *Who's Who* of state government officials, all good Democrats. An impressive packet of letters from important Texans arrived at the White House in January 1945, assuring Roosevelt, just elected to his fourth term, that George Parr was a great American and a civic benefactor who deserved to have his lost citizenship rights restored.

The writers included almost all of the state's most powerful officeholders: the lieutenant governor, John Lee Smith; the attorney general, Grover Sellers; the treasurer, Jesse James; the comptroller of public accounts, George H. Sheppard; the commissioner of the General Land Office, Bascom Giles; the chairman of the Railroad Commission, Olin Culberson; the state superintendent of education, L. A. Wood; the chairman of the Highway Commission, Brady Gentry; the chairman of the Board of Control, Weaver H. Baker; two state senators, James A. Stanford of Austin and Rogers Kelly of Edinburg; and the secretary of the state senate, Bob Barker, who addressed the president as "Dear Franklin." One of the few important people in state government who did not endorse George's application was the governor, Coke Stevenson.

Whether out of cynicism or naiveté, most of these public officials made glowing representations about the civic contributions of both George and his father, Archie. In a masterpiece of understatement, Lieutenant Governor Smith told the president that Parr, during the seven years since his sentence terminated, had been "very active in the business and civic affairs of his native Duval County and generally over South Texas."

State Board of Control Chairman Weaver Baker, whose ignorance of South Texas history seems to have been matched by his ignorance of Texas geography, assured Roosevelt that "Judge Parr and his distinguished Father and other members of the family, have rendered a service to the people of the Lower Rio Grande Valley, unequalled by that of any other family, and by reason of such humanitarian service, Judge Parr is entitled to a full measure of consideration that he may again render, unimpaired, his full duty as a citizen."

Senator Rogers Kelly, representing Archie Parr's old district, said George had led "an exemplary life" since his sentence terminated in 1938. Senate Secretary Bob Barker told "Dear Franklin" about Archie's twenty years of service "with honor" in the Texas Senate. "My good friend, George," Barker wrote, "has been very busy attending to his private business in South Texas, but he always finds the necessary time to devote to the best interests of his town, county, state and nation."

The most florid praise of all, though, came from Land Commissioner Bascom Giles, who proclaimed his "abiding faith in the honor and integrity of Mr. Parr, whose conscientious efforts to demean himself as an honorable and upright citizen, worthy of the trust that is placed in him by his fellow men, who know him best, have been noted and have impressed me with their sincerity." The commissioner went on to express his belief that the "conduct, demeanor and habits of thought of Mr. Parr are those of an honest, patriotic and upright citizen." (A few years later, in one of the most notorious public corruption cases ever to rock state government in Texas, Bascom Giles would be convicted of embezzling millions of dollars in his administration of the postwar Texas Veteran's Land Act.)

These endorsements created a display of political power no Democrat who might someday need to carry Texas in a national election could ignore, and Congressman Lyle diligently shepherded his VIP constituent's application through the bureaucratic maze to the president's desk. By the time it got there, Roosevelt was dead. The man who had taken his place behind the desk was Harry Truman.

Box 13   47

On February 20, 1946, Truman granted Parr a full pardon, wiping out his criminal record with a stroke of the presidential pen. No longer a convicted felon, Parr could vote again and hold public office, and the federal banking regulators would have no authority to exclude him from control of their FDIC-insured banks.

The Duke was truly back in the saddle again, his power unrestrained. Two years later he would demonstrate the extent of that power with a brazen election theft that changed the history of the United States.

The "Box 13" election fraud perpetrated by Parr in 1948 to ensure Lyndon Johnson's win over Coke Stevenson in the race for U.S. senator has become part of our national folklore. Overnight, it put Duval County on the map and put Parr in the big league of political bossism and election chicanery with such Hall of Shamers as Boston's James Michael Curley, Chicago's Richard J. Daley, and the likes of Boss Crump of Memphis, the Pendergast machine of Kansas City, and Boss Tweed and the Tammany Hall gang in old New York.

Although it made Duval County's name synonymous with election fraud, Box 13 wasn't even in Duval County; it was in Alice, the county seat of neighboring Jim Wells County. The two counties lie side by side like a pair of adobe bricks in the South Texas sun, with Duval on the west and Jim Wells on the east. Along Duval's western flank is big, irregularly shaped Webb County, sprawling westward across fifty or more miles of sparsely populated sand, mesquite, and cactus to Laredo, the Rio Grande, and Mexico.

Adjoining Jim Wells on its notched eastern edge are Nueces and Kleberg counties, both ending in bays and beaches at the Gulf of Mexico. San Diego sits at the extreme eastern edge of Duval County, its city limit ending almost where Jim Wells County begins, at the county line that stretches as straight as a surveyor's chain for sixty miles, north to south. Alice, four times the size of San Diego, but still a small town, is ten miles due east of San Diego on State Highway 44, near the geographic middle of slender Jim Wells County.

To George, like his father before him, Duval County's borders were not the territorial limits of his political and economic domain. Alice, with its commerce and its temptingly convenient bank, was simply too close to San Diego to stay outside Parr's field of gravity.

George had political enemies in Jim Wells County, but he had friends and employees too. By 1948 he was the president and principal shareholder of both the First State Bank of San Diego and the Texas State Bank in Alice. His strength in Jim Wells was less than the absolute power he possessed in Duval, but plenty of people there were financially dependent on him, directly or indirectly, and his political clout in Alice was substantial. Nevertheless, Parr's choice of any county other than Duval to accomplish the risky Box 13 larceny for Johnson begs an explanation, or at least a plausible hypothesis.

Texas author and newspaper columnist John Knaggs theorizes that when Johnson's urgent call for help came, Parr had "already voted just about every eligible name in Duval County" and couldn't come up with the 200 additional votes he was asked to deliver except by using the Jim Wells County voting rolls.

"Duval County's turnout in the runoff was bigger than in the first primary," Knaggs points out. "Parr had used most of the eligible names in Duval County before he knew Johnson would need more. That would explain why he took the chance of using a box in Jim Wells, where he didn't have quite as much control as he had at home, instead of just padding the Duval count a little more. It would also explain why he added all 200 votes in one box instead of spreading them out over several boxes, which would have been a lot less obvious. By using only Box 13, he limited the number of people who could ever testify what really happened."

The election statistics tend to support Knaggs' theory. Duval County reported a hefty 4,662 votes cast in the runoff, all but 40 of which went to Johnson. It is doubtful that Parr could have found 200 additional eligible names to further inflate Johnson's Duval County total. In a legal pleading filed in the post-election litigation, Stevenson's lawyers argued that "such claimed unanimity of opinion reflected by said returns bears the evidence of fraud upon its face." (Actually, Duval's total was padded by about 400 votes in the same way the Jim Wells tally was padded, but the Duval ballots and records were burned — "by mistake," of course — immediately after the election. Thus, the evidence of fraud in Parr's own county was destroyed.)

As runoff primary election day approached in late August 1948, the race between Congressman Lyndon Johnson and former governor Coke Stevenson for the Democratic Party's nomination for

Box 13   49

U.S. senator grew increasingly ugly. The nomination was more than a mere chance to win the office; Texas was a one-party state in 1948, and the November general election would be an anticlimax, a mere formality required by law. There were national implications too.

Stevenson was a traditional fiscal conservative, considerably to the political right of President Truman and most of the Democratic Party outside the South. Johnson, on the other hand, had first been elected to Congress in 1937 as an unabashed New Dealer and had remained true to Roosevelt's cause. There was no question, either in Texas or in Washington, which man Truman and the national Democrats would find more compatible with their philosophy.

In July, Stevenson had outpolled Johnson by more than 71,000 votes in the first primary, but a third candidate, George Peddy, had received enough votes to deny Stevenson the required majority and force him into a runoff with Johnson. As the runoff campaign wore on in the relentless August heat, Johnson helicoptered frantically around the state, necktie askew and coattails flapping. Making increasingly shrill charges calculated to erode the popular former governor's support, Lyndon Johnson worked himself and his exhausted staff around the clock to close the gap.

Stevenson stubbornly held his fire, reluctant to dignify Johnson's rhetoric with a reply. Late in the campaign, however, Stevenson broke his stony silence about Johnson's charges and fired back. Strong personal dislikes flourished on both sides. The race grew suffocatingly close and everyone sensed it, but probably no one anticipated it would all come down to the fraudulent count in a single precinct, corruptly controlled by the Duke of Duval, in one of the most audacious election frauds in American history.

In the legal battles that began almost immediately after the belated results from Box 13 made Johnson the surprise winner, an august array of lawyers came to Coke Stevenson's aid. They were led by former governor Dan Moody of Austin and Josh Groce of San Antonio. Moody, a reform-minded ex-prosecutor from rural Taylor, had ousted incumbent governor Miriam ("Ma") Ferguson and her impeached husband, Jim, from the Governor's Mansion in 1927. With his splendid reputation for integrity and his brilliant legal mind, former governor Dan Moody was one of the most respected courtroom lawyers of his time.

Josh Groce, a member of the State Democratic Executive Committee, was a name partner in a prestigious San Antonio law firm and an acknowledged master of courtroom skills. Groce later explained in a letter to Dallas attorney Gordon Rupe, who helped raise funds to cover part of the litigation expenses, "I was more or less placed in charge of the fact angle and Dan Moody the law angle of this case." Other members of the Stevenson legal team included C. C. Renfro of Dallas, W. E. Allen and T. R. James of Fort Worth, Henry Brooks and Clint Small of Austin, and Wilbur Matthews of San Antonio.

Two younger lawyers, Kellis Dibrell of San Antonio and James T. Gardner of Austin, both tenacious ex-FBI agents, were quickly dispatched to Jim Wells, Duval, and Zapata counties to dig out the facts and keep an eye on the players. The sworn statements Dibrell and Gardner obtained from election officials and purported voters days after the election provided the factual basis for Moody's legal challenges to the fraud.

Meanwhile, Lyndon Johnson was not without a countervailing array of talent in his corner. Austin legal and political heavyweights John Cofer, Alvin Wirtz, and Everett Looney were joined by former governor James Allred and John Crooker of Houston, Raymond Buck of Fort Worth, and Dudley Tarlton of Corpus Christi. And when the Johnson forces had to pull a rabbit out of their hat to avert disaster, Washington insiders Thurmond Arnold and Abe Fortas engineered the emergency injunction application to U.S. Supreme Court Justice Hugo Black that stopped U.S. District Judge T. Whitfield Davidson's investigation in its tracks. At a hearing held earlier in Dallas, Judge Davidson looked at the opposing legal forces standing before him and remarked, "I have rarely observed or been present in a case where there were stronger or more able attorneys on each side."

Stevenson's lawyers fought doggedly to keep Johnson from being certified as the party's nominee because of Parr's fraud. For a time it appeared they might win, but in the end they lost. Shortly before the general election, when all legal avenues had been sealed shut, Stevenson announced that he would vote for the Republican nominee, Jack Porter. His supporters were divided on the issue. Some viewed his decision as treachery to the Democratic Party; others joined him, saying they had no choice. Some party loyalists who could not bring themselves to vote for even one Republican announced they would not cast a vote in the race for senator.

Dan Moody declined to make his intentions public. In answer to

Box 13   *51*

a letter from an inquiring friend, Moody said only that he would not vote for "any candidate on the Republican ticket," thus leaving open the possibility that he, too, would vote for no one in the senate race.

Josh Groce wrote and delivered a speech that told the Box 13 story with concise but impassioned eloquence to his fellow Democrats to explain why he, as a member of the State Democratic Executive Committee, could not vote for his party's nominee for U.S. senator:

> How do you do, ladies and gentlemen. At the request of former Gov. Coke R. Stevenson, I am going to tell you an amazing story. I am going to tell you a story that will shock every Texan who believes in the sanctity of the ballot, every Texan who reveres the sacred principles upon which our state and our nation were founded.
>
> My friends, I am going to tell you the sordid story of ballot box Number 13 in the town of Alice in Jim Wells County in the run-off primary held August 28th, 1948.
>
> It is a story based on fact — on the authenticated record of trial court hearings. I have all these certified records in my possession. As one of Gov. Stevenson's attorneys in his fight to shed light on the shameful proceedings at Box 13, I gained first-hand knowledge of the facts.
>
> At 8 o'clock on the evening of August 28th, 1948, one hour after the closing of the polls in the town of Alice in the run-off primary, the election judge of precinct 13 went to the office of the town newspaper. The final vote for box 13 as reported to and carried by the Alice paper was 765 for Lyndon Johnson — 60 for Coke Stevenson. This was also the vote included in the report to the Texas Election Bureau.
>
> Six days later, when the vote was reported to the county Democratic Executive Committee, Lyndon Johnson had mysteriously acquired 200 more votes. The figure reported this time was 965 for Johnson and not 765.
>
> Naturally curious over the fact that Lyndon Johnson had picked up 200 more votes between the time the polls closed in Precinct 13 and the time the returns were reported to the Executive Committee, Coke Stevenson's friends sought to peer into the circumstances.
>
> They urged Gov. Stevenson to go to Alice and demand copies of the records of Box 13.
>
> Apparently somebody at Box 13 had something to hide.

Coke Stevenson was bluntly refused copies of the record; he was even prevented from making notes.

He was permitted to look at the list of voters. A peculiar fact was noted. According to the sworn testimony of witnesses, the names of the first 841 voters on the list were written in black ink, but the remainder were written in blue ink.

Furthermore, it was later testified under oath that in the returns "the figure 765, on the first figure '7,' the 7 had been worked over in pen and ink from a 7 around to a 9" . . . a quick and easy 200 additional votes for Lyndon Johnson.

Meantime, Harry Lee Adams, who had been elected new county chairman of Jim Wells County, and who is an honest man, demanded of the old county chairman and his secretary the election supplies. By law these should have been in his possession. But he was refused after consultation with Attorney Ed Lloyd. It is significant that Ed Lloyd also is the attorney for George Parr, whose political machine is so well known to all of you.

Harry Lee Adams, however, did succeed in looking at the poll list. He copied at random the names of several alleged voters between the numbers 842 and 1041.

Coke Stevenson's friends immediately began to contact these alleged voters whose names were on the poll list.

Lyndon Johnson, on the other hand, was desperately attempting to keep the goings-on in Box 13 behind an iron curtain. He ran to court. He filed suit for an injunction in the local court of Jim Wells County. He sought, by legal maneuver, to prevent the righting of any wrongs which may have been uncovered in Box 13.

Johnson obtained this injunction. It restrained Coke Stevenson and his friends — I quote directly from the injunction itself — "from eliminating or attempting to eliminate any votes on the ground of illegality, irregularity, or fraud. . ."

Now, my friends — let me ask you this: If the votes in Box 13 were honest votes — if the 200 mysterious votes which were somehow added to Lyndon Johnson's total were votes honestly cast, why should Johnson have anything to fear? Why was Lyndon Johnson so fearful of the entire state learning the truth about only one precinct — a precinct where political bosses who are his allies and associates maintain ironclad political rule?

Lyndon Johnson also carried his fight to prevent disclosure of the truth to the State Executive Committee. When the committee met in Fort Worth September 13 the so-called official returns from Precinct 13 in Jim Wells County were presented. There were some committee members, including myself, who sought to shed

Box 13   *53*

light on the mystery of Box 13, but Johnson contended that under a Supreme Court ruling the committee was powerless to act, and he gained his point. The committee by a vote of 29 to 28 declared Johnson the nominee of the Democratic Party by 87 votes out of a million cast.

This setback did not deter Coke Stevenson's friends in their efforts to find out the truth about those mysterious 200 votes bestowed upon Lyndon Johnson.

On September 15, in the form of a petition sworn to by Governor Stevenson, we presented the startling facts in this case to Judge T. Whitfield Davidson of the United States District Court for the Northern District of Texas. He granted a restraining order preventing the Secretary of State from certifying Lyndon Johnson as the nominee and the matter was heard September 21 and 22.

According to the testimony, a man named Eugenio Solis was voter number 841 in Precinct 13. His testimony, in the form of affidavit, was that he voted shortly before seven p.m. when the polls closed. He said when he left, there was no one else coming up to the polls.

Alleged voter number 842 was Mrs. Enriqueto Acero. On the witness stand in Fort Worth and under oath, Mrs. Acero stated that she was 38 years of age and was the only person of that name in Precinct 13. When I asked her the question, "State whether or not you voted on August 28, 1948, in the second primary," she stated unequivocally, "no."

Listed by Mr. Adams as voter number 891 was Juan Martinez. Juan Martinez in response to questions propounded by me testified under oath before Judge Davidson that he had not voted, although he was listed as having cast a ballot in Box 13.

Appearing on the same list as voter number 911 was Louis Salinas. He went to Fort Worth and testified he had worked at night, slept during the day and was the only Louis Salinas in Precinct 13. When I asked him the question, "Did you vote in the August 28 primary of this year," under oath he testified, "no."

Hector Cerda, a student at Texas A & I at Kingsville was likewise listed as voter 920 in Box 13. On the witness stand he testified that on August 28 he was not even in Alice during the legal voting hours, but, instead, was in the town of Pharr, more than a hundred miles away. When I asked him whether or not he had voted August 28, Cerda answered, "I did not vote."

Also listed as voter number 1041 at Box 13 was Tomas Garcia. I hold in my hand the original affidavit of Tomas Garcia, in which he says, "I did not vote in the August 28 primary election in Jim Wells County this year."

Based upon the evidence before him, Judge Davidson granted the injunction sought by Coke Stevenson. Judge Davidson's statement from the bench is one that deserves the thoughtful consideration of every Texan. He reviewed the early efforts of Governor Stevenson to investigate the source of the mysterious 200 ballots and the injunction obtained by Lyndon Johnson to prevent that inquiry.

Judge Davidson said — and these are his words — "In cases of fraud the rule is — throw open the doors and let the light in."

Then reviewing the unsuccessful efforts of Coke Stevenson and his friends to investigate Box 13, Judge Davidson added — "All of that throws such a cloud on the fairness of the election that we think it should be gone into and that the parties concealing this information must have been conscious of the fact that it would probably change the result of the election."

Judge Davidson then continued — "Whenever I steal, whenever I misappropriate, whenever I stuff a ballot box, we are taking from a man that which is his. We are not only taking from him that which is his, but we are depriving other voters of the right to choose, by offsetting the vote they cast."

Judge Davidson thereupon appointed a commissioner to go into Jim Wells County to investigate further this matter of alleged vote frauds. On Monday, September 27, the commissioner opened his hearings at Alice.

The commissioner, W.R. Smith, former United States District Attorney, promptly sought the poll lists for Box 13. The law requires that three copies of the list are to be made by the election judge and his assistants. Subpoenas were issued for the election judge, the county chairman and the secretary of the County Democratic Executive Committee, requiring them to appear and bring copies of the poll lists.

But mystery was heaped on mystery at Box 13 and Lyndon Johnson's 200 additional votes. Neither the election judge nor the committee secretary could be found.

The former chairman did appear but he said he had turned his copy of the poll list over to the secretary, B. F. Donald, cashier of the bank of Alice, of which George Parr is president. George Parr's brother, Givens Parr, executive vice-president of the bank, testified that the very morning the subpoena was issued for Mr. Donald, Donald had been at the office in the bank. But he suddenly left for parts unknown. Mrs. Donald was subpoenaed. She testified her husband left the day before, without telling her where he was going. She said he had called her that night from somewhere in Mexico.

Box 13   55

Then came the climax in the strange series of events which shroud the origin of Lyndon Johnson's 200 votes. Luis Salas, election judge of precinct 13, took the stand. Salas volunteered the information that in his own home about midnight he had witnessed the changing of ballots in a previous election.

Salas testified that he had personally obtained the poll list which had been in possession of Mr. Donald. He said he had left both this list and his own list in his car on the night of September 15, while he was in a tavern drinking beer. When he came out of the tavern, he testified, the lists had mysteriously disappeared. Now mind you — this took place on the night of the very day this suit was filed in the Federal court.

This, then, left only one list supposedly remaining — a list required by law to be in the ballot box. But when the commissioner appointed by Judge Davidson opened the box — lo and behold! — that list also was missing . . . so all three poll lists now are missing — a most convenient coincidence indeed for Lyndon Johnson.

It is also a peculiar coincidence that most of the names on the poll list which the new county chairman at Jim Wells County managed to copy before the originals disappeared, run in alphabetical order after voter number 841.

It is interesting to observe that throughout this struggle to drag out into the light of day the truth about the mysterious 200 votes added to Box 13, Lyndon Johnson has never once to my knowledge denied that fraud occurred — fraud of which he was the beneficiary.

It is significant that Lyndon Johnson was rescued from the embarrassment of additional facts coming out by that eminent Justice of the United States Supreme Court, Mr. Hugo Black, who issued an order at Johnson's request preventing further investigation into vote fraud in the Democratic senatorial contest.

My friends — I have been a Democrat all my life. I have never voted against a Democratic nominee for United States Senator. But in view of what I have just related to you about the shocking events at Box 13, I know that you will agree with me that Lyndon Johnson was not elected by the Democrats of Texas as their nominee.

I therefore refuse to support Lyndon Johnson for United States Senator. I know that the great mass of Texans will never bestow the privilege of high office on a man whose place on the ballot was produced by these means.

I thank you.

In the stormy days just after the election, many of Stevenson's supporters eagerly volunteered what they knew or had heard about South Texas voting practices to Stevenson's lawyers. W. V. Smith, an elderly client of Dan Moody's from McKinney, Texas, wrote to Moody to relate some information he had obtained on a family visit to Laredo:

> While there one day 2 friends of my Brother from Alice and Corpus Christi came to see & visit my Brother.
>
> One was from Alice. He had contracted with Johnson for a certain number of illegal votes which were to be cast in the County that the ballots & Records were accidentally burned by the Court House janitor (Naturally). The man from Corpus Christi ask the man from Alice if Johnson had kicked in with the money, and he says "Yes everything was taken care of." There was enough of these votes contracted for to get Johnson elected. Since the Election is over, I feel like nothing more can or will be done, but I have followed the efforts you put forth in the case but here are 2 interesting matters in connection with Case & you all might like to know about it.
>
> My Brother & both of the said friends were ardent supporters & worked for the election of Mr. Stevenson to the Senate.
>
> We all recall that O'Daniel beat Johnson in these same Counties before. We all wondered why this Happened, and it was unknown to many people. This same party had contracted enough votes to elect Johnson and defeat O'Daniel, but for some reason Johnson did not kick in with the money so as a result O'Daniel was Elected by legal votes.
>
> My Brother had told me about this before.
>
> You can readily see this game is well plotted and in most cases well carried out. Its a Shame & Disgrace for such to be allowed to happen in this or any other state.

Alice attorney Gerald Weatherly sent Moody a copy of a letter he wrote to Coke Stevenson on September 7, describing himself as "almost the only lawyer in this county who openly and actively opposes the Parr-[Ed] Lloyd gang domination here," and offering information about the way voting was conducted in Jim Wells County on August 28:

"A[n election] supervisor opposed to the Parr-Lloyd gang here states that, while he was mainly interested in the county offices, he nevertheless noticed that many votes that were plainly against John

Box 13   57

Lyle (supported by the Parr-Lloyd gang for Congress), — ballots with Lyle's name plainly marked out, — were counted for Lyle. He says the number of votes so miscounted was large. And, since this is the method of this gang, I have no doubt that votes were likewise counted against you."

From San Antonio, W. C. Linden, Sr., a retired state judge, wrote to Moody to apprise him of vote-buying in the shadow of the Alamo by the Johnson forces. "If either Coke or you will come to me personally," Linden urged, "I can furnish evidence to prove that the Bexar County vote was bought by a $45,000 slush fund."

C. G. Krueger, a commissioner of the Texas Court of Criminal Appeals, sent Moody a more circumspect note, handwritten on court stationery: "I am informed that Tom Gambrell of Lockhart has some very valuable evidence or at least has learned of it, concerning the Stevenson-Johnson case. I think if you will call on him he may come over and relate to you all he learned."

H. L. "Ike" Poole, secretary of the Jim Wells County Democratic Executive Committee and a Stevenson supporter, passed on to both Stevenson and Moody an intriguing, albeit third-hand, story that had made its way to him by telephone from a small East Texas town nearly 400 miles away:

"A few days ago, I talked with Lloyd Wheelock, an oilman from Corsicana, Texas, who was the campaign manager for Jack Porter. At that time he advised me that some man in East Texas has a wire recording of a phone call made by Lyndon Johnson to him shortly before the August 28th primary asking for a few additional votes. Johnson advised him that Jim Wells and Duval County had already come through. This man, according to Mr. Wheelock, plans to use this recording in order to keep Mr. Johnson from being seated."

Some who wrote to Moody knew him, and probably Stevenson as well, only by reputation. Their letters often were addressed simply to "Dan Moody, Austin, Texas," but in those less automated times that was enough to ensure delivery by the post office to the popular former governor's law offices on the twelfth floor of the Capital National Bank Building, just off Congress Avenue on West 7th Street.

Typical of those correspondents was Mrs. Albert Neff of San Benito, deep in the Rio Grande Valley, who addressed Moody as "Dear Sir." Voters in her part of the state, she said, were frustrated by decades of crooked elections and a lack of honest investigations.

Like many others, she hoped Moody's efforts for Stevenson would somehow change all that. "This part of Texas has grown accustomed to the power of the whitewash and greased palm," she wrote. "The 'powers that be' are expert in Xplanations, deviations, and fixed-up records. A thorough, exhaustive investigation in this case would help Americanize the Valley."

As the divisive legal battles raged in courtrooms from Alice to Fort Worth to Austin to Atlanta to Washington and back again, partisans on both sides cheered the efforts of their champions and booed the opposition. Lyndon Johnson's followers, and many of the newspapers that had endorsed Johnson in the election, castigated Stevenson and his lawyers as poor losers and disloyal Democrats for contesting Johnson's nomination. Stevenson's backers retorted angrily that the party had no lawful nominee because the election had not been won, but stolen.

Standing steadfastly beside his client as the political controversy swirled around them, Dan Moody found comfort and reassurance in a flood of incoming letters and telegrams thanking him for championing Stevenson's cause. When Gus Lundelius, president of the Farmers State Bank of Round Rock, sent a letter of encouragement and gratitude, Moody responded by expressing his pleasure that "at least some" of his friends were siding with him. "My willingness to participate in this litigation is because I believe that there has been corruption in the election returns," Moody wrote. "The testimony has gone far enough already to warrant this belief, and in my opinion every legal and legitimate step should be taken to prevent fraud in elections."

In letters to El Paso lawyer Robert L. Holliday, an old friend who had supported Johnson in the election, Moody later explained why he devoted himself so passionately to the effort to deny Johnson the fruits of his tarnished victory. The Stevenson-Johnson litigation involved "something more than the personalities of the two candidates," Moody wrote. "With me, it partook of the character of a crusade to defeat fraud in the nomination of a candidate for high office. That was a cause to which I could cheerfully devote my efforts regardless of the personalities of the candidates."

Because the Box 13 scandal marked the first time George Parr had altered the result of a statewide election by fraud, Moody con-

Box 13 59

sidered the offense to be much more serious than the Duke's previous election thefts.

"There is a difference in what is now alleged and what has happened in the past," Moody wrote to Robert Holliday. "In previous elections the vote of these counties has been reported fairly early in the returns, and I have never heard it charged before that a change had been made in the vote or returns after the polls had closed and it was evident that some contest was a close one. To me, the allegations now made — and certainly there is a lot of proof to sustain them — present a different issue from the threat that has existed so long in this block voting."

Most of those who thanked Moody for leading Coke Stevenson's legal challenge to Johnson's nomination probably assumed he had taken on the exhausting litigation because of a strong political commitment to Stevenson, but that was not his principal motivation. "In the first primary I voted for George Peddy," Moody wrote in a personal letter to Tom Gooch of the *Dallas Times-Herald.* "In the second primary I voted for Stevenson. He and I have never been intimate; when he was in the legislature and I was in the Governor's office, we did not get along very well." To Moody, a principled man above all else, the purpose of the crusade had not been to deny Johnson the nomination merely for political reasons, but to deny him the nomination because it had been secured through corruption in the election process. In fact, Moody told Tom Gooch, because he was "completely and totally convinced" that the election result was fraudulent, he had given his effort to the litigation "without compensation either for time, labor or expense."

Upon receiving the court clerk's telegram informing him that the federal courts had closed the final door on their legal efforts to deny Johnson the nomination, Moody, deeply disappointed, apologized to his professional colleagues. "I developed the theory of the case and I regret that I led you gentlemen into a case that met such an end," he wrote to all of them on October 7. W. E. Allen responded immediately from Fort Worth, "Don't worry about leading us into a case that appears to have been lost. I say 'appears' because I feel that the trial of this case has opened the eyes of the people of Texas to a rotten condition that should not exist." T. R. James, also of Fort Worth, took issue with Moody's *mea culpa*. "I think apologies from you with reference to this case are entirely out of order," James replied by return mail. "We were simply sitting in a game with a stacked deck and everything was done that could be done, and the result is not the fault of anyone."

Luis Salas would break his long silence in late July 1977. He told the Associated Press all about Box 13: how he had lied under oath in the 1948 investigation; how 202 votes had indeed been added fraudulently, all but two of them to Johnson's tally, to give LBJ the election; and how, as election judge, he had certified the returns. Salas confirmed that Parr had directed the fraud, which surprised no one. His allegation that Lyndon Johnson was present when Parr gave Salas the order, at Parr's San Diego office three days after the election, stirred up a flurry of denials by Johnson's friends and former aides.

Once again, twenty-nine years after it happened, Box 13 put Parr's empire back in the national news as *The New York Times* followed the debate about Johnson's knowledge of the fraud. Johnson's former personal secretary, Mary Rather, told the press on August 14, "Salas is an old Mexican man. He just thinks he's somebody important. But anybody who knows Mr. Johnson knows it couldn't be true."

Luis Salas in the 1940s was referred to by his colleagues as "El Indio." A massive, menacing figure with a badge on his khaki shirt, a scowl on his face, and a big pistol on his hip, Salas was the stereotypical picture of a South Texas *pistolero*. Before immigrating to Texas from his native Mexico, he had served briefly as a conscripted teenage telegraph operator for Pancho Villa's revolutionary army. A telegrapher's job with the Texas-Mexican Railroad brought him to Duval County, where he met George Parr. In time "El Indio" became one of his most dependable soldiers, so much so that Parr had him commissioned as a deputy sheriff in three counties. "We had the law to ourselves there," Salas reminisced. "It was a lawless son-of-a-bitch. We had iron control. If a man was opposed to us, we'd put him out of business. Parr was the Godfather. He had life or death control."

It was not until 1973, while under indictment for income tax evasion, that George Parr admitted to his San Antonio attorney, Anthony Nicholas, that he had been in "direct telephone contact" with Lyndon Johnson during the critical days immediately after the 1948 election. Parr said that Johnson had told him how many votes to add to his total to pull the election out of the fire.

Chapter 4

Turbulent Times

Archer Parr and his son George, the first and second Duke of
Duval, were overblown caricatures of the South Texas patron. If
Hollywood made the Parr story into a movie, the critics would
say they were unbelievably violent and corrupt.
— The Texas Observer, *April 25, 1975*

GEORGE PARR'S SUCCESSFUL hijacking of the 1948 United
States Senate race for Lyndon Johnson brought him immediately to
the attention of national news publications. In a story headlined
"The Duke Delivers," *Time* magazine on September 27, 1948, called
Parr "a powerful king-maker" and credited him with being "the man
most responsible for Congressman Lyndon Johnson's nomination
over Coke Stevenson for the U.S. Senate." Although Johnson's
margin in Duval County was no better than usual for one of
George's chosen candidates, *Time* was impressed: "How Parr could
deliver was shown in Duval County's return: Johnson 4,622;
Stevenson 40."

What made those figures really impressive is that in past elections Parr had delivered similar margins for Coke Stevenson.

On a nod from the Duke, the electorate had reversed course as
quickly and as mindlessly as a school of minnows and flashed away
in the opposite direction.

In 1949, a full citizen again after President Truman's pardon,
Parr broke his own rule by having himself appointed county judge
of Duval County to fill the unexpired term of Dan Tobin, Sr., who
had the misfortune (or the good sense) to die in office. Parr also
went through his second divorce from Thelma Duckworth that

year; this time she got $425,000 in cash and $1,000 a month for the support of the couple's daughter, Georgia, in addition to her community property interest in real estate and oil and gas interests. In 1950 Parr chose to continue as county judge; to no one's surprise, he was elected to a full term without opposition, only to resign the office in early 1952 to have himself appointed sheriff.

By 1951, when *Collier's* magazine printed an exposé titled "Something is Rotten in the State of Texas" in its June 9 edition, the popular weekly was able to report that Judge Parr was doing very well for himself. "Parr . . . denies he owns the slightest interest in any business," *Collier's* reported, but "public records prove the contrary." Besides controlling both the San Diego State Bank and the Texas State Bank of Alice, according to *Collier's*, Parr owned an interest in at least 200 oil wells, about half of those through his partnership in Parr-Delaney Oil Company.

In addition, the magazine reported, Parr owned control of the San Diego Distributing Company, the only beer wholesaler in Duval County. "Before anyone can get a beer retailing license, incidentally, his application must be approved by the county judge, who also can revoke any license. And Boss Parr, of course, is county judge," *Collier's* pointed out.

Another Parr business interest that attracted the magazine's attention was the Duval Construction Company. It was formed in 1946 and was "owned entirely by Boss Parr," *Collier's* reported. "Since then it has been awarded every road-building, repair and improvement project on which Duval County has embarked — four major plums, totaling $1,115,741.52." A recent bond issue to finance an additional $1.9 million in road construction, the magazine said, "was voted with Duval's customary rubber-stamp approval of anything Boss Parr wants: 1,376 to 8." *Collier's* was also impressed with Parr's office — not his modest county judge's office in the courthouse, but his nearby private office: "Directly across the street from the courthouse, Parr has an air-conditioned one-story private office building, working quarters for his sizable staff. The building is constructed to withstand a siege. The doors are of solid oak, several inches thick; the outer doors and the windows all are shielded with heavy steel grilles."

Collier's was appalled by the contrast between Parr's imperial standard of living and that of his loyal "Latin" subjects:

His palatial San Diego mansion is situated on walled, lushly land-scaped grounds with swimming pool, multiple garage and large servants' quarters. Nearby are stables for his 25 blooded quarter horses — and his private race track, complete with automatic starting chutes and judges' stand, where he frequently races his horses with those of neighboring ranches . . . Against the pleasant, luxurious living all this represents, the way of life of the mass of Latin Americans in the Land of Parr — from whose political control Parr has, to such a considerable extent, *made* his enormous fortune — is drab indeed.

The article described the "Latin shantytowns" of Duval County's scattered communities as "treeless, grassless sections of dilapidated one- and two-room shacks crazily crowded together, frequently without plumbing or electricity." *Collier's* also noted that Parr had increased his ranch holdings to 70,000 acres with his 1945 purchase of the 57,000-acre Dobie Ranch. "He lives there part time, entertaining political associates in baronial splendor," the magazine said.

Had *Collier's* discovered the source of the funds Parr used to buy the ranch, it would have been three years ahead of its time with a scoop and a sensational lead for its story. It didn't come to light until 1954, but George had paid for the Dobie Ranch by helping himself to a half million dollars from the county's accounts in his bank. The first $250,000 was disbursed on April 24, 1945, when the county commissioners approved a Road and Bridge Fund check in that amount to Parr. The second installment came on June 13, 1945, when the county issued a $250,000 check to Wilder Construction Company, a defunct partnership in which Parr was the only remaining partner. In March 1947 Parr hit the county again, this time for $172,000 to pay his 1946 income taxes. When he was caught, he contended he had only borrowed the money.

The 1948 election theft has been called the high-water mark of George Parr's reign — the ultimate, arrogant display of his power. Ironically, it also marked the beginning of a tempestuous era in which he was severely buffeted by unprecedented legal and political setbacks and his machine suffered a temporary weakening of its chokehold on the empire.

Most of Parr's problems in the 1950s grew out of the disclosure of the world outside to Duval County's young Mexican-American men through military service in World War II. Fear and apathy had kept political resistance in Parr's domain at negligible levels for many years, until these brave, young veterans of the big war began to return. No longer boys, no longer afraid of bullies or guns, they came home as free men wanting their say in government and willing to take personal risks to get it. Across South Texas a "New Party" reform movement stirred.

In Duval and Jim Wells Counties the organizers called it the "Freedom Party," although it really wasn't a political party there or elsewhere, but only an opposition group that recruited and backed some reform candidates in the Democratic primaries. Nevertheless, after the 1948 election scandal showed how Parr's venal politics could defraud the entire state, the angry voices of the reformers attracted increasing attention, both locally and in Austin, and even a few influential Anglos (especially in Alice) became open, active supporters of the daring new movement.

The establishment machine, the "Old Party," recognized the growing threat and fought back. When W. H. "Bill" Mason, the outspoken program director at Alice's radio station KBKI, began to criticize Old Party public officials in his on-air commentaries in 1949, he was harassed by threatening phone calls and beaten up by two deputy sheriffs. When he concentrated his fire on Jim Wells County Sheriff H. T. Sain, Parr's man, and accused Deputy Sheriff Sam Smithwick of owning a nightclub where gambling was carried on, Smithwick stopped Mason on Alice's San Felipe Street the next day and shot him in plain view of a passenger in Mason's car. As a result of the backlash over Mason's murder, Sain lost his job to an Anglo candidate backed by the Freedom Party in the 1950 primary. Although Parr's candidates won everything else on the ballot in both Duval and Jim Wells counties that year, Sain's defeat meant things were changing, and Parr knew it. Just a few years earlier, nothing could have prevented a Parr candidate's reelection.

The loss of Bill Mason was felt keenly by the New Party and its friends, and the epitaph on his tombstone in an Alice cemetery reflects their appreciation for his courage. It says:

HE DIED BECAUSE HE HAD THE NERVE TO TELL THE TRUTH FOR A LOT OF LITTLE PEOPLE.

In that same 1950 primary election a spiteful George Parr

taught Governor Allan Shivers the political price of Parr's enmity, even though nothing was at stake but Parr's pride. Shivers, who was running for election to a full term after moving up from lieutenant governor when Beauford Jester died in office the previous year, had incurred George's wrath by appointing the wrong men to three vacant South Texas judicial offices.

The popular new governor carried 253 of the state's 254 counties in the Democratic primary by huge margins, losing only in Duval, where he got a mere 108 of the 4,347 votes reported. Parr enjoyed spitting in the governor's eye to make a point, but two years later, when another political murder drew statewide attention to the region, he may have regretted going out of his way to make enemies in high places.

Jacob "Jake" Floyd, an Alice lawyer, was one of the Anglos who despised the Old Party's corruption and supported the New Party's reform ideas. From the sheriff's office in San Diego, George Parr was very much in control of Duval County and the Old Party, and the Old Party was still largely in control of Jim Wells County. Parr recognized, however, the dual threat Floyd represented: As a respected community leader, his support lent credibility to the New Party; and as an able lawyer, he strengthened the dissidents' effectiveness by giving them good political and legal advice. Clearly, Jake Floyd was a serious, long-term problem for George Parr.

Parr had already served notice that any opposition to his rule, even by the little people who had no power or influence of their own, would be crushed. Small business owners identified with the Freedom Party were ruined financially, their parking lots and front doors blocked and their customers harassed by Parr's bullies in deputy sheriff uniforms until the whole community got the message that it wasn't smart to patronize their establishments. Welfare recipients were warned about losing their benefits if they traded with the wrong merchants. Children of Freedom Party members were shunned by their schoolmates and shut out of extracurricular activities.

In scores of ways large and small, systematically and ruthlessly, Parr used the community's fear of his power and the vindictive side of his nature to turn Freedom Party members and their families into economic and social lepers. A word, a frown, a raised eyebrow from the Duke — the same man whose generosity in handing out jobs and cash to those in need was legend — was all it took to mark them as his enemies, and to ruin them.

In the late afternoon of September 8, 1952, a dark green Packard was seen near Jake Floyd's home, moving slowly along the quiet neighborhood streets, turning corners and circling blocks in a seemingly aimless fashion, but returning repeatedly to the block where Floyd's house stood.

At about 9:00 that evening, as Floyd sat in his living room, reading, he received a phone call from one of George Parr's closest associates, Nago Alaniz, a lawyer who lived in San Diego and had a law office in Alice. Floyd and Alaniz were not friends, but there were only a handful of lawyers in Duval and Jim Wells counties, and the two men knew each other well. Twenty-one years later the swarthy, sinister Alaniz would be one of George Parr's defense attorneys in a federal income tax evasion case, but that night he was putting his relationship with Parr, and probably his own life, in serious jeopardy.

"Jake, I'm glad to hear your voice. I want to talk to you," Alaniz said hurriedly. Floyd invited his caller to come to his home. Alaniz demurred, insisting instead that Floyd meet him as quickly as possible at Jewel's Drive-In, a short-order restaurant on the outskirts of Alice. "Take a taxi, Jake," Alaniz said. "I don't want anybody to see you. Come right away, Jake. Do me that favor." From the top of the stairs a dozen feet away, Jake Floyd's son, Buddy, a law student, paused to listen as he heard his father say, "Nago, I've always told you when you called me, I would come. I'll be right out." The uneasy tone of Jake's voice and the guarded nature of his responses indicated that this was no ordinary conversation.

Friends of the Floyds often remarked on Buddy's striking resemblance to his father. At twenty-two, his height and build were almost the same as Jake's, but it was the similarity in the way father and son walked that was uncanny, those who knew them said; that, and the peculiar way both men carried their arms. Skeptical, cautious, knowing how close Alaniz was to Parr but unable to ignore the near-desperation in Nago's voice, Jake Floyd did as his caller instructed. Telephoning impatiently for one of the few taxis in Alice, he succeeded at last in summoning one to his home. "I'm going to meet a Parr man," Jake told Buddy on his way out the door. Buddy and his fiancée, who was visiting at the Floyd home, watched Jake get in the cab and drive away. Jake's wife was out, but was expected home soon.

Arriving at Jewel's Drive-In, Floyd found Alaniz waiting, as agreed, in a car behind the restaurant. "Jake, I've called you out here to tell you they are going to have you killed," Alaniz said. "I can't tell you who they are, Jake; they would kill me. They would kill me if they knew I was talking to you now."

Floyd listened with growing alarm as Alaniz told him there was a death contract on his head, to be carried out that night. "They have imported two professional killers from Mexico to kill you, Jake, and to kill Judge Reams." Alaniz was referring to Sam Reams, a lame-duck district judge who was viewed as an enemy by George Parr. "They're afraid you're going to put Judge Reams back in office in November with a write-in."

Alaniz wouldn't say who was responsible for the contract. "I don't know whether George Parr has anything to do with this," he told Floyd, "but you know that somebody is putting up the money." Alaniz assured Floyd he was speaking from firsthand knowledge of the death plot. "I'm a part of this, Jake," he told Floyd. "I'm supposed to be the killer's alibi. I've agreed to testify that the man that killed you was with me." Alaniz leaned closer, his voice dropping to a near-whisper. "But I'll give you a lead, Jake: The leader of the killers is Mario Sapet, known as 'The Turk.' He's driving a green Packard."

Jake Floyd was accustomed to the political establishment's enmity, and to their recurring harassment, but this was taking things to a new depth. Shaken, he took a taxi to the Jim Wells County jail, hoping to find the sheriff. Failing, he hurried home, where he encountered a parent's worst nightmare: His lookalike son was sprawled in the driveway, dying from a gunshot wound to the head. Buddy Floyd had exited the house shortly after his father left, telling his fiancée he was going to the garage to work on his car. In the dim light the killer had mistaken him for his father and fired two shots. When Buddy's mother drove into the driveway a few minutes later, and found her stricken son lying in a pool of blood, her screams brought neighbors running. The young man's fiancée hadn't heard the shots.

The murder weapon, found in a nearby trash can, was traced to Mario Sapet, a San Antonio bar owner who was also a special deputy sheriff of Duval County. The triggerman was Mexican national Alfredo Cervantes, who beat a hasty retreat across the border. Mexican authorities refused to extradite Cervantes, preferring instead to prosecute him at home. His 1964 murder conviction in Mexico City resulted in a thirty-year prison sentence. Sapet, tried on a change of

venue in North Texas for his part in the scheme, drew a ninety-nine-
year sentence. Alaniz, tried separately in Waco as an accomplice to
the crime, was acquitted by a jury because of his last-minute attempt
to deprive Sapet of his intended target.

The suspicion that George Parr was behind the botched murder
would not subside. Mario Sapet was tied to Sheriff Parr by his special deputy commission, and everyone knew Jake Floyd was a thorn
in Parr's political side. Alaniz was extremely close to Parr, and
though he never admitted that Parr was involved, no one but George
would have had the power to assign Alaniz a role in the conspiracy.

Parr was rumored to have paid for Sapet's defense, but no proof
ever saw the light of day in court. Parr denied any knowledge of the
murder, but the gossip was so pervasive that on September 11 he
delivered a written statement to the *Corpus Christi Caller*: "It is true
that Jake Floyd, Sr., and I have been on opposite sides politically for
over 20 years, but contrary to rumors that have been circulated, I
have always played the political game open and above board . . . I
have never taken an undue advantage either legal or illegal of my
opposition . . . And despite the rumors current at the present time
my conscience is absolutely clear and [the Floyds] have my heartfelt
sympathy and compassion."

Although state officials had been alternately unwilling or unable to do anything effective about the lawless condition of the Parr
empire for forty years, the Buddy Floyd murder, with its connection
to the political stirrings of a long-somnolent electorate, prompted
them to try. Lacking any real power under the state constitution,
Governor Allan Shivers nevertheless used his position and his personal popularity to turn a spotlight on the corruption by denounc-
ing Parr and calling for a thorough investigation into his autocratic
regime by the state's attorney general.

Price Daniel was an honorable man, an able lawyer, and a realist.
As attorney general, he knew the limits of his power; as an honest
public servant, he knew something had to be done and resolved to
find a way to do it. Daniel was the Democratic Party's nominee for
the U.S. Senate and thus was preparing to change jobs after the November election, but John Ben Shepperd, another man of demonstrated ability and integrity who had been secretary of state for the
preceding two years, was primed to succeed him as attorney general.
Daniel and Shepperd were veteran Texas politicians who had long

known and despised the amorality of Parr's regime, but only once, in 1950, had they been able to help thwart its evil machinations.

In the 1950 general election George Parr had pulled off an astounding upset, reminiscent of his Box 13 feat in 1948, but for a much less visible office. The victim in 1950 was Sam Reams, appointed by Shivers in 1949 as judge of the 79th Judicial District and running unopposed for election to the remaining two years of his predecessor's term. On election night the surprised judge discovered from returns in three of the four counties in his district that Parr had quietly ordered a write-in campaign against him, seeking to defeat him with a previously unannounced and little-known opponent.

Still, Reams led by more than 4,000 votes when all the returns were in from those three counties, and it looked as if Parr had attempted an uncharacteristically ill-planned coup. Ominously, however, there were no returns from Duval County. The silence continued for six days until finally the results of the official county vote canvass were released. The news was stunning: With straight faces the county election board announced that Parr's stealth candidate had carried Duval by a mind-boggling 4,739 to 43. It was the largest total vote the county had reported in any election up to that time, and probably a margin of world-record proportions for an unannounced write-in candidate. With the Duval vote accounted for, Parr's man had won the election by more than 200 votes.

To their credit, the members of the state canvassing board, a statutory panel consisting at that time of Governor Allan Shivers, Attorney General Daniel, and Secretary of State Shepperd, refused to certify Parr's man as the winner, thus requiring Parr to decide whether to force the issue. Realizing he would have to litigate in Austin before a judge he didn't own, Parr let the matter drop and Reams remained in office. Parr made light of the rebuff by having his candidate declare he didn't want the job after all, but Allan Shivers, Price Daniel, and John Ben Shepperd earned the Duke's lasting enmity for their act of integrity.

The year 1952 didn't start well for George, and it didn't get any better as it went along. The political opposition grew bolder, and he knew the Old Party's officeholders would have Freedom Party opponents in the primaries in both Duval and Jim Wells. In April, Judge Reams gave notice that things were going to get worse: He empaneled a grand jury that owed no allegiance to George Parr, and it was obvious he expected them to do some investigating. Parr knew there was no predicting what an independent grand jury might decide to meddle in, but there were plenty of possibilities, none of them good.

Reams was on the ballot again, seeking his first full term, and Parr put him at the top of the list of those targeted for defeat in the primary. After George's unsuccessful attempt to steal the election from him in 1950, the judge could hardly be counted as an ally, and Parr simply couldn't afford to let anyone except a dependable member of the Old Party team occupy the crucial 79th District bench. Parr's choice to succeed Reams was the county judge of Jim Wells County, C. Woodrow Laughlin. The process, however, couldn't be hurried; Laughlin would have to win the primary in July, which in turn would guarantee his election in November, but he couldn't take office until January 1, 1953. Until then, the troublesome Reams would still be the district judge.

As things heated up between the insurgents and the Old Party in the Democratic primary campaigns, Parr became increasingly annoyed. In a display of defiance, Freedom Party candidates filed for every local office on the ballot in Duval County, and rallies were held openly to stir up support for them. Parr struck back with a fear campaign. His deputies haunted Freedom Party gatherings, ostentatiously noting who was there, harassing those in attendance just as they harassed dissident merchants and their customers. Parr did his best to make life difficult for the brave souls who showed up at Freedom Party events to hear speeches about liberty and constitutional government.

In July the mysterious (and still unsolved) murder of a U.S. Border Patrol officer, found shot to death in a burning automobile on a Duval County road, sent political assassination rumors racing around the region once more because the dead lawman had clashed with Duval County authorities on occasion. Apprehensive about being identified as Parr's enemies, but determined to have a voice in their own government, the dissidents held their rallies and talked up their candidates despite Parr's efforts to intimidate them, while the storm clouds of impending violence gathered over the area. Governor Shivers ordered in the Texas Rangers to keep the peace and to ensure the First Amendment rights of those who wanted to speak out publicly for or against candidates. The man Shivers put in charge was Capt. Alfred Y. Allee, a tough lawman by anyone's definition, and one who had an enthusiastic dislike for George Parr.

While the Rangers investigated Buddy Floyd's death in the fall of 1952, an investigative team of state lawyers and accountants under Attorney General Price Daniel's direction descended on Duval County. They were there to search for evidence of corruption where Daniel knew it must exist: in the official records of Duval County and its school districts, the local tax-collecting entities that a political boss like Parr would use to rake in, and then rake off, public funds.

Judge Sam Reams' defeat by C. Woodrow Laughlin in the 1952 Democratic primary was a setback for the reformers, though not an unexpected one. Despite the prospect of having eventually to deal with a thoroughly pro-Parr judge, the state's team of determined investigators, working first under Daniel and then under the new attorney general, Shepperd, kept up the search for evidence of criminality in the public records for more than a year, and along the way they were joined by federal agents from the Internal Revenue Service and the Post Office Department. By early 1954, despite mysterious disappearances of crucial records and the handicap of working in the virtual equivalent of a hostile foreign country, the team had made substantial progress toward assembling a criminal case with the potential to send Parr and a dozen or so of his associates to prison.

George was reelected sheriff in 1952, along with the rest of the Old Party candidates; later, though, in another round of political musical chairs, he resigned the sheriff's office and had the county commissioners appoint his nephew and adoptive brother, Archer Parr, to succeed him.

As events closed in on him, George's hostility toward the political dissidents in his realm intensified, and his volatile temper sometimes overcame his better political judgment. In mid-January of 1954, he showed up at an opposition political rally in Alice and provoked an angry confrontation with a Freedom Party partisan. The ensuing events put the drama on the front page of *The New York Times* on February 5, 1954. An article by Gladwin Hill, datelined Alice, Texas, carried an eye-catching headline: *"Pistols, Rangers, Indictments Mix In Old-Time Texas Political Row."*

After recounting the ongoing struggle between Parr, the governor, and the insurgent political forces opposing Parr's iron-fisted control, the *Times* article described the incident that threatened to trigger open warfare between Parr and the Texas Rangers:

One of the bitterest political imbroglios in recent history is racking this South Texas oil-and-cattle region.

No one would be surprised if it suddenly boiled over in another outburst of the gunfire and bloodshed that have intermittently punctuated the politics of the area for more than a generation.

The conflict is between the administration of Gov. Allan Shivers and the almost feudal regime of the Parr dynasty, which has long been an awesome curiosity of Texas politics.

* * *

Today, in scenes reminiscent of the old-time West, bepistoled Texas Rangers walked the streets of Alice and nearby communities.

* * *

Governor Shivers capped a half-dozen investigations and legal actions by both state and Federal agencies aimed at parts of the Parr empire by declaring yesterday that he would impose martial law on the area if necessary to assure the proper functioning of regional administrative and judicial machinery.

* * *

The present crisis in local affairs began January 16 when Manuel Marroquin, a tortilla maker, Spanish-language newspaper writer and member of an anti-Parr political group, reported that George Parr had brandished a pistol at him outside a political rally.

With the implicit backing of the Rangers, he took his complaint to the Jim Wells County Court. Mr. Parr said it was a pair of binoculars he had brandished, but was placed under $1,500 bond for trial March 15 on a charge of illegal gun carrying.

When he came to court, accompanied by his nephew, Archer Parr, sheriff of Duval County, harsh words flew between them and the Rangers in the corridor. A brief scuffle ensued that ended in only a few bruises. However, the Jim Wells County grand jury found probable cause that, on the Rangers' part, the fracas constituted assault with intent to murder. Their arraignment date is indefinite.

Two days later the *Times*, sensing a change in the winds from half a continent away, continued its coverage of events in Duval under the headline "PARR POWER EBBS IN TEXAS POLITICS." The lead sentence put it dramatically, if a bit prematurely: "Day by day, almost hour by hour, the power of what is probably the last of the nation's old-fashioned political baronies is perceptibly ebbing away."

Buried near the end of the story was brief mention of a highly significant battle in the war between Parr and the outside world: "Also, the final stage has been reached in State Supreme Court proceedings to remove from office one of the principal beneficiaries of Mr. Parr's support, Judge C. Woodrow Laughlin, presiding judge of the 79th judicial district, embracing Duval, Jim Wells, Starr, and Brooks Counties."

An obscure provision of the Texas Constitution had been invoked by enough lawyers in the district to require the Texas Supreme Court to consider removing Laughlin from office, and on March 18, 1954, the *Times* trumpeted, "*'Parr Empire' Judge Ordered Off Bench.*"

> The Texas Supreme Court, after hearing arguments, ordered C. Woodrow Laughlin off the 79th District bench by noon today.
>
> Lawyers on both sides told the Supreme Court that Mr. Parr ... was at the root of the trouble in the stormy Seventy-Ninth District.
>
> ⁂
>
> Eleven South Texas lawyers had challenged Judge Laughlin's fitness to serve. Among other things they contended that the judge showed favoritism to Mr. Parr's political forces.
>
> The Supreme Court said it was basing its removal of Judge Laughlin on the fact that his first act upon taking office was discharging the Jim Wells County grand jury while the jury was investigating matters involving his brother.

Once again the crucial 79th District Court was in unfriendly hands, as the governor designated Judge A. S. Broadfoot, of Bonham, in north central Texas, to preside temporarily in the four-county South Texas district. Under Texas law, the 79th District Court was vacant and the office would be on the ballot that year.

Parr followed up on the Jim Wells County grand jury's indictment of Rangers Allee and Bridge by filing a civil rights suit against both men in federal court. *The New York Times* reported that Parr told the court the two Rangers wanted to kill him.

Meanwhile, Parr's other troubles were multiplying. On March 23 a Jim Wells County Court jury listened first to Manuel Marroquin's testimony about being threatened with a gun, and then to George's testimony that he was merely carrying binoculars and trying to see who was attending a political rally. After deliberating an hour the jury found Parr guilty of illegally carrying a gun and fined him $150. The *Times* again carried the story.

In late March, the state dismissed the charges against Joe Bridge. On April 20, with a jury in the box ready to start the trial of Captain Allee, Parr surprised the courtroom crowd by asking the presiding judge to dismiss the indictment "for the good of the community." The *Times* noted that although it was Parr's "personal plea" that resulted in the dismissal of the charges against him, "Captain Allee refused to shake Mr. Parr's hand for photographers." In his characteristically plain-spoken manner Allee growled, "I just don't like George Parr or nothing about him. He's a dangerous man who would do anything under the sun, and I don't treat a tiger like I do a rabbit. I'm not sorry I hit Mr. Parr."

Between appearances in court, Parr kept a watchful eye on elections in April for three seats on the Benavides school board. His Anglo candidates won every seat, but their two-to-one margins of victory were anemic by past standards. Parr, however, said it showed that his detractors would never prevail; the Old Party would go on winning, he predicted confidently, "in spite of anything they can do."

As important as control of the school board was to Parr, the 79th District Court remained the most important office in the region, and the politically astute watched closely for clues to Parr's plans for that position. Attorney General John Ben Shepperd explained Parr's style of government, and the district judge's role in it, this way: "By controlling elections, you control the sheriff, the district and county attorney, and district and county judges. The district judge appoints the grand jury commissioners and they appoint the grand jury. You cannot be arrested, indicted, prosecuted, tried, convicted or sentenced."

George teased reporters and opponents in early May by announcing that he would run for the office himself. *The New York Times*, still fascinated with the man and his machinations, quoted George as saying he would run because of the many attacks made against ousted Judge C. Woodrow Laughlin, and charges that Parr controlled Laughlin. "My opponents said I control the district judge," Parr told the *Times*. "Why not let me be the district judge? Then no one will control the district judge but me."

Parr's real plan, though, was to put the disgraced but eminently dependable Laughlin back on the bench, and it was Laughlin who filed in, and won, the Democratic primary on July 25, 1954.

The New York Times reported the day after the 1954 primary that Parr, "under attack by the Shivers regime, had received perhaps his biggest electoral setback. The voting was closely watched by a detachment of Texas Rangers." The Rangers' close scrutiny took its toll on the Old Party's election-day efficiency and wounded its pride; Sheriff Archer Parr, George's nephew, lost a race for state representative by a narrow margin — but lost, nonetheless, as did George's candidate for district attorney of the 79th Judicial District, Raeburn Norris.

Elsewhere in the state, Governor Allan Shivers was forced into a runoff with a liberal former state district judge, Ralph Yarborough, and the mayor of Fort Worth, Jim Wright, won his first race for Congress. Both Lloyd Bentsen, Jr., and George's own congressman, John Lyle, chose not to seek reelection to Congress.

July 1954 produced more than electoral setbacks for Parr, however. The extended investigation by state and federal forces finally bore fruit, as the Duval County grand jury empaneled by Judge Broadfoot returned the first indictments against Parr and a score of his Old Party functionaries for stealing money from county government and the public schools. John Ben Shepperd predicted it was just the beginning, but it hadn't been easy. George and his cronies had pulled most of the tricks old Archie had used to frustrate earlier investigations, putting one obstacle after another into the path of Shepperd and his staff of lawyers and investigators. Critical bank records subpoenaed by the grand jury mysteriously disappeared, and witnesses suffered severe memory losses, denied knowledge of facts they obviously knew, or left the county to avoid questioning.

Shepperd predicted the state grand jury might indict as many as 200 people before it finished its term in November. "The gist of the allegations," the *Times* reported, was that "the Parr machine, or individuals involved in it, siphoned large sums of money out of county coffers by various devices.

"These allegedly included keeping people on the public payroll at substantial salaries for doing nothing; handing out contracts to the group for goods and services rendered the county, and cashing checks made out to fictitious persons or to persons who did not earn the money and never saw the checks. Some checks were made out to 'John Doe et al' and endorsed the same way — and honored by one of Parr's banks that was a repository for public funds," the *Times* said.

State and federal banking regulators took a dim view of the disappearance of subpoenaed public-entity bank records from George's two banks in San Diego and Alice. By July, under orders from the FDIC to divest himself of ownership, Parr had sold one of the banks and was negotiating the sale of the other.

Shepperd and his federal colleagues worked feverishly into the fall of 1954, racing against C. Woodrow Laughlin's return to the bench. Laughlin would have the power to dismiss the grand jury as soon as he took office again on January 1, 1955, and would surely do so. For the state to prosecute its cases, it was essential to get the indictments returned, arraign the defendants, and get the cases moved on changes of venue to other districts before Laughlin could undo everything the reform forces had worked so hard to accomplish. The information unearthed by the investigators had been shared by state and federal authorities, and on November 15 a federal grand jury in Houston indicted George for income tax evasion, charging that he had understated his income for 1949, 1950, and 1953 by half and owed more than $85,000 in taxes for those three years.

In one of his rare political mistakes, Parr tried to defeat Laughlin in the 1954 general election by running a write-in candidate against him, fearful that Laughlin would be disbarred after taking office and Shivers would again appoint an anti-Parr judge in his place. The attempt failed, and Laughlin responded to George's perfidy by allowing the anti-Parr grand juries to continue their investigations. George was also sued by the state to recover the money he "borrowed" from the county to buy the Dobie Ranch and pay his income taxes in the mid-1940s.

Duval County government was reduced to a state of confusion and disarray as Parr and the Old Party fought the legal and political battles of their lives for control of the empire. Events tumbled over one another like boulders bouncing down a mountainside in an avalanche. All four county commissioners and three of the seven Benavides school trustees resigned abruptly when the school district's former bookkeeper, Diego Heras, was granted immunity from prosecution and ordered to testify before the state grand jury.

When the first of the indicted Benavides School District officials was tried and convicted in December, no one had to remind George that he was facing similar charges. As the legal battles raged on, lifelong Parr confidant Dan Tobin, Jr., a second-generation Parr man and Old Party officeholder, cast his lot with the political insurgents. Archer Parr, foreseeing years of bloody courtroom battles ahead, resigned as sheriff and entered law school at the University of Texas.

By 1956, the political revolution was in full swing. The Old Party faction still dominated the Democratic Party and its candidates dominated the primary election, but the opposition, running as independents, won most of the offices in the November general election. They did not defeat George at the polls, however; he ran successfully for one of his old jobs, sheriff, only to have the reformist county commissioners declare him ineligible for the office because of the money he owed the county as a result of the Dobie Ranch transaction.

As if that were not trouble enough, George was facing serious criminal trials in both state and federal courts as 1956 drew to a close. The federal income tax charge against him had been put on the back burner by federal prosecutors while they prepared to go forward on a massive mail fraud conspiracy case against Parr, eight of his key confederates, and both of his former banks. In addition, the state was ready to try him on the same charge of stealing public funds that had already resulted in convictions of two Benavides School District officials.

All of the cases, state and federal, were based on similar facts; all grew out of the efforts of state and federal attorneys and investigators that began shortly after Buddy Floyd was murdered; all involved the systematic looting of Benavides School District funds. The federal mail fraud case, though, was by far the most ambitious and comprehensive of all the cases, and the most dangerous for the defendants.

In that case federal prosecutors were getting ready to show the world how local government, Duval County style, worked — to paint a detailed picture of Parr and his co-conspirators in action over a period of years, collecting school taxes, writing fraudulent checks on the district's accounts in one of Parr's banks, and converting the checks into cash, no questions asked, at both of Parr's banks. The angle they planned to use to make the whole larcenous operation a federal crime was the defendants' use of the United States mail to send out the tax statements and rake in the money.

The government's first attempt to get a conviction in the mail fraud case fizzled out in early December 1956, after three grueling weeks of trial, when the jury deadlocked 11–1 in favor of convicting most of the defendants on most of the charges. George and his defense team had little time to celebrate his temporary escape, however, as they had to turn their attention almost immediately to the January trial of the state's theft case 165 miles north of San Diego in New Braunfels, the county seat of predominantly conservative, ethnically German, law-and-order-oriented Comal County.

Parr's conviction in the New Braunfels trial on January 29, 1957, was reported by newspapers from Corpus Christi to New York. In the understated language of the criminal statutes, he had been charged with stealing "more than $1,000" from the Benavides Independent School District. It was, of course, a lot more, and the jury had little difficulty determining his guilt. The *Times* noted not only his five-year sentence in the state penitentiary, but also the two related charges on which he was still awaiting trial in connection with misappropriation of school district funds — a state charge of forging checks and the federal mail fraud indictment.

On January 28, the day before he was convicted in New Braunfels, Parr sought refuge from his expensive problems by filing a voluntary bankruptcy petition. In it he declared that his assets amounted to $532,106 and his debts totaled $1,925,093. The debts included the state's civil claim against him for the public funds he admitted using to buy the Dobie Ranch and the federal government's claims for income taxes owed, which he denied.

With his appeal from the New Braunfels conviction pending in the Texas Court of Criminal Appeals, George and his lawyers returned in the spring of 1957 to United States District Court in Houston, where he was to stand trial again with his friends in the mail fraud case.

After an unsuccessful effort by all of the defendants to have the trial moved to Corpus Christi, and a couple of false starts because of procedural problems, a jury was seated and the trial got under way before Judge Joe Ingraham in May. Lead counsel for Parr was Percy Foreman, the most renowned criminal law practitioner in Texas and one of the best in the country. Flamboyant and charming, pugnacious and vociferous, resourceful and supremely self-confident, Foreman as a righteously indignant champion of the accused was as effective with juries as he was difficult for opposing counsel to joust with and judges to control. As lead counsel for the most important defendant, Foreman was the field commander who led the combined defense forces into battle.

Although they were lesser figures and thus lesser targets, all the other defendants were George's cronies: the president of the Benavides School Board, Octavio Saenz; school board members Jesus G. Garza and Santiago Garcia; the board's secretary, Oscar Carrillo, Sr.; O. P. Carrillo, the board's attorney; D. C. Chapa, the board-appointed tax assessor and collector, who was also the father of Oscar and O. P. Carrillo; Jesus Oliveira, a director of Parr's Texas State Bank of Alice; B. F. Donald, the bank's cashier; the Texas State Bank itself; and Parr's other bank, the First State Bank of San Diego. Malcolm Wilkey, the United States attorney for the Southern District of Texas, headed the prosecution. The stage was set for a battle of heavyweights.

The government's evidence showed that the Benavides Independent School District operated schools in Benavides and Freer in a distinctly unconventional way. The population of the town of Benavides was more than ninety percent Hispanic, and the four Hispanic board members lived in that community. Freer, with its larger Anglo population, was the home of the three Anglo members, and the seven men seldom met as a board. The two groups functioned as two more or less separate entities, each running its own schools and preparing its own budget, although the two budgets were combined to create a single district budget on which tax assessments were based. The district's administrative offices were located outside the district, in George Parr's San Diego office building; there, offices were maintained for Parr, Chapa, and Oscar Carrillo. The district's authorized bank accounts were maintained outside Duval County, in Parr's Texas State Bank of Alice.

The government's principal witness concerning the long-running theft of school taxes was Diego Heras, the district's bookkeeper and sometimes "acting secretary." W. M. Benson, the district's auditor until mid-1950, also testified as a prosecution witness. Heras was no angel, as the defense showed in five days of withering cross examination. He had been a small but essential cog in the tightly knit group's money machine, handling the school district's books and checking accounts as Parr directed, and now he was trading his intimate knowledge of the scheme for his freedom.

For years Heras had been the willing recipient of substantial cash payments in excess of his salary, most of it paid to him at Parr's direction. He had lied to government investigators about those payments initially, and even at the trial, still reluctant to admit he was an unmitigated thief, he sought halfheartedly to explain the extra cash as "advances" of his salary and expense allowance.

It is not uncommon for prosecutors, out of necessity or expediency, to strike bargains with minor but knowledgeable figures such as Heras in criminal schemes, agreeing not to prosecute them if they will testify truthfully about the crimes of more important defendants. Prosecutors in those situations usually try to counter the predictable defense argument about tainted witnesses by reminding the jury that although they would prefer to prove a defendant's guilt with the testimony of choirboys and saints, none had been found with firsthand knowledge of the facts. Among themselves, prosecutors use a more callous aphorism to explain why lesser crooks must sometimes be allowed to testify against greater crooks and go free: "Somebody has to drive the hearse." Judge Ingraham instructed the jury that Heras was an accomplice in the scheme as a matter of law, and that they might determine from the evidence that Benson was an accomplice too.

Besides suggesting to the jury that Heras' previous lies made his testimony untrustworthy, the defense tried to depict him as a political opportunist. The Court of Appeals for the Fifth Circuit, commenting later on the evidence, observed that the defendants "largely pitched their defense on the basis of this being a fight between two political factions, implying that Heras was either personally, or as a tool for others, interested in sending the defendants, especially Parr, to jail in order to get him out of local politics."

The government's evidence in the lengthy trial opened the doors of the school district's offices and gave the jury an appalling picture of what had long been done in secrecy on the inside, out of public view. For years the defendants had contrived to collect the district's taxes, deposit the money in Parr's bank, and drain out hundreds of thousands of dollars for themselves, allowing only about half of the tax revenue collected to be spent on the education of the district's children.

Despite Heras' admitted role in the conspiracy and his lame attempts to justify the illegal payments he accepted, the jury found his testimony about the scheme believable, perhaps largely because his story was corroborated by a handful of canceled checks the defendants had sought to keep out of the investigators' hands. The

Court of Appeals noted that "All but 23 cancelled B.I.S.D. checks for the actual period [1948 to 1954] were destroyed or missing. Heras kept possession of 20 of these. The microfilm records of all transactions in the two Parr controlled banks mysteriously 'disappeared' immediately following the start of the investigation by Federal authorities." Thus Heras, the mere hireling bookkeeper who wrote the checks and reconciled the bank statements, had saved himself from prison and handed the prosecution a sword to use against the empire and its rulers by simply holding out a few canceled checks when the bank records were spirited away. It was a lesson George Parr would never forget.

On July 17, 1957, after more than two months of trial, the jury found all of the defendants guilty, some on only one or two of the twenty counts in the indictment, others on many counts, and all on the conspiracy count. Parr, D. C. Chapa, Oscar Carrillo, Sr., and the Texas State Bank of Alice were convicted on all counts. On July 30 the defendants stood before Judge Ingraham again, this time to be sentenced. Parr drew the stoutest sentence, ten years in prison and a $20,000 fine. D. C. Chapa, the tax assessor and collector appointed by the school board, was sentenced to five years in prison, and board member Oscar Carrillo, Sr., one of Chapa's sons, to four years. Others assessed prison terms were Texas State Bank cashier B. F. Donald (four years) and Octavio Saenz, the school board president (three years). Board members Garza and Garcia, board attorney O. P. Carrillo (another of D.C. Chapa's sons), and bank director Oliveira all were given suspended prison sentences and placed on probation. Both banks were assessed fines.

On August 8, 1957, the Department of Justice announced that it would defer the prosecution of its civil and criminal tax cases against George, pending the outcome of the appeal from his mail fraud conviction. At the same time the IRS announced it had concluded that Parr's ex-wife, Thelma Duckworth Parr, played no part in his tax evasion and that it would not assert its tax lien against her property. George was not so lucky; on March 10, 1958, the IRS filed a $754,000 tax lien against him for tax years 1949 through 1956, raising the total of its civil claims against him to $1,340,000.

The defendants' appeal to the Fifth Circuit was based on their contention that the evidence against them was insufficient to support the jury's verdict and on the legal argument that even if they did steal the money, their actions didn't constitute mail fraud. On April

6, 1959, that court ruled against them and issued its written opinion affirming their convictions. On September 15 all of the defendants filed a petition for writ of certiorari, urging the U.S. Supreme Court to exercise its discretion to review the case.

Abe Fortas, who had pulled both Lyndon Johnson's and George Parr's chestnuts out of the fire by stopping the investigation of the Box 13 vote fraud eleven years earlier, was called on to work his magic with the high court again. On December 7, 1959, the court granted the writ, agreeing to hear oral argument on the question whether the defendants' conduct constituted the federal crime of mail fraud.

The Supreme Court reviewed the sixteen-volume, 6,000-page transcript of the trial, and on June 13, 1960, by a vote of 6–3, it reversed all of the convictions. The defendants, the majority reasoned, had indeed "devised and practiced a brazen scheme to defraud by misappropriating, converting and embezzling the District's moneys and property," but they had been required by Texas law to send out the district's tax notices by mail, and there was "no evidence . . . that the taxes assessed were excessive, 'padded' or in any way illegal"; thus their use of the mail was not "for the purpose of executing the scheme," as required for a mail fraud conviction, but merely incidental to the "essentially state crimes" they planned to commit by stealing "an indefinite part of the receipts."

Justice Charles Whittaker's twenty-four-page majority opinion summarized some of the squalid facts on which the jury in Judge Ingraham's Houston courtroom had found all of the defendants guilty:

> Petitioners Saenz, Garza and Garcia were three of the four Benavides members of the Board. Petitioners Oscar Carrillo, Sr., and O.P. Carrillo were, respectively, the secretary of and the attorney for the Board. Petitioner Chapa was the assessor-collector. Petitioner Parr was the president and principal stockholder of petitioner Texas State Bank — the authorized depository of the District's funds — and of petitioner San Diego State Bank, and there was evidence that, although having no official connection with the District, he practically dominated and controlled its affairs, kept its books and records in his office, outside the District, until July 1951, and counter-signed all its checks after June 1950. Petitioner Donald was the cashier and administrative manager of

the Texas State Bank, and petitioner Oliveira was a director of that bank.

There was evidence that throughout the relevant period the District's funds, in large amounts, were misappropriated, converted, embezzled and stolen by petitioners. It tended to show that four devices were used for such purposes:

(1) At least once each month numerous district checks were issued against both its building and maintenance accounts in the depository bank payable to fictitious persons and were presented in bundles, totaling from $3,000 to $12,000, to the depository bank and, under the supervision of petitioner Donald, were cashed by it, without endorsements, and the currency was placed and sealed in an envelope and handed to the presenting person for delivery to petitioner Parr. The evidence tended to show that no less than $120,000 of the District's funds were misappropriated in this way.

(2) At least once each month large numbers of district checks were issued to petitioners, other than Donald and the two banks, often in assumed names or in the names of members of their families, purporting to be in payment for services rendered or materials furnished to the District but which were not rendered or furnished, which checks were presented to the depository bank and, under the supervision of petitioner Donald, were cashed by it, often without or upon forged endorsements. The evidence tended to show that no less than $65,000 of the District's funds were misappropriated in this way.

Petitioners Saenz, Garcia, Garza, Oliveira and Chapa regularly received district payroll checks, sometimes in their own names but usually under one or more fictitious names, for services not rendered. Saenz regularly received eight payroll checks in various names; Garcia regularly received payroll checks in the name of his daughter, so did Garza; Oliveira regularly received such checks, sometimes payable to him and at other times to his implement company. Chapa regularly received three such checks each month in various names. All of the checks mentioned were for from $100 to $125. A payroll check for $500 was issued monthly in the name of Parr's brother-in-law, who rendered no services for the District.

(3) Petitioner Chapa converted district checks received by mail in payment of taxes, cashed the same — some at a local bank and some at the depository bank — upon unauthorized endorsements, and misappropriated the proceeds.

(4) Petitioners Oscar Carrillo, Sr., and Garza obtained gasoline and oil for themselves upon the credit card and at the expense
of the District . . . There was evidence, too, that petitioner O. P.
Carrillo procured the remodeling of his law office and new office
furniture and equipment on the credit and at the expense of the
District to the extent of about $2,500.

Given the facts they knew Diego Heras could testify about, it isn't
surprising that school board members Saenz, Garza, and Garcia all
resigned immediately when Heras was granted immunity and subpoenaed to testify before the state grand jury in 1954.

Justice Whittaker's opinion concluded with a paragraph indicating the majority's mild discomfort with the reversal.

The strongest element in the Government's case is that petitioners' behavior was shown to have been so bad and brazen, which,
coupled with the inability or at least the failure of the state authorities to bring them to justice, doubtless persuaded the Government to undertake this prosecution. But the showing, however
convincing, that state crimes of misappropriation, conversion,
embezzlement and theft were committed does not establish the
federal crime of using the mails to defraud, and, under our
vaunted system, no man, however bad his behavior, may be convicted of a crime of which he was not charged, proven and found
guilty in accordance with due process.

Justice Felix Frankfurter blistered his colleagues with a pep-
pery dissent in which he was joined by Justices John Marshall Har-
lan and Potter Stewart, condemning "the fraudulent enterprise of
which this record reeks." Frankfurter didn't buy the petitioners'
major premise. "[T]he heart of petitioners' effort to escape their
conviction," he wrote, "is the claim that the skulduggeries of which
the jury found them guilty do not fall within the scope of the Mail
Fraud statute because in sending out the tax bills they were the neutral vehicles of legal compulsion"; i.e., because Texas law required
the district's tax statements to be mailed, their use of the mails
couldn't be considered part of the scheme. Frankfurter was indignant. The miscreants "controlled the entire conduct of the District's
fiscal affairs," he pointed out, and they had "predetermined that the
[tax] proceeds were not to be fully applied to school purposes but
were in part to be diverted into their private pockets." By demanding and collecting what they intended to misappropriate, he argued,

"they made the process of collection an inseparable element of their scheme."

Justice Whittaker's reference to the state's "inability or at least the failure" to bring the defendants to justice was a reference to the disappointing fate of all the state prosecutions that had originated from the same round of investigations that culminated in the federal mail fraud case. The majority opinion commented in a footnote that "Petitioners Parr, Chapa and Donald were several times tried in the state court on charges growing out of matters involved in this case. Parr and Donald were ultimately found guilty but their convictions were reversed . . . Chapa was tried on two other indictments returned in the state court, both charging fraudulent conversion of the District's funds. He was acquitted on the first indictment and convicted on the second but his conviction was reversed."

The failed mail fraud case was the last hurrah for state and federal prosecutors for more than a decade in Duval County. Nevertheless, George's problems weren't over. He still had tax liens and civil claims to contend with, he was in bankruptcy, the Old Party was largely out of power, and the federal tax evasion indictment against him was still pending — but at least he wasn't going to prison any time soon, and he had lost none of his cunning.

In November 1960, the state foreclosed on Parr's Dobie Ranch to satisfy his "debt" to Duval County for the half-million dollars he had dipped out of the Road and Bridge Fund in 1945 to buy the huge spread. The foreclosure sale on the steps of the Duval County Courthouse brought $1,575,000 from the successful bidder, and Parr pointed to the price as evidence that he had invested the county's money wisely.

Before long the sun emerged from behind the storm clouds and began to shine on George and the Old Party again. Judge C. Woodrow Laughlin returned to the fold, Archer Parr was elected county judge and took control of the election process, and the Old Party's candidates began winning back offices they had lost in the turbulent 1950s.

The complete collapse of all the prosecutions was demoralizing to the political reformers; they saw it as proof that no matter how hard they tried, George Parr would always prevail in the end, and without quite saying so they gave up the struggle. Events seemed to have validated what *Time* magazine had reported on February 15, 1954, about the early stages of the Freedom Party's revolution in Duval: "[M]any a southeast *[sic]* Texas politico guessed that the palm-studded empire of Parr was crumbling. 'Don't bet on it, though,' said one. 'This is mesquite country. You know how hard it is to kill a mesquite tree; you can chop it, you can burn it, but the roots go way down deep, and it'll keep coming up again.' "

In its series titled "DUVAL: A TROUBLED DUKEDOM," the *Dallas Morning News* commented on August 18, 1974, "[T]he tide turned when the Supreme Court reversed his mail fraud conviction, and when a new Democratic administration took power in 1961, George Parr, the 'Mr. Democrat' of South Texas, began to function as he had in the past."

In 1963 Parr emerged from bankruptcy after settling the huge claim of the Internal Revenue Service for a few cents on the dollar, and the remaining state criminal charges still pending against him were dismissed. His legal problems had cost him his big ranch, but that had been bought with money stolen straight out of the county treasury. He still had his elegant home in San Diego, and some of his smaller real estate holdings were restored when Archer Parr bought a batch of lots and mineral interests from the bankruptcy trustee and sold them back to George for the same nominal prices. John Kennedy and Lyndon Johnson carried Duval County by a 12–1 ratio in 1960, and Navy Secretary John Connally, in his first run for governor, swept the county by an even stronger 14–1 landslide in 1962. In March 1963, the *San Antonio Express-News* reported that Attorney General Robert Kennedy had ordered the dismissal of the government's 1954 tax evasion indictment after his "thorough review" of the case, and for the first time in nine years George was free of the threat of criminal prosecution.

The Parrs' return to political respectability was signified by the prominence of George's nephew, Archer Parr, the Duval County judge, as a Texas delegate to the 1964 Democratic National Convention in Atlantic City. In 1969 the Texas legislature created the 229th Judicial District, comprising Duval, Starr, and Zapata counties, giving George a chance to reinforce his strong bond with the Carrillo family and ensure continuing control of the local judiciary. With Parr's blessing, State Representative Oscar Carrillo got the bill passed, and Oscar's brother, O. P., became the judge. After all the painful reverses of the 1950s, George was sitting in the catbird seat again.

The Old Party reclaimed every aspect of Duval County government in the 1960s as inexorably as mesquite reclaims idle South Texas pasture land. George and Archer created a new governmental entity to play with — the grandly named Duval County Conservation and Reclamation District — and settled down to an uninterrupted decade of running the county for fun and profit. Not until 1972 would the empire be challenged again.

Chapter 5

The Austin Connection

Although men flatter themselves with their great actions, they are
not so often the result of great design as of chance.
—Francois Alexandre Frédérick, Duc de La Rochefoucauld

AFFIDAVIT

United States of America, Western
Judicial District of Texas

I, Carl H. Stautz, state that:

I reside at 1704 Exposition Boulevard, Austin, Texas.

1) I am a registered architect and a member of the American
Institute of Architects and the Texas Society of Architects. I
have been a registered architect for the past 36 years. I
specialize in school design and construction throughout the
state of Texas.

So begins the twenty-three-page affidavit that marked the beginning of the end of George Parr's reign in Duval County.

Carl Stautz signed the affidavit on May 22, 1972, in Austin. It
was witnessed by two special agents of the Internal Revenue Service,
Charles S. Volz and Gerald T. Culver, and it was the culmination of
several frustrating months of work with a badly frightened, tem-
peramental witness.

Stautz's Exposition Boulevard address was indicative of a certain level of gentility and affluence. In Houston it would have been

River Oaks, or in Dallas, Highland Park. In Austin it was Tarry-town, a posh, west side enclave subdivided early in the century from a few great estates, including that of Governor Elisha M. Pease, by several prominent landowners. When Lyndon Johnson moved his family into the neighborhood during his years in the United States Senate, the sedate little area found itself transformed into the pre-ferred place for power brokers and politicians to live.

Shaded by stately oaks and silvery elms, the old guard and the new (but not *too* new) money of Austin lived side by side along broad boulevards and serpentine lanes with names that ranged from descrip-tively functional, such as Exposition Boulevard, to quaint, like Pos-sum Trot, in comfortable pursuit of their ambitions and avarices. And so it was in Tarrytown that Carl Stautz lived, pursuing his.

In the early fall of 1971, Carl Stautz was in a sweat. The IRS computer had selected Stautz's 1966, 1967, and 1968 income tax re-turns for audit, and he was finding it difficult to come up with satis-factory answers to some very sensitive questions about expenditures he had made through his sole-proprietorship business, Triangle Construction Company.

Stautz's bank records showed that he had written checks to cash totaling more than $350,000 on the Triangle checking account during those three years. He had claimed as business deductions a few minor items that weren't allowable but he hadn't deducted any of the cash disbursements, and the revenue agent examining the returns was puzzled: Why would any businessman spend that much money with-out trying to get the benefit of some business deductions for it? The agent's curiosity was heightened by the $2,500,000 that Stautz's records showed he had been paid during those same three years by the San Diego and Benavides Independent School Districts, of Duval County, on school construction and remodeling contracts.

The checks payable to cash became the real focus of the exami-nation. The more questions he was asked on that subject, the more ill at ease Stautz grew and the more evasive and unconvincing his answers became. Finally, suspecting some kind of illicit connection between the cash flowing out and the construction payments flow-ing in, the revenue agent referred the file down the hall to the Intel-ligence Division and its criminal investigators, the special agents. Today that division of the IRS is more descriptively named the Criminal Investigation Division, or CID, but the special agents' title and duties remain the same. With a touch of gallows humor, the decision of the United States Court of Claims in a case styled *Peden vs. United States* suggests how an audited taxpayer should react to the referral of his case to a special agent: "The special agent is the unobtrusive fellow casually introduced to you midway in the audit of your income tax return, as the one who is now taking over. If you grasp the significance of his title, you gather your wits together and rush out to hire the ablest criminal lawyer you can obtain, at any cost. You know the prison doors are yawning for your reception."

Stautz was naturally high-strung anyway, but his anxiety level rose to new heights when he learned that his civil audit had become a criminal investigation. His tax attorneys, Sander Shapiro and Mike Cook of former ambassador Edward Clark's big Austin law firm, argued with some justification that no matter how Stautz had spent the cash, he had violated no tax laws because he had deducted none of it. Stautz, however, was burdened by a guilty conscience and was despondent over an assortment of personal problems unrelated to the IRS' inquiry. He became desperately afraid the government was going to learn his darkest secrets and send him to prison in his twilight years. By December he had had his fill of worrying; he was ready to throw in the towel and get it over with. At Stautz's insistence, Shapiro and Cook appeared in the office of the IRS regional chief of intelligence, George Stephen, with a proposition: If Stautz were given assurance that he wouldn't be prosecuted, he would answer all the agents' questions about the cash.

Carl Stautz's life was already in disarray when the IRS examination began, and Special Agent I. A. Filer, who came to know Stautz better than he wanted to, thinks personal problems led to his decision to make a clean breast of things. "I'm convinced," Filer says, "that if Stautz hadn't had that series of personal tragedies — his wife died, and his son got married and moved away, and he was by himself, and his mother was real ill — and if all those things hadn't been weighing on his mind, I doubt if he would have ever talked to us."

To entice law enforcement authorities to grant immunity from prosecution, the potential defendant has to convince the prosecutors it's more important to get the information he can provide about others than it is to convict him for his own offenses. What crimes has he committed that will go unpunished if his proposal is accepted? Whom is he offering to implicate, and what crimes have they committed? Does he have only information that law enforcement already has, or is he offering something new? Does he have personal knowledge and hard evidence, or is he merely seeking to trade in gossip and rumors? In law enforcement's perspective, is the target a smaller fish than the one he offers to put into the government's net? The prosecutor's analysis goes to the ultimate question whether the public interest is served by letting the target go free in exchange for his help in bringing someone else to justice.

Immunity negotiations are delicate. The target must disclose enough information to enable the prosecutor to evaluate the proposed bargain, but in doing so he risks being denied immunity after handing the prosecutor a sword to use against him. A sort of ritual mating dance occurs; ultimately, however, the target must accept the risks inherent in disclosing something of real value or no decision can be made. Stautz's lawyers told George Stephen the agents' suspicions about the cash were essentially correct: Stautz had used most of it to pay kickbacks on his school construction contracts in Duval County. The recipients included county school officials and the Duke himself, George Parr.

Parr's name stirred an immediate reaction. Stephen went to his boss, IRS District Director Robert L. Phinney, with the news, and Stephen and Phinney held meetings with lawyers Shapiro and Cook in December 1971 and January 1972 to discuss Stautz's proposal. An IRS internal progress report on the investigation reflects that at those meetings, "Stautz, through his attorneys, agreed to testify fully before a Federal Grand Jury, provided he was first given immunity." Stautz and his lawyers had more than one concern on their minds, however, as the report reveals: "The attorneys seemed to be sincerely concerned concerning STAUTZ' personal safety, stating he had received a telephone threat on his life during the Christmas holidays of 1971, and that a .22 caliber slug, or pellet, had been shot through STAUTZ' window. As regards the granting of immunity, STAUTZ' attorneys seemed to be clearly concerned about state prosecution of STAUTZ for making graft payments to public officials if he testified without the grant of immunity."

Having done business with the Duval County establishment for years, Carl Stautz knew the folklore of the region. Whether George Parr was having him harassed or not was immaterial; Stautz believed it, and he knew it was dangerous to cross the Duke, and he was scared.

Bob Phinney had been the IRS district director in Austin for nearly two decades when George Stephen put the Stautz matter on his desk. A shrewd, genial Irishman with an engaging personality, Phinney had sold advertising time for Lyndon Johnson's Austin radio station, KTBC, before Johnson had him appointed Austin's postmaster. A few years later Johnson was instrumental in his former employee's move to IRS, and in 1972 Phinney was only a few years away from retirement. Like the postmaster's job, the office of district director was a political patronage appointment when Phinney joined IRS, and Johnson, the most powerful Democrat in Washington, never missed an opportunity to take good care of his friends.

In the case of Bob Phinney, LBJ made a commendable choice; a man of integrity as well as charm, Phinney knew everyone in town and he understood the role he had been chosen to play. The district director's most important responsibility at that time was maintaining good public relations for an inherently unpopular agency, and Phinney ("Sweet Old Bob," as he referred to himself with a wry smile) was a natural at it.

Phinney and Stephen realized immediately the enormous potential of Carl Stautz's story: It meant there was a good chance the Duke of Duval and some of his friends had left themselves open to the assessment of additional income taxes and civil penalties, and maybe even to prosecution for tax evasion, because public officials on the take typically don't report bribes as income. Parr, after all, had made the mistake of not reporting bribes in the 1930s, with unfortunate consequences for him that had required a presidential pardon to cure. Stautz's story would have to be carefully verified, Phinney knew, but it was a legitimate lead that justified opening a new IRS investigation to see if Parr owed more income taxes than he had admitted to, and whether he might be vulnerable to another federal prosecution for tax evasion.

But if Stautz's proposal offered Phinney and his staff a once-in-a-lifetime opportunity to investigate a notorious public figure — the kind of opportunity the IRS cherishes because of the visibility it gives the income tax enforcement program — it also required them to think seriously about the downside of that undertaking. The IRS had invested thousands of agent-hours and many thousands of dollars in expenses in the ill-fated 1950s crusade against corruption in Duval County, and in the end it had nothing to show for it. Parr and his cronies had emerged unscathed from that bitter struggle, and law enforcement had been the big loser.

Phinney and Stephen weren't interested in presiding over a repeat of that costly disaster, and they knew another investigation of Parr would be lengthy and hard fought. ("There were some [IRS] people who got burned pretty bad in that earlier investigation," one veteran agent observed. "Nobody wanted to rush into another one on George Parr without being pretty sure they were on solid ground.") Ironically, by the time Stautz sent his attorneys to George Stephen under a white flag, to make a deal, Special Agent Dave Clore had already concluded the evidence wouldn't support a criminal tax charge against Stautz and the intelligence division had withdrawn from the case. The issue at that point, so far as the IRS was concerned, was not whether Stautz had any criminal liability, but whether his potential testimony would justify launching a major tax investigation of George Parr and several public school officials.

Phinney read the reports, listened to the views and recommendations of his staff, and decided to act. The chance that his team might be able to strike a blow for liberty in Duval County, he concluded, was simply too important not to risk the effort.

In the federal law enforcement system, decisions to grant or deny immunity requests are made by the Department of Justice on the recommendations of United States attorneys. Having decided that Carl Stautz's information was worth acting on, Phinney called the U.S. attorney for the Western District of Texas, William S. Sessions, in San Antonio. "Bill," Phinney said, "we've got a little matter here that's kinda out of the ordinary, and we'd like to tell you about it, but not on the phone. Do you suppose you could come up to Austin and meet with George Stephen and me to talk about it?"

Bill Sessions was six feet tall and lean, with almost grimly serious features that belied his generally cheerful outlook and outgoing personality. Dressed in his customary dark suit, white shirt, and conservative tie, he was the very image of a federal prosecutor with important things on his mind. His confidence in those he chose to serve on his team was matched by his personal enthusiasm for every task he assigned to himself, and his energy knew no bounds. When Sessions set out to travel from one place to another on foot, whether it was three blocks down the street to a restaurant or thirty feet down the hall to his office, only the well-conditioned could keep up with him. His drive to accomplish the task at hand and his confidently assertive personality were reflected in the tempo and vigor of his movements. Whenever the going got tough, Sessions found inspiration in the words of the Old Testament prophet, Isaiah: "They will run and not grow weary; they will walk and not be faint."

Sessions was in his early forties, his hair just beginning to show a bit of salt-and-pepper at the temples. A native of Arkansas and the son of a Christian Church minister, he had grown up in Kansas and served as an air force officer during the Korean War. Instead of sending him overseas, the air force stationed him in Waco, Texas, where he stayed on to earn undergraduate and law degrees at Baylor University after his tour of duty ended. Then he settled down in Waco to practice law.

Unlike Sessions, I was a third-generation Texan and had lived in the state most of my life. After earning an undergraduate degree in business administration at Lamar University, in Beaumont, I had served two years in the army as an enlisted man and worked for three years in the business world before perpetuating a family link with the University of Texas by moving to Austin and enrolling in law school. Although Sessions and I had practiced law for several years in two Central Texas cities only a hundred miles apart and had both been active in the Republican Party, we did not meet until 1969.

As the incoming Nixon administration assembled its team in Washington in early 1969, Senator John Tower spearheaded the emerging Texas Republican Party's drive to fill as many important positions as possible with Texas Republicans. One of those appointed by the new president at Tower's suggestion was ex-Democrat Will Wilson of Austin, the former Texas attorney general and Texas Supreme Court justice, who was chosen to head the criminal division at the Department of Justice.

Seven years earlier, in 1962, when the ink was barely dry on my law license, Will Wilson had offered me a job in the Texas attorney general's office, and I had opted instead to take a job in private practice. Because we both lived in Austin and I had friends who worked for him, I saw Wilson occasionally over the next few years. After he changed parties in 1966, I saw him more often in the context of Republican political activities.

Although Wilson had no Washington experience, he had enough familiarity with government bureaucracies to know that he wanted some familiar faces around him in the big, gray building at 10th and Constitution — preferably Republicans, because the Democrats had controlled the executive branch of government and done all the hiring for the past eight years. From Waco, he enlisted

Sessions, who by that time had been elected to the Waco City Council. From Austin, he recruited me. In early 1969 I flew to Washington for the first time in my life, to find out what he had in mind for me at the Department of Justice.

The weather that week, typical of Washington in winter, as I would learn later, was cold and wet. "John, this department is top heavy with lawyers from East Coast law schools," Will Wilson said as we sat before the fireplace in his second-floor Justice Department office. "I'm sure they're good lawyers, most of 'em, but they all have that East Coast perspective on everything. I want to bring in some lawyers from our part of the country to give this place a little more balance." He paused. "Besides," he said, "I need some people around here that I can count on to be loyal to *me*. I don't really know anybody here. Bill Sessions is coming up from Waco, and I'd like for you to come too."

For the next two years, Sessions was my immediate superior at Justice. In 1971, when Seagal Wheatley, who had been President Nixon's first U.S. attorney for the Western District of Texas, resigned to return to private practice, Sessions was appointed to succeed him, and I relocated to San Antonio with Sessions to serve as first assistant. We'd been in our offices there less than six months when we got Bob Phinney's intriguing request to visit him in Austin.

On the morning of January 19, 1972, Sessions and I made the seventy-five-mile drive up Interstate 35 to Austin, accompanied by Sessions' wife, Alice, and their young daughter, Sara. Alice dropped us off at the Federal Building while she and Sara went off to shop and visit friends.

Bill Sessions and I were ushered into Bob Phinney's office for a briefing by his chief of intelligence, George Stephen. After Stephen explained the unexpected dividend the Stautz audit had turned up and what Stautz was requesting as a guarantee against prosecution, Sessions and I discussed immunity considerations and investigative strategies with Stephen and Phinney. We explained the ground rules for obtaining an immunity grant for Stautz: Sessions would have to make a recommendation to the Department of Justice, giving detailed information about Stautz and the anticipated substance and effect of his testimony. If Justice approved, the attorney general would authorize us to apply to the U.S. district court for an order requiring Stautz to testify before a federal grand jury and prohibiting the government from using his own testimony, no matter how incriminating, against him. Stautz was insistent on one condition, Stephen said: He absolutely would not testify before a grand jury in Austin or Corpus Christi. "He's scared to death of George Parr," Stephen explained. "He's convinced Parr has so much influence in Austin and Corpus that he could find out what Stautz said to a federal grand jury in either place. He thinks Parr could even plant somebody on the grand jury. We've tried to convince him that's just not so, but he's adamant."

The meeting was productive. We agreed to seek immunity for Stautz and discussed the principal players identified as recipents of his payoffs, school superintendents Bryan Taylor and Eunice Powell, and George Parr, who was then a member of the San Diego school board. (Powell was a man, not a woman; I had mistakenly assumed at first that "Eunice" was an exclusively feminine name.) Because all three men were potentially liable for additional taxes on unreported income if Stautz's claims could be proved, it was agreed that Phinney's office would conduct a joint investigation of civil and criminal liability. The criminal investigation, however, would be put on hold pending approval of the immunity grant for Stautz. Stautz's fear of testifying in Austin and Corpus Christi wouldn't be an obstacle, we decided; he could tell his story to a grand jury in San Antonio. We realized that if we indicted Parr and the others on tax charges in the Western District of Texas they would have the right to insist on being tried in the Southern District in which they lived, but we could cross that bridge if we ever came to it. After lunch with Phinney and Stephen at La Tapatia, on East 6th Street, we drove back to San Antonio to start drafting an immunity request to the Department of Justice.

The bland scenery between Austin and San Antonio on Interstate 35 was familiar to Sessions and me; Austin was part of our Western District jurisdiction, and we had a satellite office in the federal courthouse on West 8th Street. Although the trip back to San Antonio was scarcely more than an hour's drive, it seemed interminable that afternoon. Sessions and I were bursting to talk about our new project, but we had to limit the conversation to other topics until we dropped off Alice and Sara at home and headed downtown.

The surprise package Bob Phinney dropped into our laps that morning had given me feelings akin to *deja vu*. My first job as a brand-new lawyer, in early 1962 — the job for which I had declined Will Wilson's offer to join the state attorney general's staff — was in the law offices of Dan Moody, Jr., who had practiced with his famous father until failing health forced the governor to retire. The offices were still on the twelfth floor of the Capital National Bank Building, virtually unchanged since the day Governor Moody first occupied them. The entire firm in those days consisted of Dan and me, and a secretary.

Shortly after I went to work for him, Dan had shown me his father's file on the Box 13 litigation. "Knowing your interest in politics," Dan said with a smile, "I think you might like to look through this file." I consumed it in a single afternoon, fascinated, as history came to life page by page, in letters, telegrams, courtroom transcripts, legal briefs, and notes scrawled on legal pads and hotel stationery. I had known since my sophomore year at Beaumont High School who George Parr was, but the governor's file transformed him and Box 13 from the stuff of distant legend into immediate, verified fact.

On the way back to San Antonio after the meeting with Bob Phinney, images from Governor Moody's Box 13 file came flooding back into my memory. It is truly a small world, I mused. Ten years earlier, when I had been privileged to read the details of the election fraud that changed American history, it hadn't occurred to me that someday George Parr's path and mine might cross. Between occasional exchanges of casual conversation as Sessions drove south toward home, I thought about the possibility that we might actually have a chance to prosecute Parr, and it seemed almost too implausible to be true.

I thought also of the tiny delegations of diehard activists from Duval County who began showing up at Republican state conventions in the early 1960s in spite of harassment and ridicule and the midnight vandalism of their small businesses, and of all the candidates, Republicans and Democrats alike, who had been the powerless victims of rigged voting and phony election returns in George Parr's domain, and the prospect of bringing the Duke of Duval before the bar of justice had great appeal.

We needed an answer from Justice quickly on immunity for Carl Stautz. Any prosecution based on a failure to report payoffs received in 1966 would be barred by the statute of limitations if not initiated by April 15, 1973. We had to clear some big hurdles before that date: First, we needed the immunity grant to get Stautz's story under oath before a grand jury; second, we needed to complete what might turn out to be a long and difficult investigation; third, any recommendation for prosecution growing out of the investigation would have to be reviewed and approved by IRS regional counsel — a notoriously painstaking, slow process — and then by the tax division of the Department of Justice, before we could seek an indictment. Parr's lawyers could be expected to try to delay us at every opportunity in hopes of knocking out the 1966 tax liability, and on top of everything else, Parr was seventy-two years old. Time was not on our side.

Our immunity application for Stautz went to Washington and vanished into the bowels of the Department of Justice while George Stephen and his agents grew increasingly anxious about the shortness of time. An entry in the IRS Sensitive Case Report on March 6, 1972, reflects the Service's frustration over the delay:

> The grant of immunity has been recommended but not approved. Conferences have been held with the U.S. Attorney for the Western District of Texas, WILLIAM S. SESSIONS, and his first assistant, JOHN CLARK. At this time we are awaiting the grant of immunity and [Stautz's] Grand Jury testimony before proceeding actively in the investigation of the POWELL case, and the other cases yet to be numbered.
>
> As $255,000 of the alleged graft payments were made during the year 1966, we are faced with a statute case situation even before actively beginning our investigation. Since it is usually necessary to have the final reports in statute case situations in the hands of the Regional Counsel by August 15, a hurried investigation involving more than the ordinary number of special agents and revenue agents will be required. Beginning the active investigation prior to securing STAUTZ' testimony has been considered and rejected. If the investigation was begun first, it is likely that a great deal of pressure would be asserted on STAUTZ in an attempt to keep him from testifying. However, if the immunity grant is long delayed, we may be forced by the pressure of time to take investigative actions which might be most detrimental to the case.

Technically, a witness testifying under a federal "use immunity" grant is not excused from liability for his crimes; he is protected only against the use of his own testimony against him and can be prosecuted even after giving compelled testimony if the government can prove his guilt with other evidence not discovered as a result of his testimony. But the government's burden of proving that its evidence is not derived from the witness' forced testimony is heavy, and Justice Department policy considerations do not favor prosecution in those circumstances. As a practical matter, therefore, the immunized witness ordinarily has no cause for concern about prosecution for crimes he admits in testimony.

Those principles were familiar to Carl Stautz's attorneys, and they were explained again to them, and in turn to Stautz himself. Stautz understood, but he was a chronic worrywart — the kind of client who needs a lot of what lawyers refer to as "handholding." Having made the decision to cooperate with the government to avoid the possibility of prosecution, Carl Stautz continued to fret about the wisdom of that decision while awaiting word that his immunity request had been approved. From time to time he pestered Barry Bishop, his regular attorney at the Clark, Thomas law firm, for reassurance that he had made the right choice. In Carl Stautz's case, there was no danger to him from the government; his bribery of local officials was not a federal crime, and we had nothing to prosecute him for, with or without his own testimony. If he had reason to worry, it was because of George Parr.

Because a federal immunity grant also immunizes the witness against any state crimes he may admit, the Department of Justice considers state law enforcement interests as well as federal in deciding whether to grant an immunity request. We had explained in the Stautz application that we could not furnish the customary waiver of objection from state prosecutors because the officials we would have to approach were all closely tied to the principal target, George Parr. That wrinkle, we learned, was principally responsible for the delay we were experiencing. Stautz's payments, if true, amounted to bribery under Texas law, at least as to the two school superintendents. Unless we could show that the state had no objection, departmental policy didn't permit giving him immunity. More discussions followed as we attempted to resolve the impasse. Finally, Justice had a constructive suggestion: A waiver from the state's attorney general would suffice; did we think he would consent? We were back in Austin the next day.

Before his election as attorney general, Crawford Martin had served as a state senator and as secretary of state. He was a veteran Texas public official, a conservative Democrat, and a gentleman. Distinguished in appearance, with silvery hair and a black eye patch, Martin welcomed us to his seventh-floor office in the modern pink granite attorney general's office building, located just northwest of the handsome old State Capitol, and listened attentively as we explained our mission. "You know I don't really have any independent authority to prosecute anybody," he smiled when we finished, "but if you need my consent to give this Stautz fella immunity to testify about making payoffs in Duval County, you've got it. You can tell 'em the State of Texas has no objection."

As we said our goodbyes, Martin shook hands again and wished us well. "You boys think you might get ol' George Parr, do you? Now, that would really be *something*. I remember when John Ben Shepperd tried so hard and couldn't make anything stick; I hope y'all have better luck."

Chapter 6

The Kickoff

I was a stranger in a strange land.
— Exodus 2:22

The reluctant witness

ON ST. PATRICK'S DAY, March 17, 1972, we received the Justice Department's blessing to obtain a court order granting immunity to Carl Stautz. I called IRS Intelligence Chief George Stephen that Friday morning to give him the news. The criminal tax investigation of George Parr, which we had put on hold while waiting for the attorney general to approve our request, could go forward. Still feeling the pressure of time imposed by the approaching statute of limitations on Parr's 1966 tax return, Stephen lost no time scheduling Stautz for his long-awaited debriefing.

At 9:00 the following Monday morning, Carl Stautz walked into Room 367 at Austin's highrise federal building with tax attorney Sander Shapiro, a partner of Lyndon and Lady Bird Johnson's personal attorney, Donald Thomas. Stautz was there to begin answering the questions he had dodged for months. If George Stephen and Special Agent Dave Clore expected Stautz to reveal everything immediately, though, they soon discovered it wasn't going to be that easy.

What Stautz really wanted to tell them about was the anonymous threats he claimed to have received by telephone since his lawyers began negotiating immunity for him. He produced a monthly planning calendar meticulously inscribed, in one-inch square date boxes, with cryptic little entries reflecting his business and personal activities. Additional details written on pages from a small memo pad bearing the logo of the Daughters of the Republic of Texas supplemented some of the calendar entries and were stapled to the calendar pages.

The first of the telephone calls, according to Stautz's notes, came at 6:30 P.M. on January 3, 1972; the caller spoke in a low voice, saying, *"Your days are numbered if you talk."* Stautz's entry indicates he called the police and told his lawyer, Shapiro. The calendar and notes reflected a second call at 9:30 P.M. on February 16 from "the same low voice," telling Stautz, *"This is your second warning. Don't talk."* Stautz's records also included a third entry, at 11:45 P.M. on March 15: "In bed. Phone call — didn't recognize voice. Music & talking in background. Sounded like heavy breathing. Voice said *'This is the Last Warning* — pause — *don't talk to anyone about South Texas. Tell your lawyer to lay off* — pause — *Last Warning, OK?'* Hung up."

Stautz supposedly was ready to speak openly, but the interview with Stephen did not go well. Even though it was obvious from their questions that George Stephen and Dave Clore already knew much of what he had been involved in, Stautz was evasive and defensive, finding it difficult to shake off his inhibitions and admit what he had done. Stautz identified a few sums, most of them small, as cash payments to one or another of the three subjects of the investigation, but he repeatedly pleaded confusion and lack of memory as to other, mostly larger, figures in his calendar entries. Before losing patience with his witness, Stephen maintained his composure for nearly two hours as he continued to press for straight answers. As the internal memorandum of interview reflects, at around 11:00 the IRS intelligence chief let Stautz know his immunity option was about to expire:

> At this point in the interview STEPHEN told attorney Shapiro that it was obvious that Mr. STAUTZ was not telling us about the payments that he had made in Duval County and that under these circumstances we might as well terminate the interview and call Mr. STAUTZ before a grand jury. Mr. STAUTZ asked if he could go to the rest room prior to continuing.

Upon returning to the interview room, Stautz identified cash payments in 1966 and 1968 totaling $53,500 to San Diego Independent School District Superintendent Bryan Taylor and $10,000 to Benavides Independent School District Superintendent Eunice Powell, and a single payment of $40,000 to George Parr in 1966. After listening to Stautz whine that he needed to review all of his records and look up his 1967 travel expense diary to identify the other transactions Stephens and Clore had asked him about, Stephen made these notes:

> STEPHEN then advised SHAPIRO that he would like for Mr. STAUTZ to review his check stubs, his diary and other records that he might have to refresh his memory as to payments he made to various Duval County officials in 1966, 1967 and 1968, and that the government would like to then have Mr. STAUTZ' affidavit or his testimony before a Federal Grand Jury. STAUTZ stated that if he had to appear as a witness, he would disappear, and he then discussed the threats he had received and the fact that he was afraid to go to South Texas, and that it would be easy for them to contract a sharp-shooter out of Mexico.

Stephen asked Sander Shapiro to notify him immediately if Stautz received any more threatening telephone calls and agreed to look into the possibility of giving Stautz "some form of protection." Shapiro agreed to have his client review all of his records carefully in preparation for a continuation of the interview.

Carl Stautz had been much less candid in his responses to Stephen than in his disclosures to his attorney, but Stephen's reference to having Stautz appear before a federal grand jury got the contractor's attention. Pondering the implications of Stephen's blunt insistence that he become intimately familiar with his 1966, 1967, and 1968 records, Stautz left the federal building at 11:30 A.M., frazzled and glum. The diary entry Stautz made on his planning calendar later that day said, "*To IRS with Shapiro. Rough. Go back over everything.*" Two days later Stautz drove to Dallas to visit his son, David. His subsequent account of the Duval County-connected harassment he encountered in Dallas would be one of the most bizarre stories to come out of the investigation.

In spite of Stautz's unartful dodgery on some of the suspect transactions, his records lent enough support to his reluctant admissions to justify opening both civil and criminal tax investigations of Parr, Taylor, and Powell. Stautz had personally negotiated all of the suspicious checks to cash — twenty-two checks totaling $353,500, from March 1966 through October 1968 — usually at the same teller's window at the Capital National Bank, where Lady Bird Johnson sat on the board of directors with her lawyer, Donald Thomas, and Texas financier Jim Nash, one of President Johnson's most effective fundraisers. All except two of the checks were for amounts of $10,000 or more. The teller, Lucille Spreen, had given Stautz stacks of bills neatly banded and labeled each time, and he had kept many of the wrappers in his safe at home.

The enigmatic notations in Stautz's diary that appeared to be coded references to payoffs tended to fall within a few days after one of his big cash withdrawals from the bank. Although the pieces seemed to fit together, Stephen realized that Stautz's testimony alone would not be sufficient to prove the payments had actually been made. Corroborating evidence, such as corresponding bank deposits by the recipients, or the testimony of another witness to the payoffs, would be needed.

Stautz obviously had more information to give, but because the biggest payments had been made in the 1966 tax year, time was running short. As Bill Sessions, George Stephen, and I had reminded one another and the Department of Justice repeatedly while our immunity request for Carl Stautz was pending, the deadline imposed by the statute of limitations for filing criminal charges based on George Parr's 1966 tax return was April 15, 1973, and the normal review process for criminal tax cases was notoriously slow. We had barely twelve months left to complete a difficult investigation, jump through all the hoops in the IRS and Department of Justice review protocols, and secure an indictment. It was going to take more than hard work; it was going to require a little luck, as well.

Assembling the team

The potential importance of the Duval County investigation was not lost on IRS District Director Phinney, or on Chief of Intelligence Stephen. They both knew it would take the best investigative team they could field to bring down the Duke of Duval. As chief of intelligence for the Austin District, Stephen exercised his prerogative to select the team and direct it personally, functioning as the initial group supervisor. Bill Sessions and I didn't try to influence Stephen's choices; he knew his agents, and it was his call to make. How soon our office would become involved with the investigators on a day-to-day basis would depend on what the agents encountered when they went looking for the rest of the puzzle pieces.

Stautz's statements implicated three people — George Parr, and San Diego and Benavides school superintendents Bryan Taylor and Eunice Powell — as those who demanded and got school construction payoffs from him. Because the investigations were to look into both criminal and civil tax liability of all three, Stephen picked for his team four special agents and three revenue agents. Like other federal law enforcement officers, every special agent carries a government-issue handgun — a Smith & Wesson .38 revolver with a four-inch barrel — as standard equipment. Revenue agents, because they are responsible for civil tax liability only, are not classified as law enforcement officers and do not carry firearms. In conducting an investigation in Duval County, the revenue agents probably would have felt more comfortable if they, too, could have had handguns. Stephen's agents, except for two, were young, but all were experienced investigators. They were, to a man, widely acknowledged to be among the brightest and best agents the Service had.

I. A. Filer, one of the special agents selected for the team, was known to everyone simply as "I. A." because he wasn't fond of, and never used, his first name. Filer was a native of Houston with undergraduate and law degrees from the University of Houston, and he had been a special agent in his hometown since 1965. He was tall, raw-boned, and affable, with a down-home East Texas accent, curly hair, and a ready smile. At thirty-one he was already a seasoned veteran of several major criminal investigations, including the Billie Sol Estes case. (Still discreet about his undercover role in one of the most extraordinary investigations in the history of the IRS, Filer says only that he "spent several days with Mr. Billie." Estes achieved banner-headline notoriety during Lyndon Johnson's administration, when he exploited his status as a politically connected Texas wheeler-dealer to bilk greedy lenders and investors out of millions of dollars in a get-rich-quick scheme involving agricultural fertilizer tanks and Department of Agriculture crop allotments. When Estes' house of cards collapsed, investigators discovered that most of the fertilizer tanks either didn't exist or had been pledged as security for multiple loans, and that most of the allotment deals had been illegal. The few city-slicker backers who bothered to come out west to check on Estes' fertilizer tank operations had been duped: The wily Estes confused them by driving long distances in circuitous routes

over the flat prairie roads, approaching the same tanks several times
from different directions, thus multiplying the number of tanks his
gullible guests thought they were seeing.) Filer never used his law
degree to practice law. "I'm gonna do that when I retire," he would
say, "when I don't need to make a living at it."

Jerry Culver, another native Houstonian, was only a few years
older than Filer. Like Filer, he was a graduate of the University of
Houston, and the two men had worked together previously on investigations in Houston and Austin. Besides being an able criminal
investigator and an impressive expert witness on the fine points of
the Internal Revenue Code, Culver was a dedicated fisherman.
When he wasn't stalking tax violators, he could usually be found
wading the saltwater flats of the Texas Gulf Coast, stalking speckled
trout and redfish with tackle he kept handy in the trunk of his car.

Charlie Volz, in his fifties, was within a year or two of retirement when the investigation began. Unlike most of the other team
members, he lived in Waco and was detailed to the Houston office
for the investigation. Tall, white-haired, and genial, Volz had the
appearance and demeanor of a good-natured, youngish grandfather.
He and Harold Freeman, the other senior special agent, added decades of criminal investigative experience to the team.

The three revenue agents chosen by Stephen to assess the civil
tax consequences of the payoffs from Stautz were equally impressive. Joining Dudley Beaven, also a Houstonian, and Santos Galvan,
of deep South Texas, was Ed Watts, a black-haired Tennessean with
a country twang, who was stationed in San Antonio. "I had never
met [Watts], but he had a terrific reputation as a revenue agent
working in criminal cases," Filer said. "It was a natural selection."
Watts had remained in San Antonio after a tour of duty there with
the air force, marrying a girl from nearby Mathis and taking a job
with the IRS. So impressive was his performance that the agency had
tried to interest him in becoming a special agent, but Watts pre-
ferred instead to specialize in analyzing the civil liability side of tax
evasion cases. As the investigation progressed it became apparent
why Stephen had drafted Watts for the team and assigned him specifically to the investigation of the primary target, George Parr:
Watts was that good.

Heading the team was George Stephen, the fourth native
Houstonian. Stephen had worked his way up to a group manager's
position in Houston after graduating from South Texas College of

Law and then was tapped for the intelligence chief's position in the district office in Austin.

"George [Stephen] summoned us all to Austin one day," recalled I. A. Filer. "I don't know how the specific assignments were made. George asked if anyone did *not* want to work on this investigation, and one of the revenue agents — he was Hispanic, but I don't remember his name — said, 'Yes, I've got relatives in Duval County, and I don't want to work on this one.' And so they brought in Santos Galvan from McAllen [to replace him]." Stephen decided on double coverage for Parr, assigning two special agents, Filer and Volz, to his case, along with Revenue Agent Watts. Special Agent Culver was assigned to investigate Bryan Taylor, superintendent of San Diego I.S.D., with assistance on the civil side from Revenue Agent Dudley Beaven. Special Agent Harold Freeman and Revenue Agent Santos Galvan were assigned to the other school superintendent, Eunice Powell.

Because federal criminal investigators are classified as law enforcement officers, and typically retire from government service in their mid-fifties, Stephen, Volz, and Freeman all could see retirement on the horizon when the investigation began. None of them wanted to leave the IRS, however, without successfully completing the business at hand.

George Stephen's reputation among the agents who worked for him was mixed; they respected his ability, but they dreaded the occasional displays of his mercurial temper. Although he was not the sort of chief who ordinarily gave his agents a great deal of autonomy, Stephen seemed to realize that these carefully selected agents were an all-star cast of self-starters and overachievers who needed little more than to be pointed toward the appropriate goal and left to their own devices, and he gave the team considerably more freedom in this investigation than was typical of him. "George contributed, mainly, by letting us alone," said I. A. Filer. "There were a few times he meddled, but basically he left us alone, which was what we needed. We told him what was going on, and there were some things he got mad about, but the actual supervision from him was very limited."

In the early stages of the investigation George Stephen apprised Sessions and me by telephone what the agents were doing in Duval County to pursue the leads Stautz had reluctantly provided at his turbulent meeting with Stephen on March 20. A few weeks later, circumstances caused us to begin calling witnesses before the grand

jury in San Antonio. At that time the tone of the investigation became more intense and the agents began to work directly with Sessions and me on planning and strategy. "Once the grand jury phase
of the investigation began, George [Stephen] basically left you and
Bill [Sessions] alone, too," Filer told me. "We kinda figured, really,
we were working for y'all at that point. The things that were done
that were not what you would normally think to do were things that
you and Bill suggested."

Filer's mention of measures that were "not what you would
normally think to do" in an investigation was a fond remembrance
of some unusual steps we took in the grand jury phase to solve special problems as they arose — such as our use of a helicopter to
photograph evidence on George Parr's ranch, and our seizure of
bank microfilm to prevent evidence from being destroyed. As the
investigation progressed, the agents enjoyed having the ability,
through our office and the power of the grand jury, to overcome
obstacles that might have thwarted a more conventional investigation by the agents alone.

Advice of rights

IRS procedures require that a taxpayer be notified promptly, in
person, upon becoming the subject of a criminal investigation. The
intelligence division had opened formal criminal and civil tax liability investigation files on George Parr, Bryan Taylor, and Eunice
Powell shortly after George Stephen interviewed Carl Stautz on
March 20; now, with the four special agents and three revenue
agents freed of other duties, briefed, assembled in Corpus Christi,
and assigned office space there, it was time to notify the subjects of
the investigation.

On Monday, April 3, 1972, the agents met at the IRS office in
downtown Corpus Christi to go over a notification plan that was
almost military in detail and precision. George Stephen directed the
agents to work in pairs and call on all three investigative subjects
simultaneously, at 9:30 the next morning, to prevent one target
from alerting another that unwelcome visitors were on the way.
Each notification team consisted of one special agent and one revenue agent, and each team was given a copy of its designated target's
tax returns for 1966 through 1969, to be identified by the taxpayer if
he chose to be that cooperative after hearing the special agent advise
him of his rights.

After an early dinner the agents returned to their favorite Corpus Christi motel, an obscure little place in the North Beach area that featured kitchenettes in the rooms and rates compatible with the government's modest *per diem* allowance. Most of the men watched television in their rooms and turned in early. They weren't sure what kind of reception they would get in Duval County the next day, but they were going to be well rested and ready for anything.

After an early breakfast the next morning and some light-hearted banter about synchronizing watches and fastening flak jackets, all three teams prepared to head west from Corpus Christi on State Highway 44 into hostile territory. Special Agent Jerry Culver and Revenue Agent Dudley Beaven would drive to San Diego, fifty-four miles away, to find Superintendent Bryan Taylor. I. A. Filer and Ed Watts were also headed for San Diego to see the Duke of Duval himself, George Parr. Because Special Agent Harold Freeman and Revenue Agent Santos Galvan were going to call on Eunice Powell in Freer, twenty-five miles west of San Diego, they left ahead of the others.

Each team had a shiny, new AMC sedan. "Jerry Culver negotiated the deal for those cars in San Antonio," Filer recalled. "We talked [the government's General Services Administration] into not putting their GSA stickers on the doors, and we put on regular license plates. We were trying to make 'em look just like all the other cars on the road." But their efforts at anonymity failed. "After we'd been in Duval County a time or two," Filer said, "it seemed like they had somebody assigned to watch for us whenever we crossed the county line, because whoever we went to see was always expecting us when we got there. Of course, there wasn't another AMC vehicle in all of Duval County, either, and ours were a real ugly chocolate brown; that made it pretty hard to be inconspicuous."

Ed Watts and I. A. Filer had no trouble finding George Parr's enormous house. It dwarfed every other building in San Diego except the high school. What the two agents found was an elegant, Mediterranean-style villa with expensive iron grillework, a graceful, red tile roof, and clean, white stucco walls that contrasted with dark wood beams. Its three acres of grounds were surrounded by a low masonry wall, with massive pillars of buttressed masonry to mark the entrance of a wide drive that divided and passed under tiled twin arches. These arched passageways led to a shaded, spacious courtyard, serenely complete with fountain and swimming pool. The broad front of the house, with its two-story elevation, looked out imperiously on the street.

Filer described what happened when he and Watts arrived: "We parked out in front and walked to the front door, but the front door obviously hadn't been opened in years; there were spider webs all over it. So we walked around to the back, through a sort of carport thing, and were looking around and didn't see anybody. And then all of a sudden George drove up. We identified ourselves and he invited us into the house."

The two young agents entered the house with Parr. "George let us in the back door and locked it behind us," Filer said. "It was one of those locks that you leave the key in, in case you have to get out." (At a pretrial hearing two years later, Parr's attorney accused Watts, then on the witness stand, of having had Parr "in custody" on that occasion, which Watts stoutly denied. Later, after testifying, Watts said it had been hard to resist the temptation to tell Parr's attorney that he and Filer, in truth, were the ones in custody that day.)

The agents found the house impressive but the housekeeping disappointing. "The den across the back of that house must be fifty feet long, and there's a big kitchen area with walk-in refrigerated lockers," Filer observed. "It's a nice house, but not extremely well kept; it looked like a Mexican villa, but it could have been maintained much better."

Behind the house was a six-car, metal garage with three double doors. "The garage was floor to ceiling with deer heads and deer horns, on all the walls," Filer said. "I asked George how many he had, and he said the last time he had counted, he had 109, and he'd added some since then." At one end of the building, Filer noted, was "a complete laundry, with big commercial washers and dryers, and a complete shop too."

Parr was a cordial but wary host to his official visitors. Following the prescribed script, Filer began to explain that Watts was a revenue agent and that he, Filer, was a special agent, with responsibility for conducting criminal investigations. Parr waved him off. "I know what a special agent does," Parr interjected. Filer pressed on with the obligatory admonitions about Parr's right to consult an attorney, his right not to furnish records or information that might incriminate him, and a warning that any records or information he might furnish could be used against him. Parr listened silently until

Filer finished. "I understand all of that," Parr said, "and I'll talk about anything else, but I'm not going to talk about my business."

Parr volunteered that he always turned over all of his tax records to Norman Ransleben, a Corpus Christi CPA, to take care of his tax affairs and prepare his returns. The three men made small talk, and Parr's young daughter, Georgia, made a brief appearance in the room. "We talked for a while about his house and about his little daughter. She must have been about eight or nine years old," Filer recalled. (Parr had two daughters, both named Georgia; the first Georgia was born of the first of his two marriages to Thelma Duckworth, which ended in divorce in 1933. The younger Georgia was born of his later marriage to Evangelina Perez.)

When the agents rose to leave, Parr unlocked the door, walked with them down the driveway to their car, smiled ironically, and extended his thick, stubby hand to give each man a firm handshake. "I want to wish you gentlemen good luck," he said, "but not on me."

The next order of business was to find out if Carl Stautz's tales of bribery could be corroborated. That effort began immediately with a careful look at the income tax returns of George Parr, Bryan Taylor, and Eunice Powell.

It would have been astonishing if any of the three men had reported the money as bribes or payoffs, or if they had listed Stautz or his company as a source of income of any kind, and none of them did. In fact, none of the returns showed any income items that appeared to correspond with the payments Stautz claimed to have made.

Parr's tax returns for 1966 through 1969 were relatively uncomplicated, showing only modest income consisting mostly of "consulting fees" and oil royalties, offset in some years by losses from ranching operations and a cattle partnership with his nephew, Archer. George did not itemize his deductions; he took only the standard deduction each year. His adjusted gross income, before annual reductions of approximately $3,000 for personal exemptions and the standard deduction, was $16,480.27 in 1966; $23,235.90 in 1967; $36,503.28 in 1968; and a mere $3,850.18 in 1969.

Although it appeared unrelated to Carl Stautz's allegations, one item on Parr's 1967 return did strike the agents as curious: a long-term capital gain of $40,000 on the sale of City of Benavides bonds. Their investigative instincts were stirred not so much by the capital gain itself as by the fact that Parr's reported basis in the bonds was zero. The entire proceeds of the sale represented clear profit; George had received $40,000 for municipal bonds that had cost him nothing. The agents pondered the untold story behind the bonds. Why had they cost Parr nothing, and who bought them from him, and why were they worth $40,000 to the buyer?

Because two special agents, I. A. Filer and Charlie Volz, were assigned to the investigation of George Parr, Revenue Agent Ed Watts worked and traveled with each of them from time to time. On April 7, three days after Filer and Watts paid their official visit to Parr at his San Diego home, Watts and Volz called on Parr's CPA, Norman Ransleben, at his Corpus Christi office. Ransleben's file included copies of worksheets and penciled copies of forms used in preparing returns for George and for the cattle partnership with George's nephew, Archer, as well as limited records of one of George's personal bank accounts at the First State Bank of San Diego.

All of the information used to prepare Parr's returns, Ransleben said, was supplied by Parr himself, either from Parr's own records and oral statements or in the form of third-party records. Parr had told Ransleben that the $40,000 in bonds were "worthless City of Benavides bonds" he acquired in 1939 and declared as worthless in his 1957 bankruptcy. The buyer was Harris Fender of Tyler, Texas. Watts and Volz resolved to look at the court file in George's bankruptcy proceeding, and to find out more about Harris Fender, whose Tyler home was some 400 miles away in northeast Texas.

Another subject noted for further inquiry was the indication in Ransleben's records that in 1969 Parr received a total of $15,000 from the Duval County Conservation and Reclamation District in two tax-free transactions. The two transactions were reflected in the CPA's notes as a $12,000 "salary advance" and a $3,000 "check swap." According to Parr, Ransleben said, the items were loans or advances from the district toward Parr's $1,000 monthly salary or "consulting fee" as the district's legal counsel, and thus were not reportable as income. Volz and Watts resolved also to look into Parr's relationship with the Duval County Conservation and Reclamation District, and to find out more about the district itself.

Four days later, on April 11, Watts searched county and municipal records in Duval County for descriptions of all the bonds authorized and issued by local governmental entities. On April 13 Watts and Filer flew to Dallas, rented a car, and drove 100 miles east to Tyler, deep in the piney woods of East Texas, to find and interview Harris Fender.

"We were trying to make the first visit [with Fender] sort of a surprise," Watts explained. "[Parr and his friends] knew the investigation was going on, but I think they didn't realize how much information we had put together from the old bankruptcy records about the City of Benavides bond transactions. We were concerned that they'd get together [with Fender] and make up a story if they had known we were looking for him."

Filer and Watts arrived unannounced at Fender's Tyler office at 1:00 P.M. Don Horton, Fender's CPA, explained that Fender was at that moment on his way back from Dallas. Fender arrived an hour later to find an unexpected welcoming committee. As the agents had hoped, they had gained the advantage of surprise.

Harris Fender was a large, self-assured, fiftyish man of generous girth and expensive tastes who looked as if he had been born to wear a gold watch chain and smoke imported cigars. He was also shrewd, gregarious, bombastic. (Because I grew up in the Golden Age of radio, Harris Fender always evoked my old mental images of Harold Peary's grandiloquent character, "The Great Gildersleeve.")

The agents displayed their credentials and Filer told Fender that he and Watts wanted to talk to him about his business dealings with George Parr. Fender was immediately on his guard. "What is it that you want to know about my dealings with Mr. Parr?" he asked. Filer explained that they wanted to know "the means of payment and the purpose" of all of Fender's payments to Parr, direct and indirect. Harris Fender paused. "I want to cooperate with you," he said, "but I want you to understand that George Parr is my friend, and I've made money doing business in Duval County. I'll answer your questions, but I'm not giving you any records without a summons. You give me a summons, and you can have whatever information and records you want."

An IRS civil summons is a formal, written, administrative demand for documents, designed to be served on individuals and entities in possession of records material to an investigation. It can be enforced by a federal district court, if necessary. Fender's request indicated he was a sophisticated taxpayer, knowledgeable about IRS procedures and policies. It may also have meant that he wanted to be able to tell George Parr he had had no choice but to give the agents the information they wanted.

For the task of obtaining information from a wily witness such as Harris Fender, the Internal Revenue Service could hardly have picked two agents better suited than I. A. Filer and Ed Watts. Their southern accents were as thick as Fender's own, and their manner, though businesslike, was informal, chatty, good-humored, and un-hurried. As they talked, Fender warmed to the subject of the discussion. He seemed to take pride in his unusual role as an outsider who had become George Parr's trusted consultant and business associate in Parr's own county.

Though few people in Duval County except the ruling elite knew it, Fender owned seventy-seven percent of the stock in the First State Bank of San Diego and was the chairman of its board of directors. His principal business was investment banking, conducted in the name of James C. Tucker & Company. His specialty was underwriting municipal securities for public entities in Texas, and since 1962 he had handled every bond issue of every governmental entity in Duval County, with one minor exception. Without Parr's blessing, Fender could never have gotten his foot in the county's door. For an Anglo who lived nearly 400 miles away, in a region of Texas much closer in culture and customs to the Old South than to Old Mexico, Harris Fender was a uniquely important man in the duchy of Duval.

The agents' memorandum of interview indicates that although Fender was proud to be the county's financier, he was careful to disclaim any responsibility for the county's stewardship of its bond funds. The memorandum reported the following about Fender: ". . . [A]ll work and bonds he had any dealings with in Duval County were properly recorded and issued in accordance with all state regulations. He explained that for him to be able to market the bonds after he purchased them it was necessary to make certain the bonds were correctly issued." Fender denied knowing anything about the handling of the bond funds in the county. He said he "handled the bonds correctly for his part and what they did on the other end (Duval County) was not his concern."

Fender readily admitted paying $40,000 to George Parr in 1967 for the worthless City of Benavides bonds. The city went through bankruptcy in the 1950s, he explained, and the bankruptcy court gave bondholders a deadline to turn in their bonds. Bonds totaling more than $139,000 were not turned in, and the court declared them void. Sometime later, he said, George's nephew, Archer Parr, was appointed liquidator of the only bank in Benavides, and Archer found the missing bonds in the bank vault and kept them as his fee. In the early 1960s, Fender continued, he was hired as an adviser on the formation of a new governmental entity, the Duval County Conservation and Reclamation District, the purpose of which was to furnish municipal water and sewer service for most of the county, including the cities of San Diego and Benavides. (Everybody in Duval County has always referred to the Conservation and Reclamation District simply as "the water district," Fender explained, because the official name was just too complicated and didn't have anything to do with the district's functions anyway.)

According to Fender, "the bond attorneys" told him the new water district could not acquire title to the San Diego and Benavides water and sewer systems until those cities' previously issued utility bonds — including the missing Benavides bonds that had been barred by the bankruptcy court — were reacquired and canceled. Because the cities had no money, Fender spent several years tracking down and buying the bonds by "horse trading" with the owners, finally completing the acquisitions in late 1966. Ultimately, Fender would recoup his money and make a profit when the water district was legally able to buy the cities' water and sewer systems and the cities could use the water district's money to buy back the old bonds from him. Fender denied the scheme was circuitous. "It was the only way they could do it," he insisted.

The last bonds Fender acquired were the barred City of Benavides bonds Archer Parr turned in. There was no negotiating on those, Fender said; he paid the full face amount plus all accrued interest. In May 1967, Archer Parr told him "George's share" of the Benavides bonds was $40,000, and on Archer's instruction Fender wrote his check to George in that amount. Fender told the agents he paid Archer for the remainder of the bonds. He pulled out his old files and produced a copy of his canceled check dated May 24, 1967, payable to George Parr, in the amount of $40,000; a bank stamp on the back side showed that it had been deposited in George's account at the First State Bank.

The word "Legal" was written in the explanation column on the face of Fender's check. Fender explained that he made that notation to be sure his accountant, Don Horton, would deduct the expense on his tax return. Horton, who had been sitting in on the discussion, added that as Fender's CPA he made a special trip to Duval County to satisfy himself that the $40,000 payment was deductible when he prepared Fender's income tax return. (In reality, Fender's recollection of the total amount he paid the two Parrs was too modest; the actual figure turned out to be $210,000, all but $40,000 of which went to Archer.)

Horton was never able to determine what bonds Fender got from George Parr for his money, but he did determine that the $40,000 payment was "a cost of doing business in Duval County." Although Horton chose his words carefully, using the antiseptic argot of accounting, the effect of the transaction was unmistakable: for the privilege of handling the water district's bond issue, Fender had to give George Parr $40,000 in cash. The worthless bonds, if George ever owned any, had been merely a ruse.

Fender answered questions earnestly and expansively, breaking off from time to time to conduct whirlwind business negotiations on the telephone. "While we were interviewing him he bought a carload of salt, then authorized the drilling of an oil well, and bought a bunch of cattle. He was wheeling and dealing the whole time we were interviewing him," Watts marveled. Filer remembered Fender taking a telephone call, listening in silence for perhaps half a minute, and then hanging up after saying, "Okay, sell two." Filer's curiosity prompted him to ask Fender what he had sold. "Two carloads of hogs off my farm," Fender replied. "We got too many of 'em."

Modesty was not Harris Fender's strong suit, and he relished dropping the names of the politically powerful in both parties. He told Filer and Watts about a recent meeting with Lyndon Johnson, and he claimed to have been asked to head U.S. Senator John Tower's 1972 reelection campaign in Tyler. "Now why would I want to do a thing like that?" Fender asked rhetorically. "If I need anything from him, I'll just *buy* him; I don't have to run his campaign."

As the afternoon wore on, Fender became a fountain of information, some of it unsolicited, about the Parrs and their fiefdom. He wanted to explain the relationship of Archer Parr and George, he said, recounting Archer's birth in Mexico City to George's sister, Marie, and his later adoption and change of name by his grandfather, Senator Archie Parr, who wanted to ensure having a male heir to carry on the Parr name. He produced a $10,000 promissory note signed by George, reflecting a 1968 loan from Fender. George had not repaid any of the principal, nor had he paid any interest, Fender said, "but I don't plan to ask him for it; he'll repay it when he wants." He explained Duval County's practice of issuing warrants instead of checks for normal operating expenses "when it's not on a cash basis," and the First State Bank's practice of honoring the warrants by creating, in effect, overdrafts to be covered later by interest-bearing time warrants or bonds. Filer's memorandum of interview sums up Fender's understated familiarity with the unconventional ways of Duval County and the Parrs: "Fender stated that Duval County, Texas is like a foreign country in that things are done differently. He explained that when he referred to Duval County records he meant George Parr's records, because he is the county."

As the afternoon wore on, the two agents grew concerned about getting back to Dallas in time to catch their scheduled flight. "You didn't just interview Harris Fender," Filer said. "It took lots of listening, because he loved to talk. When we explained about our flight, he said, 'Hell, don't worry about it. I've got a plane. I'll have my pilot fly you back.'" Three and a half hours after they began the interview, Filer and Watts put away their notes and thanked Fender for his cooperation. "Always glad to help the government," Fender replied.

Upon returning to South Texas, Watts continued his efforts to nail down whether Parr had actually owned any City of Benavides bonds. Searching through the court records in the two bankruptcy cases filed by Parr and the city, he found that Parr had not claimed to own any City of Benavides bonds, and that the city had not listed him as a bond owner. Watts went further, seeking information about the Benavides bonds from officials of the state comptroller's office, the state attorney general's office, and the Texas Water Rights Commission. Finally, after finding no evidence that George Parr ever owned any of the bonds and satisfied that he had given Parr the benefit of every doubt, Watts concluded in his report that "[i]f Parr did in fact sell City of Benavides bonds to Fender as he and Fender allege, it had to be part of the bonds which were not refunded and became worthless."

Thus far, the agents had found nothing to corroborate Carl Stautz's bribery allegations, but in the Fender transaction they had discovered $40,000 of income that Parr had falsely reported as a capital gain on the sale of bonds he never owned. It wasn't much, but it had both civil and criminal tax ramifications.

The Duval County Conservation and Reclamation District was housed in a little, flat-roofed building at 304 South Dumas Street, less than three blocks from the First State Bank of San Diego, in a backstreet location where weeds flourished in a vacant lot next door and poked through cracks in the sidewalk out front. The building's once-white brick exterior was dingy and streaked with gray. An extra course of brown bricks ran a little more than halfway up the front of the building before stopping abruptly, as if construction money had run out. Ceramic tile in a dark shade of burgundy outlined the lower half of the front entrance as well as the windows, which were covered by heavy black metal grillework. The same heavy grillework covered the panes in the upper half of the dirty front door and the transom above it, giving the shabby little building a vaguely secretive look.

Directly over the front door a sun-weathered sign, extending at right angles from a metal pole, proclaimed in neon letters no longer capable of lighting that the dreary little structure had once been the home of the C. G. Palacios General Insurance Agency. A spiny television antenna sprouted from a short metal mast affixed to the front of the building, above the window nearest one end of the building. The dangling antenna lead twisted halfway down the face of the building and around a corner, disappearing into another window. Hanging a little less than evenly from the bottom of the insurance agency's sign was a much smaller sign, with black letters painted on a white background. It said, "Duval County Conservation & Reclamation District." On April 18, 1972, Charlie Volz and Ed Watts came calling.

The agents' mission was to find out more about the water district and Parr's relationship with it. Harris Fender had given Watts and Filer his version of the history and the statutory purpose of the district, and they had learned from interviewing Norman Ransleben, George Parr's CPA, and studying Parr's tax returns that Parr was on the district's payroll as a $1,000-a-month consultant. They sensed that there was much more to learn.

Two employees comprised the district's entire clerical and administrative staff. Leopoldo Sepulveda, a slight, wiry man whose ever-present sunglasses made it difficult to tell whether he was thirty-something or maybe a decade older, was the business manager; on occasion he was also referred to as the office manager, or the bookkeeper. Maria Barkley, a veteran of other local government payrolls before the water district was created, performed secretarial duties and assisted Sepulveda with recordkeeping. C. G. Palacios, the same man whose insurance agency sign had top billing on the front of the building, was officially the district's general manager, but because of his advanced years and poor health he had long been a *de facto* retiree. In the casual tradition of Duval County, the district simply continued to pay his salary.

Sepulveda explained the district's operations in general terms and showed Volz and Watts the rudimentary books he kept. The district had four checking accounts, Sepulveda said: the Operating Fund, the Payroll Fund, the Social Security Fund, and the Interest and Sinking Fund. The operating fund, he explained, was the district's general-purpose account, used for most receipts and disbursements. Still curious about the $12,000 "salary advance" and the $3,000 "check swap" Ransleben had noted as tax-free transactions with the water district in 1969, Volz and Watts searched through Sepulveda's records to see how they were classified on the district's books. To their mild surprise, there was no trace of either one. Sepulveda professed complete ignorance. Hoping to find something helpful in the original documents, the agents asked to see the bank statements and canceled checks for the four accounts.

"I don't have them," Sepulveda replied. "The bank keeps them. I have to go over there to reconcile the bank statements, and I'm not allowed to take them out of the bank."

For San Diegoans who wished to bank in their hometown, Harris Fender's First State Bank was the only choice. The one-story, tan brick building was of recent vintage, lacking the architectural distinction and charm of many older small-town banks. Without its identifying signs it could easily have been mistaken for a restaurant or a real estate agency. However, the building's bland appearance belied the bank's importance as the financial nerve center and clearinghouse for the Parr machine's operations, a complex role we would eventually come to understand better — but never fully — only after getting a crucial investigative break.

Before interviewing Leopoldo Sepulveda and looking for records at the water district office on April 18, Charlie Volz and Ed Watts had stopped at the bank and served its vice-president, Fletcher Brown, with a handful of civil summonses for bank records. Volz and Watts didn't know it then, but they were firing the first shots in what would become a protracted legal battle with the First State Bank.

The summonses were worded to capture a broad array of bank

records pertaining to the accounts of George Parr, Bryan Taylor, Eunice Powell, and the Parr Cattle Company — everything from signature cards, canceled checks, and bank statements to loan applications and safe deposit box records. After discovering later in the day that the water district's records didn't reflect the $12,000 and $3,000 "non-taxable" payments George Parr had reported to his CPA, and that all of the district's canceled checks were retained by the bank, the agents returned to the bank the following day, April 19, and served an additional summons on the bank's president, B. O. (Barney) Goldthorn, for copies of all checks the water district had issued to Parr from 1966 through 1969. The summonses required the bank to assemble the records and turn them over to the IRS on May 1.

During the public corruption investigations that threatened George Parr's empire in the mid-1950s, Texas Attorney General John Ben Shepperd had stationed Texas Rangers inside the First State Bank to stop the mysterious disappearance of bank records subpoenaed by the grand jury. This time it didn't take long to find out that even though the ownership of the bank had changed since then, it still wasn't going to be easy to pry loose any records that might aid an investigation of George Parr and his friends. The bank immediately retained Houston attorney John Heard, a partner in the powerful Vinson & Elkins law firm (where former governor and LBJ confidant John Connally had been a high-profile partner until President Richard Nixon appointed him secretary of the treasury), to deal with the IRS demands, and Special Agent Harold Freeman called Heard to inquire whether the bank would turn over the records before May 1.

An entry in the Sensitive Case Report compiled by the special agents describes the response Freeman got from Heard: "After numerous telephone calls to HEARD Special Agent FREEMAN contacted him, at which time HEARD advised him that the bank would not comply with the summons in the PARR, POWELL and TAYLOR cases. When questioned as to his reasons for non-compliance HEARD stated he would rather not discuss the details, that he would prepare a letter discussing their position in the matter."

All of the agents knew, or knew of, John Heard. He had opposed them in other summons enforcement cases, for other clients, and his tactics had often cost them precious time. Their investigative focus was still on Carl Stautz's bribery allegations, and they feared delay because time was running out on their ability to put together a prosecutable case for 1966, the year in which Stautz made the bulk of his cash payments. The Sensitive Case Report reflects the agents' frustration over the prospect that the investigation was about to be stalled by summons enforcement litigation:

> Based on a completion date required for a case concerning the tax year 1966 it now appears a lengthy summons enforcement to obtain the basic bank information required in this case (including "Public Records" — County, City and Water District checks — retained in the FIRST STATE BANK of San Diego) would be fatal to a prosecution case for that year.
>
> Based on similar cases in the past such enforcement could destroy any possible prosecution case for the year 1966. As can be seen in the initial sensitive case report filed in this case the year 1966 is of utmost importance in that $255,000 of the $353,000 alleged kickback payments were in 1966.

On May 1, 1972, Harris Fender and his attorney, Leroy Lasalle, showed up emptyhanded at the IRS office in Corpus Christi. On John Heard's advice, they explained, the bank was declining to produce any of the required records. At the request of IRS regional counsel the Justice Department's tax division reacted quickly, filing a summons enforcement petition in federal court in Corpus Christi. When U.S. District Judge Owen Cox promptly ordered the bank's president, Barney Goldthorn, and its vice-president, Fletcher Brown, to appear in his Corpus Christi courtroom on the morning of May 18 to show cause why the summonses should not be enforced, the stage was set for the first courtroom skirmish of the investigation.

Twenty-four hours later, on Tuesday afternoon, May 2, we issued the first grand jury subpoena of the investigation. It commanded Carl Stautz to appear before the federal grand jury at the U.S. Courthouse in San Antonio on May 9 at 9:30 A.M., and to bring with him "any diaries, spiral notebooks used to record road and travel expenses, cancelled checks, calendars, memoranda, letters and any and all other documents relating to payments made to any public official or any other individual in connection with the procurement of school building construction contracts during the period January 1, 1966 through December 31, 1969."

Special Agent J. E. McElroy found Stautz at his Tarrytown

home in Austin at 11:00 the next morning and put the subpoena in his reluctant hand, then drove seventy-five miles south to San Antonio to bring me a copy showing the date and time of service.

Stautz wasn't surprised at being served, but he certainly was distressed. Ever since his gut-wrenching meeting with George Stephen in March, he had known that eventually he would have to testify against those he claimed to have bribed, and the knowledge that they would see him as their betrayer had kept him chain-smoking furiously by day and sleeping fitfully by night. For those few long weeks, while things had seemed to him to be on hold, Stautz had kept a tenuous grip on his equilibrium by telling himself it would never actually happen, that somehow the investigation would go away if he could just stop worrying about it.

But now, suddenly, he was holding a subpoena with his name on it, and the reality of his predicament hit him between the eyes. He was scared. Stautz saw himself trapped between the conflicting demands of two terrible forces, each worse than the other. In his mind "the feds" represented the cold, dark specter of prison gates closing behind him if he failed to cooperate as promised, while George Parr represented the appalling prospect of physical retribution against him and his frail, octogenarian mother if, to avoid going to prison, he kept his bargain with the government. He wanted desperately to find a way to satisfy both sides, so both would leave him alone.

At 9:00 A.M. on May 2, 1972, thirty-eight people occupied the first few rows of wooden benches in the high-ceilinged main courtroom on the third floor of San Antonio's federal post office and courthouse building, awaiting the entrance of the Honorable Adrian A. Spears, Chief United States District Judge for the Western Federal Judicial District of Texas. Spears, an appointee of President Kennedy, was proud that he had been recommended for the lifetime position by a man he knew personally, Lyndon Johnson; and though some had had misgivings about his political background when he was appointed, Spears had managed to win widespread respect as an able judge.

Each person waiting had received a summons to report for grand jury duty. They came from Bexar County and the surrounding Hill Country and South Texas counties in the San Antonio Division of the Western District of Texas, and their names had been selected at random from the voter registration rolls. Twenty-three of them would be chosen by lot to make up the grand jury; those whose names were not drawn would be held over for petit jury duty.

The federal courthouse at the corner of Alamo and East Houston streets was representative of the many combination post office-courthouse buildings constructed in cities across the nation by the federal government during the Great Depression. The stately building, with its buff-colored six stories and red tile roof, occupied a full city block. Its pink granite steps swept down to busy Houston Street, the Menger Hotel, and historic Alamo Plaza. Just across Houston Street, within a stone's throw, were the restored walls of the Alamo itself. Inside the courthouse, brass and marble fixtures, varnished wood, and terrazzo tile gleamed softly in the first floor lobby and the public corridors, beneath lofty, vaulted ceilings and massive bronze chandeliers. The overall effect was a reassuringly permanent ambiance that said, "This building, like the government that built it, is here to stay."

Dan Benedict, the United States district clerk, drew twenty-three names from the jury wheel, calling each one aloud and directing them to come forward. Twenty-three right hands were raised as a deputy clerk administered the stilted oath prescribed by federal law:

> You do solemnly swear that you will diligently inquire into and true presentment make of all such matters and things as shall be given you in charge for the Western District of Texas. The government's counsel, your fellows' and your own you shall keep secret, unless required to disclose the same in the course of a judicial proceeding in which the truth or falsity of evidence given in the grand jury room in a criminal case shall be under investigation. You shall present no person from envy, hatred or malice; neither shall you leave any person unpresented for love, fear, favor, affection, or hope of reward, but you shall present things truly as they come to your knowledge, according to the best of your understanding, so help you God.

Judge Spears continued with an orientation he had given dozens of times, about regularly scheduled meetings of the grand jury and the customary length of grand jury service in the San Antonio Division (the second and fourth Tuesdays of each month, for four months), the principles of the Fourth, Fifth, and Sixth Amendments to the federal constitution (freedom from unreasonable searches and seizures, the right not to incriminate oneself, and the

right to counsel), and the grand jury's traditional function of deciding whether the government's evidence, standing alone and uncon-
tradicted, is sufficient to justify charging a person with a crime. He
did not dwell on the grand jury's broad investigative powers, but he
did touch on its autonomy:

> Now, of course, the Grand Jury is pretty much the master of its
> own fate. It is very seldom that the Court orders the Grand Jury
> to do anything. Sometimes it is necessary if there is a special type
> of investigation that is going on that needs the service of the
> Grand Jury at some time other than a regularly scheduled time, or
> it may be necessary from time to time to change a time for the
> Grand Jury to meet, but, as I say, it is primarily up to you as to
> when to meet, except for the stated meetings that the Court has
> indicated.

Judge Spears appointed Alvin B. Jones, a Joske's department
store executive, as the grand jury foreman, and a San Antonio
plumbing contractor, Dale E. Johnson, as deputy foreman. No one
present in the courtroom could have anticipated it at the time, but
the grand jury empaneled that morning would remain in session
eighteen months and learn more about the inner workings of Duval
County than outsiders had ever known before.

Minutes after Special Agent J. E. McElroy left Carl Stautz's
house on the morning of May 3, Stautz called Bryan Taylor in San
Diego and told him about the subpoena. Stautz told no one that he
had made the call.

On May 5, Stautz's accountant called him to report that he had
just refused a demand by Archer Parr for copies of Stautz's 1966,
1967, 1968, and 1969 income tax returns. Stautz called Bryan Taylor
again, angry about being harassed, but Taylor cut him off with a
promise to see him soon. Later that day Taylor called Stautz from
Kenedy, a small town south of San Antonio. "I'm coming to Austin
tonight, Carl," Taylor said. "I need to talk to you." Stautz agreed to
meet him at the Night Hawk, a popular restaurant on the southwest
corner of the University of Texas campus, at 9:00 P.M.

Taylor arrived at the restaurant with a second man, Marvin Foster of San Diego, whom he introduced as his lawyer. After receiving
Taylor's call, Stautz had alerted Barry Bishop, his regular attorney at
the Clark, Thomas law firm, that he might need him that evening,

and now he summoned Bishop to the restaurant. "You have an attorney, so I want my attorney here too," Stautz told Taylor.

As the four men sat in a booth drinking coffee, Foster studied Stautz's subpoena and frowned. "We've got to do something to offset this investigation," Foster said.

Bishop offered no comfort. "There's not a damn thing you can do about a federal grand jury subpoena, Marvin," he told Foster.

Neither Stautz nor Bishop mentioned Stautz's cooperation with the IRS, or the immunity he had been promised. When both lawyers left the table for a trip to the restroom, Stautz asked Taylor what "the feds" were looking for in Duval.

"They're looking at building contracts," Taylor replied. "They're really digging, but they haven't found what they're after or they wouldn't still be there."

When Stautz angrily told Taylor to "get word back down there to get the goon squad off my back," Taylor raised his hands defensively, palms out. "I don't know what you're talking about, Carl," he protested.

Chapter 7

Moment of Untruth

For all we take we must pay, but the price is cruel high.
— Rudyard Kipling

WHEN JUDGE SPEARS FINISHED his orientation speech, the new grand jury followed an assistant U.S. attorney downstairs to the grand jury room, on the second floor of the courthouse. Although chosen to make decisions that would affect people's lives profoundly, the grand jury would perform its duties in very ordinary surroundings. The room was rectangular and plain, about fifteen feet wide by thirty feet long. A row of windows on the long west side overlooked North Alamo Street. Outside the grand jury room, on the opposite side of the hallway and far enough away to prevent hearing what was said inside, a wooden bench offered Spartan seating. Usually it was occupied by government agents waiting to give the formal testimony necessary to support an indictment in routine cases. Near the door used as the entrance to the grand jury room was a single wooden chair for the grand jury's bailiff, a deputy U.S. marshal. The U.S. attorney's offices were on the third floor, strung out along the peripheral corridor on the north side of the building.

Inside the grand jury room, twenty-three modest swivel chairs were arranged around an elongated "U" of sturdy conference tables, supplied by inmate labor in the federal prison system. A solitary witness chair was centered on the north wall, facing the open end of the conference tables. In one corner a stenographer's chair awaited those occasions when a court reporter would be present to record testimony and mark exhibits. On the east side of the room, the wall and both of the doors opening to the outside corridor were covered with acoustical tile, making the room virtually soundproof.

Federal grand juries have enormous investigative power. As an arm of the district court, a grand jury in any district can command anyone in the United States, its territories and possessions, to appear before it. Its subpoenas are served by deputy U.S. marshals, or by any other federal agent authorized by the grand jury to do so. Subpoenaed witnesses are entitled to reimbursement for travel expenses, and to the same *per diem* allowance for food and lodging as government employees receive. Lack of funds to travel is no excuse; tickets and travel advances are provided on request. Witnesses can even be required to appear *instanter*, or immediately, although most subpoenas specify a date and time instead of requiring the witness to drop everything and hurry off to comply. Refusing to honor a subpoena is inadvisable; because the grand jury is an arm of the federal court, failure to comply with its subpoenas is punishable as the equivalent of contempt of court.

In addition to the awesome power of its subpoenas, the grand jury also has available to it the vast investigative resources of the executive-branch agencies responsible for enforcing the laws Congress writes. The forensic laboratories and investigative skills of the FBI are legend. Less well known are those of the other federal agencies with narrower, more specialized criminal jurisdiction, such as the Secret Service (counterfeiting and currency offenses), the Bureau of Alcohol, Tobacco, and Firearms (firearms and explosives offenses, in addition to alcohol and tobacco tax violations), the Postal Inspection Service (mail fraud and mail theft), Customs (smuggling), and the Drug Enforcement Administration (controlled substances). The list of specialized agencies is long. Whenever Congress makes particular conduct a federal crime, some executive-branch agency must be given authority to investigate violations of that statute and present them to the U.S. attorney for prosecution. If the offense is a felony, indictment by a grand jury is a prerequisite to prosecution. Thus the grand jury serves one of its two principal functions by judging whether the government's case satisfies the "probable cause" test: whether the government's evidence, standing alone, is strong enough to justify initiating a criminal prosecution by charging a specific person or persons with a federal crime.

In that role the grand jury carries out its historic function, deeply rooted in the Anglo-Saxon rule of law, as a barrier against any attempt by the executive branch to initiate frivolous or improperly motivated prosecutions; it is that function that is reflected in the grand jury's oath to "present [indict] no person from envy, hatred or malice." The grand jury's other role, less frequently exercised, but vitally important to federal prosecution of sophisticated crimes, is investigative. With its sweeping subpoena power and the human and technical resources of the executive branch agencies at its command, the federal grand jury is the most formidable criminal investigative entity in the free world. If it did not already exist, federal law enforcement would have to invent it.

The balance of the morning was taken up by Bill Sessions' brief orientation on the U.S. attorney's office and its executive branch relationship to the grand jury and the federal courts, followed by the government's presentation of what prosecutors refer to as "routine cases" — the ones that are brought to the grand jury as neatly packaged solved crimes, already investigated to completion by a federal agent. Although hardly routine to the persons indicted, these are the cases that make up most of a grand jury's work. Typically, the U.S. attorney needs only the testimony of the investigating agent (a criminal investigator from the FBI, DEA, Postal Service, or any of a dozen other federal agencies) to satisfy the "probable cause" standard necessary for an indictment, and the cases are presented in almost assembly-line fashion. Bank robberies, drug transactions, firearms violations, mail thefts, and more — the cases cover the spectrum of everyday federal crimes without requiring the grand jury to exercise its powerful investigative resources.

After a few Tuesdays spent listening to cases that tend to fall into predictable categories, grand jurors also begin to think of those kinds of crimes as routine, and many wish for the opportunity to investigate something more challenging. Although federal law places an outside limit of eighteen months on the life of a grand jury, not many serve that long; most serve only a few months and are discharged without ever being called on to conduct a sophisticated investigation. Only a fortunate few begin a history-making investigation their first day on the job. Although they didn't know it yet, this new grand jury was about to do just that. Bill Sessions and I knew this particular investigation was unlikely to be completed within this grand jury's customary four-month rotation. Even so, neither of us realized how long and twisted a road the prosecutors, the grand jurors, and the IRS agents were about to travel together in search of the truth about George Parr's income tax returns.

At 1:30 P.M., returning from lunch, the grand jurors helped themselves to coffee and sat down. Knowing they were going to be asked to do something different from their morning's work, but not knowing precisely what, they looked expectantly to Sessions, who welcomed them back. To set the scene for the testimony they were about to hear from Carl Stautz, Sessions began in a confidential tone:

> Now, I want to discuss with you the background of what needs to be done this afternoon.
>
> Sometime in 1966 a contractor and builder went into Duval County and began competing for school construction contracts. In the process of doing that, he became involved in dispensing favors of various kinds to elected public officials and others in Duval County.
>
> This came to the attention of the government when the contractor withdrew large amounts of cash, supposedly for his business operations, but which he did not deduct as business expenses on his tax records. The man I have subpoenaed here today is the contractor. He has indicated that he will not testify unless he is given immunity from prosecution. I have not talked with him personally. I have not met him.
>
> The Internal Revenue agents who have dealt with him say he may refuse to testify even if he is granted immunity. He has received threats on his life three different times, and if he does testify today he will tell you about those. But I have no assurance whatsoever that he will testify.

Although this grand jury would be the first to hear testimony in the investigation, Sessions told them, they would probably not be the last; the investigation was likely to last longer than their customary four-month tenure. Before bringing Stautz in, Sessions reminded the grand jury their oath of secrecy was intended to protect not only the integrity of the investigation, but also the rights of witnesses and possible defendants. Furthermore, Sessions added, the grand jury "stands between the government and any improperly brought indictments" as a safeguard to those who might be accused of crimes. He went on:

The matter I hope to have this witness tell you about is the most serious type of corruption that can affect government, so I don't take it lightly. I will not ask you not to ask questions; things that come to your mind that you want to know, you may feel free to ask. If he will not testify, the Department of Justice has authorized me to offer him immunity. And if he does not testify after being granted immunity, I will ask the court to hold him in contempt, and I will pursue it. I don't take lightly what I am doing here, and I would ask you not to take it lightly, either.

Again, secrecy is highly important for the protection of all the people involved. The man I will bring before the jury is Carl H. Stautz, S-t-a-u-t-z, and he lives in Austin. As soon as he gets down here, we will proceed.

Carl Stautz had arrived at the federal courthouse in San Antonio earlier that day with his attorney, Barry Bishop. Because Stautz was worried about what he considered threats on his life, we put him and his attorney in a secure room inside our office complex until it was time for Stautz to appear before the grand jury. George Stephen and Special Agent Dave Clore had driven down from Austin for the occasion, and Special Agent I. A. Filer had driven up from Corpus Christi.

Stautz approached the door to the grand jury room, his palms sweating. Then he hesitated, almost imperceptibly. On the bench across the corridor, where Stautz couldn't fail to notice him, sat the man he had met at the Night Hawk with Bryan Taylor just four days earlier: Marvin Foster, the lawyer from San Diego. The government's attorneys didn't know Foster. Stautz saw him but said nothing.

Bill Sessions introduced Stautz to the grand jury. While Stautz stood stiffly, right hand raised, grand jury foreman A. B. Jones administered the oath. Stautz's eyes darted around the room, taking in every face, while Sessions advised him of his rights:

> Mr. Stautz, it's my responsibility to warn you that this grand jury is investigating allegations of income tax evasion and a conspiracy to evade income tax in which you may be involved. Under the Constitution of the United States you have the right to refuse to answer any questions which may tend to incriminate you. If you do testify, anything you say may be used against you in a court of law.
>
> You have the right to consult an attorney, and although he may not be present in this room, at any time you want to consult

him, you may ask to be excused and Mr. Jones will excuse you to
go out and consult with him.

The questioning began. Under Sessions' examination, Stautz
described the history of Triangle Construction Company. It had
originally been a three-way partnership, he explained. He and two
associates created it after World War II to get in on the school construction boom they saw coming. One partner was a roofing contractor. The second, a general contractor, was also a state representative and had a knack for getting construction business from rural
Texas school districts. Stautz was an architect. Through their combined talents, Triangle offered a complete service, from design to
construction. Much of their business involved remodeling and adding on, which was all some rural school districts could afford. As his
partners died off over the years, Stautz became the sole owner of the
business. The company had no employees, Stautz said, but "later on
when the work load became too heavy, I did make a — shall we say,
a labor contract with another man."

The other man was Amador Sendejo, of San Diego, Texas. Sendejo's role, Stautz explained, was to furnish labor for certain Triangle jobs. "Where it was required by the owner to use local labor, or
certain things of that type, why, he furnished the labor and everything, and I bought the materials," Stautz said. What Stautz didn't
say was that Sendejo was useful to him in one particular county:
Duval. School construction jobs were political capital in George
Parr's empire. Sendejo knew which laborers to hire and which to
refuse.

The chief purpose for bringing Stautz before the grand jury
with his records was to further develop and nail down those limited
admissions he had made to George Stephen about kickbacks to
George Parr and others for school construction contracts. Among
the records Stautz brought along in compliance with his subpoena
were two dog-eared books of scrawled entries covering dates from
1966 through 1969. One of the books Stautz called his "road diary";
the other he identified as his "road cost book." He traveled with his
road diary, Stautz said, and he used it to record his travel expenses
and brief notes about each day's activities and the people with whom
he met. For reasons known only to him, Stautz copied the information from his diary into his road cost book after returning home

from trips. "In other words [the two books] would more or less match," he explained, "but I'm not saying they're exact." As soon as Sessions began asking questions about Duval County school construction contracts, Stautz invoked his Fifth Amendment privilege against self-incrimination.

"Are you familiar with the construction contracts you had, either through Triangle Construction Company or otherwise, in Duval County in the years 1966, 1967, and 1968?" Sessions asked.

"I'm familiar with them, but on the advice of my attorney, I'm not going to answer on the grounds that it might incriminate me."

To better define the scope of Stautz's claim of privilege, Sessions inquired whether Stautz had had any "business dealings, arrangements, or transactions" with a list of persons who might, in one way or another, figure into the investigation. Although Stautz was willing to identify each of them (including school superintendents Eunice Powell and Bryan Taylor; George's nephew, County Judge Archer Parr; State Representative Oscar Carrillo and his brother, State District Judge O. P. Carrillo; and Harris Fender of Tyler, majority shareholder of the First State Bank of San Diego), he would not answer questions about his relationship with any of them. Concluding those questions, Sessions addressed the subject of immunity:

> I have asked the Department of Justice for the right to ask the court to grant you immunity so that we might have the benefit of your testimony. Before I go any further, I want you to know that the court has entered an order, which I will ask the foreman of the grand jury to read to you, that will grant you immunity and compel you to answer the questions that are propounded to you today.
>
> After the foreman reads it to you, you may want to consult your attorney. If so, you will need to tell the foreman, Mr. Jones, and then we will resume.
>
> I anticipate that after the immunity order is communicated to you, there will be no further refusals on the ground that your testimony might tend to incriminate you.

Judge Spears had signed the immunity order one day earlier, on May 8, 1972, at our request, in anticipation that it would be needed. The foreman read the document aloud, slogging through the mire of unfamiliar legalisms almost as if he were translating a foreign language, but managing somehow to get the point across. Stautz heard himself ordered by the court to appear before the May 1972 grand jury to "testify and produce evidence" notwithstanding his anticipated refusal on the basis of possible self-incrimination. The order concluded with the specification that "no testimony or information compelled from the said Carl H. Stautz under this order may be used against him in a criminal case except in a prosecution for perjury, giving a false statement, or otherwise failing to comply with this order." Jones put aside the order, looked intently at Stautz, and asked, "Do you still refuse to testify, sir?"

Stautz asked for and was granted permission to talk with his attorney. Returning to the grand jury room a few minutes later, Stautz indicated he was ready to answer, so Sessions resumed the questioning by asking about the threatening telephone calls Stautz had told George Stephen about in March.

Stautz allowed that after the last threatening call, he consulted with his attorney and then called the IRS intelligence chief, George Stephen. He'd given some thought to Stephen's suggestion that he disappear for a while, preferably to a place that offered both security and limited access, such as a military installation, where he could work in safety and seclusion on his books to prepare for his meeting with the federal grand jury. Stautz chose, instead, to drive to Dallas to stay with his son.

"I was there approximately three weeks," said Stautz, looking up at Bill Sessions. "Shall I tell you how I think they found me?" Sessions told him to go on.

It was all related to the threatening phone calls, Stautz explained, and a dark car with a light top. He had called his lawyer, Barry Bishop, after the last of those calls, which had come at 10:00 at night, just five days before his meeting on March 20 with George Stephen. He couldn't tell his mother about the calls, he said; she was eighty-six, and in such poor health he was afraid she would worry herself into yet another heart attack. So he called Barry Bishop and told him about it, and then, to get a breath of fresh air and a little exercise, he decided to get out of the house for a few minutes, to take a little walk on a cool March evening in Tarrytown. He was sitting on the concrete wall across the street from his house on Exposition Boulevard when he saw it, Stautz said: a dark car with a light top, moving slowly. As he watched, it circled the block. He waited a bit, smoking a cigarette, while it circled again. When he saw it a third time, making its steady approach for another slow trip around the block, Stautz hurried back into his house.

It had been twenty years since Jake Floyd's son had been shot in the driveway at the Floyd home in Alice, Texas. Stautz hadn't thought about that in years, but he thought about it that night. Just about everyone had agreed at the time, though no one could prove it, that George Parr was behind that murder.

Locked behind his heavy front door, Carl Stautz called Barry Bishop again. Bishop, whose house on Spring Lane was only a few blocks away, hurried to Stautz's home and stayed with his frightened client until 1:00 A.M.

Stautz broke off his narrative for a moment. "This thing still has me scared to death," he said, his voice dropping. The look in his eyes and the tone of his voice said it was true. Carl Stautz was scared. Perplexed, because he knew what he wanted to say next but didn't know quite how to say it, he stared for a moment at the grand jury, studying some of its Hispanic faces. Prompted by Sessions, he continued his story, finally admitting the reason he had declined the suggestion of the IRS to take refuge on a military installation was that he was afraid of Hispanics, and he knew a lot of Hispanics were employed, as well as stationed, on military bases in South Texas.

Stautz had described some of the voices in the threatening phone calls as "Latin," and he seemed to fear that every Hispanic person he saw might have ties to Duval County and George Parr. "I don't know how far those tentacles extend in this part of the country," he explained. "I don't want the jury to think I'm a coward, but I've heard of other things happening in South Texas. So I decided to go to my son's house in Dallas, and I left at 9:00 P.M. the next day and took a rather roundabout way to get to Interstate 35."

In spite of the circuitous route he took, Stautz said, the same car was waiting for him at Round Rock, some twenty miles outside Austin, when he entered Interstate 35 northbound from Burnet Road. The mysterious car followed him the one hundred miles to Waco, where he lost it by leaving the interstate and going around the traffic circle on the Old Dallas Highway. Stopping at a Central Texas landmark, the old Elite Cafe, he told a waitress he was honeymooning and needed to give some pursuing friends the slip; she gave him directions for detouring around Waco and rejoining Interstate 35 north of town. "She told me, 'If you can get to the Y on the other side of Hillsboro, they won't know which way you went, whether you went to Fort Worth or Dallas,'" he said. Stautz claimed to have left Waco at 11:15 P.M. and reached Dallas, a hundred miles away, in time to call his son at twenty-five minutes past midnight from the Hilton Inn on Central Expressway. "So if anybody knows anything about speeding, they know I was hitting ninety to a hundred miles an hour, and there wasn't any car following me, though I did pick up traffic at Waxahachie."

It was while taking another walk one night, this time in Dallas, after he had spent a week reviewing his records at his son's apartment on Preston Road, that Carl Stautz saw it again: the dark car with a light top. The car passed him, then swung around in a U-turn to head back in his direction. "I ducked between some of the apartments and got back to the alley, and finally got myself back to my boy's apartment," he told the grand jury. Nine days later, venturing out of the apartment for a late-evening snack, he would meet the men in that dark car with a light top.

"I went down to the Betty Crocker Tea House and got myself a little bite to eat," Stautz explained, "because I didn't eat any supper. When I came out and started walking back up, this car pulled up beside me — it was the same car — and they told me to get in. I told them I didn't have any reason to get in, that I was just out walking." Stautz paused, probably aware he was in the middle of a great story, to look at Bill Sessions. "If I'm boring you, please say so, because this —" But Sessions invited him to continue.

Stautz's words tumbled out in a disorderly rush. "Because this is a thing which has completely torn me to pieces. They opened the glove compartment light — no, not the light, the glove compartment door. And in the light, you see, I could see that it was a Colt .45 laying there on the glove compartment door. The two men had silk stockings, or something, pulled over their heads. And I told them, I said, 'Well, I guess that does say that I get in.' I said, 'What do you want from me?' They said, 'Get in.' So I got in."

Stautz described a two-hour ride around north Dallas, during which his captors reminded him repeatedly that he had been warned to stay away from his attorneys and to stay away from the IRS. He tried to explain that his visits to the IRS were necessitated by IRS questions about the tax return for his late wife's estate, Stautz said, but the two men didn't believe him.

The anguish in Stautz's voice was becoming acute. "They said,

'That's not the only reason.' I said, 'That's the only reason I know of. I don't know what you guys are talking about.' And they said, 'You know good and well what we're talking about. Stay out of South Texas.' I said, 'Well, I haven't been to South Texas.' They said, 'What we're talking about is stay out of the business of South Texas.'"

On a dark street a few blocks from his son's apartment, the two men dumped Carl Stautz out of the dark car with a light top. Two hours had passed since he was ordered to get in. As the car drove away, Stautz strained to read the muddy license plate. All he could make out were the letters T-A-M, but he figured he knew what that meant: They were probably from Mexico. (The Mexican state of Tamaulipas stretches along the Rio Grande from Laredo to Brownsville, and cars with its license plates are often seen in South Texas.) The men's voices, he said, were "similar to the voice of someone who might be of Latin or Mexican extraction and used the English language also. In other words, it was broken."

Stautz insisted the car was the same one he had first seen in Austin, the same one that had followed him on his way to Dallas. He assumed the occupants of the car were the same each time, he said, because the two men told him, "We have been hunting all over for you, and we finally found you."

When this long tale of intrigue wound down, Sessions sought to bring the line of questioning back on point. "All right, sir," said Sessions. "Now you indicated earlier that they wanted you not to deal with the IRS or with your lawyers?"

Stautz acknowledged that was true.

"So," asked Sessions, "who is 'they'?"

Wide-eyed with seeming innocence, Carl Stautz replied, "Well, I don't know who 'they' is. I'm not a quizzical sort of fellow, and I didn't ask the question."

It was impossible to know whether all or any part of Stautz's story was true, but he had come to San Antonio determined to tell it, and the grand jury, though perhaps skeptical, had listened intently. Probably none of them had ever heard a story like Stautz's before. In fact, neither Sessions nor I had ever heard a story like Stautz's before, but neither had we ever investigated happenings in the Duchy of Duval before.

Having given Stautz immunity from prosecution and the opportunity to describe his curious misadventure, Sessions directed his attention to the limited admissions of bribery he had made to George Stephen in March. Frankly, our expectations were high. Even though Stautz might have been frightened by the unwelcome attention he received in Dallas (if, indeed, that story was true), he had by his own account spent weeks going over his records — his diary, his road book, the Triangle Construction Company checking account — and all those records were at hand to help him answer detailed questions about the number and size of the payoffs, the persons who had received them, and George Parr's role in all of it.

Responding to Sessions' questions, Stautz explained that the Benavides Independent School District had awarded him three construction contracts in 1966, totaling approximately $2,200,000. Stautz denied paying any member of the school board to get the contracts. Sessions inquired next whether Stautz had paid any money to the superintendent of schools, knowing Stautz had previously told George Stephen he had done so.

"Did you in fact, Mr. Stautz, pay any money to Mr. Eunice E. Powell between the dates of January 1, '66 and December 31, '69?"

"I gave him some money, some cash."

He didn't remember the date, Stautz said, but it happened while he was in the middle of a school construction job for Powell's school district. Eunice Powell came into Austin on school business often, and on one of those trips, Stautz said, "he called me and said he needed $500."

He gave Powell the money in cash, Stautz told the grand jury. He remembered one other occasion, several months later, when he had given Powell another $500, "because he could make me or break me down there." He was sure, however, that there had been no other payments to Eunice Powell.

On March 20, Stautz had told George Stephen that he paid $10,000 in bribes to Powell in 1966.

Sessions tried another subject. "All right, sir. Let me ask you about Mr. Bryan Taylor. Was there any occasion when Mr. Bryan Taylor, superintendent of the San Diego Independent School District, received money from you?" Stautz agreed there was, and Sessions asked him to tell the grand jury the occasions.

"Well, Bryan Taylor, now, he was a gambler. I guess he inherited it," Stautz began. "You know, his father was a professional gambler. And the school superintendents, like they still do, meet about twice a year in Austin for their convention.

"And quite a number of them get in big poker games, up there in Room 1201 of the old Stephen F. Austin Hotel. As I said, Bryan was a gambler, and if they, so to speak, broke him in a game — well, he'd call me for some money. Usually, it was at night, and I'd get some money and take it down to him."

When Sessions asked Stautz if he remembered specific occasions when he had given Bryan Taylor money, Stautz tried to dodge the issue by saying he couldn't remember specific dates. Sessions stayed after him, asking if he remembered specific amounts.

"Well, one time," Stautz recalled, "I know I gave him $500, and another time he wanted $1,000."

"Did he simply call you and ask you for the money?"

"Yes, sir."

"Did you, in fact, take it down to him?"

"Yes, sir."

"Mr. Stautz," Sessions continued, "was this in the period from January 1, '66 through December 31, '69?"

Stautz began to fidget in his chair. "Yes, sir," he said.

When Sessions asked if he remembered the total amount of money he might have given Bryan Taylor during that three-year period, Stautz's fidgeting escalated to active squirming. "I was asked that same question by the IRS," he said uneasily, "and my best recollection would be about $2,000."

On March 20, Stautz had admitted to George Stephen that he gave Bryan Taylor $53,500 in bribes in 1966 and 1968.

From the moment he entered the grand jury room, Carl Stautz had exhibited all the signs of acute nervousness. Now his anxiety was about to increase. When Sessions turned to the subject of payoffs to George Parr, Stautz looked about as happy as a martyr when the fire gets hot.

"Do you remember any occasion," Sessions inquired, "between January 1, 1966 and December 31, 1969 when you delivered any amounts of money to George B. Parr in Duval County?"

"Yes, sir, I remember one occasion. I received a phone call from Bryan Taylor that Mr. Parr needed a couple of thousand dollars."

Asked for more information, Stautz could recall only that it was in the spring. He couldn't remember the year. With every additional question, he was having more trouble sitting still.

On March 20, Stautz had told George Stephen about making a lump-sum cash payment of $40,000 to Parr in 1966.

Using Stautz's checking account records, Sessions confronted him with his frequent withdrawals of tens of thousands of dollars in cash in 1966 from Triangle's checking account at the Capital National Bank. Yes, Stautz agreed, he had made all those withdrawals, and he had kept the cash in a safe at his home. Sessions pressed him for more details, asking what amount of money he had kept at home in cash from 1966 through 1969. Stautz struggled to avoid being pinned down.

"I didn't have any specific amounts," he said evasively. "It varied." Sessions persisted, asking for the the high and low ends of the range. The least amount, Stautz said reluctantly, would have been "possibly $15,000, $20,000"; the maximum would have been "possibly as much as $150,000." The grand jurors exchanged glances, silently seeking confirmation from one another that they had heard the answer correctly.

Stautz confirmed the curious circumstance that had led the audit agent to question his cash withdrawals in the first place; it was true, he said, that he had reported and paid income tax on all the cash withdrawals, but had not deducted them as business expenses of Triangle Construction Company. Sessions asked Stautz to explain. If he had kept $15,000 to $150,000 in cash at home, what had he used that money for?

"Nothing," Stautz replied.

"I beg your pardon?"

"Nothing," Stautz said again.

Sessions pointed out to Stautz that his answer didn't make sense; he must have used the money for something, or else he'd still have it. Stautz thought about the irrefutable logic of that proposition and gave another answer.

"Well, I used it when they called me up, wanting a few thousand. I would get it out of there," he said.

This wasn't at all the kind of testimony we had expected. Sessions tried again.

"So far, Mr. Stautz, you've told us you gave about four or five thousand dollars, maximum, to three people, and yet you were maintaining between $15,000 and $150,000 in cash at your home. There must have been some other payments to Mr. Powell, or Mr.

Taylor, or Mr. Parr, or to somebody. I want you to tell me frankly, the occasions when you paid money to any of those people."

"I can't remember," Stautz said, hoping a poor memory would get him off the hook.

But Sessions would not be put off. Firmly, though never discourteously, he patiently confronted Stautz with the specific diary entries Stautz had previously identified to George Stephen as coded notations of cash payoffs made in connection with the Benavides and San Diego school district contracts. If Stautz was going to recant his previous admissions, he was going to have to do it completely and in detail.

Sessions picked up Stautz's diary and questioned him about the entry for April 14, 1966. On that date Stautz had written: "To San Diego to see Bryan Taylor - 8M." Stautz had a perfectly innocent answer. The "8M" was a reference to the estimate on the library Taylor wanted to build at one of the schools. "It means my estimate was $8,000 too high," he explained. Frowning, Sessions referred to George Stephen's memorandum of his March 20 meeting with Stautz, in Austin. Why, he asked, had Stautz told Stephen that entry meant he had paid Bryan Taylor $8,000 in cash on that date?

"Well, I may have misunderstood his question, or something," Stautz replied lamely.

"Is it your testimony now," Sessions asked, "that you did not pay Bryan Taylor $8,000 in cash?"

Stautz gutted it up and issued a categorical denial. "I did not pay Bryan Taylor," he replied. "We were talking about his new library."

Stautz's diary entry for April 30, 1966, noted that he had traveled to Kenedy, Texas in the morning "to see Bryan on the new bond issue — 8M — and bought his lunch." Stautz had told George Stephen that entry meant he had delivered another $8,000 in cash to Taylor on that date. Now he couldn't recall giving that explanation. He had a similar memory lapse about a "5M" notation in his diary entry for May 4, 1966, which he had identified to George Stephen as a payment to School Superintendent Eunice Powell. Powell had been in San Antonio that day, the diary showed, and Stautz had taken him to dinner. When Sessions asked for an explanation of the dinner and the "5M" notation, Stautz offered a different interpretation of the same kind of notation he had previously identified as a coded reference to an amount of money.

"Well, my recollection is that this '5' means he got into town at 5:00 P.M.," he ventured. It was merely a reference to the time of day, he said, and had nothing to do with money. Sessions asked Stautz, point-blank, if he had paid $5,000 to Powell on May 4, 1966. Stautz glanced again at the diary entry and licked his lips. "No, sir," he replied.

Sessions persisted, turning to another diary entry. On June 6, 1966, Stautz had made notes indicating he was in Freer and Benavides for the award of a construction contract to Triangle. Sessions prodded him about a portion of the entry that said, "Eunice — 10 — to dinner." Again, Stautz had an innocent explanation. "Eunice Powell told me I was $10,000 above what he had set up for the building," he said. When Sessions reminded his witness that he had told George Stephen the June 6 entry memorialized the delivery of $10,000 to Powell on that date, Stautz disavowed his earlier statement.

Sessions was about to reach a more important transaction in his progress through Stautz's diary. Summing up the surprising essence of the architect's testimony to that point, Sessions inquired whether Stautz really wanted the grand jury to believe that his previous admissions to George Stephen about two $8,000 payments to Bryan Taylor and a $10,000 payment to Eunice Powell had been untrue. Stautz, growing ever more defensive, tried to hedge.

"Well, bear this in mind, Mr. Sessions, I had no records. I had none of these records that I could refer to," he whined.

"I'm not asking you about your records," Sessions shot back. "I'm asking you whether or not you delivered these amounts of cash to these persons."

Stautz committed himself to denying it. "No, sir," he said at last.

Sessions turned to the diary entry for July 11, 1966, and pulled out the Triangle Construction Company checking account records for that month. Stautz had made a $20,000 cash withdrawal at the Capital National Bank on Monday, July 11, the records showed, and an identical $20,000 withdrawal on the preceding Friday, July 8. Stautz thumbed the pages of the Triangle bank statement, stared at them briefly, and acknowledged making the two withdrawals. At Sessions' request, Stautz read the July 11 diary entry aloud. It said, "Left at 6:00 P.M. for Alice and San Diego. Meeting with George and others (40)." Stautz put down the diary and braced himself for the questions he knew this entry would raise.

"All right," Sessions began. "Who was George?"

"That was George Parr," Stautz said weakly.

"And who were the 'others'?"

"That was the school board at Benavides."

"What was the '(40)'?"

Stautz looked away. "That meant it was $40,000 more than what they wanted to spend," he said.

Sessions reminded Stautz he had previously admitted to George Stephen that he paid $40,000 in cash to George Parr on July 11. Stautz equivocated. "I don't remember that," he replied. Sessions demanded to know whether he had delivered $40,000 to George Parr on that date or not. "I did not," Stautz said, his voice rising. "I don't remember telling Mr. Stephen that. I don't remember anything."

In contrast to his earlier statement to George Stephen, Stautz told the grand jury he had paid Bryan Taylor "possibly $6,000 to $8,000," mostly to help Taylor cover gambling debts, from 1966 through 1969; that he had given Eunice Powell "about $1,000" during the same period of time; and that he gave George Parr "around $2,000." Our great expectations were dashed. After spending weeks reviewing his travel diaries and canceled checks, Stautz had disavowed or minimized most of his previous admissions to George Stephen. His credibility was damaged, perhaps irreparably.

Completing his questions about the diary entries, Sessions was convinced Stautz had chosen to lie to the grand jury because he feared for his and his mother's safety if he told the truth. He reminded Stautz of the penalty for perjury, and then surprised him by inquiring why he feared for his life. Stautz groped for words. "I don't know," he said haltingly. "I just don't know." When Sessions asked if he was seeking "protection" as a witness, Stautz brightened a bit. "Yes, sir, if I can still get it," he said eagerly.

"Mr. Stautz," Sessions said, "do you think someone is out to get you?"

Stautz looked around the grand jury room again. "Let me answer it this way," he began. "In 1951, I believe it was, it was a killing down there. A boy was killed when they were after his father, who was an attorney doing some investigating —" Stautz's voice grew shaky and trailed off. "That boy was killed for no reason whatsoever," he resumed, "and that sticks in my mind, Mr. Sessions." Testifying about what he termed "that group of people down there" scared him, Stautz said, because "if they feel that I am going to say something, my head can roll as easily as that boy's head rolled in 1951." Although he was off by a year on the date, it was clear the Buddy Floyd murder had made a lasting impression on Carl Stautz.

Sessions inquired whether Stautz genuinely thought any of the people he had been asked about would try to harm him if they feared he would testify against them. Stautz's face was ashen, his hands trembling. He asked permission to go to the restroom before answering, and hurried to the door when it was granted. Sessions handed him over to George Stephen; I. A. Filer and Dave Clore accompanied him to the restroom.

Returning a few minutes later, Stautz begged for "protection" and a chance to redeem himself with the grand jury. He had a lot of notes at home about how much money he "passed to them down there to keep their good will," he said, and he could reconstruct all of those transactions if he could have some protection. "I need protection for my house and everything," Stautz said, warming to the subject. "I don't mean just a court order protection, now, because that isn't the way they work. I've seen it down there."

He was still being harassed, Stautz told the grand jury. As an example, he cited Bryan Taylor's phone call just four days earlier, on May 5, and the meeting he had attended with Taylor and Marvin Foster at the Night Hawk that evening. And there was more, he indicated.

"I had a phone call last night at my house," Stautz said, pausing for dramatic effect. "I recognized the voice."

"Who was it?"

Stautz eyed Sessions, watching for a reaction. "Archer Parr," he said, naming George Parr's nephew, the county judge of Duval County. To avoid talking to Archer, Stautz said, he pretended to be someone else and told Archer that he, Carl, wasn't home.

Without actually admitting he had lied to the grand jury when he repudiated his earlier statements to George Stephen, Stautz attributed his disappointing testimony to the terrifying abduction in Dallas and the harassment he had received since then. "They're not stopping it, Mr. Sessions," he wailed. "I want you and this grand jury to know that what I told you today, I told you under stress of all these threats and everything." He promised to do better if he could be protected while reviewing his records.

"Well, I'll honor your request," Sessions told him. "This is the first time you've communicated it to me, and I'll make arrangements for you. We'll discuss it."

As Sessions prepared to excuse Stautz to report to our offices with his attorney, it was apparent that whether the grand jurors believed Stautz's testimony or not, they had already developed a proprietary interest in the investigation and wanted assurance that they would have a chance to hear more. The deputy foreman, Dale Johnson, raised his hand.

"Mr. Sessions, I've got to ask this question," he said earnestly. "Is this going to be continued on the thirtieth, where this grand jury is going to hear the end of this thing?"

"I'll discuss that further when the witness has left," Sessions replied. "We will have Mr. Stautz back again. He will continue — "

Johnson interrupted. "The same grand jurors?"

Sessions smiled. "The same grand jurors, that's correct."

Chapter 8

Favors

It is better to know some of the questions than all of the answers.
— James Thurber

THE MEETING IN Bill Sessions' office with Stautz, Bishop, and the IRS agents was intense. Stautz, still trembling, insisted on repeating the story of his abduction in Dallas and detailing the telephone threats he claimed to have received before his appearance in front of the grand jury. He wanted everyone to know he was in fear not only for his own safety, but for his eighty-six-year-old mother's as well. While Stautz babbled, George Stephen seethed. Bill Sessions, though angry, remained composed, telling Stautz in stern terms that he had put himself in jeopardy by lying to the grand jury, and that his professed fear of "those people in Duval County" was no excuse for perjury. Nearly three tense hours had elapsed since Stautz first entered the grand jury room. Visibly distraught, Stautz did what he usually did in stressful situations: He asked to be excused to go the restroom. Dave Clore and I. A. Filer accompanied him. There, Stautz threw up.

After shuffling back to the U.S. attorney's office, Stautz tearfully repeated his pledge to go over all of his records and tell the truth about every transaction if he could have protection. He said he had seen "at least one or two" Hispanic jury members whom he feared might have Duval County connections, and he insisted once more that he feared for his life. "I'm not saying for sure," he said defensively, "but they looked familiar, like maybe it was somebody I had seen down there before."

Sessions and I were still guessing whether Stautz's stories about threats were true, but we knew his cash withdrawals and his travel diary tended to support his earlier admissions of paying big kickbacks to George Parr, Bryan Taylor, and Eunice Powell. That part of his story, we felt, was true. Whether the rest of it was fact or fiction or a little of both, there was no denying that Stautz appeared to be genuinely frightened. After a brief conference between Bill Sessions and George Stephen about the logistics of witness protection, the decision was made. Beginning immediately, the IRS would furnish around-the-clock security for Stautz while he reviewed his records and prepared to testify truthfully about all of the illicit payments. The ground rules were that Stautz couldn't hold anything back, and he would have to return and face the grand jury again in two weeks, on May 23, 1972.

Stautz left the U.S. attorney's office with an armed escort, in the form of I. A. Filer and Dave Clore, who drove him back to Austin. It was early evening when they arrived at the big house on Exposition Boulevard. "Dave and I got Stautz back to his house that day sometime after six o'clock," Filer recalled. "I stayed at the house with Stautz. Dave went to a motel, and then he relieved me at the house at one A.M. It was a big house, very nice, but it was an unbelievable mess from him living in it. It looked like he still had every magazine and newspaper he had ever gotten in the last twenty years. They were everywhere. By two o'clock Stautz's mother had become very sick, and we had to check her into St. David's Hospital that morning."

If the first evening at Stautz's home had been unsettling, the second night turned into absolute chaos when the special agents and their ward were jolted awake by urgent pounding noises at the front door, accompanied by flashlight beams intruding through the windows. The house was on a large lot, thick with trees, and the evening was dark. George Stephen was alerted and rushed over in his pajamas and bathrobe, armed with his service revolver, to help protect his witness, only to find that the mysterious night visitors were two out-of-uniform Travis County sheriff's deputies carrying official identification and sidearms. "Things were a little tense until they stepped out of the shadows and showed their badges," said Special Agent Buddy Adams, who was based in Corpus Christi and occasionally was assigned to assist in the Stautz investigation. Adams had been told by those who were there what had transpired. The two deputies' stories didn't match. "One of the them said it was just a routine attempt to serve a subpoena," Adams recounted, "but the other one said that was nonsense, because they had just gotten the subpoena that day and had others that had been waiting months for service." The subpoena they wanted to serve was issued at Marvin Foster's request. It called for Stautz to appear at the First State Bank's summons enforcement hearing in Corpus Christi on May 18. The agents suspected that George Parr arranged the incident to harass Stautz.

George Stephen was furious. He gave orders to move Stautz into a secure location. The next day I. A. Filer and Dave Clore moved their terrified witness to an apartment in the highrise West-gate Building, just across the street from the southwest corner of the State Capitol grounds.

Stautz was convinced that Parr arranged the incident. "Stautz was paranoid about Parr," Buddy Adams remembered. "He kept saying George Parr had 'tentacles' that could reach anywhere, and he was obsessed with the idea that every 'Mexican' he saw belonged to Parr and was there to get him. And when we visited his mother in the hospital, Stautz would become incensed if he saw 'Mexican' nurses, or 'Mexican' orderlies or cleaning personnel, on the floor where his mother was staying."

To help him prepare an affidavit detailing all of the kickbacks he had paid to the targets of the investigation, the agents were instructed to help Stautz review his bank records and diaries. Stautz was not an easy person to work with in the best of circumstances, and protecting him twenty-four hours a day "wasn't one of the more enjoyable assignments I've had in my career," Filer said. All of the agents found Stautz gloomy, stubborn, opinionated, and argumentative. Filer described him as a lonely man, craving attention and company, an "extreme chain smoker" who was high-strung and nervous. Although Stautz was in his early sixties at the time, he looked and acted like a much older man — so much so that the agents referred to him, though not within his hearing, as "the old man."

Because of the routine Stautz insisted on following, work on the affidavit proceeded at an agonizingly slow pace. Filer explained:

With Carl, the meals took about eight hours a day. First, we had to take him out to breakfast every day, and then we had to go by the hospital to see his mother, and then we'd get back and maybe work an hour, and then it was time to go to lunch. And we kept having to go to different places; he might want to go someplace down on the south side of Austin, so we'd have to haul him down there. And then we'd have to drop by and see his mother again on the way back.

We'd get back to the apartment and maybe have time to work another hour or so in the afternoon. By then it was time to eat the evening meal, and then we'd have to go by the hospital to see his mother again, so most of the work we'd get done on the affidavit was from about seven-thirty to ten o'clock at night.

Most of the detail work on Stautz's affidavit was done by Filer and by Jerry Culver, the agent whose primary target, Bryan Taylor, received more than $50,000 in kickbacks, according to Stautz. Other agents, including Dave Clore, Buddy Adams, and Charlie Volz, provided welcome relief for Filer and Culver on a regular schedule. The good-natured Volz, who was the agent nearest Stautz's age, got along with the irascible architect better than any of the other agents, but even Volz found him difficult to tolerate for long periods of time.

Stautz liked to eat at Wyatt's Cafeteria, in Austin's Hancock Shopping Center, Buddy Adams recalled. Adams and another agent were with him on one occasion when Stautz insisted on sitting by the windows, as had been his habit for years. Adams told him that wasn't advisable, but Stautz persisted. "We're here to keep you from getting killed, not to get killed with you," Adams finally told Stautz. "You can sit here if you want to, but we're going to sit over there by that partition in the dining room." Stautz stubbornly refused to budge, and when he asked to go back to the same cafeteria a few days later, Adams refused to take him.

When Stautz called George Stephen to complain, Stephen asked to talk to Adams, who explained the reason for the refusal. Stephen listened, then told Stautz, "Do what the agents tell you to do, or I'm pulling them off right now and you can do without the protection." Stautz agreed to comply.

It was no fun to take Stautz out in public, Adams said: "He was loud and crude, and he seemed to enjoy drawing attention to himself. I think he liked having us go everywhere with him. It made him feel like a Mafia kingpin or something, having two armed government agents protecting him all the time."

While the agents endured the frustrations of their unremitting togetherness with Carl Stautz, the approaching summons enforcement hearing in Corpus Christi before Judge Cox, to compel the recalcitrant First State Bank of San Diego to turn over its records on the accounts of Parr, Taylor, and Powell, required Justice Department and IRS officials to make some important tactical decisions before May 18. "We knew that if we won [before Judge Cox], they'd appeal it and that would drag it out for a couple of years," Filer said. "Bob Phinney wanted to avoid that. He knew we needed to get the records right away and start reviewing them, and the way to do that was through the grand jury in San Antonio." Phinney, the IRS district director in Austin, talked to the IRS regional counsel in Houston, who talked to U.S. Attorney Tony Farris, also in Houston, who in turn talked to Sessions and me in San Antonio. Everyone agreed the summons enforcement effort should be abandoned to avoid giving the bank an opportunity to keep the records out of our hands for months, if not years, through appeals, and that the records should be subpoenaed for our grand jury instead.

On May 16, IRS Assistant Regional Counsel Robert Liken of Houston wrote to Scott Crampton, the head of the Justice Department's Tax Division in Washington, D.C., to make that recommendation:

> After the above summons enforcement actions were filed in Corpus Christi, a key witness concerning the transactions in question appeared before a federal grand jury . . . at San Antonio.
>
> It is recommended that in view of all the circumstances, particularly the pressing need for a speedy conclusion of the investigation, the summons enforcement actions at Corpus Christi should be withdrawn. This recommendation is made to you with the understanding the First State Bank of San Diego, Texas, will be subpoenaed to appear before the grand jury at San Antonio to produce the records and testimony sought in the summons enforcement cases.

Crampton quickly agreed, and by the morning of May 18 the federal government was ready to file a motion in the United States District Court in Corpus Christi to dismiss the pending summons enforcement actions. To carry out the second step in the plan, I was standing by in San Antonio to issue a grand jury subpoena for the same records as soon as the summons enforcement case was dismissed. In Judge Owen Cox's courtroom that Thursday morning was Vinson & Elkins attorney John Heard, who had come 200 miles to Corpus Christi from Houston to represent the First State Bank of San Diego. Assistant U.S. Attorney Ted Pinson of Houston, who had filed the summons enforcement actions for the IRS to begin with, had returned to Corpus Christi to file the motion to dismiss them and was present to represent the IRS in the hearing before Judge Cox.

Because records were being sought solely from the bank and not from the individuals, the only parties to the summons enforcement suit were the IRS and the First State Bank. On May 15, just three days before the hearing and six days after Carl Stautz's grand jury appearance in San Antonio, George Parr and Eunice Powell, represented by Houston tax attorney Taylor Moore, and Bryan Taylor, represented by San Diego attorney Marvin Foster, had filed a motion to intervene in the case, claiming that the summonses violated their rights and should not be enforced because there was no civil tax purpose behind them. Moore had come from Houston, and Foster from nearby San Diego, to Judge Cox's courtroom that morning to represent their clients. They had attempted to subpoena both George Stephen and Carl Stautz to the hearing, hoping for a chance to question one or both of them about the investigation to find out precisely what the government was looking for and how much it knew. They had also issued a subpoena for Ed Watts.

The government's motion to dismiss the enforcement actions had rendered the bank's opposition moot before the hearing started, and Judge Cox had already decided not to allow Parr, Taylor, and Powell to intervene. Their motion was supported by Marvin Foster's affidavit, which revealed, surprisingly, that Foster and Bryan Taylor knew before May 9 that Stautz had been promised immunity from prosecution in exchange for testimony about his transactions with Parr, Taylor, and Powell.

Foster's affidavit also recited that he was present in the federal courthouse in San Antonio on May 9, 1972, and saw Stautz enter the grand jury room with records and documents and remain there "with only brief appearances outside for water and restroom breaks, for a period of three hours." Stautz wouldn't have been before the grand jury that long if he hadn't been telling them what they wanted to hear, Foster reasoned. He asserted his belief that Stautz "gave inculpatory testimony concerning [Parr, Taylor, and Powell], and my belief is based on information furnished to me by [Stautz's] attorney [Barry] Bishop, prior to said appearance."

Judge Cox granted the government's motion to dismiss the summons enforcement actions, gathered up a few papers, and rose to leave the bench. Foster, still eager to ferret out what the government was up to, tried to enlist the judge's assistance to gain some insight into what the IRS intended to do next. Would there be additional civil summonses, he wanted to know, and more enforcement actions filed and then dismissed when his clients showed up to oppose them? It would cause his clients considerable inconvenience and expense to have to come back to court to challenge the IRS again and again over civil summonses, Foster argued. Judge Cox paused to listen, papers in hand, but remained poised to exit the courtroom. These matters "are not actually before your honor yet," Foster told the judge, but "we would like to have an opportunity perhaps to discuss [them] with the court in chambers, or we'd be glad to bring the matter up here in open court. May I be heard about it, your honor?"

Judge Cox was having none of it. At age sixty-two, Owen Cox was in his second year on the federal bench. In 1970 he had become the first federal judge ever appointed from Corpus Christi when U.S. Senator John Tower recommended him to President Richard Nixon. Judge Cox was generally soft-spoken and courteous to lawyers and litigants who appeared before him, but Marvin Foster was testing his patience. "I have got so many things on my desk that are before me, and in proper form, that I hesitate to get involved in something that is not on file in this particular division at this time," he told Foster as he exited the courtroom.

Later that day, as planned, I issued a grand jury subpoena for the same bank records that had been listed in the IRS summonses. Charlie Volz served it on the bank's cashier, Karl Williams, the following day; it required the bank to deliver the records of the Parr, Taylor, and Powell checking accounts to the grand jury in San Antonio the same day Carl Stautz was scheduled to return, May 23.

Earlier in the month Ed Watts and Charlie Volz had obtained from Norman Ransleben, George Parr's CPA, copies of the accounting workpapers and all the supporting documents used to prepare Parr's income tax returns. When they returned to Ransleben's office later with questions about oil royalty payments Parr had reported, the CPA handed them an envelope full of oil run tickets and suggested the agents check the numbers themselves. Back in Corpus Christi, making a detailed examination of the records, Watts discovered a penciled notation indicating the $12,000 "salary advance" Parr had told Ransleben about was paid from a water district account the agents hadn't heard of — the "Special Account." Watts pointed it out to Filer. "Did you ask Leo Sepulveda about it?" Filer asked. It was Friday morning and the agents would be heading home at the end of the day, Filer to Houston, Watts to San Antonio. "It wouldn't be much out of your way to go through San Diego on your way home and see what Sepulveda knows about it," Filer suggested.

That afternoon Ed Watts made the increasingly familiar fifty-four-mile drive from Corpus Christi to San Diego and found the water district's business manager in his office. "You told us the district had four checking accounts, Leo," Watts said, "but you didn't tell us about the Special Account. What's it used for?"

Sepulveda looked at him blankly. "I don't know anything about any special account," he replied. "That's not something I have." Sepulveda displayed the endorsement stamps for the four bank accounts he maintained and imprinted them on Watts' yellow legal pad. "That's it," he said. "That's all I have."

Sepulveda's answer raised new questions. Volz and Watts had inquired about the $12,000 "salary advance" on their first visit to the water district office, on April 18, only to find that it wasn't reflected on the district's books and that Sepulveda seemed to have no knowledge of it. Discovering the name of the account from which the $12,000 was paid had given the agents new hope of finding out more about the transaction, but Sepulveda's professed ignorance of the account left them frustrated again. "Let's subpoena the bank to produce all the checks ever written to George Parr on the Special Account," Charlie Volz suggested. "That's the only way we're going to find out anything about that $12,000 check."

I prepared the subpoena, and on May 19 Volz served it on the First State Bank along with the other subpoenas for the bank account records of the three individuals, Parr, Taylor, and Powell.

With the grand jury's May 23 meeting date fast approaching, I. A. Filer and Jerry Culver struggled to finish Carl Stautz's affidavit. As Sessions and I made plans for the next grand jury meeting, I stayed in touch with the agents to be sure Stautz would be ready to testify as scheduled. There were other obstacles slowing progress on the affidavit besides the great blocks of time lost in escorting Stautz on meal excursions and visits to his hospitalized mother. Filer recalled the difficulty of dealing with the cantankerous architect's insistence on salting the affidavit with his excuses for the kickbacks, and George Stephen's angry reaction to the final document:

> The problem was that Stautz kept a contemporaneous book with him in his car — his "road book," where he wrote down his payments — and he had a "permanent" book back at his house. He'd stay down there [in Duval County] three or four days a week, and he'd record things in his road book, and then he'd transcribe them — Heaven knows why — in his permanent book when he got back home, and there were discrepancies between the two. The payoffs weren't written in the permanent book; they were just in the road book. And there were two or three occasions when the road book would say he was in Duval County, and the permanent book would say he was in Detroit or somewhere, and the old man would say, "I might have made some mistakes when I transcribed it, but the road book is the record I made contemporaneously, and it's the one that's right." So Culver and I wrote, gosh, a twenty-some-odd page affidavit setting out all the payments and all the history, and every so often the old man would insist, "You've got to put this in," and it would be some self-serving statement about how they forced him to pay kickbacks, and how he really didn't make any money, and we'd put it in if we couldn't talk him out of it, because he'd say, "I'm not going to sign it unless you put that in there."
>
> Obviously, the kind of affidavit we wanted could have been written in a few pages, but we had to put in all this other stuff for him, and we had to try to explain the discrepancies. It was obvious that he'd kept two sets of records, and Culver and I tried to face that head-on and explain the differences — give the old man's version of the discrepancies — and that's what Stephen got mad about. He threw the affidavit and the books across the room. He said, "Y'all have ruined it. The whole case is gone. Y'all should have thrown those books away." And he was cussing for about two hours. The biggest ass-chewing I ever got from George Stephen was over that affidavit.

The affidavit — all twenty-three pages, plus at least that many more pages of exhibits — was finished May 22, less than twenty-four hours before Stautz was due to face the grand jury again. There were times when all the agents had doubted it would ever happen, but at last Carl Stautz swore to it before Jerry Culver, and Charlie Volz signed it as a witness. One of the low points, Filer said, occurred when George Stephen "dropped in at the Westgate apartment one day and told Stautz, 'Carl, they've figured out how much tax you owe. You owe $340,000,' or something like that. That was about the worst thing George could've said to him. That old man was so tight he wouldn't even get his clothes cleaned; he was in shock. It took us a couple of days to get Stautz settled down again so we could finish up his affidavit."

Stautz was one of two witnesses scheduled to testify before the grand jury on May 23. The other was Karl Williams, cashier of the First State Bank of San Diego. Williams was there as the bank's custodian of records, and we didn't expect his testimony to consist of anything more than the identification and turnover of the subpoenaed records, so we had scheduled him to appear first.

Karl Williams was about six feet tall, bespectacled, and appeared to be in his fifties. He was soft-spoken and articulate, choosing his words carefully and enunciating them clearly, in smooth, reassuring tones that were always studiously polite. Of all the First State Bank officers and employees we had any contact with in the course of the investigation, Williams was easily the most professional, with a good grasp of basic banking operations and a thorough knowledge of the First State Bank, although he had been employed there for only a couple of years. In his quiet gray suit, immaculate white shirt, and neatly patterned tie, he was the kind of bank officer whose conservative appearance and pleasant demeanor make small-town depositors feel good about the safety of their savings accounts. He was also a skillful witness.

Listening carefully to each question, he answered as succinctly as possible only the specific question asked, then stopped and waited for the next one. That kind of witness makes the questioner work much harder for helpful information than one who, because of nervousness or eagerness to please or innate loquaciousness, rambles on, inadvertently raising issues or dropping clues his questioner might not have thought of. Although we believed Williams was being truthful, we also realized, because he framed his answers with such great care, that he knew much more than we were likely to develop from him that day. Our problem, especially at that early stage of the investigation, was that we didn't know the right questions to ask, and Karl Williams was much too shrewd to volunteer any information. Throughout the investigation, Williams protected himself effectively: By being truthful he avoided being charged later with perjury; by being circumspect he avoided being accused by George Parr, Bryan Taylor, and Eunice Powell of unnecessarily disclosing any damaging secrets.

Williams entered the grand jury room with a handful of manila folders. None of them, I noted, were thick enough to contain more than a few of the bank records called for by the grand jury's subpoenas.

We began to face off. "Mr. Williams," I asked, "within the last week or so you have received certain subpoenas issued by this grand jury for some records of your bank, have you not?" He answered yes.

"And as the cashier of the bank," I continued, "you are the custodian of the bank's records, are you not?" He agreed that was correct. I looked again at the handful of thin manila folders in his hand. "Mr. Williams," I said, "have you brought those records with you this morning?"

He replied, "In part, yes, sir."

In part?

The six subpoenas had called for an exhaustive list of bank records on Parr, Taylor, and Powell, their business entities, and, as to both Taylor and Powell, their children — copies of all their bank statements, canceled checks, and deposit tickets for the years 1966 through 1969, as well as every other kind of record we could imagine the bank having on each of them. In addition to checking and savings account records, the subpoenas called for loan records, financial statements, safe deposit box records, cashier's checks and records of CDs purchased — and, as to Parr, copies of the regular monthly retainer checks paid to him by the water district, and copies of all checks paid to him from the water district's Special Account. *And all Karl Williams could say was "In part"?*

"Let's start with this first subpoena, Mr. Williams," I continued. "It calls for all checks payable to George B. Parr on the Duval County Conservation and Reclamation District Special Account during the years 1966 through 1969, and all deposit tickets on that same Special Account for the same years, showing any funds from George Parr that were deposited to that account during those years."

"I have those records," Williams said. "I believe they are complete." He handed me a skinny folder.

"All right," I continued. "So what you have for us here is photocopies of the front and back sides of the canceled checks that are described in that subpoena and photocopies of the deposit tickets showing deposits on that account from George B. Parr; is that correct?"

"Yes, sir," replied Williams. "Those original documents were in the bank. The subpoena asks for photocopies. Therefore, we produced photocopies."

The questioning continued, painstakingly identifying every document Williams produced in response to each item specified in each subpoena. After going through everything this witness had brought with him, we had only a disappointing handful of paper: some signature cards and a few liability ledgers, cashier's checks, and account ledger sheets. Except for the water district's monthly retainer checks to Parr and one check payable to Parr on the Special Account, Karl Williams had managed not to produce canceled checks for us. How was this possible? Williams explained that he had produced everything covered by the subpoenas that existed in the bank in original form. Because the bank mailed canceled checks and deposit slips back to checking account customers with their monthly bank statements, he said, the bank's only record of those documents was on microfilm, and the bank did not have a reader-printer machine to make copies.

"The only thing you haven't brought us, then, in response to these subpoenas, is records that exist only on microfilm in your bank?" I asked. Williams said that was correct; he had brought us copies of everything else. Although Williams gamely tried to put a good face on the bank's meager compliance, he had failed to produce most of the documents we had subpoenaed. There were no copies of canceled checks and deposit slips from the accounts of George Parr, Bryan Taylor, and Eunice Powell, among which we hoped to find evidence corroborating Carl Stautz's testimony about kickbacks.

The bank could make the check copies the grand jury wanted if it were furnished a microfilm reader-printer machine, Williams said, and in the next breath he volunteered an alternative solution so that he could shoot it down himself before we suggested it: The copies could be made from the microfilm by a commercial firm, outside the bank, Williams said, but he couldn't recommend such an irregular procedure because of the expense and the danger of loss or damage if the microfilm were taken out of the bank.

Suppose the bank were supplied a reader-printer machine, I inquired; how much time would the bank need to go through the microfilm and make copies of the Parr, Taylor, and Powell checks and deposit slips for 1966 through 1969, as required by the subpoenas?

"I would hate to hazard a guess," Karl Williams said carefully. "Mr. Taylor alone has over two thousand items to be copied. Those must be found on the spool of film and then photographed. It would be only a guess, but my thought now would be some ninety days."

Members of the grand jury exchanged looks of shocked disbelief.

When I inquired if it wouldn't shorten the process considerably if the bank could be furnished more than one reader-printer machine, Williams ducked behind another excuse. "It's highly unlikely we would have the personnel to operate more than one machine," he said. "We're entering into a period of vacation, and our personnel is limited."

Whoever prepared Karl Williams to testify had anticipated our interest in getting the records quickly, because Williams had a ready supply of reasons why it couldn't be done. The bank could make one person available to run a reader-printer, he offered. Suppose the government could provide four machines and personnel to operate three of them, he was asked. Wouldn't that make the job go much more quickly? Yes, Williams agreed, but the bank's senior officer would have to give permission for "outside people" to look at records in the bank. As an alternative, Williams suggested, "We can continue to furnish you on a periodic basis such information as we have compiled during the given period." Like a diplomat trained in the art of conveying offensive messages in sugarcoated terms, Williams was telling us in bureaucratic doublespeak that we would simply have to be patient and let the bank make the copies its own way, at its own pace.

I reminded Williams that the records he claimed to need so much time to locate and copy were the same records the bank had been ordered to produce a month earlier, when the IRS began its subsequently abandoned summons enforcement procedure. I wondered what the bank had done in the weeks before the summons enforcement hearing in Judge Cox's court. "Did you assemble any of those records in preparation for responding to the IRS summons?" I asked him. Williams made vague references to locating some of the records inside the bank and some in a storeroom outside the bank. The bank had copied some of the documents in preparation for responding to the civil summonses, Williams conceded, but he believed it would all have to be redone.

For every time-saving suggestion we made, Williams had already thought of an objection. It would cause "severe crowding" to put four reader-printer machines in the bank; the confidentiality of other bank customers' records would be compromised by allowing "outside persons" to assist in searching the microfilm for records of the three investigative targets; removing the bank's microfilm to another location would entail the risk of loss or damage.

The grand jurors, growing impatient, challenged Williams' professed concern about the safety of the microfilm if it were taken out of the bank to be copied. The government would be responsible, one juror pointed out, if anything happened to it; why not just bring the microfilm to San Antonio and let the IRS do the copying?

"If anything happened to the microfilm, it would be small comfort to our bank customers to know the government was responsible if their records could not be reproduced," Williams countered.

"But isn't this film kept for exactly this purpose?" the grand juror persisted. "What's the use of keeping it if not for this purpose?"

Williams smiled tolerantly at the tenacious juror, as if she were an unhappy bank customer he had been assigned to placate. "That's correct," he said reassuringly, "and the bank is willing to produce the records if given reasonable time."

Williams was asked to wait outside while the grand jury discussed its options with Sessions and me. It didn't take long. The grand jury wanted to see those checks. They were in no mood to let the bank stall. Williams was called back into the room and advised by the foreman that the grand jury would direct the Internal Revenue Service to place four reader-printer machines and three agents in the bank as soon as possible. The bank would be expected to assign one person to operate the fourth machine.

It was apparent Williams had been instructed by his superiors to avoid this result. "I'm represented by counsel," he said, addressing himself to me. "Would you care to speak to my counsel?" He was referring to the bank's attorney, John Heard, who was waiting outside the grand jury room in case his client needed help.

"I'll talk to him," I told Williams, "but you're the bank's representative and the custodian of the records, and I want to be sure you understand the grand jury's wishes."

Williams, though looking pained, remained calm. "I understand it," he said.

The foreman set June 13, three weeks away, as the deadline for Williams to return with the copies. Williams was unhappy. It would not be "humanly possible," he protested, even with four machines, to have the information that soon.

The foreman was resolute: "Mr. Williams, would you give us your assurance that you will do everything in your power to cooperate with the Internal Revenue agents and get the records ready for us by that time?"

"Yes, sir. I have expressed a willingness to cooperate with this grand jury in every way we can. I believe that's on the record. But I would like very much for Mr. Clark to discuss this matter with my counsel and perhaps appear again at a later date, or later on today."

Williams was eager to avoid the result that was being forced on him, that of having three IRS agents stationed in the bank with reader-printer machines to copy canceled checks from the bank's microfilm. "My counsel has advised me that it will be very improper to have outside personnel come into our bank," he said. "In fact, they strongly advise that I do not agree to any such arrangement."

Sessions and I met outside the grand jury room with the bank's counsel, John Heard, and Williams, to discuss the bank's compliance. Williams stood silently, hands clasped behind him, and let the bank's lawyer take us on. Heard was adamant: No one except bank employees would be allowed to make copies from the bank's microfilm, period. We were equally adamant: The grand jury would not allow the bank to dictate the timing of the investigation; we would subpoena the microfilm and insist on the grand jury's right to have it produced immediately. Voices rose. The grand jury wasn't entitled to the microfilm and the bank wasn't going to turn it over, Heard insisted. Moreover, he vowed, the bank wasn't going to comply with the grand jury's instructions to Karl Williams, and it would fight any attempt to force it to put the government's machines or its agents in the bank.

The meeting ended in an impasse. Williams and Heard left the courthouse, and Sessions and I returned to the grand jury. We would deal with the bank's recalcitrance later. It was time to bring in Carl Stautz.

Stautz entered the grand jury room warily, holding his newly completed affidavit in front of him as if it were a shield. He had been afraid for his life when he appeared before, he told the jury, and his testimony had been less than candid and complete. Since then, he said, he had been given protection, and he was ready to testify truthfully about the kickbacks he had paid on school construction contracts in Duval County.

Rather than drag the story out of him in question-and-answer form, Sessions and I had come up with a damage control strategy that would avert any more backsliding by Carl Stautz. We had decided to read the signed affidavit into the record ourselves and let him affirm its accuracy. As Sessions read aloud from the original, Stautz read along silently, line by line, from a copy.

The affidavit detailed Stautz's relationship with Duval County and its two school districts all the way back to the late 1930s, when he had inspected school construction projects in San Diego and Del Rio for a San Antonio architectural firm. The first of his more recent Duval County jobs had started in 1962, after the formation of the Triangle partnership, with the remodeling of a school for the San Diego Independent School District. Other jobs followed in 1964, 1965, and 1966, and Stautz claimed the two school districts still owed him more than $44,000 on the 1966 jobs.

Throughout his affidavit, Stautz had insisted on cataloging not only the substantial kickbacks he paid, but also the petty demands over the years by an assortment of public officials in the county. The Benavides school board, he wrote, asked for six season tickets to the Houston Astros baseball games; O. P. Carrillo, when he was the county attorney and president of the school board, had demanded a concrete slab for a building on his ranch; whiskey had to be supplied to the office of Rodolfo Couling, the county tax assessor-collector, who disbursed both school districts' periodic payments on Triangle's contracts. When the Benavides school board insisted that he use Sherwin-Williams paint, Stautz found that "to have the Alice, Texas dealer furnish me the paint, I had to pay off the bill of Oliveira Implement Company (defunct but owned by Couling)."

Bryan Taylor first asked him for money in 1964 or 1965, Stautz said, in amounts of $500 to $600, to cover gambling debts incurred while attending school superintendents' meetings in Austin. He explained he made the payments to Taylor because of Taylor's control over labor in the county. "When labor was needed I had to send word through the proper channels, usually through Bryan Taylor, that I needed labor and how many. This procedure was a MUST. If I did not do it, I did not get the labor. My understanding was that only certain men were to work. Others were in trouble with 'the powers' and were not to work on the jobs." Stautz said he learned "through the construction grapevine" that "the powers in Duval County could and would bankrupt me if I didn't go along with their demands."

Stautz described the system he and "the powers" devised to award construction contracts to Triangle in what was required by state law to be a competitive bid process. Stautz, as architect, would design the project, and Triangle would bid the job as contractor; other carefully selected contractors who had absolutely no desire to work in Duval County would then be solicited to submit "complimentary" bids, intentionally inflated so they would not be accepted, as a "courtesy" to the architect. The net result was no taxpayers' bargain: The contract price was set without the benefit of competition, and it was inflated by Stautz's surcharge for the kickbacks he expected to have to pay.

"In my normal architectural contracts I tried to figure in a profit of approximately six or seven percent," Stautz said. "In my contracts in Duval County, Texas, it was necessary for me to increase my profit percentage by approximately five to ten percent in order to cover anticipated demands for kickbacks by individuals and officials in Duval County." There was no prearrangement for kickbacks, Stautz said. He never knew when or how much he would be required to pay, but he knew the demands would come.

Stautz listed the dates, amounts, and circumstances of the payments he claimed to have made to George Parr, Bryan Taylor, and Eunice Powell in 1966, 1967, and 1968, relying on his diary and his bank records for corroborating details. No one had given him the right kind of pocket calendar for 1966, so when the thrifty architect ran out of homemade calendar pages in late July he discontinued keeping a diary for the rest of the year rather than buy one. "I think I did make other kickback payments" during that period of time, Stautz recalled, but "I am not certain as to the amounts of those payments or to whom they were made." Even without data for the last five months of 1966, however, the figures were substantial.

For each payment Stautz claimed to have made, the agents had required him to identify supporting diary entries and cash withdrawals from Triangle's checking account. Stautz said he had been instructed to make the payments in cash only, and in every instance he had delivered bundles of $50 and $100 bills.

"It was a continuing problem for me to maintain a sufficient supply of currency in my safe which could be used to meet their continuing and increasing demands for money at various non-banking hours or at night," Stautz's affidavit read. "In order for me to maintain a sufficient reserve of currency in my house it was necessary for me to cash numerous checks at the Capital National Bank, Austin, Texas, drawn on the Triangle Construction Company checking account."

Stautz made fifteen cash withdrawals totaling $255,000, each by check on the Triangle Construction account, between March 30 and September 27, 1966. The smallest amount was $4,500. All the rest were $10,000 or more, and he made three consecutive withdrawals of $25,000 each on August 18, September 25, and September 26. Because he was a creature of habit, Stautz usually dealt with the same teller, Lucille Spreen, who occasionally asked him what he was going to do with "that much money." His 1967 cash withdrawals amounted to $75,000, all on five dates from July 11 through September 29. In 1968 he withdrew $23,000 more, in two checks cashed September 30 and October 23.

In his affidavit Stautz explained his procedure: "It was my practice to write a check payable to the Capital National Bank or to cash, cash the check at Capital National Bank, obtain currency, and then keep the currency in the safe until a kickback was required and made. Prior to delivering the currency to the individuals from Duval County, Texas, I sometimes would remove the money wrappers from the currency."

In the safe at Stautz's Tarrytown home the agents had found a blue Capital National Bank money bag containing sixty-nine currency wrappers in denominations totaling $102,100. The coded entries in his diary, Stautz now admitted, were his way of memorializing the kickbacks he paid. "My diary entry for April 14, 1966, shows in part: '. . . To San Diego to see Bryan Taylor, 8M . . .' The corresponding entry dated April 14, 1966 in my road costs book shows, '. . . to San Diego — Bryan to lunch . . .' These entries show that I met Bryan Taylor in San Diego and delivered him $8,000 as he had demanded."

In similar fashion Stautz documented additional payments to Bryan Taylor: $8,000 on April 30, 1966, at a restaurant in Kenedy,

Texas; $25,000 on July 13, 1967, in San Diego; $10,000 on July 17, 1967, in Austin; $30,000 on September 26, 1968, in Austin; and $7,500 on November 11, 1968, in San Diego. He identified only two payments totaling $13,000, both made in Freer, to the other school superintendent, Eunice Powell. The first payment, $10,000, was made on June 6, 1966, the records indicated. The second payment, $3,000, was made on October 28, 1968.

What the grand jury really wanted to hear about was Carl Stautz's dealings with the Duke himself. Stautz stated that, to his knowledge, George Parr never held a position with either the Benavides or San Diego school districts in the period Stautz worked in Duval County (1962–1968). Nevertheless, Stautz added, "Although Parr was not an elected member of the school boards, it was necessary that I deal with and have his approval on various phases of my work in the cities of Benavides, San Diego and Freer."

Stautz was able to document only two payments of cash to Parr, both in 1966:

> In early May, 1966, I had a discussion with George Parr concerning a San Diego Independent School District bond issue. Several days prior to May 5, 1966, someone (I don't recall who) informed me that George Parr wanted and expected $20,000. My diary for May 5, 1966 shows in part: "Left at 9 A.M. for Alice, San Diego. Saw George to check on new San Diego bond issue . . ." In the upper right hand corner of the daily diary entry for May 5, 1966 appears, "20M." The 20M signifies that $20,000 was delivered to George B. Parr on that date by me, and which was a kickback on the work I had in Duval County, Texas. My road costs book shows that on May 5, 1966, I was in "Freer, San Diego, Alice" and that I incurred expenses while there.

The second payment to Parr occurred one evening in July, on the steps of the Duval County Courthouse. Between mid-April and early June, Stautz had already paid out $16,000 to Taylor, $10,000 to Powell, and $20,000 to Parr. The next demand was the largest he had ever received.

> On July 11, 1966, I received a telephone call from an unidentified individual. I don't recall who the caller was, but I do remember that at the time of the call, the voice sounded familiar. The caller said, "Papacito needs 40,000." I then replied, "Oh, my god!" The caller then explained that the money was needed that night. I

then replied, "Jesus Christ, how much more?" The caller instructed me to go to the Duval County Courthouse in San Diego, Texas to meet "him." The caller also stated that "he" wanted to talk about the Benavides plans. During this time, I had been working on drawings and plans for the construction of a new high school in Benavides, Texas. I told the unidentified caller that I would be in San Diego around 9:30 P.M. The caller explained to me that "Papacito" would be in a water district meeting at the court house that night and would be out at approximately 9:30. I understood the caller's instructions to mean that I was meeting George B. Parr who was known to me as "Papacito."

I left Austin, Texas at approximately 6 P.M. on July 11, 1966, for Alice and San Diego, Texas, and met with George B. Parr on the west side of the Duval County Courthouse, San Diego, Texas, at approximately 9:30 P.M. At that time, I delivered $40,000 in $100 bills wrapped in a brown grocery sack to George B. Parr. I said to Parr, "Here is $40,000, that is what they told me to give to you. Do you want to count it?" Parr replied, "We will count it later." Parr put the paper sack with the $40,000 in it inside his shirt. I do recall telling Parr that was "a hell of a lot of money to be carrying around." Parr said, "I am not worried about that down here."

After giving Parr the money, Stautz drove around San Diego for a few minutes and then met briefly with Parr and some of the Benavides school board members at Parr's home to discuss how to hold the Benavides High School construction costs within the budget for the job. There was no mention of the cash that had changed hands a few minutes earlier. Stautz said he would have to "cut something out of the structure" to deliver the building at the contract price. Parr and the board members talked among themselves in Spanish, and Parr told Stautz, "We'll let you know." Stautz spent the night at a motel in Alice and made the 200-mile drive back to Austin the next day. The $40,000 was paid to Parr only, Stautz said; he made no payments to school board members.

Stautz's records lent some credence to his story. The Triangle Construction Company checking account records showed that he had cashed $20,000 checks on May 3, July 8, and July 11. Stautz's travel expense records, which he kept in true pack-rat fashion, were consistent with his diary entries: They included cash receipts for food and gasoline purchases in Alice on May 5 and July 11, and bills from the Americana Motor Hotel in Alice showing that he was registered there on both dates.

Sheriff's deputies remove George Parr's body from his car after Parr's suicide at Los Horcones Ranch, April 1, 1975.
— Courtesy Corpus Christi *Caller-Times*

Top: *George Parr struck a confident pose on June 3, 1936, just before U.S. District Judge Robert J. McMillan revoked his probated sentence for income tax evasion. The young Duke spent the next ten months in federal prison at El Reno, Oklahoma.*
— Courtesy UTSA–Institute of Texan Cultures — San Antonio *Light* Collection

Below: *The Duke of Duval, always a masterful politician, poses with a blue ribbon winner at a South Texas stock show.*
— Courtesy *Corpus Christi Caller-Times*

Top left: *George Parr's mother, Elizabeth Allen, married Archie Parr in 1891 after her graduation from the state teacher's college in Huntsville, now Sam Houston State University.*
— Courtesy *Corpus Christi Caller-Times*

Top right: *Senator Archie Parr, George's father, circa 1936.*
— Courtesy *Corpus Christi Caller-Times*

Bottom: *The De Alcala hotel was a busy San Diego hostelry when Archie Parr arrived in the early 1880s.*
— Courtesy the South Texas Museum, Alice, Texas

Top: *Archie Parr's mentor in political godfathering, Brownsville attorney James B. Wells (standing, second from left), poses in 1910 with a group of Texas Rangers.*

— Courtesy UTSA–Institute of Texan Cultures–San Antonio *Light* Collection

Below: *In 1914 Archie Parr burned down this courthouse, Duval County's first, to thwart an investigation that was getting too close to him.*

— Courtesy the South Texas Museum, Alice, Texas

Top: Collier's *magazine described George Parr's office building in San Diego as "built like a fortress."*

— Courtesy *Corpus Christi Caller-Times*

Below: *George Parr's house, built in 1927 just outside San Diego, on the Benavides highway.*

Top: *George Parr appears unconcerned as the investigation of Box 13 swirls around him.*
— Courtesy *Corpus Christi Caller-Times*

Right: *What price dissent? Outspoken broadcaster W. H. (Bill) Mason, murdered in 1949 after criticizing the Parr machine, is buried in an Alice cemetery.*
— Photo by Author

Left: *Texas State Bank of Alice, site of Benavides School District accounts looted by George Parr. Its cashier, B. F. (Tom) Donald, fled to Mexico when subpoenaed in the Box 13 investigation.*
— Photo by Author

Top: *Attorney Percy Foreman (left) confers with Texas State Bank cashier B. F. (Tom) Donald and bank president George Parr in the Comal County Courthouse, October 1956. Parr and Donald were among twelve defendants awaiting trial on state charges of conspiring to steal Benavides School District funds.*
— Courtesy UTSA–Institute of Texan Cultures–San Antonio *Light* Collection

Three more defendants in the Benavides school funds case: (from left) George's brother, Givens Parr, executive vice-president of Texas State Bank; Jesus Oliveira, a bank director; D. C. Chapa, school district tax assessor-collector.
— Courtesy UTSA–Institute of Texan Cultures–San Antonio *Light* Collection

Top: *(From left) U.S. Attorney William S. Sessions, San Antonio attorney Roy Barrera, Sr., Chief U.S. District Judge Adrian A. Spears, 1972.*
— Courtesy UTSA–Institute of Texan Cultures–San Antonio *Light* Collection

Below left: *Office of the Duval County Conservation and Reclamation District, 1972.*
— Photo by Ed Watts

Right: *The First State Bank of San Diego held the county and water district accounts George Parr and his cronies looted in the late 1960s and early 1970s.*
— Photo by Author

Right: *Archer Parr (left) and Benavides mayor Octavio Saenz stroll toward San Antonio's federal courthouse in September 1972 to appear before the grand jury investigating George Parr.*
— Courtesy *Corpus Christi Caller-Times*

Below: *D. C. Chapa, patriarch of the Carrillo family, climbs the stairs at San Antonio's federal courthouse with attorney Roy Barrera, Sr., for Chapa's fourth appearance before the grand jury investigating George Parr.*
— Courtesy *Corpus Christi Caller-Times*

Ranch house complex at Los Horcones, photographed by the author August 11, 1972. Beyond the house are fields irrigated by sprinkler system purchased by George Parr with public funds.

— Photo by Author

Left: *Main Street, Benavides, Texas, 1972. City Hall is on the corner at left.*
— Photo by Ed Watts

Below: *When IRS agents finally located the Zertuche General Store in 1972, it didn't look like the center of commercial activity indicated by its reported sales to local governmental entities.*

— Photo by Ed Watts

Right: *Duval County Court-house, 1972.*
—Photo by Ed Watts

Right: *County Judge Archer Parr strides through the Duval County Courthouse to attend a hearing in his stormy 1974 divorce suit against Jody Martin Parr.*
— Courtesy *Corpus Christi Caller-Times*

Left: *Jody Martin Parr with Texas Rangers John Wood (left) and Jim Peters. Before committing suicide during her bitter divorce suit with Archer Parr, Jody exposed his monthly rakeoff of Duval County funds.*
— Courtesy *Corpus Christi Caller-Times*

George Parr leaves Corpus Christi's federal courthouse March 19, 1974, after a jury found him guilty of income tax evasion. In the foreground is Clinton Manges. Nago Alaniz, in a dark suit, is behind Parr.
— Courtesy *Corpus Christi Caller-Times*

Ramiro Carrillo, in shirtsleeves, talks with Archer Parr in the Duval County Courthouse.
— Courtesy *Corpus Christi Caller-Times*

Attorney Douglas Tinker arrives at the federal courthouse in Corpus Christi in March 1974 to lead George Parr's defense against income tax evasion charges.
— Courtesy *Corpus Christi Caller-Times*

Top: *Ramiro Carrillo (left) and O. P. Carrillo (second from right) hurry to court with attorneys Richard (Racehorse) Haynes and Arthur Mitchell (right).*
— Courtesy *Corpus Christi Caller-Times*

Below: *Ramiro Carrillo's son, David (left) listens as the three Carrillo brothers, O. P., Oscar, and Ramiro, confer on political strategy.*
— Courtesy *Corpus Christi Caller-Times*

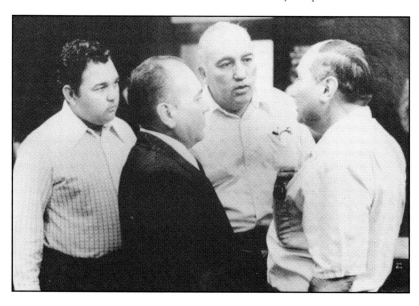

O. P. and Ramiro Carrillo
arrive at the federal courthouse
in Corpus Christi.
— Courtesy *Corpus Christi
Caller-Times*

Former judge O. P.
Carrillo flashes a
politician's smile
while being led away
in handcuffs by
Texas Ranger
Ray Martinez.
— Courtesy *Corpus
Christi Caller-Times*

Arturo Zertuche, proprietor
of the mythical Zertuche
General Store, walks between
his cousins, Ramiro (left) and
O. P. Carrillo, en route to a
hearing before U.S. District
Judge Owen Cox.
— Courtesy *Corpus Christi
Caller-Times*

George Parr with his close friend and attorney, Nago Alaniz, in 1974.
— Courtesy *Corpus Christi Caller-Times*

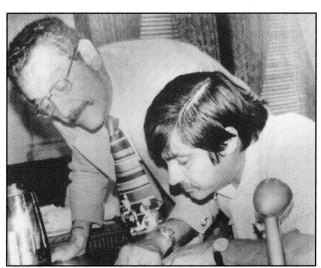

Archer Parr, escorted by Texas Rangers Rudy Rodriguez (left) and Ray Martinez, returns home in federal prison attire for arraignment on state criminal charges.

— Courtesy *Corpus Christi Caller-Times*

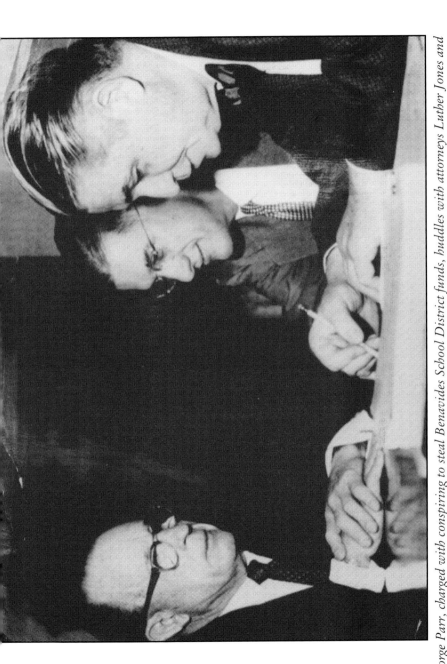

George Parr, charged with conspiring to steal Benavides School District funds, huddles with attorneys Luther Jones and Percy Foreman in the Comal County Courthouse, October 1956.

— Courtesy Corpus Christi Caller-Times

Above: *George Parr's sister, Marie Parr Thompson, talks with her daughter, Mary Elizabeth Ellis, in an empty courtroom during a break in the action.*
— Courtesy *Corpus Christi Caller-Times*

Right: *Archer Parr and Syleta Hawn had to reschedule their wedding when Archer was whisked off to federal prison August 21, 1974. Here, Syleta pauses outside the Duval County Courthouse.*
— Courtesy *Corpus Christi Caller-Times*

Dust rises from the ranch road as the 150-car funeral cortege departs Los Horcones for George Parr's burial in the Benavides cemetery.
— Courtesy *Corpus Christi Caller-Times*

(Inset) The Parr family plot in the Benavides cemetery. George Parr's headstone is prominent in center foreground. — Photo by Author

Racetrack built on Archer Parr's land by Duval County employees using county roadbuilding machinery. — Photo by author

George Parr used public funds to install miles of self-propelled irrigation systems at Los Horcones ranch, south of Benavides.

U.S. District Judge Owen Cox was the trial judge in 1974 for George Parr and O. P. and Ramiro Carrillo in Corpus Christi. Here Judge Cox shares a moment of relaxation with his dog.

— Courtesy Corpus Christi Caller-Times

THE PARR DYNASTY — *Father, grandson, and son (left to right)*
Archie, Archer, and George Parr, who controlled the political machine of
Duval for three generations. Duval County Courthouse at top.
                                        —Courtesy *Corpus Christi Caller-Times*

Stautz said he couldn't recall the specific occasions or conversations on all the kickbacks, but he did remember that "generally when a demand for money was made upon me the caller would say something similar to 'We need ten,' or whatever the amount demanded was. I would then explain to the caller that I could or could not be there at the stated time, and arrangements would be made for the delivery."

Stautz's payments may have kept him in construction contracts, but they earned him only perfunctory expressions of gratitude from the recipients. He explained:

> I recall that on occasions George Parr would come up to me and pat me on the back and say "Thank you for the favor." I don't recall any specific date or year in which such occurrences happened, but I do remember that they would be within a day or so after a kickback which I had made to one of the three individuals in Duval County. All of the above kickbacks made to either Parr, Powell, or Taylor were also made when no other individuals were present. I recall that on occasions Bryan Taylor and I would in fact, get in my car or his car and ride out of town so that I could make the delivery of currency to him.

When Bill Sessions finished reading the affidavit, Carl Stautz solemnly reaffirmed that it was his own, true statement. Stautz also wanted to restate the reason for his denials of the same payoffs two weeks earlier. He had been looking at Sessions while his affidavit was being read; now he looked directly at the grand jury. He had lied on his first appearance two weeks earlier because he was afraid he might be killed if he told the truth, Stautz said plaintively. "My mother is eighty-six years old and I'm the only one she has left, and I was just scared to death because of all of this."

The grand jurors had listened carefully and kept a close watch on Stautz while Sessions read the affidavit. When Stautz finished his little curtain speech, a few jurors still had questions about the way the kickback scheme worked. The requests for money would begin after he had one or two jobs in progress, Stautz explained, and because he never knew how much money he would be asked for, he would bid each job at an artificially high price that he hoped would leave him an after-kickback profit.

"No one else would bid?" an incredulous grand juror asked. Not really, Stautz explained; he was able to get other contractors who didn't want Duval County construction jobs to submit "courtesy bids" that were even higher than Stautz's inflated bids. Sometimes, Stautz said, he factored in too little money for kickbacks and then had to cut corners on a job to avoid a loss. "On the Benavides High School job, I had to cut down on the building when they asked me for that $40,000," he said.

When a juror asked Stautz whether he got receipts on the kickbacks he paid, Stautz smiled faintly for the first time in his two appearances before the grand jury.

"Did I get a receipt? No, sir," he replied. "That was out of the question."

Before the grand jury recessed for the day, John Heard called from Houston in a more conciliatory frame of mind than when he had left the federal courthouse in San Antonio. The bank had reassessed the amount of time it would take to copy the records the grand jury wanted, he explained. They now thought it could be done in thirty days with no outside assistance, by having one bank employee work overtime and on weekends. He wondered if the grand jury would accept that as a reasonable compromise between its position and the bank's. Excusing Stautz for a few minutes, we discussed Heard's proposition with the grand jury. Reluctantly, they agreed to give the bank a chance to perform. The date of June 20 was selected for the next meeting, and the grand jury would expect the copies then.

When the grand jury ran out of questions for Stautz he was excused, drained and pale but relieved that his ordeal was at least temporarily behind him. This time he made the seventy-five-mile return trip to Austin without an armed escort. No one was more relieved than the agents who had spent what seemed like months with their difficult ward.

"Charlie Volz and I had been with Stautz for a week one time," Filer said, "and the relief people came in on a Thursday night, because we were going to be off for the weekend. Charlie and I went down to Scholz's Garten [a traditional Austin watering hole favored for decades by students, politicians, and professionals] and had some sauerkraut and knockwurst and drank some beer, and that was one of the best meals I ever had, because we got away from the old man."

I. A. Filer was the principal liaison between our office and the agents assigned to the investigation. It was not unusual for the two of us to talk on the telephone several times each week about the slender leads they were trying to follow, and occasionally he would come to my office in San Antonio to pick up or deliver documents, or to secure grand jury subpoenas to be served on witnesses. In one of our conversations I remarked to Filer that we had a lot riding on the genuineness of Carl Stautz's handwritten notes and records.

"We've got a dandy expert we could get to look at 'em," Filer responded. "I could send all those diaries and calendars and road cost books off to him and see if he can tell us if all the entries are in Stautz's handwriting, and whether the paper and ink are the right age for the dates on the entries."

The expert was Phillip A. White, a questioned documents examiner with the Bureau of Alcohol, Tobacco, and Firearms (like the IRS, an agency of the Treasury Department), in Washington, D.C. White, I would learn firsthand later, was the kind of witness prosecutors dream of being able to use: superbly qualified in the science of his special field and highly skilled in explaining it clearly to a jury of ordinary people.

Chapter 9

Disappearances

Effort supposes resistance.
— Charles Sanders Peirce

WE MADE A DEAL with John Heard: The bank would be permitted to do the necessary copying from its microfilm, using its best efforts to complete the task and deliver the records to the grand jury exactly four weeks later, on June 20. We made it clear that the bank was on probation so far as the grand jury was concerned; if it couldn't satisfy the grand jury's need for copies, the only alternative was to surrender the microfilm.

Because bank microfilm records are a complete photographic file of the daily transaction items on every bank customer's account (the checks, deposit slips, and other debit and credit items affecting each account), it is possible to locate every transaction affecting a bank customer's account, and then to look at and copy both sides of every item charged or credited to that account. As the bank's complete, fail-safe record, the microfilm is always available as a backup, or as a source of hard copies when needed. Reader-printer machines allow an operator to look at the photographs one by one and make copies with the touch of a button; because the items are organized only by date of receipt, and not by name or account number, locating a particular bank customer's transactions can require examining a lot of records. Consequently, we knew it would be no small task to locate and copy all the documents the grand jury wanted to see.

IRS agents immediately delivered a reader-printer machine and a supply of copy paper to the bank, and in the days leading up to June 20 they regularly renewed the paper supply. "I'd always ask Karl Williams if they were having any problems whenever I took more copy paper to the bank, and he'd always say no, things were going all right," I. A. Filer said. "They didn't like having us in the bank. Barney Goldthorn, the bank president, would get scared every time we showed up; his face would turn bright red, and you could just tell he was going to have a drink as soon as we left. Barney thought he was going to jail."

Bill Sessions and I instructed the bank to begin by making copies of the transactions for the oldest year, 1966, in the George Parr, Bryan Taylor, and Eunice Powell bank accounts. Special Agent I. A. Filer called me on June 14 to tell me the bank had completed the 1966 copies and turned them over to him and Special Agent Harold Freeman for delivery to the grand jury. After the agents spent the rest of the week examining them for transactions that would corroborate Carl Stautz's story, Filer brought the copies to my office on June 19 for delivery to the grand jury the following day.

On June 20 Karl Williams, the bank cashier, made his second appearance before the grand jury, bringing with him a brown envelope containing more photocopies from the bank's microfilm. These, he said, were copies of the transactions in George Parr's checking account for the period December 27, 1966, through March 19, 1968. Copying was still in progress, he emphasized, and the bank was making every effort to complete the project as quickly as possible. He gave us a hopeful smile.

But the grand jury wanted a lot more than smiles from Karl Williams and the First State Bank. Immediately before Williams entered the room, the grand jury had spent a half hour examining the copies the bank had turned over to the agents on June 14, and had found, to their dismay, most of the copies were of such poor quality as to be useless. The grand jurors were indignant. The bank had taken nearly thirty days to copy only one year's checks, and most of the copies were illegible. Their frustration increased when they looked at the additional copies Williams had brought. They were not appreciably better.

Karl Williams' appearance before the grand jury that day was to have been a mere formality, to turn over copies of checks and deposit slips, identify them, and leave. Instead, he found himself walking on hot coals. Yes, he said, there were "some problems" with the quality of the copies, but the bank had done the best it could; they had adjusted the machine to the best of their ability. Perhaps, he ventured lamely, the 3M reader-printer machine furnished by the IRS was incompatible with the bank's Recordak microfilm. The grand jury eyed him coldly.

Williams acknowledged that he had supervised the copying and spot-checked the results. He admitted that in those instances when he had compared illegible copies with the images on microfilm, the microfilm was readable. The copies of 1967 and later transactions were a little better than the 1966 copies, he said; perhaps the older microfilm had faded. The foreman brusquely directed Williams to wait in my office for further instructions.

The grand jury was of one mind: It was time to get the microfilm and let the IRS copy the checks. I returned to my office, prepared the subpoenas, and served them on Karl Williams, explaining what they required. These were "forthwith" subpoenas, I pointed out, by which the grand jury meant that he was to proceed immediately to San Diego, some 140 miles away, gather up the microfilm, and bring it to San Antonio as quickly as possible.

"I'm sure Mr. Heard will take the matter to court," Williams responded.

"You'll certainly want to tell him about this," I replied, "but the grand jury is insistent; they want that microfilm, and they want it now."

Heard called Bill Sessions the next morning, expressing surprise at the grand jury's new demand. "I thought we had an agreement that the bank would make the copies," he said. Sessions explained why the grand jury had changed its mind. Heard repeated the bank's position; according to Williams, the government had supplied old copying paper and a machine that was in poor condition, and the bank had done the best it could. He expected to file a motion to quash the subpoenas within the next couple of days, he said.

On June 9, while we were awaiting the turnover of check copies by the San Diego bank, Bryan Taylor's attorney, Marvin Foster, had demonstrated his ingenuity and persistence once more by opening a new front in what was now an intensifying legal war. On behalf of Bryan Taylor, he filed with the U.S. district clerk in San Antonio a "Pre-Indictment Motion to Suppress and Return Evidence Illegally

Seized, and for Affirmative Injunctive Relief." The law was against him, but Foster was still trying to persuade a court that the IRS could not legally conduct simultaneous civil and criminal tax investigations. The motion was assigned to U.S. District Judge John H. Wood, Jr., for determination, and six days later Judge Wood held a hearing on Foster's motion in his courtroom on the third floor of the San Antonio federal post office and courthouse building. Judge Wood listened to Foster's argument and ours, and then turned down Foster's request. Foster gave notice of appeal. Whether Foster really thought he could prevail or was merely trying to slow us down and complicate our task, he did create a diversion that had to be dealt with; the investigation was barely under way, and we were already writing and filing briefs, responding to Foster's emergency appeal to the Fifth Circuit.

On June 23, Judge Wood got his second exposure to the investigation of George Parr, when Heard, true to his word, filed a motion to quash the subpoenas I had served on Karl Williams. Judge Wood scheduled a hearing for June 28. Ordering the bank to surrender its microfilm would be an extreme and unnecessary step, Heard told Judge Wood at that hearing; it would completely disrupt the bank's business, and (because the IRS agents would have to look at every check on every reel of film to identify those of the three subjects of the investigation) it would violate the confidence of the hundreds of depositors whose records had nothing to do with this investigation. Let the bank conduct the search and make the copies, he urged.

The bank has already demonstrated that it can't, or won't, do the job, I countered, and the grand jury wants and needs the records now.

Judge Wood was persuaded the grand jury had both right and reason on its side of the controversy. He ordered the bank to produce the microfilm "INSTANTER in San Antonio, Texas, at any recognized banking institution of its choice . . . and then and there allow the agents of the May, 1972 Grand Jury to make photographic copies from said microfilm reels of the records specified in the said Subpoenas." The judge also gave the bank the right to have an observer present while copies were being made.

It was a pivotal victory for the grand jury, as events of the next few weeks would demonstrate. Copying began the next day, when the microfilm was delivered to San Antonio's century-old Frost National Bank, and the IRS delivered three reader-printers and assigned personnel to operate them.

Except for what Carl Stautz had told us, we knew very little about the relationships between Superintendents Bryan Taylor and Eunice Powell and their respective school districts. To learn more, we subpoenaed the presidents of the San Diego and Benavides school boards to appear before the grand jury on July 5, one week after we obtained the San Diego bank's microfilm, and to bring with them their districts' personnel files, payroll records, and records of any other financial transactions with the two men, and the minutes of their school board meetings. We knew equally little about George Parr's relationship with the Duval County Conservation and Reclamation District, except that he served as its legal counsel on a retainer of $1,000 monthly, and that in 1969 he had received a $12,000 "salary advance" from an account its business manager claimed to know nothing about.

The president of the San Diego school board was Dan Tobin, Jr., whose father, as a Parr loyalist, had been a Duval County officeholder before him. The president of the Benavides board was D. C. Chapa, the patriarch of the Carrillo clan, with whom the Parrs shared power. Chapa's three sons (surnamed Carrillo) all held office in Duval County: Oscar was a state representative, Ramiro was a county commissioner, and O. P. was a district judge. (In the tradition of Old Mexico, Chapa's complete name was David Carrillo Chapa, the third name being his mother's family name. After living in Mexico during World War I, reputedly to avoid compulsory U.S. military service, he returned to Duval County as "D. C. Chapa." His sons, however, used the Carrillo name.) Because Chapa was also the president of the Duval County Conservation and Reclamation District, he received two subpoenas, one for school district records concerning Eunice Powell and one for water district records concerning George Parr.

Tobin, it turned out, had brought next to nothing in response to his subpoena. Bryan Taylor's personnel file consisted of his college transcript, copies of his teaching certificates, and a TB chest x-ray record. Tobin had obtained Taylor's official personnel file from Taylor, and he had not looked to see if any of the other subpoenaed records were in the school district's files; he had merely asked Taylor, and Taylor had told him there were no other records responsive to the subpoena. Among the items conspicuously missing from the documents Tobin delivered were records of payments from the school district to Taylor, including payroll checks. The grand jury quickly sent Tobin packing, back to Duval County, with instructions to conduct his own search for the "unavailable" records and bring them back the following day.

The appearance of the dual-office president, D. C. Chapa, was equally unproductive. It began with Chapa's request for an interpreter, which took us by surprise; we located the district court's official interpreter, Louis Marquez, and began again with his help, allowing Chapa to speak through Marquez. Chapa had both of his subpoenas, but no documents.

"Have you brought no documents whatsoever with you?" I asked.

"No, sir," Chapa replied. "I had none of those things in my possession."

Chapa was completely emptyhanded: He had no school district records and no water district records. Moreover, he had made no attempt to locate any of the records required by either subpoena. "I have never had them; I don't know what it's all about," Chapa said, blinking his owlish eyes and shrugging his shoulders. Like Tobin, Chapa was ordered back to Duval County to search for the records he should have produced, with instructions to deliver them to our office the next day.

Whan I asked I. A. Filer, during a recess, why he hadn't told us Chapa would need an interpreter, Filer was incredulous. "When I served him with those grand jury subpoenas at his house the other day, we had a twenty-minute conversation about his sons, and his hunting trips to Wyoming, and a lot of other things," Filer said, "and I don't know three words in Spanish. He doesn't need an interpreter any more than you or I do."

Old D. C. Chapa was shrewd. By using an interpreter, he gained the advantage of hearing each question in English, then listening to the Spanish translation, thus gaining extra time to formulate an answer. When asked a question in English, Chapa would look intently at the questioner, betraying not the slightest glimmer of understanding. He would then look expectantly to the interpreter, answering only when the translation was complete. We came to regard Chapa as one of the craftiest people we encountered in the investigation; he was in his eighties, and he played his chosen role of "dumb old Mexican" convincingly when it suited his purpose, especially when he was within sight or earshot of a court, but all of us who dealt with him became convinced that he was only dumb like a fox.

"I suspect old man Chapa was the reason George was able to keep control of things down there," I. A. Filer later assessed. "He was able to keep a lot of the Hispanics under control. He took care of himself and his boys, and he was a sharp old man."

When Harris Fender was interviewed by I. A. Filer and Revenue Agent Ed Watts at his office in the East Texas city of Tyler, 300 miles from Duval County, about his 1967 purchase of worthless City of Benavides bonds from George Parr, Fender explained that he had bought all of the city's outstanding bonds to comply with a legal prerequisite to the creation of the Duval County Conservation and Reclamation District (which Fender, like the residents of Duval County, referred to as the "water district.") Shortly after that interview, while checking details of entries in George Parr's tax returns, Ed Watts learned from Parr's CPA that the source of the modest rental income Parr reported was a business called Oil Belt Chevrolet, in San Diego. Watts and I. A. Filer called on the owner, J. C. King, to ask some routine questions about his business relationship with the Duke.

J. C. King, they learned, had owned Oil Belt Chevrolet for more than twenty years. It had been San Diego's only Chevrolet dealership, a storefront Chevrolet agency in a decrepit facility that looked like the automotive counterpart of *The Last Picture Show.* By 1966 King had virtually given up trying to sell cars, but continued in the auto repair business at the same location. George Parr had been his landlord since 1952, and the rent on the ramshackle building had never changed: $250 per month, half of it payable to George, the other half payable to George's first wife, Thelma.

King was friendy, talkative, and unconcerned about being interviewed. Realizing they were talking to a man who had known and dealt with George Parr for decades, Filer and Watts used their good ol' country boy charm to engage the car dealer in a long, rambling conversation about Duval County and Parr himself. Before the conversation ended they discovered to their great surprise that J. C. King had bought the City of Benavides water and gas systems in 1967, at the same time Harris Fender was buying up all the city's old bonds to facilitate the creation of the Duval County Conservation and Reclamation District. King couldn't recall the exact price, but he remembered it was "about $700,000" — far more than he had ever had in the bank at one time. The whole transaction, it seemed, was something he had been recruited into and simply consented to on faith, without knowing how it would affect him.

Filer and Watts called to brief me soon after interviewing King. "John, we oughta let the grand jury hear his story," Filer urged after giving me a summary of the highlights. "It's vintage Duval County. Let's put him on the grand jury list."

Hoping to learn more about the creation of the water district, and intrigued by both agents' descriptions of J. C. King's unique role in its creation, I issued a subpoena for Duval County's only Chevrolet dealer and prepared to question him about his purchase of the Benavides water and gas systems.

Actually, King knew very little, because he had not been in the inner circle of people who planned and carried out the complicated creation of the water district. He had merely lent his name to the purchase of the Benavides water and gas utilities and followed instructions. Nevertheless, his testimony painted a compelling picture of the absolute obedience and blind trust George Parr commanded among his subjects.

In response to our subpoena, King brought with him his canceled check for $717,478.21, payable to the City of Benavides. He also produced a deposit ticket, not in his handwriting, reflecting a deposit to his account in the same amount by the Duval County Conservation and Reclamation District. He had no other documents related to the transaction. When he signed the check, King told the grand jury, he didn't know what it was for, and he knew he didn't have that much money in his account. "They called me from the bank to come over and sign some papers," King explained. "Maybe a day or two later they told me I bought the City of Benavides water department and gas system, and then sold the water department to the Conservation District, and I was ending up with the gas system and owing a $15,000 note on the gas system."

King had arrived at the bank to find Mayor Octavio Saenz, several of the city councilmen, County Judge Archer Parr, and bank president Barney Goldthorn waiting for him. All they wanted from him was a signature on some papers. "I don't believe I was there five minutes," he said. "After I found out I owned the gas system, though, I got scared, because they told me about the terrible gas lines in the system, and how they might blow up and I'd be sued, and all I wanted then was to get out of it. It took me a long time to get out of it too."

The warnings about liability hadn't come from those who set him up in the transaction. When Ed Watts and I. A. Filer interviewed King before his grand jury appearance, Filer asked what he had done when he found out that he owned the Benavides gas system. King replied that he drove to Alice and asked his son-in-law, an attorney, about it. "He said, 'You damn fool, that thing will blow up and kill everybody, and you'll get sued for everything you're worth,'" King told the agents.

The interview of King was "a hell of scene," Ed Watts recalled later. "We were sitting there in the Chevy dealership of San Diego, Texas, which reminded me of one of those old movies — maybe once a year they had a car in the showroom, and there was no fancy furniture, and just linoleum on the floor. J. C. King was dressed like an old farmer, and his bank accounts had very small balances, like $100 or $200 average at all times, and he was telling us about writing a $700,000 check on his account because they told him to do it. Any normal individual would ask a lot of questions, like 'Where is the money coming from?' but he was just nonchalant about it."

King told the grand jury that when he saw Archer Parr at the meeting in the bank, he assumed George Parr was behind the transaction. An earlier experience with Parr made him think he would make some money out of the deal, he said.

"Didn't it strike you as unusual that somebody would have you sign papers and sign a check for a substantial sum of money and not tell you what it was all about?" I asked him.

"No, it didn't," King replied, "for I've done that before, and I made money out of it, and I thought I was going to make some money out of this too."

He was referring to a 1949 transaction in which he had let Parr use his name to acquire a royalty interest from Standard Oil Company of Kansas, King said. "After the deal was completed I made $4,900 on it, and that's about as much as I ever made on any deal. I thought something like that was going to come out of this Conservation District deal, but it didn't."

Eventually, King said, with the help of his attorney son-in-law and "a lot of hollering" at O. P. and Ramiro Carrillo, he was able to get rid of the Benavides gas system by transferring it to Ramiro Carrillo's son, who also assumed the $15,000 note. Although it took "quite a while" to get rid of his purchase, King testified, he never went to Benavides to inspect what he owned and "never got a nickel" in revenue from it. In the meantime, he said, he relied on an unwritten understanding with the city secretary that the gas revenue would be applied on his $15,000 note, and that the city would file all the regulatory reports and "take responsibility for the liability of any blowup or anything like that."

Dan Tobin of the San Diego school board reported back to our office the next day, July 6, still emptyhanded, with bad news: The school district records for the years we wanted, 1966 through 1969, were missing. No one could explain to him why only those records were gone, he said, but they were. The whole school board wanted the records found, Tobin said, but they simply weren't available. Come back on July 18 and tell it to the grand jury, we told him.

Later in the day D. C. Chapa showed up at our office with Roy Barrera, Sr., a prominent San Antonio criminal defense attorney. Chapa looked very uncomfortable as we gathered in Bill Sessions' office. "Bill," Barrera said, "Mr. Chapa has something to tell you about the records the grand jury subpoenaed. He can't bring you the water district records. When he got back to San Diego, he found out there had been a burglary at the water district office and somebody has stolen all the records. Everything. And on the Benavides school district records, he tried to get those, too, but he found out they'd been stored in an old, vacant school building, and when the school was torn down about a year ago, apparently all of those records were thrown away."

The First State Bank's microfilm was still at the Frost National Bank, where IRS agents were copying checks on the accounts of George Parr, Eunice Powell, and Bryan Taylor, with a representative of the San Diego bank observing. With the original records of the two school districts and the water district now unavailable, it appeared the microfilm pictures of their checks and deposits would be the only remaining source of record information about the financial transactions between those governmental entities and the three individuals, and the current copying job was nearing completion. To hold the microfilm at the Frost Bank and ensure its availability for another round of copying, we served new subpoenas on the bank for original and microfilm records and filed an application for a temporary restraining order to prevent the removal of the microfilm from the Frost Bank. John Heard responded for the First State Bank by filing a motion to "modify and limit" the grand jury's subpoenas. Judge John H. Wood, Jr., scheduled a hearing on July 13.

I. A. Filer and Ed Watts returned to the water district office on July 11 to interview Leo Sepulveda about the burglary reported by D. C. Chapa, and to serve Sepulveda with a grand jury subpoena.

"They only took records, papers," Sepulveda told the agents in a voice tinged with bewilderment. "They didn't take things that might be worth some money, like these two typewriters, or the adding machine, or the copier." As we had planned, Filer served Sepulveda with a grand jury subpoena for July 18.

On the following day, July 12, Sessions and I drove to Austin for a meeting at the IRS district director's office with Intelligence Chief George Stephen, Group Supervisor Hugh Loventhal, who had taken over in that capacity to allow Stephen to concentrate on his broader responsibilities, and Special Agents Jerry Culver and I. A. Filer, to review our progress and chart the course of the remainder of the investigation. Still of great concern to all of us was the short time remaining — only nine months — before the statute of limitations would bar any prosecutions for 1966, the tax year in which Carl Stautz had paid his largest single kickback to George Parr. Because of the long and singularly unsuccessful history of investigations into Duval County corruption, we had all known from the beginning that we were facing a difficult task, and it was living up to our expectations. In a little more than two months of grand jury activity aimed principally at obtaining public-entity financial records (a task that ordinarily would be quick and easy), we had been frustrated by the alleged loss or theft of documents from the two school districts and the water district, and delayed by the stalling tactics of the First State Bank of San Diego. So far, we had little to show for our efforts.

The next grand jury meeting was scheduled for two days, July 18 and 19. At the meeting in Austin on July 12, we made plans to use those two days to question Leopoldo Supulveda and D. C. Chapa about the water district burglary, and Karl Williams and Barney Goldthorn about water district bank records. In the meantime, we agreed, the IRS agents would continue to pursue all leads developed from the ongoing check-copying project in San Antonio, and interview witnesses in the field. Based on the limited leads we had, we estimated that we could schedule all remaining witnesses to appear before the grand jury by late August.

As the microfilm copying project produced copies of checks and deposit slips, agents sorted, scheduled, and analyzed the transactions, hoping to find something in the three individuals' bank accounts to corroborate Stautz's kickback testimony. While poking around in the Duval County deed records on a hunch that Parr, Taylor, or Powell might have bought real estate with Stautz's money, Ed Watts made an important discovery: Both Bryan Taylor and Eunice Powell had made cash deposits on Duval County ranches, on dates and in amounts corresponding closely to the dates and amounts of kickbacks testified to by Stautz. Nothing in the checking account records or in the Duval County deed records, however, tended to corroborate Stautz's testimony about kickbacks to George Parr.

With each day that passed, our prospects for success faded. "What we've got on George so far," Filer remarked to Watts one day, "is Carl Stautz's affidavit, and Fender's $40,000 that George should have reported as ordinary income instead of capital gain. That's nowhere near enough evidence for a prosecution. I think old man Stautz is telling the truth, but if we don't find something else that supports his story pretty soon, we're going to have to fold our tent."

The agents were wearing out State Highway 44 between Corpus Christi and San Diego, pursuing first one hunch and then another without success. "For example, we knew George had some racehorses," Filer said, "and we ran all over South Texas, tracking down money he spent on them. He was buying and selling them all the time, but whenever he bought one, he wrote a check on his own account, and they all turned out to be legitimate, arms-length transactions." The chocolate brown AMC sedans were getting a workout, according to Filer. "We put 20,000 miles on each one of those cars in a few months. Thank goodness the air conditioning worked in those things."

At the Duval County Courthouse one afternoon, while leafing through county purchasing records, Filer and Watts were shown the county's master payment records. "We've got them here on cards, by vendor," Walter Meek, the county auditor, said. "You're welcome to look."

The two agents had a microfilm camera with them. "We always carried it with us," Ed Watts recalled, "and when anybody in Duval County showed us any kind of records, we usually photographed 'em." With no specific purpose in mind except to study the records later, at their leisure, they photographed the entire card file. It was an unremarkable occurrence at the time, but it would have profound consequences for three of George Parr's cronies in the future.

On July 13, for the second time in two weeks, we were in Judge John H. Wood's courtroom, jousting again with Houston attorney John Heard over the First State Bank's noncompliance with grand jury subpoenas. The bank's irreplaceable microfilm had already been out of its hands too long, Heard argued. He characterized the grand jury's investigation as a mere fishing expedition, and its demand to keep the microfilm still longer as burdensome, oppressive, and unreasonable. Judge Wood was almost visibly skeptical.

As a successful lawyer and a socially prominent Republican in heavily Democratic San Antonio before President Nixon tapped him for the federal bench, Wood knew all the folklore about the Duke of Duval and his corrupt control of people and institutions in South Texas. Throughout the hearing I had the feeling that the judge was enjoying the show, discreetly toying with the San Diego bank's lawyer, surmising that the bank was actually worried about protecting George Parr, not the microfilm.

Judge Wood listened attentively as I explained why we issued the new subpoenas, and he pressed Heard to justify the bank's opposition. The bank's resistance to the grand jury's earlier subpoenas for microfilm and Marvin Foster's efforts to snuff out the investigation for Bryan Taylor had already piqued the judge's interest. The mysterious disappearance of subpoenaed public records regarding George Parr raised his interest to the level of outright suspicion.

When the judge had heard enough he looked intently at Heard. Surely, he suggested in a "let's get serious" tone, the microfilm was safe in the custody of the venerable Frost National Bank. The Frost was San Antonio's oldest national bank, and one of the most respected financial institutions in the state. It was also the correspondent bank for the First State Bank of San Diego. The copying of the records of George Parr, Bryan Taylor, and Eunice Powell had been in progress there for weeks with no reported problems and no apparent inconvenience to the San Diego bank, Judge Wood noted. How would the bank be harmed, he asked Heard pointedly, by leaving the microfilm at the Frost Bank a while longer?

The bank's lawyer had already made his best points, but the bank's legal position was weak and Judge Wood was obviously not swayed. Heard argued again that the grand jury was merely "fishing," with no real reason to think it would find anything significant in the bank's microfilm records. The records were "voluminous," Heard told the court. "We'll be here for weeks getting them copied." Having its microfilm tied up in San Antonio for no good reason, he urged, would violate the bank's property rights without due process of law, and it would also give the IRS an unwarranted opportunity to look at the records of all the bank's hundreds of customers, when only a few were under investigation.

"Well, in some cases, Mr. Heard, I would agree with you," Judge Wood said, "but where three governmental entities have been subpoenaed to bring records before the grand jury, and the records have utterly disappeared, either burglarized or lost, it's just too coincidental not to arouse the suspicions of any investigatory body." Because of the repeated efforts that had already been made to restrict the grand jury's investigation, the judge announced, he would order the microfilm held in San Antonio as the grand jury requested.

But the bank, Heard protested, was concerned about the privacy of all those other depositors, unrelated to the investigation, whose checks the IRS could scrutinize at its leisure if the government were allowed free reign to prolong its inspection of the microfilm. Judge Wood was unmoved. He had made up his mind to let us keep the microfilm, and his patience was running low.

"Let's get to the meat of the coconut, Mr. Heard. How would you have me limit this order I'm about to enter?" Wood asked. Heard, realizing he had no choice, fell back to a damage-control position for his client. The government should be required to identify the specific transactions and the specific individuals and entities it is investigating, he told the judge, and its examination of the bank's microfilm should be limited to looking at those specific records.

A specification of the persons and transactions the United States was interested in would have been immensely valuable to the targets of the investigation -- indeed, it would have identified for them the additional records they needed to hide or destroy and the witnesses they needed to control — but it would have been irrelevant to any legitimate interest of the bank. It seemed obvious the First State Bank was trying to run interference for its most powerful depositor, George Parr, and his friends.

Judge Wood stood firm: The microfilm would remain at the Frost Bank until the grand jury had the copies it needed. The government would bear the expense of maintaining one bank officer in San Antonio as an observer while the copying was done.

As the hearing wound down, I reminded the judge that we had asked the court to hold the bank and its vice-president, Fletcher Brown, in contempt of the grand jury for refusing to comply with the subpoenas. Heard urged the judge to deny that request.

"Well, I'm not going to rule on that at this time," Judge Wood said. "I'll keep this contempt matter under advisement until I see how well Mr. Brown and the bank react to this order. Do I make myself plain to you, Mr. Heard?"

"Yes, sir, you surely do. I'll be back in touch with my client to talk about this, but my recommendation to them, your honor, is to take an appeal from your order to the Fifth Circuit."

Judge Wood knew that even if the bank did appeal, the federal appellate court in New Orleans was sure to uphold his discretion to protect the grand jury's investigative prerogative. The judge's blue eyes twinkled, and the slightest hint of a smile tugged at the corners of his mouth. "That's what I have overseers for, Mr. Heard," he said with mock humility. "I want to give you every opportunity to have your exception."

There was more than a touch of irony in the consequences of the San Diego bank's efforts to minimize the grand jury's scrutiny of the microfilm. The effect on the grand jury, the IRS agents, and the prosecutors was predictable: If the bank didn't want us to see it, we wanted it all the more. But while we had carefully kept the investigation out of public view for more than two months, the bank's thrashings about in Judge Wood's court finally caught the attention of the press, just as the struggle of a hooked fish attracts sharks.

Both of San Antonio's daily newspapers, the *Express* and the *Light*, had reporters regularly assigned to cover the federal courthouse beat. In their quest to glean newsworthy tidbits from the arcane and usually mundane business of the federal courts, they roamed the corridors of the courthouse daily, schmoozing with court staffers and bureaucrats, and scanning the pleadings and motions filed by lawyers in the district clerk's office.

Principally because of criminal prosecutions, our office generated most of the dramatic news stories in the federal courthouse, week in and week out. Geography and demographics made San Antonio a convenient distribution center for enormous quantities of smuggled Mexican heroin and marijuana, and those illicit activities gave rise to a steady stream of high-profile drug prosecutions that often involved undercover penetrations into criminal networks stretching from Mexico into several American states. (A few years later, Judge John H. Wood would be murdered by Charles Harrelson, a killer hired by drug kingpin Jimmy Chagra, just before Chagra was scheduled to be tried in Wood's court. The drug underworld had dubbed Wood "Maximum John" because of the heavy sentences he invariably assessed in drug cases, and Chagra, anticipating a conviction, wanted to avoid being sentenced by him.) Because cameras were not allowed in the federal courthouse, and because Bill Sessions was a hard-nosed believer in protecting the accused, as well as the merely suspected, from unnecessary pretrial publicity, our office, despite being a prime generator of news, was also a chronic source of frustration for the press.

During our two years at the Department of Justice, Sessions and I had been thoroughly trained in the department's policies for dealing with the press on investigations and indictments. Those rules required strict secrecy concerning grand jury investigations, and they permitted the disclosure of only basic facts — name, age, city of residence, offense charged, and maximum possible punishment upon conviction — about persons named in indictments.

Some elements of the press, particularly among San Antonio's television news community, yearned to get from us the kinds of prisoner-and-evidence "photo opportunities" and off-the-record information leaks they often found available to them in the more political atmosphere of San Antonio's Bexar County Courthouse. Instead, we disclosed information about criminal cases by issuing written press releases directly attributable to the U.S. attorney. Because I was the designated writer of press releases, followup questions from reporters seeking clarifications and additional information were customarily directed to me.

On July 12, the day before the hearing in Judge Wood's court, *Express* reporter Wilson McKinney found in the district clerk's records the motions John Heard had filed that week for the San Diego bank. McKinney was young, but he was no cub reporter. Digging a little deeper, he found in a separate file the bank's earlier motions opposing the grand jury's first request for the microfilm. The bank's motions identified George Parr, Bryan Taylor, and Eunice Powell, and their wives, as subjects of the grand jury's investigation.

Like every other courthouse reporter in Texas, McKinney knew who George Parr was, and the San Diego bank's motions told him that the May 1972 grand jury had been leading two lives from its inception, conducting an investigation of a Texas legend in addition to acting on run-of-the-mill criminal cases every two weeks. After doing a little more research, McKinney came to see me the day before the hearing in Judge Wood's court. Over cups of barely tolerable office coffee, we talked briefly about trivia. Then, getting down to business, McKinney put the question to me directly: Why was our grand jury investigating George Parr?

When I declined to confirm that Parr was being investigated, McKinney persisted. He had done his homework, he indicated, by reading the San Diego bank's motions, and by finding out all he could about the IRS summons enforcement action in Corpus Christi.

"Look, I already know you're investigating him, and I know it involves his income taxes and his bank accounts. But how did it get started? And why is it being investigated here in San Antonio?"

"I can't elaborate on what's available to you in the public record, Wilson."

"Well, I figured you'd say that, but I had to ask. I'll keep my eyes and ears open."

Phillip White's laboratory report came back to us with encouraging news: The age of the paper and ink in Carl Stautz's diaries, calendars, and "road cost books" was consistent with the dates of the entries, White concluded, and all of the handwriting matched known samples of Carl Stautz's handwriting. We still were short on corroborating evidence that Stautz actually made the payoffs he claimed to have made, but at least we knew the diary entries could be defended as genuinely his, and as having been made close to the dates they reflected. It was a start.

Chapter 10

Special Account

I have heard the key
Turn in the door once and turn once only.
— T. S. Eliot

WHILE READING THE *San Antonio Express* at breakfast the next morning, an hour or so before the hearing, I spotted Wilson McKinney's first story about the investigation. It carried his byline, and the headline said, "George Parr's Bank Records Eyed."

McKinney attended the hearing that day, listening carefully and taking notes as Heard and I verbally thrust and parried and Judge Wood asked questions. The *Express* printed his followup story the next morning under a headline that said, "George Parr Case Records 'Missing.'"

Bill Sessions and I were disappointed that the investigation had become a news story. For more than two months we had enjoyed the luxury of conducting a sensitive grand jury investigation without attracting the attention of the press, but now the cat was out of the bag. Neither of us had ever known publicity to aid a grand jury investigation. Conversely, in other investigations we had seen prospective witnesses try to avoid "getting involved" because they feared publicity.

The Federal Rules of Criminal Procedure protect grand jury witnesses by prohibiting prosecutors, grand jurors, court reporters, and interpreters from disclosing their testimony, but nothing prevents reporters from observing who the witnesses are and pursuing other sources — including the witnesses themselves — to learn the

185

inside story. With a tantalizing subject as newsworthy as George Parr, we knew the press would camp outside the grand jury room to monitor the comings and goings of the grand jury and the witnesses who appeared before it, as long as the investigation continued.

On Monday, July 17, the eye-weary agents who had copied thousands of checks and deposit slips from the bank's microfilm for nearly three weeks finished copying George Parr's records. "One of the guys the bank kept in San Antonio to watch us copy checks had worked for the bank as a cattle appraiser," I. A. Filer recalled. "He just sat there all day and never looked at a thing. When we found something, we'd make two copies and give him one. He wanted us to go slow, because he was making $25 a day, plus expenses."

The first witness before the grand jury on July 18 was there on unfinished business. Dan Tobin, Jr., was back to tell the grand jury what happened when he returned to San Diego to find the school district records they wanted to see.

He didn't get any records, he said. He went to the school district's tax assessor, A. V. "Blondie" Barrera, and the superintendent, Bryan Taylor, because they were in charge of the district's records, he explained, and they told him they simply couldn't find the particular records the grand jury wanted. He had made no search himself, Tobin said, but he insisted that he had done "everything he could do" to comply with the grand jury's instructions. Asked if he thought it was satisfactory to take Bryan Taylor's word that Taylor's own records were missing, Tobin replied defensively that he hadn't taken just Taylor's word for it; he had also asked Barrera, who gave him the same answer. (Long after our investigation was over, one of George Parr's attorneys confirmed for me what I had been told earlier by other sources: that Barrera had been one of the trusted Parr lieutenants who inscribed the 202 fictitious signatures on the Box 13 voter list in 1948, at Parr's direction, to make Lyndon Johnson a United States senator.)

It did seem strange, Tobin admitted, that the only school district records missing were those for the particular years in which the grand jury was interested. Nevertheless, he said, it didn't cross his mind to conduct his own search, because Barrera and Taylor were the custodians of the records, and they said the records weren't there.

I pushed a little harder. "Mr. Tobin, isn't the real answer, you took their word for it because you know Bryan Taylor is George Parr's boy? Isn't that really why you wouldn't probe further for this grand jury?"

"No, sir. No. No, I tried. I tried all the influence that I could use to get those things — the records."

In addition to being president of the San Diego school board, an elected position in which he had served more than ten years, Tobin was a county commissioner, a rancher and farmer, an oil and gas lessor, and the county's only Lone Star beer distributor. He had run for the school board because of his interest in the schools, he said. I asked if he had secured approval of his candidacy from anyone else before running for the office.

"Oh, yes, sir, naturally, sure," Tobin nodded. "You have to have George Parr's support down there to run. He holds most of the political influence down there." In fact, Tobin admitted, the school district is really run by George Parr. Being president of the school board, he said, was "more titular than anything."

At ten minutes before noon, Tobin was excused with emphatic instructions from A. B. Jones, the grand jury foreman, to return to San Diego once again, conduct a physical search for the subpoenaed records, and report back at 10:00 the next morning.

"Do you understand that thoroughly, sir?" Jones rumbled.

Tobin's shoulders sagged. "I understand it," he replied tonelessly.

Through the court's interpreter, Louis Marquez, octogenarian D. C. Chapa, president of both the Benavides school board and the water district, repeated for the grand jury the same, sad story he had told Sessions and me through his attorney on July 6: The Benavides Independent School District's records had been thrown away, he was told by school board secretary Rodolfo Couling, and the water district's records had been stolen.

Chapa's attorney had seen to it that his client would at least get credit for making an effort to find the missing papers. Chapa testified that he did go to the site of the unused school building where the school district's records had been stored. "Yes, sir, I went there," Chapa testified. "There is no school there. They knocked it all down, made it into little pieces, about a year ago."

Next, Chapa described his visit to the water district office, where a disconsolate Leopoldo Sepulveda, the business manager, showed him the empty file cabinet in the empty walk-in safe. Sepulveda opened the door and said, "Look, look," Chapa explained. "Where I looked in there, there was nothing. There was not even a pencil." Chapa said he did not notice whether the building or the safe had been entered by force, but he did verify that Sepulveda had reported the incident to the sheriff.

What the water district called a "safe" was little more than a walk-in closet with an ordinary window on the back wall. The door, which was rarely closed, could be secured by a combination lock, but the combination was taped to the door for the benefit of the forgetful and the uninformed.

To the IRS agents who had dealt with him up to this point in the investigation, Leopoldo Sepulveda had been something of an enigma. When they discovered there might be a fifth water district checking account after he had told them there were only four, they assumed that Sepulveda had held out on them. But his claim of ignorance about a "Special Account" had impressed them as genuine, and the bank's tight control over the canceled checks and bank statements for the four accounts he had admitted handling raised the possibility that Sepulveda was not an insider, but only what he purported to be: a mere bookkeeper with limited knowledge of his employer's business.

The existence of a Special Account had been confirmed on May 23, when banker Karl Williams produced copies of the $12,000 and $3,000 items the agents had spotted in CPA Norman Ransleben's workpapers, identified there as nontaxable payments to Parr from "DC&RD Special Account." Though we still didn't have the Special Account bank statements and canceled checks, the grand jury was eager to see Sepulveda, to hear what he would say under oath about the Special Account and the reported burglary of the water district office. With help from Agents I. A. Filer, Ed Watts, Charlie Volz, and Jerry Culver, Sessions and I had prepared a laundry list of things Sepulveda might be able to shed some light on.

Leopoldo Sepulveda was a slender man, a little less than average height, with dark hair and sharp features. Judging from his appearance, he could have been in his late thirties, but he was probably at least ten years older than that. He was dressed that day as the agents had seen him on their visits to the water district office: in neatly pressed jeans, a tailored Western shirt, cowboy boots, a Western belt, and sunglasses.

He lived in San Diego, he said, and had been the Duval County Conservation and Reclamation District's office manager since November 1966. He was polite, mild-mannered, understandably nervous, and so soft-spoken that I had to ask him to speak up. His principal duties, he said, were to keep the district's payroll records and its water and sewer line installation expense records, and to file its Social Security and payroll tax withholding reports. He was not an accountant, but he had worked for thirteen years as a bookkeeper for International Harvester Company, in Alice, before joining the water district. His role with the water district, he told us, was "sort of an all-around bookeeper," maintaining cash disbursement journals, making revenue deposits, and reconciling bank accounts. His salary was $650 a month. He was a Rotarian, he added.

Although both he and his assistant, Maria Barkley, prepared checks, neither had authority to sign them. During the years in question, Sepulveda said, all of the district's checks had to be signed by the president, D. C. Chapa, and the secretary, Jose Tovar. Tovar managed to die in early 1972, apparently of natural causes, shortly before the grand jury investigation began. The agents speculated that although Tovar might have lost the authority to sign checks, his death would not prevent him from continuing to vote in Duval County elections.

The water district, Sepulveda explained, owned the water and sewer systems in the cities of San Diego and Benavides, and supplied water to all the municipalities in the county except the city of Freer. The district's business was run by its four-man board of directors, Sepulveda said. Besides Chapa and the late Jose Tovar, the other directors were Julio Benavides and Humberto Garza. Sepulveda prepared minutes of the board meetings in English, but all the meetings were conducted in Spanish.

As Sepulveda described his duties in more detail, we learned that the district's sources of revenue were property taxes, and water and sewer sales. He did not collect or deposit taxes, Sepulveda told the grand jury, nor did he handle water and sewer collections. The bookkeeping system Sepulveda described was primitive at best, consisting of a cash disbursements journal and no ledgers. Sepulveda handled no money and prepared only basic revenue and expense reports for the board of directors.

All of his records, Sepulveda said, had been cleaned out by whoever burglarized the office over the Fourth of July holiday.

There was no sign of forced entry. "They had to have broken in with a key," he said. "The office used to be an abstract company, and there's bars on the windows and strong locks and doors."

Sepulveda acknowledged that he and his co-worker, Maria Barkley, had keys, as did C. G. Palacios, the unofficially retired former general manager, who no longer came to the office because he was "physically and mentally deteriorated." He had no idea how many other keys there were, Sepulveda said, because no one bothered to change the locks when the district rented the building.

Bill Sessions pressed him for more information. "What was in the records that were stolen, please, sir?"

"The whole works, sir. My monthly report that I present to the board, my statement of revenue and disbursements, Social Security and IRS records, individual employee records, you name it; I lost everything."

The burglary must have occurred between Monday, July 3, and Wednesday morning, July 5, Sepulveda concluded. "The janitor saw everything as it usually was Monday morning; my desk was cluttered as usual. But when I came in Wednesday there was nothing on top of my desk." The burglars did a thorough job, by Sepulveda's account. All the water district records were gone, he said, as well as all the personal papers he kept in a separate file cabinet on his desk. He seemed particularly miffed that his book club records had been stolen.

Sepulveda reported the burglary to Deputy Sheriff Israel Saenz, who promised to try to solve the crime. He also reported it to the district's legal counsel, George Parr.

"What did Mr. Parr say?" Sessions inquired.

"He asked if I was involved in it, and I said, 'No, sir, I was out of town that weekend.' And he said, 'Well, I'll try to find out who did this.'"

One thing the burglars did not get was the water district's bank statements and canceled checks. Sepulveda told the grand jury, as he had told Charlie Volz and Ed Watts previously, that the district had four checking accounts — the Operating Fund, the Social Security Fund, the Interest & Sinking Fund, and the Payroll Record Fund — and that he was required to go to the bank each month to reconcile them. Usually, he said, Barney Goldthorn, the bank president, was the officer who sent for the checks and showed him where he could work. Sepulveda didn't know why the bank kept the district's monthly statements and canceled checks. "I was informed that they were supposed to be at the bank," he said. "I figured it was some kind of law."

Sepulveda was intelligent enough to figure it out: The restrictions on his access to bank statements and financial data were obviously calculated to limit his knowledge of things he didn't need to know. It must have occurred to him, though, that his salary was very comfortable by Duval County standards and his job was indoor work with no heavy lifting. Perhaps that explained why he was willing to prepare financial reports for the board based on deposits he never saw, and to troop to the bank each month, hat in hand, to ask humbly for his bank statements and a place to examine them, without so much as asking if they could simply be sent to his office. Nevertheless, he seemed to be answering our questions truthfully, even if his knowledge was limited by his seemingly voluntary ignorance of what may have been going on around him. I wondered what he would say about the Special Account when confronted with a Special Account check.

"Mr. Volz asked me about a Special Account when the agents were at my office, and I told him I didn't know anything about that account, that I didn't handle a Special Account," Sepulveda said. But Sepulveda was bookkeeper enough to realize there had to be another account that he didn't have access to. "I figured there was bound to be a surplus account," he said, "because I'm just given the amount of money I requisition to operate the system for the year. I figured that if there was more tax collections than that, there had to be another account where that money was kept."

I handed Sepulveda a photocopy of a Duval County Conservation and Reclamation District check for $12,000, payable to George B. Parr. It apparently was the same $12,000 "DC&RD" item noted on CPA Norman Ransleben's work papers. Karl Williams had brought us the photocopy in response to a subpoena when he appeared before the grand jury on May 23. Sepulveda confirmed that the check had apparently been an "Operating Fund" check, with that account title appearing immediately above the signature line, but the words "Operating Fund" had been crossed out, and the words "Special Account" had been typed in. He was also able to confirm that the check had been written and protected with the check protection device in the water district office.

The explanation on the face of the check identified it as "advance salary." The check was dated April 18, 1969.

"Were you ever made aware that Mr. Parr received an advance of $12,000 on his salary in April of 1969?" I asked.

"No, sir. I didn't have it in the Operating Fund, sir."

He had no record and no knowledge of any salary advance to George Parr, Sepulveda said. He did keep a record of short-term loans the water district sometimes made to its employees to cover unexpected medical bills and other minor financial emergencies, he said, but he seemed mystified by the check to Parr.

Frowning, Sepulveda studied the photocopy, turning it over and over in his hands, scrutinizing first the front side and then the back, and then he looked back at me. There was no doubt it was a genuine Operating Fund check, number 3454, taken from the checkbook Sepulveda maintained. All of the signatures on the check were familiar, he said. Just below the altered account title was the signature of the late Jose Tovar, as secretary of the board of directors. In a box at the left margin of the check was the countersignature of the board's president, D. C. Chapa. On the back, in a large, flowing hand, was the endorsement of the payee. Sepulveda had no difficulty recognizing it as George Parr's signature.

George Parr's treatment of the $12,000 payment as a nontaxable salary advance raised additional questions. Sepulveda had testified a few minutes earlier that Parr had been paid his $1,000 monthly salary at every board meeting since Sepulveda became the district's office manager in late 1966, by checks written on the Operating Fund. Parr attended board meetings regularly, Sepulveda said, but he knew of no legal work that Parr had ever done for the district.

The U.S. attorney took up the questioning. "So far as you know, Mr. Sepulveda, was there any interruption of the month-by-month payment of a $1,000 retainer to Mr. Parr? Does he receive $1,000 a month every month?"

"Yes, sir."

"So far as you know, has he been paid each and every month since you came on?"

"Yes, sir."

"Has there been a year's interruption?" a grand juror interjected.

"No, sir."

Sessions persisted, demanding to know how Sepulveda could have failed to notice that check number 3454 was removed from the Operating Fund checkbook. Sepulveda speculated that the check stub probably indicated that the check was voided. Usually, but not always, he said, voided checks were folded and stapled to the stub, in the checkbook. If Maria Barkley voided a check when he was away, he said, it was possible the check would not be returned to him.

Sepulveda insisted a missing check would have caused him no concern if the stub showed that it was voided, even though the check was not folded and stapled into the checkbook. He admitted having seen that happen "maybe three, four times." He did not report those instances to the directors because the checks never showed up as charges against the Operating Fund, Sepulveda said. "As long as it doesn't come out on my Operating Fund as a check, well, I figure it has been destroyed."

Sessions was appalled by Sepulveda's casual bookkeeping procedures; the open invitation to fraud was obvious. Because Texas law requires that public agencies have their books audited annually, Sessions inquired who performed the district's audits. "We haven't had an audit since we started, sir," Sepulveda replied.

"Since 1966, when you came on board, there has never been an audit?"

"Right."

Sepulveda was aware of the legal requirement, he said, and he had urged the board of directors to have it done, but "there has never been one."

Sepulveda came across as sincere, and the grand jurors seemed to have accepted his testimony as true, although many of his answers left them shaking their heads over the realities of local government in Duval County. Their assessment of the directors of the water district, though, was less charitable than their attitude toward the hired hand, Sepulveda.

"Do any of the board members that serve on this board get paid?" a grand juror inquired. Yes, Sepulveda explained, each one was paid $100 per meeting. "They do get paid?" the grand juror asked again, incredulously. Sepulveda nodded. "Each meeting," he said.

Sepulveda's subpoena had directed him to produce the district's bank statements and canceled checks, but, believing the bank

would not release them to him, he had not asked for them. His testimony had substantially enhanced the investigative importance of
the Special Account. It was now clear that the district had not four
checking accounts at the First State Bank, but five. The grand jury
instructed Sepulveda to go back to the bank, secure the bank statements and canceled checks for all five known accounts, and return
with them to San Antonio by 1:00 P.M. the next day.

Sepulveda was apprehensive about his unsolicited assignment.
He knew his place in the pecking order of Duval County, and he was
not accustomed to confronting either the water district's directors
or their bankers. He responded like a schoolboy who had just been
ordered to tweak the nose of the class bully.

"Do you think I have the authority to go to the bank?" he asked
anxiously, directing the question to Bill Sessions.

"You may have to consult counsel," Sessions replied. "I can't
advise you, but the grand jury has ordered you to bring those checks
in."

Sepulveda was very uneasy. What would happen, he wanted to
know, if the bank refused to give him the checks? "You'll have to
report back to this grand jury who refused you, and under what circumstances," Sessions told him, "and we'll try to support you in
that, sir."

We, too, were skeptical that the bank would honor a request by
Sepulveda for the water district's bank statements. During a break, I
prepared a subpoena requiring the bank's cashier, Karl Williams, to
bring to the grand jury the next morning every water district bank
statement and canceled check in the bank's possession, including
those on the Special Account. Charlie Volz served the subpoena on
Williams that evening at his home in Alice, some 140 miles south of
San Antonio. It wasn't the first subpoena we had served on the bank
for water district bank statements, but with the benefit of Sepulveda's testimony, it was the most specific one to date.

After seeing D. C. Chapa's signature on a Special Account
check, we had more questions for him in his capacity as the water
district's president. He followed Leopoldo Sepulveda as a grand jury
witness the afternoon of July 18. With court interpreter Louis
Marquez at his side, Chapa sat with folded hands and regarded us
and the grand jury with an expressionless look. In response to my
questions, he told the grand jury that the late Jose Tovar, who had

been the secretary of the board of directors until his death earlier in the year, had once "mentioned" a Special Account to him. "What did he say about it?" I asked.

"All he said was that there was an account. He worked at the bank. I believe he was a director of the bank."

Chapa was equally uninformative about the $12,000 "salary advance" to George Parr. Shown the Special Account check that had puzzled Leo Sepulveda, he identified his own signature without hesitation, but professed uncertainty as to Jose Tovar's, which also appeared on the face of the check, and George Parr's, which appeared as an endorsement on the back. Parr was the district's lawyer, and it was "possible" he had given legal advice or rendered other legal services to the board, Chapa said; he could not remember.

Chapa knew Parr's salary was $1,000 a month, and that it was paid to him each month at the board of directors meeting. His responses to questions whether the directors authorized a salary advance for Parr in 1969 alternated between "I don't know" and "I don't remember." I put the $12,000 check in his hands and asked him why it had been written to Parr. "I don't remember," the old man said nervously. "He might have asked for it. They might have just given it to him."

Additional attempts to elicit more definitive answers from Chapa resulted in a request by him to confer with counsel, followed by his invocation of the Fifth Amendment. By the time he was excused, I was convinced he knew far more than he was willing to admit. I was also beginning to feel, however, that it would take an immunity grant to pry any more information out of him.

On the morning of July 19, Dan Tobin, Jr., returned. This time, he said, he had personally searched the school district's buildings and files for the records the grand jury had directed him to find. Probably no one was surprised that he had found none, but the grand jurors had already heard more than they wanted to hear about the unavailability of public records they wished to see. Their hostile attitude toward Tobin reflected their growing frustration with the difficulty of getting information from these experts at obfuscation and delay.

A. B. Jones, the foreman, was angry, and he let Tobin know it. It appeared to him, Jones growled, that the records the grand jury needed were "conveniently" missing.

"You don't serve much function down there, as president of the school board," a grand juror told Tobin, "if you can't get those people to keep records like they are supposed to be kept." Tobin meekly agreed.

"This grand jury is going to find out about those records. All you're doing is delaying it," another grand juror chimed in.

Karl Williams took Leopoldo Sepulveda off the hook the next morning, July 19, by showing up with two large cardboard boxes stuffed to overflowing with water district bank statements and canceled checks. Records of all five accounts — including the Special Account — for 1966 through 1969 were carried into the grand jury room and inventoried, on the record, to be sure no statements were missing.

To our astonishment, Williams claimed he had not known until he and Barney Goldthorn, the bank's president, searched the bank's basement storeroom the previous evening, after our subpoena was served, that the water district's monthly statements and canceled checks were being held at the bank. When reminded that he had produced forty-two of the same checks on May 23 — the Operating Fund checks for George Parr's monthly retainer — and taken them back to the bank with the grand jury's permission, leaving photocopies for our use, Williams suggested that apparently "a clerk in the organization" had located the records and later replaced them in the bank's storeroom. He had not conducted that search, he said, and he insisted he had not known that Leopoldo Sepulveda always returned the documents to a bank officer so they could be returned to storage after reconciling his accounts.

His explanation was so hollow it was unlikely anyone in the room believed it, but we were more interested at that moment in turning over the records to the agents for a long-delayed examination. In particular, we wanted our investigators to take a close look at the elusive and mysterious Special Account.

The final witness on July 19 was B. O. ("Barney") Goldthorn, president of the First State Bank of San Diego. Barney was making his first appearance before the grand jury, but it wouldn't be his last. Goldthorn appeared to be in his sixties. He was a small man whose florid face suggested hypertension, or a drinking problem, or both. His hair matched his ruddy complexion, and in his light-colored, patterned slacks and dark green blazer he looked like the popular

stereotype of a used-car dealer. The distinctive sound of pills rat-
tling in hard plastic vials in the pocket of his jacket suggested he was
on one or more medications. From 1934 to 1936, Goldthorn had
been employed by the Parr family's Texas State Bank of Alice. From
1936 until he joined the First State Bank in 1962, he had been the
John Deere implement dealer in Alice, and he had enjoyed a minor
political career.

Though Goldthorn seemed extremely nervous, he fielded questions adroitly, limiting his answers to disclose as little information
as possible while exhibiting a consistently deferential manner to the
grand jury and his questioners. He had helped Karl Williams search
for the water district bank statements and canceled checks the previous evening, he said, to comply with the grand jury's subpoena, and
he had been surprised to find they were stored in the bank. Like
Williams and the bank's vice-president, Fletcher Brown, Goldthorn
insisted he had not known Leo Sepulveda always left the water district's statements and checks at the bank after reconciling the accounts. Since he, Brown, and Williams all agreed that Sepulveda customarily asked one of them for his bank statements and a place to
reconcile them each month, it hardly seemed credible that not one
of the three was aware Sepulveda always left the statements at the
bank when he was finished. Perhaps my own impression of Goldthorn's credibility was tainted by the knowledge that in 1948, when
George Parr used Jim Wells County's Box 13 to steal an election,
Barney was the mayor of Alice, where it all happened.

After the grand jury adjourned, Sessions and I met with Filer
and Watts to talk about the day's events and plan for the next grand
jury session, in early August. We didn't know exactly what we had,
we concluded, but there was bound to be something special about
the Special Account.

Years later, long after the investigation and its aftermath were
history, our old adversary Marvin Foster acknowledged over lunch
at Mama's Hoffbrau in San Antonio that our capture of the Special
Account was a turning point in the investigation. A grin creased his
face as we reminisced about the hectic days of the investigation.
"When y'all finally got hold of the Special Account," Marvin
drawled, "I knew y'all had done hit the mother lode."

Chapter 11

Breakthrough

I'd rather be lucky than smart.
— Anonymous

IT WAS THE CHANCE audit of Carl Stautz that triggered the investigation of George Parr, but it was the serendipitous discovery of the Special Account that kept our efforts from ending in frustration and failure in the summer of 1972.

"It was almost sheer luck we ran across the Special Account," Revenue Agent Ed Watts admitted. "Of course, everything that happened after that was pure investigative skill," he grinned, "but finding out about that account in the first place — well, we got a break."

Had George Parr's CPA, Norman Ransleben, not jotted a reference to the Special Account on his work papers for Parr's 1969 tax return, we almost certainly would never have heard of it. None of the three or four people who knew the nature of the account would have breathed a word of it to us voluntarily, and the First State Bank of San Diego hadn't produced it for us even though our subpoenas had called repeatedly for records of all of the district's checking accounts. Not until we knew enough to demand the Special Account by name did the bank admit its existence.

In the account records we expected to find documentation of the $12,000 "salary advance" and the $3,000 "check swap" Norman

Ransleben had noted in his work papers, but we didn't know whether we'd find anything else relating to George Parr. To our surprise, the account would prove to be Parr's undoing, and it couldn't have fallen into our hands at a more propitious time: before we acquired the Special Account records, the door Carl Stautz opened months earlier had led only to his own reluctant admissions of payoffs — for which we had nothing but limited, circumstantial corroboration — and to the $40,000 payment from Harris Fender for bonds that were either worthless or nonexistent, which Parr had falsely reported as a capital gain. That wasn't nearly enough evidence to win Justice Department approval for a tax evasion prosecution of the Duke, and we had just about run out of investigative leads.

Charlie Volz, I. A. Filer, and Ed Watts seized upon the Special Account and spent days reconstructing and analyzing it, transaction by transaction. Patiently, methodically, they opened each bank statement, scanned the ledger sheets, inventoried the canceled checks, deposit slips, and other contents, and compiled a meticulous schedule of every deposit and withdrawal. The account had been opened November 17, 1967, they found, and closed December 30, 1969. During that time a total of $583,748.34 was deposited to the account, all from property taxes collected for the district by the county tax assessor-collector, and every cent was disbursed.

The final withdrawal emptied the account by transferring the remaining balance, $61,320.72, to another First State Bank account we hadn't heard of before — the "Reserve Fund." That meant the bank's cashier, Karl Williams, would be making another trip to San Antonio to produce the records of still another mystery bank account. I wondered, as I prepared Williams' new subpoena, how many more there might be.

The Special Agent's Report prepared later by I.A. Filer and Charlie Volz described the peculiarities of the Special Account:

The DUVAL COUNTY CONSERVATION AND RECLA-MATION DISTRICT Special Account is unique in that it is an official bank account of a governmental body in which the business manager, secretary . . . and the majority of the Board of Directors had no knowledge of its existence. The disbursements from the account were made primarily by Advice of Charges, but when checks were written on the account, pre-printed checks from the District's operating account were used with "Special Account" written or typed on the face of the check.

"The Special Account was special, all right," I. A. Filer remembered. "We'd never seen anything like it before, and I haven't seen anything to equal it since." The records reflected a peculiar way of conducting government business: A rushing torrent of tax revenue flowed into — and out of — the account in the two years it was open, but only a handful of checks were written on it, and all of those were pre-printed Operating Fund checks that were changed, in ink or typewriting, to "Special Account" checks. All but a handful of the withdrawals were made by debit memoranda labeled "Advice of Charge" — little white bank forms about the same size as deposit slips, with space for a bank officer's initials and a few blank lines for an explanation of the charge. Each of these debit memoranda bore the approving initials of the bank's president, B. O. Goldthorn.

"What few checks there were, were written to what looked like legitimate businesses the district might have some reason to buy things from," Filer recalled. "The explanations on some of the advices of charge showed they were used to pay for cashier's checks to real businesses, too, but a lot of the advices of charge didn't show what the money was being withdrawn for." In fact, scores of these debit memoranda totaling nearly $160,000 in 1968 and 1969 reflected only that the account was being charged "per instructions."

The agents knew Parr's $1,000 monthly legal retainer had been paid from the water district's primary account, the Operating Fund. In the Special Account bank statements for 1969 they found the other two payments Parr had told Norman Ransleben about, for $12,000 and $3,000. The smaller item was evidenced by an advice of charge that read, "To transfer funds as per instructions to GBP account." The other, a $12,000 check marked "salary advance," was the only check ever written to George Parr on the Special Account. Nothing else in the account records pointed directly to him.

From the checks and debit memoranda that were sufficiently informative to be helpful, the agents identified a half-dozen businesses that had been paid substantial sums from the Special Account. When we met in my office to plan our next steps, mindful of Duval County's history of chicanery involving public funds, we all assumed those payments somehow benefited George Parr. Filer and Watts made plans to locate and interview the payees while I prepared new grand jury subpoenas to the First State Bank. We wanted to see every cashier's check ever purchased with Special Account funds, and we wanted to see the previously unknown Reserve Fund.

Filer went first to Houston, to inquire about several large purchases from Stewart & Stevenson, Inc., a major supplier of equipment and services to the oil and agricultural industries. It didn't take him long to find out we were onto something significant at last.

On July 26, 1972, a desk sergeant at the Corpus Christi Police Department fielded an unexpected telephone call. The voice on the other end of the line was young, male, Hispanic, scared. "It's about those papers from the water district in San Diego," the caller explained. "You know, the ones that were stolen. We found them, OK? I want to turn them in, but I gotta be careful." When the sergeant determined the investigative interest was federal, he referred the jittery youth to the FBI.

Special Agent Penrod Harris of the FBI knew about the water district burglary from articles in the *Corpus Christi Caller-Times*. Although he was unable to extract the edgy caller's last name, Harris felt the IRS needed to hear his story. I. A. Filer hurried back from Houston to meet with the FBI agent and two unknown witnesses in Corpus Christi the following day, stopping briefly at my office in San Antonio to pick up grand jury subpoenas for the individuals and whatever records they might have found.

Two frightened young men, "Ramon" and "Carlos" (not their real names, because they could still face reprisals today if their identities were revealed), showed up at the IRS office to meet with Harris and Filer on Thursday evening, July 27. Also present were IRS Special Agent B. H. Gilligan of Corpus Christi and Revenue Agent Dudley Beaven of Houston, a regularly assigned member of our Duval County investigative team.

From a plastic bag Ramon solemnly drew out twenty books of check stubs and a fabric-covered accounting journal with "Duval County Conservation and Reclamation District" hand-lettered in black ink on the front cover. The check stubs were from the district's Operating Fund, and they matched the disbursements recorded in the journal. The book also contained some rudimentary ledger accounts that made the agents smile: The debit and credit sides were reversed, so that assets were recorded as liabilities, and liabilities as assets. The musty-smelling records were infested with insects; they had obviously been exposed to the weather, perhaps for weeks, and they still felt damp. Filer handed grand jury subpoenas to both youths and took custody of the documents.

They had been out drinking beer with some friends the preceding Saturday night, Ramon told the agents. On the way home they took a back road, a narrow dirt lane that loops out of the southeast corner of San Diego and back into town. Stopping in a dark, secluded spot to let one of their companions relieve himself, they stumbled upon the records in tall weeds along the side of the road. "They looked like they might be important," Ramon said, "so we took them home to show my parents." He and others in the family had read about the water district burglary, he explained, and they thought these might be the records that were stolen. It had taken the boys several days to work up the courage to report their find.

Because Ramon and Carlos were members of old Duval County families, the agents initially were skeptical of their story and their motives. "I questioned them real thoroughly about how they got the records, and why they were interested in them, and what they did and what their parents did, to see if there was any kind of a vendetta between them and the Parrs, or any close ties with the Parrs," I. A. Filer said. "We finally concluded they had nothing to do with the burglary, and they were probably telling the truth about just finding the records and trying to be helpful."

Late that evening Filer and Gilligan followed Ramon and Carlos to the unlighted country road outside San Diego where the boys had found the records. Dense weeds, waist-high on each side of the narrow roadway, hid the adjoining fields. Nothing broke the silence except the chirp of crickets and the hushed conversation of the four men. "Those boys were extremely frightened about being out there with us, of possibly being seen with us," Filer recalled. "They were worried about their safety and their families' safety, because they'd heard, all their lives, about things happening to people who 'went against the system,' so to speak. They begged us not to tell anybody their names."

Although Filer and Gilligan had their service revolvers for comfort, they, too, were uneasy about poking around late at night on a deserted country road, virtually in George Parr's backyard. "We still thought it could be a setup, an ambush," Filer said. "We found a few loose papers that night, but nothing important. Best of all, nobody bothered us. We were all glad to get out of there."

At Bill Sessions' urging, the agents renewed their search the next morning, finding only a few additional documents of no particular investigative interest. IRS Intelligence Chief George Stephen was unhappy to learn that his agents had spent part of that Friday morning tramping through the weeds in Duval County, Filer said. "He wanted me to get back to Stewart & Stevenson in Houston, to be sure they didn't destroy any records. I told him, 'George, that's an international company; they're not going to do that, not even for George Parr.'"

All of the records turned over by Ramon and Carlos, as well as the scattered papers the agents found later, pertained to the Operating Fund. "What we got was just a small part of the records that were missing from the district," Filer said, "and none of it seemed to shed any light on the Special Account." The identities of the two young men were never revealed outside the inner circle of the investigation because they were so fearful of retaliation, and we believed their fears were justified. The grand jurors agreed; they declined to ask Filer to name them when he appeared before the grand jury to turn over the documents and explain how they were obtained. Initially we thought the recovered records were of little investigative interest, but the check stubs would later prove valuable in the prosecution of George Parr's nephew, county judge Archer Parr. Because the sheriff had announced he would investigate the reported burglary, Sessions wrote to invite him to examine the documents. The sheriff never accepted the offer.

Filer, Volz, and Watts had a rejuvenated sense of mission as we gathered again in Bill Sessions' office at the end of July 1972 to take stock of our progress and reassess our plans for several days of grand jury proceedings in August. Unlocking some of the secrets of the Special Account had lifted their spirits to heights I hadn't seen since the earliest days of the investigation.

"Y'all are not going to believe what we're finding in that account," a jubilant Ed Watts told Sessions and me as Filer nodded his assent. "They've been using it to buy all kinds of things for the Atlee Parr ranch — he was George's brother, and his widow lives there now, but George runs the ranch like it was his own. They've bought enough irrigation equipment to flood half the county. And that's not the only thing. There's no telling what-all we're going to come up with before we're through."

Filer agreed. "We've got a whole bunch of new leads to follow," he said. "We're not even sure what some of it means yet, but it's pretty obvious George has been getting the benefit of a ton of money out of that account." Filer had already completed a preliminary inquiry into the water district's purchases from Stewart & Stevenson, Inc., while Watts and Charlie Volz had followed up on other suspect transactions. As welcome as the emergence of the Special Account was, it also put additional pressure on all of us; time to complete the investigation was running out, and suddenly we had a lot of loose ends to tie down.

We assigned top priority to two objectives: getting the records of the Reserve Fund from the First State Bank, and getting someone from Stewart & Stevenson before the grand jury. Filer's interviews of that company's recordkeepers in Houston had confirmed that impressive quantities of irrigation equipment were paid for with Special Account funds, apparently on Parr's instructions, and we needed to know the circumstances of the transactions and the whereabouts of the equipment. Other Special Account transactions cried out for investigation too: The water district had purchased from the First State Bank a sizable note owed to the bank by George's deceased brother, Atlee; it had paid thousands of dollars to the same bank on promissory notes owed by James Dula, a helicopter pilot from Oklahoma; and it had bought huge quantities of brush killer and fertilizer. We decided to schedule as many witnesses as possible in August, using two-day sessions in the second and fourth weeks of the month. With a little luck, we thought, this could be a very productive month.

Karl Williams, the First State Bank's cashier, was all smiles as he seated himself in the witness chair on August 8. He had found all the records of the Reserve Fund, he said proudly, and he was pleased to be able to present them to the grand jury. Everything was there, he assured us, from the opening of the account on November 25, 1969, through the bank statement of July 31, 1972, only a week old. How did it happen, I asked him, that we had to learn of the Reserve Fund by finding a reference to it in the Special Account? Why hadn't the bank disclosed this account to the grand jury in response to the previous subpoenas?

Williams gave us the company line: As the bank interpreted the subpoenas, he said, that particular account was never asked for previously. That night, to prepare for bank president Barney Goldthorn's grand jury appearance the next day, our team studied the Reserve Fund.

Harold Priesmeyer of Corpus Christi had worked for Stewart & Stevenson, Inc., for twenty years, selling irrigation, agricultural, and oil field equipment. He began dealing with George Parr in 1967, he said, "right after he drilled his first irrigation well on his ranch." Priesmeyer spotted Parr as a prospective customer by being observant, the same way he spotted other irrigation equipment customers in the vast expanse of his South Texas territory.

"When I look out across the countryside and see a water well drilling, I try to get to know the owner," he said. His job was to sell Stewart & Stevenson's services to clean and test the well after completion, and then to "engineer the equipment in the hole to do whatever job the owner wants to do."

What George Parr wanted to do, Priesmeyer learned, was to grow lush coastal bermuda and Alysia grasses to fatten his cattle. George was preparing the ranch — the 14,000-acre Atlee Parr ranch, owned by his widowed sister-in-law, Hilda — for that operation by clearing the tenacious native mesquite from vast expanses of acreage, and he wanted an irrigation system installed as soon as possible. Priesmeyer's company didn't drill water wells or eradicate brush, but it was right up their alley to custom-design an irrigation system, supply all the aluminum tubing and diesel engines and pumps, and assemble, install, and test the system to be sure it functioned satisfactorily.

The equipment he sold to George Parr, Priesmeyer said, was installed at Parr's ranch, about six miles south of Benavides, beginning in May or June of 1967. He described in detail the system he designed to make use of George's two irrigation wells. Employing hundreds of forty- and fifty-foot lengths of five-inch and eight-inch aluminum pipe, dozens of seventy-six-inch aluminum wheels, and several expensive diesel engines, it amounted to a self-propelled sprinkler system of Brobdingnagian proportions. The eight-inch pipe served as the stationary "main line," Priesmeyer explained, running thousands of feet from each well at ground level, parallel to the long sides of the rectangular fields Parr was creating with his extensive brush-clearing program. Extending laterally from both sides of each main line, the five-inch "feeder" pipe was deployed across the fields as a sort of water-filled axle, in 1,320-foot "power rolls" that moved by diesel power on the huge aluminum wheels. Other diesel engines pumped water from the wells into the main line, which in turn supplied the laterals. Each of the rotating sprinkler heads spaced at forty-foot intervals along the quarter-mile lateral lines sprayed twenty gallons of water per minute onto the thirsty soil.

Priesmeyer identified each of his sales to Parr from 1967 through 1969, using records Filer had copied at Stewart & Stevenson's Houston headquarters. They totaled more than $166,000 and reflected purchases of eight miles of aluminum irrigation pipe, several $10,000 diesel engines (including a spare), and hundreds of sprinkler heads, couplers, valves, wheels, and other accessories. The system grew, Priesmeyer explained, as Parr drilled a second water well about three-quarters of a mile from the first one and cleared the unwanted mesquite from additional hundreds of acres of rough land. The initial equipment order alone for the second well was in excess of $65,000 and included more than two and one-half miles of aluminum pipe.

I asked Priesmeyer if his company had many accounts that bought irrigation equipment in such large quantities. "Not in South Texas," he replied.

Priesmeyer drew a diagram for the grand jury, to show how the system was laid out. One of the grand jurors quickly calculated that Parr was irrigating two full sections — 1,280 acres, or two square miles — of recently cleared land.

I took up the matter of billing, knowing the agents had identified most of the Stewart & Stevenson purchases as charges against the water district's Special Account. Priesmeyer's transactions with Parr had been written up as sales contracts. Each called for delivery at "Parr Ranch, six miles south of Benavides." Each was signed by George Parr as "Owner." Each specified "Duval County Conservation and Reclamation District, San Diego, Texas," as the party to be billed.

"At the time this contract was entered into, did you know what the Duval County Conservation and Reclamation District was?" I asked Priesmeyer, showing him one of the orders.

"No."

"Did you have any dealings with the Duval County Conservation and Reclamation District in connection with this sale?"

"I didn't have any dealings with anybody except Mr. Parr. He instructed me to write the contract up just as you see it there. How it was paid for, I don't know. The only time I get involved with payment is if somebody don't pay."

"Did Mr. Parr always instruct you to have these bills sent to the Duval County Conservation and Reclamation District?"

"Right. Just like that."

Priesmeyer identified his only small sale to Parr, in the amount of $1,908.14, as repair parts for a water well at Parr's San Diego home. I asked Priesmeyer how it was billed.

"It was originally billed to George Parr, San Diego," he said after studying the records. "At Mr. Parr's request it was rebilled to the Duval County Conservation and Reclamation District."

He never did know what the Conservation and Reclamation District was, Priesmeyer told the grand jury; so far as he was concerned, it was just a name and address Parr wanted the bills sent to. Although the irrigation system was designed specifically for Parr's ranch, it would be possible to dismantle it and move it elsewhere, Priesmeyer said in answer to a grand juror's question. He was "pretty sure" it was still on the ranch, he said, because he had seen some of the equipment just a week earlier when he was in that vicinity, and he had sold Parr another diesel engine for the system sometime in 1971. He hadn't told Parr he was appearing before the grand jury that day, and he had no reason to think Parr knew, he said.

Maybe so, I thought to myself, *but Marvin Foster monitors the corridor every time this grand jury is in session. George Parr will know you were here before you leave this courthouse, if he doesn't know already.*

I hoped Priesmeyer was right when he said it would be difficult to dismantle and move the irrigation system, but it struck both Sessions and me that Parr might be tempted to put that expensive equipment out of sight before we could get a look at it. Not knowing how difficult it might be to find it, I had Priesmeyer give us detailed directions to the ranch. Although he consistently referred to it as "George Parr's ranch," what he described was the location and the layout of the Atlee Parr ranch, Los Horcones, a few miles south of Benavides.

Much of the grand jury's time the next day was taken up with the president of the First State Bank, Barney Goldthorn, as we questioned him in detail about the Special Account and its successor, the Reserve Fund. Barney seemed even more ill at ease than he had in his first grand jury appearance, before we got our hands on the two secret accounts. His face glowed red above the collar of his white shirt and his hands fluttered nervously as I read his constitutional rights to him. One of the outer pockets of his sport coat bulged, and from it the muffled rattle of pills in plastic vials was audible as he shifted uneasily in the witness chair. He had hypertension medication or tranquilizers, or both, I surmised, in that pocket. It didn't require medical training to see that he needed it.

No more than three or four people ever had specific knowledge of the Special Account. One of those who did was George Parr. Another was Barney Goldthorn. Jose Tovar apparently had been in on the secret, too, although he probably knew only as much as Parr and Goldthorn found it necessary to tell him. The key to Parr's ability to set up and use the account was the absolute loyalty of a knowledgeable "inside man" at the bank. That man was Barney Goldthorn.

Goldthorn knew he was going to be questioned about the Special Account, and that put him in a risky position. He needed to appear truthful and cooperative without disclosing anything harmful to Parr, and he needed to avoid implicating himself in the Special Account scheme without committing provable perjury. To accomplish those goals, he cast himself in the role of a humble country banker who had merely honored his customer's requests without interfering or asking questions. Someone had rehearsed Goldthorn carefully for the part. As delicate as his task was, though, he had one advantage: No matter what story he told, he didn't have to worry about being contradicted by the late Jose Tovar.

Barney Goldthorn was acquainted with all of the water district's directors: D. C. Chapa, Humberto Garza, Julio Benavides, and the newest board member, Anacleto Valerio, who filled the vacancy left by the death of the board's secretary, Jose Tovar. Barney was also acquainted with its two clerical employees, Leopoldo Sepulveda and Maria Barkley. The water district dealt exclusively with him on banking matters, Goldthorn said, and until Tovar died in March of the current year, his dealings were always with Tovar, who was also a director of the bank. (Although he had lived in Spanish-speaking South Texas most of his life, Goldthorn pronounced the late director's name "TOW-var," placing the emphasis on the first syllable, as an East Texan like Harris Fender might have done.)

Since March, he said, he had dealt with Leo Sepulveda, who continued Tovar's custom of always coming to the bank personally to transact the district's banking business.

"Most of the withdrawals of funds from the Special Account were done by debit memorandum, rather than by check, weren't they?" I asked.

"Yes, sir."

"Was there any particular reason for that?"

"No, sir. I couldn't give you any reason other than Mr. Tovar particularly would come by and instruct me what to do. And I would carry out his instructions."

To make a withdrawal by debit memorandum, Goldthorn explained, Tovar would come directly to him with instructions, always in person, never by telephone. He would prepare the debit memo as Tovar instructed, filling in the purpose of the withdrawal if Tovar gave him one, initialing the memo as the approving bank officer, and processing it as a charge against the account. Depending upon Tovar's instructions, the money would be used to purchase a cashier's check payable to a named payee, or transferred to another account in the bank, or paid out to Tovar in cash. Debit memos reflecting withdrawals for the first two purposes would identify the payee of the cashier's check or the account to be credited. Goldthorn agreed he could also identify the debit memos that resulted in cash withdrawals, because they would bear the numbered stamp of the teller who paid out the cash. As for those that were used to pay for cashier's checks, he assured us, the canceled cashier's checks were available for our inspection.

"All the records at the bank are available, Mr. Sessions," Goldthorn said anxiously, aware of the grand jury's resentment over our struggles to obtain bank records. "I just want to tell you there is no records in that bank gone."

Goldthorn suggested banking by debit memorandum might be a cultural phenomenon ("San Diego is ninety-eight percent Latin-American," he explained, "and they would come to the bank and do things that you would expect to be done by check"), but he admitted no other large accounts at his bank were handled that way. He said he had never talked to any of the district's directors about the unorthodox practice, except that once, years ago, he had asked Leopoldo Sepulveda why they didn't write checks on the Special Account. Goldthorn paused expectantly, doubtless surmising that

Sepulveda must already have denied knowledge of the account, trying to gauge whether he had succeeded in planting doubts about
Sepulveda's credibility.

"Did you have more than one conversation with him on that
subject?" I asked.

"Not to my recollection, no, sir."

"What exactly did Mr. Sepulveda say when you asked him why
they didn't write checks?"

The banker rubbed his chin thoughtfully, as if struggling to
dredge up from memory the exact words of a long-ago conversation.
"Gee whiz," he said, shaking his head, "I'd hate to quote this wrong,
but I believe he said it was easier for Mr. Tovar to attend to it. He
said they'd have meetings and just tell Mr. Tovar what to do."

Goldthorn's story tarnished only his own credibility; if Sepulveda had been lying to us about his ignorance of the Special Account, he was the better actor of the two.

To be sure we missed no investigative opportunities, and to
commit Goldthorn to a detailed version of the facts, we led the nervous banker through a painstaking, month-by-month, transaction-
by-transaction review of the Special Account, from the initial deposit to the closing entry, one piece of paper at a time. One of the
earliest debit memos brought George Parr's nephew, Archer Parr,
the county judge, to our attention for the first time. It appeared to
be inconsistent with Goldthorn's story that no one except Jose
Tovar gave instructions for charges against the account: The typed
explanation over Barney Goldthorn's initials on a $14,000 advice of
charge dated February 2, 1968, was "To transfer funds to Archer
Parr as per instructions from Archer Parr." Surprised but resourceful, Goldthorn improvised an explanation that shifted responsibility
to the late Mr. Tovar and set a pattern for most of his answers to our
questions about the money that had flowed so freely from the account: "Archer Parr said he was due a $14,000 legal fee from the
Conservation District and that they were going to give him a check,
and he needed a deposit that day. And I called Mr. Tovar — which I
remember now — and he said that was right, sir."

The disbursements to Archer Parr from the Special Account
added up to $28,000 in 1968 and $38,700 in 1969, all by debit memoranda transferring funds to his account at the First State Bank.
None of the debit memoranda reflected any explanation for the
charges, and the banker professed ignorance. The only thing he

could tell us about those transactions, Goldthorn said, was that Mr. Tovar would have told him to do it. "I've initialed all of these things," he said, "and I certainly wouldn't have put my initials on anything I wasn't instructed to do, sir."

Goldthorn was no more informative about most of the other Special Account transactions we had flagged for inquiry. He identified twenty cash withdrawals totaling nearly $160,000 in 1968 and 1969, much of it in more or less regular monthly withdrawals of $6,000 at a time, but found nothing noteworthy about it. "Mr. Tovar would come to me at the bank, sir, and sometimes he'd tell me why he wanted the money and sometimes he wouldn't," Goldthorn explained. "If he told me, I'd put it on the advice of charge. And then I'd go to the teller's cage with him, and he'd get the money and leave."

As we went through the records of the Reserve Fund with the banker in similar detail, the picture that developed was so like the Special Account that we wondered why it was created and the Special Account closed. Barney Goldthorn's only explanation was that "Mr. Tovar came in to see me and told me he wanted to close out the Special Account and transfer the money and set up a Reserve Fund, sir, and he didn't give me any reason." Goldthorn agreed there was no difference in the way the two accounts were handled.

Opened November 25, 1969, with an initial deposit of $311,519 in property tax collections, the Reserve Fund was merely the Special Account with a different name. All deposits were tax revenues, including the $61,320 balance transferred from the Special Account. Most of the withdrawals were accomplished by advices of charge, all initialed by Barney Goldthorn. Few checks were written on it, and those few were altered Operating Fund checks. Cash continued to stream out of the account like water from a garden hose: Goldthorn identified twenty-seven cash withdrawals totaling nearly $250,000 — four of which were for the attention-getting sum of $32,000 each — yet he saw no reason for concern, or even for curiosity.

The Reserve Fund was closed July 13, 1972, just three weeks before Goldthorn appeared before the grand jury to produce the records. In a little more than four years from the time the Special Account was opened, the cash withdrawals alone from that account and the Reserve Fund exceeded $400,000. The more we saw of these transactions, the more plausible Carl Stautz's testimony about dark-of-night cash deliveries to George Parr, Bryan Taylor, and Eunice Powell appeared.

Barney Goldthorn's matter-of-fact description of a public official walking out of the bank day after day with thousands of dollars
in public funds, withdrawing the money in cash from a covert account without explanation and without stirring so much as a glimmer of curiosity in the minds of bank officials, confirmed for us that
Duval County was still being run as it had been in the 1950s — and
as it had been since old Archie Parr came to power in 1912. Because
we knew already that these secret accounts had been used to make
large purchases for George Parr, we suspected he was getting his
share of every dollar that came out of them, including the cash, but
we would have to investigate further to find out. Jose Tovar would
never be able to tell us whether he really made all those trips to the
bank and stuffed all that cash in his pockets, but there was no question the public's money was gone.

Chapter 12

Following Up

*A sekret ceases tew be a sekret if it iz once confided — it iz like a
dollar bill, once broken, it iz never a dollar agin.*
                                                    — Josh Billings

AFTER HEARING STEWART & Stevenson's Harold Priesmeyer
describe the irrigation system installed at Los Horcones, Sessions
and I discussed the advisability of getting photographs right away,
just in case George Parr decided to dismantle the equipment and
hide it. Ed Watts had taken pictures as best he could from the highway a few days earlier, but the distance to the equipment was too
great to get the perspective or the details we wanted for evidence.

Sessions called on another Treasury Department agency for
help. Bill Hughes, the district director of customs at Laredo, had a
helicopter at his disposal. We knew Hughes, a gregarious Bostonian
who went about his duties as guardian of the international border
with great exuberance, from drug smuggling cases in which his agents
often were witnesses in our district. Sessions inquired whether
Hughes would lend us his helicopter and a pilot for a photo-recon-
naissance mission to aid our tax investigation. "Hell, yes," Hughes
boomed. "We all work for the same government. Come on down."

On Friday morning, August 11, 1972, Sessions, Filer, and I
drove south from San Antonio to the U.S. Customs headquarters
complex outside of Laredo. The helicopter was a shiny, red-and-
white Bell Jet Ranger, spacious enough to accommodate all three of
us plus the pilot and another armed customs agent, and extra fire-

213

arms and ammunition. Hughes' officers knew Parr's reputation, and they knew he kept his own helicopter at the ranch. They believed in being prepared.

With Sessions in the co-pilot's seat we lifted off just before 11:00 and headed east toward Duval County, following Highway 359 across the brush country to Hebbronville, continuing along Highway 285 to its intersection with Highway 339 on the Brooks-Duval county line, and then turning north to find the ranch. Harold Priesmeyer had given very specific directions when he testified two days earlier, and Filer had seen the ranch from ground level. Three-quarters of a mile east of the highway, the sprawling, white ranch house with the red tile roof was easy to spot from 400 feet up. Between the house and the highway, contrasting sharply with the late-summer browns of the surrounding countryside, were huge, rectangular fields of shamrock-green bermuda grass. Without question, this was the place.

To facilitate photography we had removed the rear side panels from the aircraft before leaving Laredo. I sat on the right side as the designated photographer, Nikon loaded and ready. The pilot dropped the ship to scarcely more than windmill height and crossed the fenceline. Pulse rates rose as we scanned the horizon, half expecting to see another helicopter rise to intercept us. Long, silvery ribbons of aluminum tubing on giant, spoked wheels seemed to stretch for miles across the thick, green grass. I wished the sprinkler heads were turned on, but the scene in the viewfinder was impressive enough as it was. We made three or four low-altitude passes while I leaned out the open side of the aircraft and shot frame after frame of irrigation equipment, reservoirs, and grass, and a few of the ranch house. The others kept a wary eye out for signs of hostile activity in the air or on the ground. There was a lot of triumphant cheering and general excitement over what we had found, but the pilot lost no time withdrawing when I signaled that we had all the pictures we needed.

A short flight north to San Diego, to make an aerial scan for more water district documents along the unpaved road where Filer made his midnight search in late July, was unproductive. Nevertheless, we drove back to San Antonio that afternoon elated about the day's work. The color photographs of all that green grass and silvery aluminum would bring the Special Account to life for a trial court jury someday.

As the grand jury's customary four-month term drew to a close in August, they made it clear they wanted to stay on. "It's unanimous, Mr. Sessions," foreman A. B. Jones told us earnestly. "Everybody wants to get to the bottom of this thing. We don't want to quit." We prepared a letter for Jones' signature and conveyed it to Chief Judge Adrian Spears. On August 23, to the grand jury's delight, the judge granted their wish. "Since it is the preference and wish of the entire Grand Jury to continue to serve in order to complete the extended investigation it has been conducting since May," Spears wrote back, "I am glad to comply with your desires."

Fred Wright was the manager of Thompson-Hayward Chemical Company's San Antonio office in May 1969, when he received a telephone call about a huge quantity of brush killer. He remembered the incident very distinctly, he told the grand jury. The caller said she was with "a water conservation district in Duval County," Wright explained. "They wanted six or seven thousand dollars worth of chemicals. It was to go to George Parr's ranch, and they were in a rush and would pick it up in their own truck because a helicopter was waiting there to apply it."

The woman didn't want to give him a written purchase order, Wright said. "Normally we sold material to government agencies on open terms, but I was just suspicious about the whole thing. I insisted on a check in advance and tried to get a formal purchase order." The product they wanted was 2,4,5-T, a powerful brush killer designed to eradicate such notoriously stubborn vegetation as mesquite trees. A little 2,4,5-T goes a long way, Wright indicated, and they wanted 1,045 gallons — nineteen 55-gallon drums. Wright didn't stock the product in that quantity, but he located it for them at Thompson-Hayward's outlet in Llano, 115 miles northwest of San Antonio in the Texas Hill Country. The total price came to $6,134.15.

Wandah Otto, the company's office manager in Llano, remembered the transaction too. When two Duval County employees arrived in a Precinct Three vehicle to deliver a water district check and pick up the order, it was the first time she had ever seen anyone haul drums of brush killer in a dump truck.

A little later, another curious fact came to light: We had focused on the Thompson-Hayward transaction because the bill was paid by one of the few checks ever drawn on the Special Account, but the microfilm records of the Llano bank showed that when Thompson-Hayward deposited check number 3604, signed by Jose Tovar and D. C. Chapa, it was an Operating Fund check, plain and unaltered. Chapa had insisted from the beginning that he never signed a Special Account check. We hadn't believed him, but this raised the possibility he was telling the truth. It raised other questions too: Who at the First State Bank had intercepted the returning check, altered it before it was microfilmed, and sidetracked it into the Special Account? Who else, if not Barney Goldthorn?

The helicopter standing by to spray brush killer at Los Horcones in May 1969 was a three-place Bell craft that belonged to George Parr and was kept at the ranch. It was to be piloted by James Irwin Dula, Jr., of Rubottom, Oklahoma, a rural community not far across the Red River from Denison, Texas. Dula had the soldier-of-fortune manner and appearance of a born bush pilot. He would have been a natural for a 1930s movie role in khakis, leather jacket, and aviator's goggles, climbing out of the open cockpit of a biplane in a jungle clearing. Dula's entrepreneurial interests in 1972 included flying, cattle breeding, and ranching.

The Special Account records reflected dozens of payments on the notes of Dula's closely held corporation, J. C., Inc. Filer and Watts tracked him down at his ranch for an interview. They were aided in their search by a *Newsweek* magazine article about Dula's innovative technique for implanting purebred cattle embryos in ordinary cows, to be carried to term by the surrogate bovine mothers while the elite purebreds produced more embryos.

James Dula had met George Parr in 1964 while operating a flying service in Corpus Christi. In 1966 Parr helped him out of a financial bind by arranging for a loan at the First State Bank, and Dula, grateful, reciprocated by giving Parr free flying services on request for the next couple of years. By 1968 Dula had moved to Oklahoma, but he was spending as much as two weeks each month consulting and flying for Parr in Duval County. It was in 1968, Dula said, that he began receiving compensation for his services in Duval County.

Dula told the grand jury he did whatever Parr wanted done with the helicopter, "from shooting coyotes to rounding up cattle, observing cattle, looking over land sites — I didn't ask why he wanted me to do these things. I just went ahead and did it." He remembered spraying a lot of brush killer on the ranch.

"How many acres you reckon you sprayed down there on Mr. Parr's ranch?" a grand juror asked.

"It's been a while back," Dula replied, "but I'm going to say somewhere in the neighborhood of 4,000 to 6,000 acres."

He did some flying on Archer Parr's ranch, too, Dula said, but everything he did was with George Parr's approval.

"Did you do some flying for hunting purposes also?" I asked.

"Shooting coyotes, yes, sir. There have been many people who shot coyotes from the helicopter."

"Was there some deer hunting?"

"I think there's been some shooting at deer."

"Was that by George Parr?"

"Yes, he shot some."

"Archer?"

"I think so."

"Other acquaintances occasionally?"

"Yes, sir. It was in all the papers down there. I don't guess there's any use in denying it."

When Filer and Watts interviewed Dula at his Oklahoma ranch, Dula told them about the day he quit working for George Parr. "He said George had shot his thirtieth deer that day and was trying to shoot his thirty-first," Filer recalled. "It was a hot day, and Dula was having trouble holding the chopper still enough for George to get off a shot, and George yelled and screamed and cussed at him so bad, he quit. He said George would just shoot the deer and cut their heads off, and put the heads in the helicopter and leave the carcasses on the ground, and after a while the smell of blood in that hot helicopter would get to you."

Dula was compensated for his services by periodic transfers of funds from the water district's Special Account to reduce the balances owed on his corporation's notes at the First State Bank. His interest in the source of the funds was casual at best. Parr told him the notes would be "taken care of" through payments for his flying services, Dula testified. "Now, where he was going to draw the money from, I didn't know."

"Do you know what the Duval County Conservation and Reclamation District is?" I asked.

"Not entirely, no, sir. My understanding is that it handles the water needs of the city, but I'm sure it goes much further than that.

I do know Mr. Parr had something to do with it. He was either directing it, or chairman of it, or something."

"Did you consider yourself working for the Conservation District during 1968 and 1969?"

"That's a touchy question. I considered myself working for the man that was paying me to do what he wanted me to do. If that was his company and he chose to pay me out of that, that's who I was working for. I was doing what George Parr wanted me to do. I do know now that all of the payments came from the water district."

In 1968 and 1969 Special Account funds totaling $25,909 were paid on the notes of J. C., Inc., at the First State Bank, all by advices of charge initialed by Barney Goldthorn. In 1970 the Reserve Fund was tapped for an additional $6,196 for the same purpose, in the same way.

A bulk purchase of fertilizer led Filer and Watts to the piney woods of deep East Texas, and from there back to another previously undiscovered gold mine of graft in Duval County. An advice of charge dated February 6, 1968, drained $8,700 out of the Special Account to buy two cashier's checks of $4,350 each, payable to Texas Farm Products Company of Nacogdoches. That company's manager, Fred Bomar, dug out the records for the agents. It was an unusually large order of fertilizer, he recalled. It was telephoned in from the Farm and Ranch Supply store in Benavides. Bomar had required payment in advance because his company had to make a special production run to supply the quantity ordered: one hundred tons.

At County Commissioner Ramiro Carrillo's Precinct Three shop and warehouse in Benavides the agents found the Farm and Ranch Supply store. There they also found Cleofas Gonzalez, a county employee whose real job was running the commissioner's private business in the county's building. Gonzalez was young and affable, with a ready smile. Everybody called him "Buffalo." The Farm and Ranch Supply store carried only a modest inventory of merchandise, Gonzalez indicated, but they could order almost anything. He remembered the big fertilizer order. It was for George Parr.

"Tell us about that transaction," I said to Gonzalez when he appeared before the grand jury.

"Mr. Parr called me, you see, that he needed some fertilizer and asked me where did we get it. I told him who we bought it from, and he says, 'Can you order me some fertilizer?' I told him I could, so he said, 'Go ahead and call in an order, and ask them how much it will be, and tell them to deliver it to the ranch.'"

But Texas Farm Products was cautious. "They told me I had to send a cashier's check before they could start making it," Gonzalez said, "so I told Mr. Parr and I guess he sent a check for it. All I did was just order it for him." Gonzalez didn't know how it was paid for, but he recalled the delivery with a grin. Heads turned as a convoy of six big trucks roared into tiny Benavides one afternoon, flatbed trailers stacked high with enough bagged fertilizer to jump-start most of the crops in the county. "Those trucks stopped there at the Farm and Ranch store, and we told them how to get to the ranch," Gonzalez said.

Gonzalez was referring to the ranch with the big white house on it, about six miles south of Benavides. "It has a red tile roof," he explained. "It belongs to somebody from the Parrs. I think it's Atlee Parr's, or George B. Parr's."

The pieces of that particular puzzle were falling neatly into place. Brush killer, helicopter, irrigation equipment, fertilizer. The result was the sea of green we had photographed from the U.S. Customs helicopter on August 11.

Mrs. C. S. Reynolds, of Freer, was sure she would get her money eventually, but George Parr's $975 account with her small business, Reynolds Well Service, was several months past due when she saw Parr in the First State Bank and reminded him that she hadn't been paid for the work her crew had done on one of his irrigation wells at Los Horcones.

"Yeah, I'll have to do something to get you paid," Parr replied.

Vice-president Fletcher Brown greeted Mrs. Reynolds in the bank lobby a few weeks later with a deposit slip showing a $975 credit to her account. "He said Mr. Parr had taken care of it," she said in a sworn statement taken by I. A. Filer. Mrs. Reynolds didn't know it, but the money had been transferred from the water district's Special Account. The advice of charge initialed by Barney Goldthorn read, "To pay Reynolds Well Service, Invoice No. 1600." His instructions, Goldthorn told the grand jury, came from the late Jose Tovar.

Beginning with Harold Priesmeyer's first sale to George Parr in 1967, Stewart & Stevenson's account records documented the delivery of an astonishing 47,410 feet of aluminum irrigation pipe —

nearly nine miles in all — and four expensive diesel engines to Parr's ranch by the fall of 1969. The total cost was $166,860.17, and every cent had been billed to the water district on Parr's instructions. Our study of the water district bank accounts, however, left one perplexing gap in the evidence: Water district funds were not used to pay the $33,007.60 bill for George's first purchase, even though that one had been charged to the water district just like all the rest.

Sessions and I met again with most of the investigative team in mid-August to review our progress and plan our next steps. Solving the $33,000 mystery was high on the priority list. Ed Watts had already looked at Parr's own bank accounts and eliminated the possibility that the money had come out of George's funds. Stewart & Stevenson's records showed only that they had been paid for the merchandise. Their Houston bank's records showed only that the company had given the bank a collection item in that amount, and that funds were collected on it five days later. Because it was a collection transaction, the Houston bank kept no copies of any of the documents.

"We're going to have to make the First State Bank find it for us," Filer said. "Stewart & Stevenson must've drawn a draft on the water district, and it's got to be in Barney Goldthorn's bank somewhere."

It seemed as if a hundred other loose ends needed to be tied down too. We didn't know what water district directors Garza, Benavides, and Valerio would say about the secret bank accounts, or about all the money spent on Los Horcones, or the $12,000 "salary advance" that had turned up earlier. Maybe they were going to tell us these were all loans to George, approved by the directors, like the "loans" of Duval County funds George used twenty years earlier to buy the Dobie Ranch; that would violate Texas law, but it would be a defense to income tax evasion because loan proceeds aren't income under the Internal Revenue Code. We didn't know, either, what Hilda Parr would say about her arrangement with George at Los Horcones. Maybe she would try to shield him by saying the money was all spent for her benefit, since she owned the ranch. And what about the big legal fees Archer Parr had received from the secret accounts, we wondered; how much of that did he share with George, and what would he tell us about it? Filer and Ed Watts addressed still more unfinished business and unsolved mysteries: What had happened to the staggering sums of cash Barney Goldthorn said were withdrawn from the secret accounts by Jose Tovar? Why had the water district bought the late Atlee Parr's note from the bank, and why had sizable checks been written to George's sister, Marie Parr Thompson?

Also beginning to look intriguing, the agents told us, was the Farm and Ranch Supply business in Ramiro Carrillo's county warehouse. Early in the investigation, Filer and Watts had microfilmed the county's vendor records in auditor Walter Meek's office; over the ensuing months they had perused them when time permitted, looking for clues and patterns. The hundred-ton fertilizer purchase through what turned out to be a front for Carrillo was an eye-opener that served to focus their examination more closely.

"The county spends an awful lot of money on equipment rentals, and barbed wire and fence posts," Watts said. "They buy a whole lot of it from the Zertuche General Store."

The agents' instincts told them the county's purchases were suspect. "They've bought enough barbed wire and fence posts just in the last couple of years to put three strands around the whole county," Charlie Volz said.

The water district, too, was a Zertuche customer, to the tune of a thousand dollars or so each month. All of the agents were on the lookout for the Zertuche General Store. "We haven't found it yet, but we will," Jerry Culver promised. "It's supposed to be in Benavides, and that's a pretty small place to hide a business that sells as much big stuff to the county and the water district as it does."

D. C. Chapa's colleagues on the water district's board of directors paraded before the grand jury in August to proclaim their convincing ignorance of the Special Account and the Reserve Fund. Their professed lack of knowledge about George Parr's habit of using the district's funds for his own benefit, though, was halfhearted at best, particularly as to expenditures made from the Operating Fund. D. C. Chapa continued to insist he had never signed a Special Account check, notwithstanding his countersignature on the few that existed.

San Diego resident Humberto Garza, an oilfield roustabout, was one of the four original appointees to the board and had continued to serve as an elected member. Visibly ill at ease in the unfamiliar setting of the federal courthouse, he entered the grand jury room and solemnly handed me his subpoena. Because Leo Sepulveda had told us the board meetings were conducted entirely in Spanish, I asked Garza if he needed an interpreter. "No, sir," he replied. "I can speak English. It might be a little hard in my throat, but I can do it."

By the time Garza appeared before us, we knew most of the irrigation equipment purchased for Parr had been funded through clandestine bank accounts. Nearly $43,000 of the total, though, had been paid in 1968 directly from the Operating Fund. We wanted to know how the directors would explain that.

All of the district's bills were presented and approved at the directors' meetings, Garza said, on the first Monday evening of each month, at the district's office building. George Parr usually attended. It wasn't hard to imagine Garza and three other equally unsophisticated directors, all selected by Parr for their docile dependability, meeting with Papacito in the grubby little office building on South Dumas Street and mechanically approving whatever was placed before them. Indeed, any bill George did not want the district to pay would never have found its way into the meeting.

"Do you have customers who buy water for irrigation?" I asked Garza.

"No, sir."

"Do you own any irrigation equipment?"

"Yes, sir," he said reluctantly.

"Where is it?"

Garza looked around the room for help, but found none. "I guess it's at George Parr's ranch," he said.

Pressed for specifics, Garza ducked and dodged. He didn't know exactly what kind of pipe they had bought, or how much, or when, or why, he insisted. "There was a couple of bills that came in, and we approved them. That's all I know," he said.

"The district didn't have any use for irrigation pipe, did it?"

"I guess not, but they brought in that bill, and we accepted it, and that's all I know about it."

Garza remembered that the bills were from Stewart & Stevenson, for irrigation pipe, but his only explanation for approving payment was that they were presented. The directors' approval process, it seemed, might have been a bit perfunctory.

"Why did you buy it, Mr. Garza?"

"We just bought it."

"Why didn't you ask any questions about what it was for?"

"Well, it was for Mr. Parr, so it was okay."

"Did Mr. Parr ever pay the Conservation District anything for that pipe?"

"I wouldn't know."

"Did anybody ever ask him to?"

"No, sir."

"You wouldn't dare ask him to, would you?"

Garza stared out the window. "I wouldn't know about that," he said.

Garza confirmed that the directors were paid $100 each month for their services, whether they attended the board meetings or not. Grand jurors rolled their eyes heavenward. Parr's compensation was $1,000 a month, Garza said. "He advises on machinery, and whether to buy things, or something like that. He might do paperwork, I think. He says he's a lawyer."

Garza denied any knowledge of Parr's $12,000 "salary advance," or the purchase of Atlee Parr's promissory note from the First State Bank. The district didn't make any loans to George Parr or anyone else, he indicated, and it didn't buy promissory notes. Its only business was to furnish water and sewer service to San Diego, Benavides, and the tiny communities of Concepcion, Realitos, and Ramirez. Archer Parr had no connection with the water district, Garza testified; he knew nothing about any payments the district might have made to Archer.

Garza had heard the name "Special Account," he admitted, but he claimed to know nothing about the district's bank accounts or its banking business. "I mean, like, I'm a director there; I mean, I wouldn't know anything else."

Director Julio Benavides walked into the jury room, eyes wide, looking rapidly around the room as if he were trying to take in everything at once. We had been advised he spoke little English. "You do solemnly swear that the testimony you may give will be the truth, the whole truth, and nothing but the truth, so help you God," the foreman intoned. He awaited court interpreter Louis Marquez's translation and the witness's customary "I do."

Still standing, Benavides spoke urgently to Marquez in Spanish. "I wish to invoke the Fifth Amendment," Marquez translated.

I tried to clarify matters. "Mr. Benavides, you haven't been asked a question yet. You're only being asked to take the oath to tell the truth."

"To say the truth if I know it?"

"Yes."

"That's all right."

Like Garza, Benavides had been a director of the water district from the beginning. He was a lifelong resident of Ramirez, he said. "I work on the farm," he explained. "I have a few head of cattle and I also work at the aluminum plant."

When Jose Tovar died, Benavides served temporarily as secretary of the board of directors. Despite serving as an officer, Benavides was, if anything, less knowledgeable about the water district's business than his colleague, Humberto Garza. He seemed acutely muddled, or extremely inarticulate, or both. Despite the consummate skill of the court interpreter, Louis Marquez, communicating effectively with Benavides proved to be nearly impossible.

It was Benavides, accompanied by Leo Sepulveda, who trekked to the First State Bank to close the Reserve Fund and transfer the balance to the district's legitimate account after our investigation brought the secret accounts to light. I showed him the written order the bank had required to transfer the funds. It was signed by Benavides as secretary of the district.

"Who gave you that piece of paper to sign?" I asked.

"Gotone?" he said quizzically, arching his eyebrows. "What's the name of that old man?"

"Mr. Goldthorn?"

"Well, I think that's his name."

"Why did you have to sign that piece of paper?"

"Because I did not know those funds existed. I found out after the other man died, the secretary who was there."

The newest member of the water district's board of directors was Anacleto Valerio, appointed to fill the position vacated by the death of Jose Tovar. He had been on the board only five months when he appeared before the grand jury in August. Testifying through the court interpreter, he told us he lived near San Diego, on his farm.

"What is the business of the Duval County Conservation and Reclamation District?" I asked him.

"It's been such a short time that I have been there that there are many things I do not know about."

"Why did you become a director?"

"Because the salary that I have, it's really low, and this is $100 more."

"Mr. Valerio, do you not know the purpose of the Conservation and Reclamation District?"

"I don't understand it. It's the water district; handles sewers. That's all I know of."

Romeo Salinas identified himself as the assistant cashier of the First State Bank of San Diego. He went to work for the bank in 1954 and had been there ever since, he told us proudly. We had subpoenaed Salinas to test Barney Goldthorn's story about Jose Tovar's unorthodox way of doing the water district's banking business with the Special Account and the Reserve Fund. Yes, Salinas said, he was aware most of the withdrawals from those public-agency accounts were made by debit memoranda.

"Do you have many bank customers with accounts like that?"

"No, sir."

"That's a little bit unusual, isn't it?"

"Well, I take orders."

"Sir?"

"I take orders from the boss."

Like a boxer anticipating his opponent's next punch, Salinas had his defenses up, pointing out that all of the district's debit memoranda were signed by a superior bank officer before they reached him. In fact, he indicated, they all were brought to him by Barney Goldthorn.

"Do you know the officers and directors of the Conservation and Reclamation District?"

"Well, yes, I do."

"Do they come into the bank often on banking business?"

"No, sir; no, sir."

"Do any of them come to the bank?"

"If they do come in, I don't know. Sometimes I'm busy, but I never see them in there."

These answers weren't exactly in harmony with Goldthorn's song and dance about personally escorting Jose Tovar to Salinas' teller window, sometimes several times a day, so the board's secretary could withdraw cash on a debit memorandum. Goldthorn had painted a vivid picture of Tovar walking out of the bank day after day with envelopes stuffed full of $50 and $100 bills. Salinas agreed that many of the debit memoranda were used to withdraw cash, and often it was in substantial amounts. But the person he gave it to, he said, was Goldthorn, not Tovar.

"Did Jose Tovar do much banking business with you as an officer of the Conservation District?"

"No, sir."

"Did Mr. Tovar ever bring debit memos to your window to get cash?"

"No, sir."

"Did any other bank officer ever bring debit memos to your window?"

"No, sir."

"Only Mr. Goldthorn?"

"Right."

"And he always came by himself?"

"Right."

"Mr. Salinas, you're in charge of all the tellers. Have you ever seen officers or directors of the Conservation District deal with any of the other tellers?"

"No, sir."

So much for Jose Tovar and the envelopes, I thought, but with Tovar dead it was this witness' word against Goldthorn's. And no matter whom the teller had handed all that money to, we still weren't in a position to prove what it was used for.

With our growing knowledge of the Special Account and its successor, the Reserve Fund, and the exotic uses made of both, we subpoenaed Leo Sepulveda and his assistant, Maria Barkley, for encore appearances before the grand jury in late August.

It was perfectly clear that about half the tax revenue collected by the county tax collector for the water district went into the secret accounts, and that someone — whether it was Jose Tovar or Barney Goldthorn or someone else — had used debit memos systematically to bleed those accounts on George Parr's instructions. It was clear, also, that the water district's directors had rubber-stamped bills and paid them from the legitimate accounts, even if they were solely for George's benefit, whenever George told them to. Nevertheless, a lot of questions were still unanswered as we entered the late stages of the summer of 1972.

Maria Barkley had worked as a secretary for George Parr's

nephew, County Judge Archer Parr, until the water district was created in 1967. Since that time she had been on the district's payroll as half of its office staff. We felt sure she was the unidentified woman who called Thompson-Hayward Chemical Company to order brush killer for George Parr. She couldn't exactly remember doing that, she said, although she admitted she had sometimes placed calls for him. The grand jury eyed her with disbelief.

Leo Sepulveda grew on us. Each time he appeared as a witness, we became more convinced that this diminutive, soft-spoken man could be faulted only for not blowing the whistle when he could hardly escape knowing the water district was being misused for the private benefit of the powerful. And yet, we thought, how realistic was it to expect someone in his position to take on the Parr machine? From time to time, for decades, others had tried. Ultimately, all — including the mighty United States and the great State of Texas — had seen their most determined efforts dashed upon the rocks of failure in appellate courts, like waves crashing impotently against a great, granite wall. Upstart political opponents had been run out of business, and some troublesome individuals had even died under circumstances strongly suggestive of George Parr's direct involvement. When Sepulveda described himself to the grand jury as "only a pencil-pusher," he was telling us he knew and accepted his place. He was not a member of the Parr machine, but he was useful to it because he was competent to keep the water district's books and sufficiently astute to realize that his ticket to survival in that job, and in that autocratic society, was to content himself with following instructions and asking no questions.

Sepulveda understood also that volunteering information to the grand jury would be seen by Parr and his friends as unforgivable treachery, and he avoided giving more information than he was asked to give. Nevertheless, he responded forthrightly to our direct questions.

No, he said, frowning slightly as if trying to guess what prompted such peculiar inquiries, the water district had no use for irrigation equipment or brush killer, no need for fertilizer or the services of a helicopter pilot. The annual budgets he prepared had never included any of those items, and he had never heard any of them discussed at a board meeting. "We do use weed killer, though, around the plant, or around the wells," he added. Sessions inquired further.

"Approximately what amount would you use in a year?"

"I'd say about $600 worth, sir."

Sepulveda seemed baffled by our evidence of the district's bulk purchase of 2,4,5-T from Thompson-Hayward Chemical Company. He was familiar with the product, he said; it was a strong brush killer.

"The Conservation District wouldn't have bought 1,045 gallons to kill weeds around any of its wells or any of its plants, would it?"

"Not 2,4,5-T," Sepulveda said, wide-eyed. "That would bring a bunch of landowners with brush damage."

Sepulveda recognized Stewart & Stevenson as a vendor whose invoices had appeared occasionally for board approval and payment, though he was unsure what products or services that company sold to the district. Sessions had gathered several debit memoranda on the Special Account and the Reserve Fund to show him. He started with one of modest size.

"Here's one dated December 13, 1969, for $860.78, and you'll note it's identified as being issued 'per instructions from the district to purchase cashier's check payable to Stewart & Stevenson, Inc., Houston, Texas, as per statement attached.' "

"Yes, sir."

"Do you recall seeing an invoice of that size for Stewart & Stevenson approved by the board?"

"No, sir."

Sessions selected another one.

"Here's one dated April 19, 1969, for $15,388, and it says 'to pay Stewart & Stevenson statement as per instructions from district,' and there's a statement attached in that amount. Now, do you recall having seen that?"

"No, sir," Sepulveda said, a note of disbelief in his voice. "The ones I remember are $25 or $30, for connections or fittings, or something like that."

"For repair parts or replacement parts, is that it?"

"Right, which I would think they could use in repairing the lines, or in a plant."

"You don't recall seeing any large amounts?"

"Not that amount."

Sessions took a third debit memo from the file in front of him, relishing the moment. He had saved the best for last. "Let's look at this one, October 17, 1969, in the amount of $65,493.81. It says, 'to purchase cashier's check payable to Stewart & Stevenson, Inc., as per instructions from district.'" He handed it to the witness.

Sepulveda inspected it at close range, then held it at arm's length, shaking his head. "My God," he said.

It was to be an afternoon of surprises for the business manager; Sessions laid the predicate for one more.

"What kind of pipe or tubing does the Conservation and Reclamation District use in its water lines?"

"Mostly cast iron, and we use some cement-asbestos, it's called, now."

"You don't use aluminum pipe for that purpose, do you?"

"No, sir."

"Has the district ever bought any aluminum pipe from anyone that you know of?"

"Not that I know of."

"You wouldn't have any use for it?"

"No, sir."

Opening the file again, Sessions pulled out still another debit memorandum and showed it to the business manager. This transaction, we felt, even more than most of the others, reflected Parr's utter contempt for the puppets he put on the district's board of directors.

"This one is dated January 5, 1970, in the amount of $21,925.14. It says, 'transfer of funds to George B. Parr account in payment of aluminum pipe sold to district as per instructions.' I take it from what you've said that you don't have any idea what that transaction is about?"

"No, sir," Sepulveda said emphatically. He attended board meetings regularly, he said in answer to further questions, and he had never heard that transaction mentioned.

Neat trick, we thought; a "twofer." George had had the district buy the pipe for him, and then buy it from him — and the pipe was still in use at Los Horcones.

Sepulveda also denied any knowledge of the district's Special Account purchase of the late Atlee Parr's promissory note from the First State Bank for nearly $58,000. He had never heard it discussed by the directors, he had received no payments on it, and he wouldn't know how to account for it, he said. He was similarly mystified by the $12,000 "salary advance" to George Parr. It wasn't on his books, he told the grand jury, and it had never been discussed. The board occasionally approved small loans to its workers, Sepulveda said, perhaps a few hundred dollars at a time, but those were put on a regular payment schedule and he posted the payments as they were received.

"Have you received any amount of money for the district in repayment of that $12,000 advance?" Sessions inquired.

"No, sir."

"What is his current monthly salary?"

"$2,000."

This was new; it had been $1,000 a few months earlier, when our investigation began.

"When did it go to $2,000?"

"About three or four months ago, sir."

A grand juror spoke up, curious to know what George did for the district that was worth $24,000 a year. "To your knowledge, what services has he provided for the water district?"

"To my knowledge, nothing," the business manager replied flatly.

Payments from the Operating Fund to another member of the Parr family struck a more familiar note with Sepulveda. Revenue Agent Ed Watts had spotted in the records of the Reserve Fund a $5,000 "salary advance" to Marie Parr Thompson, and the purchase of her promissory note from the First State Bank for $12,150. In addition, Watts pointed out, she received a regular paycheck for $350 each month from the Operating Fund.

"Who is Marie Parr Thompson?" Sessions asked Sepulveda.

"Mr. Parr's sister," he answered. She was also County Judge Archer Parr's mother, we understood. Sepulveda knew nothing about the salary advance or the purchase of her note, he said.

"Does she work for the district?"

"Yes, sir, she is on the payroll."

"What does she do for the district?"

"I don't know, sir."

Marie Parr Thompson was in her seventies, Sepulveda estimated. She didn't work under his supervision, he said; he didn't know what her job was.

"To your knowledge has she ever performed any work for the district?"

"Not to my knowledge." He added that she came into the office at least once a month, usually to talk to Maria Barkley.

"And what does she do when she's there?" Sessions persisted.

"Visit with Mrs. Barkley."

"Did she do anything you would normally call work?"

"No, sir."

Marie Parr Thompson's monthly salary was approved by the directors annually, as part of the district's regular payroll, Sepulveda said. As usual, he had volunteered nothing to us, but he had answered our questions when we asked the right ones. It was clear he had always known she did nothing to earn a salary but had never questioned the board's annual ritual of approving one for her. Leo Sepulveda, the self-styled pencil-pusher, survived by following directions and minding his own business.

The four intensive days of grand jury testimony in August had answered some questions, opened some doors for us, and nailed some shut for George. We gathered the team again and focused on our remaining objectives. We still wanted to know what became of all the cash that left the Special Account and the Reserve Fund; whether it was handled by Jose Tovar or, as now seemed more plausible, by Barney Goldthorn, it was a great deal of money. We had decided not to attempt interviewing Hilda Parr, but to bring her before the grand jury to see what she would say about George's irrigation equipment — or would she call it hers, to save him? We would subpoena Archer Parr in September, we decided, to explore whether he had shared with George any of the money he was paid from the secret accounts as legal fees. And we couldn't ignore the growing indications that the Farm and Ranch Supply business and the elusive Zertuche General Store were fronts for some kind of graft by George's partners in power, the Carrillo family.

One especially frustrating piece of old business remained: the mystery of George's first purchase of irrigation pipe from Stewart & Stevenson, a $33,007.60 transaction. We were sure I. A. Filer was right. Somewhere in the First State Bank was a paper trail that would lead us to the source of the money used by the bank to pay a draft in that amount, drawn on the water district; and once we found the source, we could hope to discover who made it happen, and why.

Chapter 13

Perjury

I have often regretted my speech, never my silence.
— Publius Syrus

ON THE MORNING OF September 13, Karl Williams brought the grand jury part of the answer to the riddle of the first pipe purchase. He had located the collection item from Stewart & Stevenson's Houston bank, he said. It was a draft drawn on the Duval County Conservation and Reclamation District for $33,007.60. And he had identified the source of the funds used to pay the draft, he told us, just as we had requested.

Karl Williams' relationship with the grand jury had improved markedly since the difficult days of May and June, when the bank repeatedly tested our resolve by resisting compliance with our subpoenas. The bank had thrust him forward at the outset to be the lightning rod for the grand jury's frustration as the bank's masters sought to thwart the investigation through obstruction, obfuscation, and delay. Over time, however, Williams had earned our trust in his personal integrity as we came to realize that his role with the bank was similar to Leo Sepulveda's role with the water district: He was the honest and capable technician essential to the bank's legitimate operations, not a party to the looting of the public-entity bank accounts and not responsible for the bank's policy of resisting the investigation.

"Karl Williams and Leo Sepulveda didn't lie to us," I. A. Filer

232

observed. "I can't say that about a lot of other folks we dealt with in Duval County."

Williams was sufficiently astute to avoid acquiring any direct knowledge of the illegal activities in the bank and sufficiently discreet not to volunteer whatever he might have suspected. He was careful to be the proper banker each time he appeared before the grand jury, never editorializing about the bank's customers or the bank's officers or the banking practices of either, never volunteering the answers to questions not asked, always courteous, tactful, and calm. Nevertheless, I sensed an air of special satisfaction in his demeanor that morning. Williams had already complied with his subpoena by giving the IRS agents the documents he had found, and I had the feeling he was privately enjoying our success at uncovering some of the Duval County establishment's dirty little secrets.

"What was the source of those funds?" I asked. He smiled almost imperceptibly.

"We made a search of our records in the bank and found that this particular item was paid out of an account called 'City of Benavides Special Sinking Fund,'" he replied.

"Is that an account maintained in your bank by the City of Benavides?"

"Yes, sir."

"How did you determine from what account the funds came to pay this draft?"

"We just dug it out by looking at all of the public accounts for the month of August 1967, until we came upon this particular one."

"Why did you begin looking at public accounts?" I asked.

His answer was a masterpiece of understatement, avoiding the obvious response that the identity of the ultimate beneficiary made such a search logical. "Because it was a draft drawn against a public fund. We were of the opinion that perhaps public funds paid for it," he said.

Nothing about the transaction was routine. The First State Bank had paid the Stewart & Stevenson draft circuitously, by drawing a draft on its own funds on deposit with the Houston bank and offsetting the resulting credit by debiting the City of Benavides Special Sinking Fund. The only First State Bank officer whose name appeared anywhere in the records was Karl Williams' predecessor as cashier, Amelia Garcia. Contrary to normal banking practice, she had omitted from the documents any identification of the City of

Benavides as the remitter of the funds. In the space where that information should have appeared on the face of the First State Bank's
draft was only the number of the Stewart & Stevenson draft.

"Apparently Miss Garcia felt that this number would afford
sufficient identification of this item," Williams said tactfully, taking
care to avoid direct criticism of the former cashier. He had to assume, he said, that officials of the water district and the city authorized the bank to pay the Stewart & Stevenson draft by charging it
against the city's account. Because there were no other records, he
couldn't explain why or how it happened. "I would suppose the au-
thorization was verbal," he said, "and inasmuch as it happened five
years ago and there has been no complaint about it from any of the
people involved, I would have to assume it was a legitimate transaction as far as those people were concerned."

"Did any bank officer other than Amelia Garcia have to be aware
of that transaction in order for the city's account to be debited?"

"No," Williams said. "As cashier, she had complete authority."

Foreman A. B. Jones had sat silently through Karl Williams'
questioning, but as the session wound down a frown clouded his
face. As we prepared to release the banker, Jones spoke up.

"Mr. Williams, there's something going through my mind. In all
the years I've dealt with banks, and it's a pretty long while, it's very
seldom you see a cashier leave a bank unless they retire. Yet, this cashier is no longer in the bank. Why? Do you want to answer that?"

"You asked the question," Williams replied, "so I'll have to answer it." He paused, framing his response in his mind. "She was a
long-time employee of the bank," he said carefully. "It's my understanding that she had some personal financial difficulties, which was
not good for the bank's image in the community, and she was given
a leave of absence for six months. She was not returned to work."

Williams' testimony shed new light on the significance of a Reserve Fund transaction we had quizzed Barney Goldthorn about,
albeit superficially, when he was before the grand jury a month earlier. Shown a $6,000 debit memo dated September 16, 1970, bearing
the explanation "to make loan to cover checks as per instructions
from District," Goldthorn had explained it as a humanitarian ges-
ture by Jose Tovar: "I think that's the time when the cashier of the
bank — let me see, it was a lady, and what did she do?" the banker
had mused. "She had issued some cashier's checks, and they were
returned to the bank, and the bank had a loss. She had been there

some twenty years, and when I found out, I knew something had to be done. She contacted Mr. Tovar, and he came down, and the water district picked up the checks for her. She was granted a six-month leave of absence, and she was not re-elected as cashier." The cashier's name, Goldthorn had recalled with pretended effort, was Amelia Garcia. Her name hadn't meant anything to us at the time.

Listening to Barney Goldthorn's low-key explanation a month earlier, we could only speculate why someone had been motivated to use water district funds to rescue the defaulting cashier from the consequences of her breach of trust. Suddenly it made sense, either as a returned favor or as insurance against the telling of tales out of school. The foreman had one more question for Karl Williams.

"Was she ever prosecuted, sir?"

"No, sir," he replied.

The Special Sinking Fund records showed that it was opened April 2, 1967, just nine days before the Mercantile National Bank of Dallas transferred a little more than $39,000 to the city's checking account at the First State Bank. The money was the unexpended remainder of a court-ordered escrow fund that had been created years earlier to ensure the struggling city's ability to retire new bonds issued with permission of the bankruptcy court. When Harris Fender bought up all of the city's bonds in 1967 to facilitate the creation of the water district, the city became eligible for a refund of the surplus in the escrow fund. There was, however, a curious but familiar wrinkle: A few days after the $39,000 windfall was wired from the Mercantile Bank to the city's regular checking account at the First State Bank, the money was transferred by debit memorandum to the new Special Sinking Fund. Barney Goldthorn's explanatory notation said, "Mercantile National Bank remittance of bond funds deposited to wrong account; goes to Special Sinking Fund account."

To no one's surprise, Amelia Garcia had suffered a complete lapse of memory about the Stewart & Stevenson transaction. After examining the two drafts and identifying her signature on the First State Bank's instrument, the only thing she was sure of was that she would not have charged the City of Benavides account without Barney Goldthorn's instruction. Later we learned that she had been drawing a salary of $600 a month from the water district since her forced departure from the bank in 1970, though no one could explain what her job was. The directors approved her salary, Leo Sepulveda told us, but he was unaware of any function she performed.

Hilda Parr was nervous, soft-spoken, but open and direct in answering questions before the grand jury. After taking the oath she sat stiffly in the witness chair, rigidly erect, holding her purse upright in her lap and looking as if she might bolt for the door. The foreman tried to put her at ease. "Mrs. Parr, just relax," he said hospitably. "Lay your pocketbook down and just relax."

We hoped her testimony would establish that George Parr, and not Hilda, owned the improvements paid for by the water district on the Atlee Parr ranch. We didn't know what she would say about that.

Her late husband, Atlee, inherited the ranch before they were married, Hilda said, and left it to her when he died in 1967. Although she had lived on the ranch since they were married, her knowledge of ranching was limited. "My husband was in his forties when we married," she explained. "He ran the ranch and I ran the home, and when he died I knew nothing about ranching, absolutely nothing. When my husband died, my brother-in-law, George Parr, agreed to take over the operation of the ranch." The agreement was oral. In exchange for taking care of her cattle, George was allowed to run two of his own for every one of hers on the 14,000-acre ranch. She estimated her herd at 250 to 300 head. She didn't know how many cattle George had on the ranch.

Hilda was only vaguely aware of George's irrigation project. She didn't pay for ranch equipment or supplies, she said; that was George's business. I posed the key questions:

"If he buys equipment and uses it there, then it's his equipment, is that right?"

"Yes, sir."

"Whatever irrigation equipment he's using to raise grass, if he's bought it since he became manager of the ranch, I take it that's his equipment. Is that correct?"

"Yes."

Her answers put us over a big hurdle on the path to tagging George with liability for the value of the ranch improvements as income.

Hilda was aware of the water district's purchase of Atlee's note from the First State Bank, she said, but she didn't understand it. "I guess they felt sorry for me, because I couldn't pay it; I don't know.

I know they purchased the note, but I don't know why." She wasn't sure who the directors of the water district were, she indicated, and no one had asked her to pay anything on the note in the two years since Atlee died.

The water district's purchase had taken the note out of the bank, where state bank examiners soon would have insisted that it be collected, and put it safely under George's absolute control in an unregulated public entity that had never even had an internal audit. It hadn't cost George a cent, and it ensured that the ranch he was using rent-free wouldn't have to be sold to pay the debt against it. That $57,850 expenditure, we figured, would also be taxable to him as income.

Hilda didn't know why delinquent property taxes on the ranch amounted to more than $70,000 when Atlee died, she said, because Atlee didn't involve her in running the ranch. By ignoring property taxes, Atlee was continuing a family tradition. Ed Watts and I. A. Filer had noticed, while looking through the county's tax rolls early in the investigation, that the assessed valuation of George Parr's palatial home in San Diego had been lowered from an already nominal figure to nearly nothing.

"We asked why they changed it," Filer said, "and they told us, 'Because Mr. Parr asked us to; but it doesn't make any difference, because he doesn't pay taxes anyway.'"

Still searching for clues to the disposition of the cash that had been spirited out of the Special Account and the Reserve Fund, we zeroed in on the largest of those withdrawals, the ones identified on debit memoranda as "transfers" to the cities of San Diego and Benavides. We subpoenaed representatives of both cities to testify.

Mrs. F. C. Perez had been the secretary and treasurer of the City of San Diego since 1950. Since 1967 she had also sent water bills to her city's residents for the Duval County Conservation and Reclamation District and collected the payments. The city had just one bank account, Mrs. Perez told the grand jury, and she was solely responsible for keeping track of every dollar that went in or came out.

Mrs. Perez had brought with her all of the city's financial records for 1971 and 1972, as required by her subpoena. I showed her, one by one, four debit memoranda issued in those two years on the water district's Reserve Fund, which Barney Goldthorn had testified about in August. Each document bore his notation "to transfer funds to City of San Diego per instructions from the district."

According to Goldthorn, Jose Tovar had given those instructions and had walked out of the bank with the cash — a lot of cash — each time.

While the grand jury watched, Mrs. Perez scrutinized her bank statements and her cash journal, confirming for the record what she already knew: The city had not received the money.

"Now, Mrs. Perez," I summarized, "when we add up those debit memoranda — the three $32,000 items and the one $24,000 item — that's $120,000 between February 1971 and January 1972. Are you sure the City of San Diego did not get that money from the Conservation District?"

"I'm sure," she said firmly.

"If the city had received that money, you would know about it?"

"I sure would."

A grand juror followed up. "Mrs. Perez," he inquired, "what is your annual budget for the City of San Diego?"

The question took her by surprise. "I'm sorry, but I don't think we have any budget," she said uncertainly. "The City of San Diego? No, sir."

"Well, what does it cost to run the city offices, more or less? Is it as much as $100,000 a year?"

She began shaking her head before he finished the question. "Oh, no, no, sir," she said.

Santiago Garcia, Mrs. Perez's counterpart in Benavides, was equally sure his city never got the $32,000 indicated by the debit memorandum of June 4, 1971, on the Reserve Fund. Barney Goldthorn's notation said "to transfer funds to City of Benavides per instructions from district." He had explained it as another cash withdrawal by Jose Tovar, but the money never reached the city's coffers. Garcia was actually employed by the water district to bill and collect its accounts in Benavides, he said, but since the little city had no secretary, he also served as a volunteer in that capacity.

When I asked Garcia about the gift the city didn't receive, he responded with a question of his own about the money that found its way into the City of Benavides Special Sinking Fund.

"Did the city ever get $32,000 from the Conservation and Reclamation District?" I inquired.

"Heck, no," Garcia said. He looked at Sessions and me as if he had more to say. "Can I ask a question?" he inquired earnestly.

Garcia was aware of the escrow fund at the Mercantile National Bank, and he knew the city was supposed to have received a refund in 1967 when all of the city's bonds were bought up and the water district was created. "I don't know if we wrote a letter or phoned to transfer that money to the City of Benavides," he said, "and I don't know how much it was, but it was about thirty-something thousand, and I didn't ever see that either."

I showed Garcia the bank statements on the Special Sinking Fund. He looked them over carefully and announced that he had never seen them. He agreed the signature card bore his signature, and the mayor's, but he insisted he knew nothing about the account or the two withdrawals from it, one for $33,007.60 and one for $5,000.

Garcia's subpoena required him to bring all of the city's bank records and cash journals. I asked to see them.

"That's what I want to tell you about, see," Garcia began. "I brought all my records. I came yesterday, and I stayed at my brother's house. This morning when I got up, my car was broken into. They stole the records and my suit and my stereo. I called the police."

All the records he had brought with him were stolen, Garcia said — bank statements, canceled checks, cash journal, even his subpoena — and the San Antonio police had come out to investigate. The only people who knew he was coming to San Antonio, he said, were the mayor, Octavio Saenz; D. C. Chapa; and Ramiro Carrillo. "Oh, yes, and my wife," he added. "I have no secrets from my wife."

Too many things were happening for the second or third time in this investigation, our team agreed while eating a hurried lunch that day. The burglary of Santiago Garcia's car sounded too much like the burglary of the water district office. It reminded us that Garcia was among those convicted by a federal court jury in the 1950s, along with George Parr, D. C. Chapa, and the others, for looting the school system's treasury. Like all of his companions, Garcia owed his freedom to Abe Fortas' skillful advocacy before the U.S. Supreme Court.

I. A. Filer and Ed Watts had pointed out in our periodic planning sessions that for a public entity with little apparent need for lawyers' services, the Duval County Conservation and Reclamation District had paid out a lot of money in legal fees to George Parr and his nephew, Archer, in recent years. George, we knew, drew a monthly retainer that had doubled to $2,000 after our investigation began, and he had received a $12,000 "salary advance" from the Special Account in 1969. If George was indeed the district's lawyer, we wondered, why had they paid Archer — the county judge — tens of thousands of dollars in legal fees in those same years? Most of Archer's fees had come from the two secret accounts, some by check and some by debit memorandum. We assumed the money had been shared with George, or used for his benefit. To test our theory, we subpoenaed Archer to appear before the grand jury on September 13.

Archer Parr was George's nephew by birth and his brother by adoption. His mother, Marie, was George's sister. After Marie was divorced from Archer's father, N. R. Weller, Archer was adopted by his grandparents, Archie and Elizabeth Parr. Archer referred to himself in jest as "El Mojado" ("The Wetback"), because his American parents lived in Mexico City when he was born. Under the Mexican Constitution, American citizen Archer was also a citizen of Mexico.

Archer was an ex-Marine and a Korean War veteran. He had been county judge of Duval County since 1959. Like George, he was a lawyer; unlike George, he paid his State Bar dues. Archer was in his early forties, in robust good health, an active, gregarious man who reveled in the good life and the power that went with his official position as head of county government and his unofficial position as heir-apparent to the family's political and economic empire.

Archer may have been the only man in the history of Duval County to own a mink coat. The black silk label inside proclaimed the owner's identity in embroidered crimson script: "Designed for Judge Archer Parr by Anamorena Furs, Chicago." It is difficult to imagine that Archer ever wore his fancy wrap in public in his home county, but the mere fact that he owned it exemplifies the difference between his style and George's. George was too much a man of the people — and too good a politician — to have owned so pretentious a garment.

Although Archer must have felt some anxiety about appearing before the grand jury that was investigating George, he exuded confidence as he entered the room.

"We met with Archer at the Menger Hotel before he went over to the courthouse that day," Marvin Foster told me years later, describing a gathering of the stellar legal defense team engaged by George to hold the friendly witnesses' hands before they testified and to debrief them afterward. "We told him he absolutely *had* to take the Fifth Amendment on everything," Marvin said, "and he promised us he would. Unfortunately, he didn't."

For the first few minutes after taking the oath and listening to a Miranda warning, Archer fenced with us, with verbose politeness.

He wanted to cooperate with the grand jury in every possible way, he said, but he was in a quandary as to what he should do. "Being an officer of the court, as you are, sir, my livelihood depends upon my being able to have a law license plus being county judge," Archer began. He looked directly and earnestly at Sessions and me, and then at the grand jury. "It's hard for me to sit here and not answer your questions, because I do want to cooperate with you, ladies and gentlemen of the grand jury, but if some of my conduct by any chance has violated some federal law, I don't know it, sir, so therefore I would like, if possible, for you to write the questions out where I could confer with my attorney and my accountant, and I would be glad to answer any of those questions, sir."

I explained that federal grand jury investigations are not conducted that way; he could confer with counsel about any question he was asked, but there would be no written questions. Undaunted, Archer raised another objection. He was a resident of the Southern District of Texas, he pointed out, not the Western District. "It is my considered opinion," he announced magisterially, "that if I have done any act contrary to federal law, then the Southern District grand jury should be investigating me, sir, not this grand jury, and I'm willing to go before that grand jury at any time, sir." He was entitled to his opinion, I told him, but the questioning was about to begin. Archer requested and received permission to leave the room to confer with his attorney.

The advice Archer got — to invoke his Fifth Amendment privilege no matter what he was asked — was advice he should have heeded. Politicians with something to hide often can't bring themselves to accept that advice, though, perhaps because their egos overcome their better judgment. Not uncommonly, they think they can confuse or deceive a grand jury with the powers of charm and persuasion that help them win elections. It usually is a costly mistake.

Archer assumed he had become a target of the investigation, but we viewed him principally as a witness at that time. We wanted to question him because we suspected that his "legal fees" were a sham, a scheme to allow him to drain money out of the water district at least partly for George's benefit. Even if our surmise was correct, though, our primary interest would still have been in George's failure to report the money as income; merely stealing money from the water district wouldn't have been a federal crime. Had Archer really been a target of the investigation, he would not have been asked to appear before the grand jury.

"Mr. Parr," I began when he resumed his seat in the witness chair, "are you familiar with the Duval County Conservation and Reclamation District?"

Archer knew our investigation had been focused on the water district for months. He approached the question warily, like a fox avoiding a snare. "I know it exists," he said. "Let me put it to you that way."

"Did you have anything to do with the creation of that entity?"

"No, sir," he responded emphatically. "It was created by the legislature of the State of Texas, and I had absolutely nothing to do with that." Archer gave us, unsolicited, a rambling history of other legislatively created water control and improvement districts in Duval, Jim Wells, and Nueces counties. I inquired whether he had any connection with the current district.

"Only thing I did was just represent them at times, sir, in a legal capacity, when they were first formulated."

"About when would it have been that you represented them?"

"In '65. I'm not sure," he said cautiously. "About '65, along in '66."

His only function at that time, he explained, was to help the district get organized after it was created, by preparing the papers and having an accountant set up the bookkeeping system. "Very much like you and I do when we form a corporation," he said collegially. He wanted us to understand, though, that he was speaking about the past. "I haven't done any legal work for them, sir, in, oh, four or five years," he added. Currently, he said, in his official capacity as county judge and not as a private attorney, he was pressing the district to submit its annual budget to him by the approaching statutory deadline.

Archer continued to stress his lack of familiarity with the district. He understood his uncle George was one of the directors, he said, but he didn't know whether George was also its attorney.

"Are you aware of the nature of any service or consultation that he may give to the Conservation and Reclamation District?" I asked.

"I haven't attended a meeting of the Conservation and Reclamation District in five or six years, sir. I don't know. The building could burn down and I'd know about it two days later."

"Because unless they call on you for some specific thing, you have no connection with them?"

"None whatsoever."

The tenor of his answers indicated Archer might have forgotten about the fees he had received from the district's secret accounts. Reserving that topic for the moment, I inquired about the district's payments to Archer's mother, Marie Parr Thompson, and his stepfather, R. A. Thompson.

"Aside from George Parr, do any other relatives of yours work for the Conservation District?"

"Well, I've heard that my half-sister, Mary Elizabeth Ellis, works for it. She tells me that she was working there on a part-time basis, but I don't know that."

"Would you know if other persons related to you were working there?" I inquired.

"Not necessarily," he replied, keeping plenty of daylight between him and the suspect district. "I haven't been there and I haven't done anything for the district in four or five or six years, and I don't know who is or is not employed there, sir."

His mother was seventy-six years old, Archer said. I asked if she worked for the water district. "Not that I know of," Archer said. "Now, I've heard rumors that she does, but I don't really know, sir."

One of the few checks written on the Reserve Fund was written to R. A. Thompson in late September 1970 for $2,500. I asked Archer if Thompson had ever worked for the district. "If he did, I want to see him back," Archer quipped. "No, sir, he didn't. He died in 1948, or '49, or '50, somewhere back in that neighborhood."

At a brief recess, Sessions and I compared notes with Assistant U.S. Attorney Ray Jahn, the third prosecutor on our investigative team, and with our IRS agent colleagues. We agreed it was time to let Archer explain why the district had paid him so much money in legal fees in recent years, when he had done no legal work.

I showed him a $14,000 check drawn on the Special Account and made payable to him. It was dated February 13, 1968. The typed description on the face of the check said, "Legal services rendered in 1967."

Archer examined the check. "I have never seen this check to my knowledge," he said, handing it back to me. "The only thing, I was notified. I was given deposit slips. I knew I had the money at the bank. That's the first time I've seen that check."

Archer gave the same explanation for a $15,000 check dated February 7, 1969, also drawn on the Special Account. A similar purpose was indicated on its face: "Legal services rendered year 1968." He began to sound a bit testy.

"I've never seen either one of those checks in my life, sir. This is the first time."

"But you did receive the money by its being deposited in your account, didn't you?"

"Yes, sir, I received that money, and I also reported that money on my income tax if that's your next question, sir."

"Well, in any event, I don't need to ask it, do I?"

"You sure don't, sir."

I handed Archer a debit memorandum dated February 2, 1968, reflecting another $14,000 charge against the Special Account. On its face Barney Goldthorn had written, "To transfer funds to Archer Parr as per instructions from Archer Parr." When he appeared before the grand jury in August, Goldthorn had described Archer's in-person request and his own confirming telephone conversation with Jose Tovar.

Archer expressed surprise and confusion. "Isn't that the same date as the check is? 2-2-68?" he asked.

No, I pointed out, the first check I showed him was dated February 13, 1968, eleven days later.

"Have you ever asked Mr. Goldthorn to transfer funds from the water district account to your account?" I asked.

"Most emphatically not, sir," he replied sharply. "I'm positive of that." If the money was deposited to his account, though, Archer volunteered, he had paid income tax on it.

I showed him another debit memorandum on the Special Account, this one dated June 17, 1969, for the largest amount yet: $23,700. Barney Goldthorn's handwriting on the face of the instrument said, "To transfer funds to Archer Parr as per instructions from district." Archer was good at maintaining a poker face, but he could see where this line of questioning was leading. After taking great pains to disclaim any attorney-client relationship with the district in the past five or six years, he had been shown nearly $67,000 in payments from the district in 1968 and 1969 alone. He had painted himself into a corner, and he needed to find an escape route. Suddenly, his answers took a different turn.

"Could you tell the grand jury what that $23,700 transaction was all about?"

"A legal fee, sir, for paying me," he said without hesitation.

"What was the nature of the services rendered?"

"Budget work, studying up books. Just general legal work, sir."

"Over what period of time was the work performed?"

"'66, '67, '68, and '69."

"Wasn't that legal work covered by the prior checks that were written?"

"No, sir."

"In other words, $14,000 was paid on February 13, 1968, $14,000 was paid by debit memorandum on February 2, 1968, and $15,000 was paid February 7, 1969; but the work covered by this $23,700 fee on June 17, 1969, was not included in the previous checks written?"

"That's correct, sir."

Confronted with the payments, Archer had reversed course, insisting he had done a lot of legal work for the district in recent years. He was finding it difficult, though, to explain what the work consisted of. Ray Jahn handed me another debit memorandum, this one charged against the Reserve Fund scarcely more than two years previously, on June 19, 1970. The amount was $15,000. Barney Goldthorn's notation said, "Advance to Archer Parr as legal fees." It wasn't an advance, Archer said; it was for services already rendered.

"Was that a legal fee that was due and owing to you?"

"Due and owing to me," Archer affirmed. His tone of voice was as confident as ever, but his eyes betrayed anxiety.

"Not an advance?"

"That's why, when you said 'advance,' I kind of hesitated on that. It was something that was already done."

From 1967 on, Archer said, he had devoted approximately three months of his time each year exclusively to the district. Pressed for details, he could only generalize about "advice to the district, paperwork, setting the thing up in the legal sense." The entire board of directors sought and received his advice, he said. He attended some of the board meetings, and two or three times a week board chairman D.C. Chapa and directors Jose Tovar and Julio Benavides would come to his office with legal questions, "mainly about budgetary items."

"Did you participate in the budget-making?" Bill Sessions asked.

"Personally, I did most of it," Archer replied.

George Parr, too, often sought his advice on the district's legal matters, Archer said. He did submit bills to the district for his services, Archer explained, but they weren't itemized and he didn't keep copies from one year to the next.

"Did you bill them monthly?" Sessions inquired.

"No, sir, just whenever I needed some money."

Archer volunteered that some other clients also paid him only occasionally, in large amounts. Coastal States Gas Producing Company paid him a retainer of $36,000 per year in two semiannual installments, he said, and Central Power and Light Company paid him $12,000 in a single installment each year. Those retainers from two of the largest real property owners in the county dwarfed his compensation as a public official — $6,750 a year as county judge, plus $600 for serving as the county's juvenile judge.

When the questioning turned to Harris Fender's payments to Archer and George in 1967 for worthless City of Benavides bonds, Archer did what he should have done all day: He invoked his Fifth Amendment privilege.

Bill Sessions returned to the subject of legal services to the water district, offended by what sounded like perjury, and tried mightily to pry out of Archer some specification of the services he had performed to earn the money he received from the district's two clandestine accounts. It totaled $81,700 between February 1968 and June 1970. Unable to improve on the vague generalities we had already heard, Sessions instructed Archer to consult his records upon returning home and provide us with a complete account of his legal services to the district.

Archer responded in writing a few weeks later with a list of receipts that included all of the payments we had questioned him about, plus a check for $39,800 from the Operating Fund on April 13, 1970. The total amounted to an astonishing $121,500 — all for legal services, Archer insisted, and for helping the district prepare its budget, collect its taxes, and set up its bonded indebtedness schedule. Unsurprisingly, he had no records to back up his story.

Octavio Saenz had been the mayor of Benavides, an almost entirely ceremonial post, since 1955. He was retired from the Texas-Mexican Railroad in 1970 after fifty years of employment, starting as a messenger boy and ending as the station agent in Alice. His dark, slicked-back hair, though thinning a bit, made him look a little younger than his age. He wore a dark suit, a crisp white shirt, a conservative tie, and a gold watch chain, cultivating a look of importance befitting his position. Spectacles, a light gray Stetson, a determined smile, and an almost obsequious demeanor completed the picture.

Having heard the city secretary deny knowledge of the Special Sinking Fund that paid for George Parr's first purchase of irrigation pipe, we wanted to test the mayor on the subject.

He understood the account was opened to receive any money left over in a Dallas bank account after the city sold its water and sewer systems to the Duval County Conservation and Reclamation District and no longer had any bonds to pay off, he said.

"Is that an active account, Mr. Saenz?"

"I don't know. I don't think so. We never have received any statements on it."

He remembered signing the signature card on the new account, he said, but he couldn't explain why the money was first deposited into the city's regular checking account and then transferred by debit memorandum from the "wrong account" into the Special Sinking Fund. He had expected some money to be deposited in the new account, he told us, but he never knew when, or how much.

"Weren't you curious enough to at least check with the First State Bank once in a while and find out?"

"No, sir, I did not check with them."

"Well, to a city the size of Benavides, $39,000 is a pretty substantial sum, isn't it?"

"I agree with that."

"Quite a bit more money than you ordinarily had in any other bank account, isn't that true?"

"That's correct."

"And yet you made no inquiry to find out when the money got there?"

"No, sir, I did not."

The city had no budget, collected no taxes, and rarely had any significant amount of money on hand, Saenz explained; its only expenses were the replacement of a few street lights, and its only income was in the form of voluntary payments in lieu of taxes by utility companies that supplied electricity and telephone service.

The records of the Special Sinking Fund had taken little time to analyze. In the entire history of the account there had been only one deposit and two withdrawals, and the small balance remaining after the second withdrawal was still there. The records showed that Amelia Garcia charged the Stewart & Stevenson draft against the account in August 1967. Five days later Octavio Saenz drew a $5,000 draft on the account, payable to himself, leaving a balance of $1,320.45. When Saenz appeared before the grand jury in September 1972, that same, small balance remained in the account, untouched for more than five years.

"On August 17, 1967, Mr. Saenz, there was a withdrawal of $33,007.60 from the Special Sinking Fund. Did you have any knowledge of that withdrawal?" I inquired.

"No, I did not."

"Have you learned anything about it since it was made?"

"No, sir."

"Then, five days later, on August 22, 1967, there was a $5,000 withdrawal. Do you have any knowledge of that transaction?"

Saenz shifted in the witness chair. "I think I have," he said uneasily.

"What can you tell us about that transaction?" I asked, approaching him with a handful of documents.

Saenz tilted his head to peer through his bifocals at the papers in my hand, trying to see them without being too obvious about it. "Well, I don't remember in what form it was withdrawn," he hedged. "Do you have anything?"

I handed him the account ledger sheet reflecting only the initial deposit, the two subsequent withdrawals, and the long-static balance.

"I don't know anything about the $33,000," he said.

"All right. What can you tell us about the $5,000 withdrawal?"

Saenz fished again for clues to reveal how much we knew before committing himself to an answer. "Well, let's see," he said, "was it made in the form of a check, or . . ." His voice trailed off in an open-ended question.

"What I want is what you know about it, Mr. Saenz. Apparently that one does ring a bell with you?"

"Yes sir, it does."

"What do you know about that transaction?"

Saenz hesitated. "Well, in August of 1967 — well, that might be a withdrawal that I made myself."

"What was the purpose of that withdrawal?"

Saenz committed himself at last. "The purpose of the withdrawal," he said, "was a compensation that was agreed on by the city council for my services."

He had never received any compensation for his long years of service as mayor, Saenz explained, except the token $50 Christmas bonus the council voted for itself each year. He asked his colleagues if they didn't think he was entitled to some kind of compensation for his services after the sale of the city's water and sewer system to the Conservation and Reclamation District, he said, "and they agreed that if and when money was available it would be all right with them." He didn't ask for a specific amount, Saenz said; the council voted that he was entitled to some compensation and left the amount up to him.

Saenz insisted he didn't know whether there was any money in the account when he wrote the $5,000 draft to himself. He simply presented it at a teller's window and asked if it could be honored for that amount of money, he said.

"And it's your testimony that as of the time you walked up to that window you did not know how much money was in that account?"

"That is correct. I didn't know, and I don't know now."

The grand jurors' facial expressions reflected their growing irritation with the dapper little mayor's patently incredible story. The circumstantial evidence was compelling: Saenz withdrew $5,000 for himself only five days after most of the refunded bond money was paid out by Amelia Garcia, for George Parr. The $1,320.45 balance was still in the account, apparently too hot for Saenz to touch and too small for Parr to bother with.

"What the public got for that $5,000 was your services as mayor, right?" I demanded.

"Right."

"But you don't know what the public got for the $33,007.60?"

"I don't know."

"Let me tell you. George Parr got $33,007.60 worth of irrigation equipment for the Atlee Parr ranch, six miles south of Benavides. That's what the public got."

"I don't know, sir. I don't know that."

"Are you telling us you know absolutely nothing about the fact that $33,007.60 was withdrawn from that account to pay for irrigation equipment for George Parr?"

"I don't know, so help me God."

Saenz admitted he had known George Parr all his life. "As a matter of fact, you were indicted with him one time, weren't you?" I asked.

"That's correct."

"At that time you were a member of the Benavides Independent School District board of directors, weren't you?"

"Yes, sir."

"Mr. Saenz, if I seem a little bit skeptical about your statement that you know nothing about that $33,000 withdrawal, it's because what you were convicted of in the trial court — even though the Supreme Court subsequently reversed the conviction — was being part of a scheme to drain tax money away from the school district. Now, that was the charge, wasn't it?"

"I just imagine it was."

"As a matter of fact, you were convicted on thirteen of twenty counts of a mail fraud scheme designed to siphon tax money out of the school district to yourself and others. The Supreme Court reversed that conviction because you were tried under the wrong theory of the law. They said it wasn't mail fraud, but this is what they said about the facts: 'Petitioners Saenz, Garcia' — that's Santiago Garcia — 'Oliveira, and Chapa regularly received district payroll checks, sometimes in their own names but usually under one or more fictitious names, for services not rendered. Saenz regularly received eight payroll checks in various names.'"

Saenz blinked his eyes and frowned in disbelief. "Eight payroll checks? That's untrue," he protested.

"How many was it?"

"I don't remember, but it's not eight. That's exaggerating."

"I'm relieved to know that, Mr. Saenz."

"That's very exaggerated," Saenz sniffed. "In fact, I was not guilty of anything."

Sessions, offended by Saenz's transparent theft from his impoverished city and by his brazen tale of innocence, challenged his testimony that the city council had agreed he could pay himself a bonus for his years of dedicated service. Saenz stuck to his story.

"And at that time you had been mayor for twelve years?" Sessions asked.

"Something like that."

Sessions gave him a verbal needle. "The city hadn't gone bankrupt while you were mayor, had it?"

Saenz fidgeted with his tie clasp. "Well, I think there was a bankruptcy case in Corpus," he conceded after a moment.

Sessions bore down, still proper but with an edge to his voice. "There's nobody in the city of Benavides who knows how much Mayor Saenz took from that account except Mayor Saenz, is there?"

You could throw a dart at a world map, I thought, *and hit a place the mayor would rather be right now.*

"No, sir," Saenz said.

"Nobody knows how greatly they honored you?"

"No, sir," Saenz conceded. "I didn't steal that," he added, sensing what everyone else in the room was thinking.

Unfortunately for Saenz, his city council colleagues refuted his story. County Commissioner Ramiro Carrillo had been a member of the Benavides City Council for twenty years. The only compensation connected with the job, he said, was a $50 Christmas bonus and free utilities. "The city has been broke most of the time," he explained; its income was so nominal it didn't even need a budget. Carrillo was aware in 1967 that the city was to receive some funds from the Mercantile National Bank, but he didn't know how much. "I asked Mr. Goldthorn about it," he said. "I think he said it had been received, but he said he had to keep it for two or three years in case there were any other claims to be paid out of it." The banker didn't tell him how much money there was, Carrillo said.

According to Carrillo, the mayor once suggested "some kind of compensation" for all the council members if the city got some money back. No amount was discussed, no vote was taken, and nobody gave the mayor any authority to act on the idea, Carrillo said. He wasn't even sure the conversation took place at a city council meeting.

Shown the bank statements and the two drafts on the account, Carrillo expressed mild surprise. "We're rich, and then we're broke again," he said ruefully, referring to the initial deposit and the two withdrawals. He knew nothing about either of the expenditures, he said, and he felt sure the other council members would be as surprised as he was to learn the facts.

Council members Pat Gonzalez, Jose Gutierrez, and Leopoldo Chapa had served as long as the mayor. All had a vague understanding that the city would eventually receive some money, but all believed the money had never become available. All denied authorizing

Saenz to pay himself anything except the customary $50 Christmas bonus. F. H. Canales, the fifth councilman, had been a member only three years. In that time, he said, the council had met only once or twice. Like the others, he knew nothing about Saenz's generosity to himself.

The directors of the water district were equally unsupportive of Archer Parr's claim that the $121,500 he received was for legal services. Directors Humberto Garza and Julio Benavides knew nothing about payments to Archer, or about any legal services he had rendered, they told the grand jury, and they had not gone to Archer's office to discuss the district's legal affairs. "Never have I discussed that with him in his office," Benavides said. New director Anacleto Valerio wasn't associated with the district during the years in question.

Board chairman D. C. Chapa told the grand jury Archer had performed no legal services for the district in the last five years, and he denied asking Archer for legal advice at his office or anywhere else. Archer "was going around with papers here and there, to Austin and I don't know where else," when the district was being organized, Chapa said, but he had done nothing as a lawyer for the district since that time. Nor had Archer advised the district on budget or financial matters, Chapa said, addressing another of Archer's principal claims.

Taken together, the directors' testimony was entirely consistent with Archer's initial denial of any professional connection with the district since shortly after it was created. We still didn't know why the district paid him $121,500, but it certainly wasn't for legal services.

It was abundantly clear from the directors' testimony that they were directors in name only. Expenditures were made as a matter of course at George Parr's suggestion, even from the district's legitimate checking account, with no questions asked. The Parrs, George and Archer, and the banker, Barney Goldthorn, dealt mostly with Jose Tovar, Chapa told the grand jury, and he in turn relied on Tovar to manage the district's business.

"I live in Benavides, sir," Chapa explained, "and Tovar was the secretary, and a director of the bank, and his office was across the street from the water district. And he used to tell me, 'We're going to do this. We're going to do that.' And I respected his way of doing things because he understood about books and about the bank and how the accounts were. I'm just stating the facts as they are."

Questioned in detail about the purchases of irrigation equipment, fertilizer, brush killer, helicopter services, promissory notes, and the like, Chapa admitted the district had no reason to make those kinds of purchases, but he insisted he knew nothing about any of them. The same was true, he said, of such items as the checks to Archer Parr's mother and her long-deceased second husband. None of those things, he swore, were discussed or voted on by the directors. They simply approved whatever bills were placed before them, he indicated.

"They may be legal, they may not be legal," Chapa said with a shrug. "Only God knows."

The one item that struck at least a vaguely familiar note was the $12,000 "salary advance" to George in 1969. "I remember something, a little bit, that Mr. Parr said in the meeting that he needed that money and if we could give him that advance," Chapa said. "I don't know why. I don't know what it was for."

"Does the board of directors do whatever George Parr asks them to do?"

"He's asked for advice and almost all the time whatever he recommends is what's done."

"Is the board of directors afraid to say no to Mr. Parr?"

"I don't know, sir. Who knows?"

"Are you afraid to say no to him?"

"Many times I don't know whether I should say no, because I don't know whether it's legal or not."

"Have you ever said no to Mr. Parr when he asked the water district to do something?"

"Possibly sometimes yes; possibly sometimes no."

Even after we obtained an immunity grant for Chapa, hoping to open the door to more information, he continued to insist he had no knowledge of the Special Account.

"I never knew anything about that, sir, except that Tovar once told me that we had a special account. He said it was so that when something would come up, we would have it, but he never showed me any papers or anything that would say why we had to have it or how much money was in it, nothing."

"So you don't know what money went into the Special Account, or what came out of it?"

"No, sir. You can hang me, but I can't tell you because I don't know. I cannot say it. I'm an old man, and I'm not going to say any lies."

Chapa agreed his signature was on the few checks written on the Special Account and its successor, the Reserve Fund, but he was adamant about never having seen those words on any check he signed.

Because Chapa only countersigned water district checks, his signature always appeared on the line provided across the left end of the check. Jose Tovar's signature always appeared on the line above the printed name of the account, near the lower right corner of the check. Sometimes, Chapa told us, he would countersign blank checks and leave them at the district's office so it wouldn't be necessary to bring checks to him in Benavides for signature after Jose Tovar signed. At other times he countersigned after Tovar had signed; in either event, he admitted, he didn't question the purpose of any of the checks.

After finding that the check issued to Thompson-Hayward Chemical Company for George's brush killer had been an Operating Fund check when Thompson-Hayward deposited it, we gathered up all of the altered checks and sent them to our document examiner, Phillip White, in Washington.

White made a discovery that lent additional credence to Chapa's claim that he never saw "Special Account" on any check he signed. On one check, the tail of the "J" in Jose Tovar's signature overlapped the typewritten alteration. Forensic examination showed that the signature was placed on the paper first, White reported; the words "Special Account" were typed over it.

We subpoenaed typewriters from the water district and the bank and sent type samples to Phillip White, hoping to find out whose typewriter had been used to alter the checks. The effort failed; nothing matched. One water district typewriter, however, had escaped our net. Leo Sepulveda told us the story he said was related to him by Archer Parr's half-sister, Mary Elizabeth Ellis, who had begun working part-time in the water district office. He and Maria Barkley were both out one day, Sepulveda said, leaving Mary Elizabeth to staff the office alone. A typewriter repairman she didn't know came to the office and told her he was supposed to take that machine to a shop in Laredo for cleaning and repairs, Mary Elizabeth told Sepulveda, and she had let him take it. Nothing had been seen of the typewriter or the repairman since, and no one knew how to find either one. After all the other mysterious disappearances we had encountered, it was hardly surprising.

Chapter 14

The Phantom Store

Things are seldom what they seem,
Skim milk masquerades as cream.
— Sir W. S. Gilbert

BY MID-OCTOBER, 1972, a little more than five months after Carl Stautz's first appearance before the grand jury, our investigative horizon was broadening to include more of George Parr's partners in power. We hadn't planned it that way, and it wasn't entirely convenient. It was essential that we finish our work in time for the IRS and the Department of Justice to complete their reviews before next April 15, when the statute of limitations would bar prosecution for Parr's 1966 tax liability. Nevertheless, a growing body of evidence was drawing us like a magnetic field, compelling us to look more closely at the relationships between other governmental and business entities in the county and the people behind them.

If we had learned anything about George Parr's duchy by that time, it was that appearances there often were calculated to deceive. We had come to understand, also, that local government was the county's only real industry, and that every governmental entity in the county was controlled by the same, tiny coterie of insiders; a subsurface network of family, political, and business connections tied them all together like the elements of a self-contained ecosystem.

Property taxes collected from impersonal, absentee landowners such as deep-pocket utility and oil companies located in Houston and Corpus Christi provided much of the county's economic base.

255

Local government distributed the money through payrolls, projects, boondoggles, and graft, all tightly controlled by George Parr. It was a tidy arrangement, a politico-economic system designed and implemented decades earlier by George's father, Archie, the first Duke of Duval, and refined to an art form by his son and successor, George.

George Parr was unquestionably alone at the pinnacle of the county's power structure. It was clear that nothing was done by, or to, any institution of government in the county without his knowledge and acquiescence. That realization prompted our team of IRS agents, after studying the vendor account records I. A. Filer and Ed Watts had photographed in the county auditor's office months earlier, to urge that we take the time to look into the suspicious procurement patterns they had found there.

To Ramiro Carrillo's chagrin, the paper trail left by the water district's purchase of a hundred tons of fertilizer for George Parr had led back to the Farm and Ranch Supply store in the county's Precinct Three warehouse. Using a county building and county employees to house and run a private business was hardly the most egregious practice we had encountered in Duval County — in fact, it seemed rather petty alongside George Parr's abuses of the water district — but it made us wonder what else the Carrillos were involved in. Given the county's traditions and the Carrillo family's niche just below the Parrs in the establishment's pecking order, we felt sure there was a lot more to the Farm and Ranch Supply store than met the eye.

And then there was the Zertuche General Store, shrouded in a pea-soup fog of rumor, ambiguity, and obfuscation. Duval County, it appeared from the records maintained by the county auditor, was a substantial customer. The water district, too, was a faithful patron, though its purchases were on a more modest scale than the county's. Revenue Agent Ed Watts methodically scheduled the checks written by both entities to the Zertuche General Store over a three-year period and showed Bill Sessions and me the results. The water district's purchases for 1967 through 1969 ranged from $12,000 to $15,000 a year. The county was a much more active customer; its purchases from the Zertuche store were three to four times that size in each of the three years.

"We'd been saying for a while that the next time we were in Benavides, we needed to find out where the Zertuche General Store was," Ed Watts recalled. "And one day I stopped at the Benavides

Post Office to get directions to Julio Benavides' ranch, because I had a grand jury subpoena to serve on him; and just as an afterthought I said to the guy behind the counter — I guess he was the postmaster — 'Oh, by the way, I've been sort of looking for the Zertuche General Store, too, and I was wondering if you could tell me where it's located?' And he looked straight at me, and then he looked down, and he said, 'As far as I know, it's that post office box right there,' and he pointed to it."

Watts told Filer, Culver, and Charlie Volz about that conversation upon his return to Corpus Christi. "We all started looking for it in earnest after that," Watts said.

The reputed owner of the store, the agents learned after many inquiries in and around Benavides, was a young man named Arturo Zertuche. No one the agents spoke with was able to say, though, exactly where the store was, and no one could recall seeing Zertuche conducting any kind of business.

In 1972 Arturo Zertuche was a recently licensed teacher and coach in the Freer public schools, under the supervision of Bryan Taylor. I. A. Filer and Jerry Culver found Zertuche in Freer and interviewed him. They briefed me on the interview as we planned for the next grand jury meeting. "He told us he operated the store from 1966 to 1970," Culver said, "but he plainly didn't want to talk to us about it. He said he sold things to the county, and he kept telling us everything was on his tax returns. He must have said that a dozen times. The thing is, he was in college during that entire time; he wasn't even in the county." Zertuche identified the store's location as the Vaello Sales Company building, across the street from the Benavides City Hall.

On a muggy fall morning after an evening thunderstorm, Culver went to the City Hall and buttonholed Octavio Garcia, the city manager. "He said he'd been in Benavides for years and he'd never heard of the Zertuche store," Culver reported. "He said the Vaello building had been vacant for about ten years." Culver pointed across the street, where people could be seen coming out of the Vaello building with boxes, putting them in old cars, and driving away. "Oh, that's the commodity distribution for the poor people," the city manager explained. "The county welfare people use the building twice a month to give away surplus commodities, like butter and flour, from the Department of Agriculture. That's the only thing that building is ever used for."

Having found the site of the store at last, and the building open, Culver took the opportunity to examine it inside and out and to take photographs. It was a one-story, stucco building on a corner, facing east onto Benavides' one-sided main street. Its nearest neighbor was a two-story stone box of a building that in more prosperous times had been the Merchants Exchange Bank; now used as the Benavides City Hall, it occupied the adjacent corner to the north, across a side street. The forlorn little town's stunted commercial district comprised only a few buildings, as many vacant as occupied. All stood on the curbed west side of the main street, looking across to the curbless east side where dark gray asphalt blended into straw-colored sand to form a beach-like shoulder. A row of utility poles bordered the strip of barren dirt that lay between that side of the street and the railroad track that paralleled it thirty yards to the east. Beyond the railroad track was a third ribbon of commerce, State Highway 359, connecting Benavides with San Diego to the north and Hebbronville, the county seat of Jim Hogg County, to the south.

On the south side of the store building was an ill-kept vacant lot that separated it from two large, well-kept, Spanish-style houses. These were the residences of two of D. C. Chapa's sons, District Judge O. P. Carrillo and County Commissioner Ramiro Carrillo.

As Culver watched, welfare recipients entering and exiting the store building walked around dense clumps of foot-high weeds that flourished in the broken sidewalk and along the curb in front of the building. The display windows on the sides facing the two streets were gray with accumulated grime. The top half of one was broken out, leaving a margin of jagged shards around the upper window frame, and another was peppered with BB holes. A third window had been decorated, apparently by high school students, with the legends "Srs. '66–'67" and "Yea Fish '66–'67." Most of the smaller windows in a row above the display windows were shattered. A sagging canopy roof sheltered the sidewalk in front of the building, suspended by rusty cables from the building's dingy facade. Near the north end of the building a Philco sign projected over the canopy. A four-by-eight-foot political sign from Oscar Carrillo's last campaign for the Texas legislature perched precariously atop the canopy near the other end, its warped plywood backing and dull colors showing the effects of long exposure to the South Texas weather.

A wide, rectangular main room with a square column in the middle occupied most of the front half of the building. Opening from it were several smaller rooms, one separated from the main room by an arched doorway. Cardboard cartons stamped "USDA" were stacked along a back wall. Water-stained ceiling tiles sagged overhead. Above a scattering of soggy tiles that had fallen to the floor, a gaping hole in the roof explained the shallow lake covering part of the floor. Navigating the creaky wooden floor required caution: It was rotten in places, and the damp soil beneath the building was visible through holes big enough for the unwary to put a foot through.

On the column in the middle of the big room was a moth-eaten moose head, canted quizzically to one side and looking for all the world as if it had asked a profound question and were listening eagerly for the answer. Stuffing had spilled from the head onto the dirty floor below. On a nearby wall a neglected caribou head surveyed the scene impassively with its one remaining glass eye. On the back side of the arched doorway was the mounted neck of an elk. The head of the forgotten trophy lay in a puddle of water on the floor, the broken antlers a few feet away. Except for the USDA commodity boxes, an old refrigerator, and the forlorn taxidermy, the building was empty.

Jerry Culver sent me his photographs and a wry note. "Charlie Volz asked the owner of the Cash Store in Benavides about the Zertuche store," Culver wrote. "This man has operated his store for thirty-three years within 200 yards of the Vaello building, and he has never heard of the Zertuche business. I'm developing the very slightest doubt as to the existence of the Zertuche General Store."

D. C. Chapa was characteristically vague when asked about Arturo Zertuche. "He's a teacher at Freer, isn't he?" Chapa responded. He knew Zertuche had been away at college, he said, and he recalled that the young man had once had a store that "might have sold radios or something." The store was sometimes open and sometimes not, Chapa said; he thought the water district probably had been a customer, but he couldn't think of anything it might have bought.

Leo Sepulveda recognized the name of the store from invoices, but aside from that he knew virtually nothing about it. "We get invoices from the Zertuche General Store," Sepulveda told us. "They're brought in by our water superintendent in Benavides, Julian Stockwell, or sometimes by D. C. Chapa. I don't remember what's on the invoices; probably pipe connections and tools. I think there's equipment rental invoices, too, for a truck or something. Mr.

Stockwell signs most of them. I take it for granted he checks those invoices before he sends them to me for the board to approve." He hadn't seen any Zertuche invoices in the last few months, Sepulveda said; he understood the store had been closed. He didn't have copies of any paid invoices, either. They were among the records that vanished in the unsolved Fourth of July burglary.

Duval County merchants who sold goods on account to the water district, the county, a city, or a school district were accustomed to an antiquated way of billing and collecting from those customers. Elected officials made their self-appointed rounds once a month, gathering current invoices from favored vendors and handing out checks for the previous month's bills in return. The archaic custom lent a distinctly personal touch to the relationships between elected officials and their merchant constituents, emphasizing for the latter that supporting the right candidates could be essential to one's financial well-being. The practice probably was designed for an even more important purpose, however: So long as fraudulent invoices weren't sent or paid by mail, no one could be charged with the federal crime of mail fraud that nearly brought down the Parr machine in the 1950s.

Ed Watts' analysis showed checks totaling $12,758.72 from the water district to the Zertuche General Store in 1967. All were written on the Operating Fund. The largest was $1,287, issued in November. It bore the notation "Maintenance water system — Benavides." The smallest, $531, was one of two checks written to the Zertuche account in October, aggregating $1,344.57; no purpose was indicated on its face. A check for approximately $750 (one month it was a little less, another month, a little more) was written to the Zertuche General Store at about the same time nearly every month. Some of the checks bore a reference to "Benavides maintenance" or "Benavides sewer system" in the explanation column. Others revealed nothing more descriptive than an invoice number. Some were devoid of any reference to the reason for their issuance.

The pattern for 1968 and 1969 was similar, as were the monthly check amounts. "Equipment rental" showed up in the explanation column of a check written in December 1968, and alternated with "truck rental" on most of the checks issued to the Zertuche store through 1969. The water district paid the Zertuche General Store more than $42,000 from 1967 through 1969. Duval County records reflected a similar pattern but larger amounts, totaling $40,000 to

$60,000 a year. Fence posts, barbed wire, equipment rental, and contract labor accounted for the bulk of the county's purchases, according to the terse, two-word descriptions on most of the Zertuche invoices.

Julian Stockwell, the water district's maintenance superintendent in Benavides, was confused. The only equipment he had ever rented for the water district was a diesel truck, he told the grand jury, and that was several years ago. He used it only four or five days a month, for two months.

"From whom did you rent that truck?" I asked him.

"As far as I know, sir, it was Zertuche's General Store. My problem is that I'm not sure whether it was Zertuche's store or the Farm and Ranch Supply store."

"Why do you say you think you may have rented it from Zertuche?"

"Well, I'll be frank with you, sir. I didn't know there was such a thing as the Zertuche General Store. I didn't know the store existed."

"When did you first hear of Zertuche's General Store?"

"When the investigation started, seven or eight months ago, I guess."

"How did you happen to hear about it?"

"Mr. Garcia, the city secretary, said the IRS had asked somebody in the Cash Store about the Zertuche General Store, and then I asked my workers, and they were just as confused as I was." Stockwell tried to explain the source of his confusion. He and his crew occasionally bought supplies at the Farm and Ranch Supply store, he said, and when they signed for their purchases they were always given invoices headed "Zertuche General Store." He had learned recently "just from hearsay" that Arturo Zertuche owned the Zertuche General Store, Stockwell said, and because the Farm and Ranch store had Zertuche invoices as well as its own, he assumed that it and the Zertuche store were one and the same.

Stockwell's confusion grew when the unofficial Benavides city clerk, Santiago Garcia, told him the Zertuche General Store had been located in the Vaello Sales Building. Like D. C. Chapa, Stockwell recalled that there had once been "radios and stuff like that" for sale in the Vaello building, but he had never seen Arturo Zertuche there.

"Did you ever buy anything in that store for the water district?" I asked.

"Not that I know of, no sir."

Stockwell said he was acquainted with Arturo Zertuche because their homes were only two blocks apart. He had never had any business dealings with Zertuche, and he was not aware that Zertuche had ever conducted any kind of business. "He was a student before he started teaching," Stockwell said. "I don't think he did anything."

His own purchasing authority was limited to items of $100 or less, Stockwell said. The purchases he and his crew made were always in small amounts, mostly $20 to $40 at a time. "Anything over $100, I have to call Mr. Sepulveda, and he'll either approve it or sometimes he'll tell me I need to come to the next board meeting and ask."

"You never rented anything from Zertuche's General Store that would have cost $750 a month in rental?" I asked.

Stockwell seemed nonplussed. "No, sir," he responded.

"Do you think it's possible that the purchases you and your men made from the Zertuche General Store would have amounted to $15,000 a year?"

"No, sir."

"They didn't come anywhere near that figure, did they?"

"Golly, I don't think so, no, sir."

Ramiro Carrillo identified himself as a rancher and a lifetime resident of Benavides. He had been a member of the Benavides City Council for twenty years and he was the county commissioner for Precinct Three in Duval County, having succeeded the late Atlee Parr in that position in 1967. He had known Arturo Zertuche all his life, he said.

"How do you happen to know him?" I asked.

"He lives right across the street," Carrillo replied. What he didn't tell us was that Arturo's father, George, was a mechanic in the Precinct Three warehouse and shop, and that the Carrillos and the Zertuches were related.

Carrillo told the grand jury Arturo Zertuche had conducted a business in the Vaello Sales Building until "up to two years ago." He answered questions about the subject delicately, uttering as few words and divulging as little information as possible.

"What kind of business did he have?" I asked.

"It was a little bit of everything. Sold, you know, sold stuff."

"Was the business open while he was away at college?"

"I don't say that it was open all the time or part-time."

"Do you know whether he had any employees?"

"No, I don't."

"Can you tell us more specifically what kinds of things he sold?"

"Well, no. No, I couldn't."

Carrillo was similarly vague about the Farm and Ranch Supply store. "I'm an owner," he admitted when asked if he had an interest in it.

"And what kind of business is that?"

"A little bit of everything."

He ran the business mostly by himself, he said; he had no employees.

"Nobody assists you in running the store?"

Carrillo hesitated. "Yes," he said reluctantly.

"Who does?"

Another hesitation. "Gonzalez."

"Cleofas Gonzalez?"

"Yes."

"Is Cleofas Gonzalez an employee of yours?"

Carrillo's discomfort with the interrogation seemed to be growing. "He gets compensation from me," he said evasively.

Gonzalez's compensation was in the form of bonuses, Carrillo said, but it wasn't based on sales. "We don't have that many sales," he said. "He gets things wholesale and stuff like that." Cleofas Gonzalez was a county employee, Carrillo admitted. "He handles all the welfare things, and he's the foreman there at the shop."

"Does he spend his time in the store, or does he spend his time in the county shop?"

"Well, I'd say about the same."

"But he's a full-time employee of Duval County?"

"That's correct."

"How were you able to arrange to have the services of a full-time county employee to run your store?"

"Well, like I say, it's right next door. And my county commissioner office is right behind it too."

The commissioner wove a tangled web of lies as we questioned him about the ethereal Zertuche General Store.

"Are all of your invoices printed in the name of Farm and Ranch Supply?"

"I think so, yes."

"Isn't it a fact you also have at your store invoices that say Zertuche's General Store on them?"

"I don't think so. I might have."

"If you do, why do you have Zertuche invoices?"

Carrillo improvised unconvincingly. "Well," he said, "if they buy something from Zertuche somewhere else and he didn't have it, he sends them over there and I'll bill Zertuche for it."

Carrillo's explanation required him to embroider an elaborate story about customers referred to the Farm and Ranch store by Zertuche, who asked for Zertuche invoices to evidence their purchases. The water district's purchases, he said, all came through Zertuche.

"Why did you have that arrangement with Arturo Zertuche to sell merchandise in his name?" I queried.

"Well, sometimes he didn't have something."

"Did he carry the same kinds of merchandise that you carry at Farm and Ranch Supply?"

"Well, it would be mostly the same."

"Did he not have a large stock of merchandise?"

"I would not say he had a large stock, no," Carrillo said. It was the understatement of the week.

He kept track of the sales he made for Zertuche, Carrillo explained, and billed him monthly for the cost of the merchandise plus a profit margin. He didn't send Zertuche copies of the invoices or an itemized statement, he said, just a bill that showed the total amount Zertuche owed for the month, but he did keep a record of the monthly billings. He wasn't sure whether Zertuche had a post office box. "I would send the bills to him or give them to him," the commissioner said.

Sessions jumped in, alert to the possibility of mail fraud violations. "Occasionally, I presume, you mailed them?" he suggested. But Ramiro had witnessed the narrow escape of his father and his brothers from the nearly successful mail fraud prosecution of the 1950s, and the lesson had not been lost on him. "I don't think I mailed them," he replied.

Carrillo's memory failed him when I asked if he had ever rented trucks to the water district. He was vague about the number and types of county vehicles under his domain as a commissioner, and equally vague about trucks that might have been owned by the Farm and Ranch Supply partnership, or by him. Sessions persisted, pressing for an explanation of the substantial checks issued each month by the county and the water district to the Zertuche General Store for truck rental.

"Is there any possibility you used county equipment for your own purposes or your own businesses?" Sessions asked.

Carrillo's ambiguous tone conveyed a message of concealment. "I would say no," he replied.

"I'm asking you specifically, did you ever use county trucks?" Sessions demanded.

"Not that I remember, no."

"So your testimony is that you never did?"

"No, that's not my testimony. My testimony is that I do not remember."

"So you might have used the county equipment?"

"I might have."

Over the noon hour we prepared and served on Ramiro Carrillo a subpoena requiring him to bring the grand jury all of his business records on the Farm and Ranch Supply store. We looked forward to hearing from South Texas entrepreneur Arturo Zertuche after our usual quick lunch at Schilo's, a couple of blocks away on Commerce Street.

When Ramiro Carrillo returned later to produce records, he told us he had not kept a record of his billings to Arturo Zertuche; he had simply been mistaken about that, he said, in his earlier testimony.

Arturo Zertuche looked like a typical young Texas high school coach with teaching duties. He was in his mid- to late twenties, moderately tall, with dark hair and an athlete's trim physique. San Antonio criminal defense attorney Harry A. Nass, Jr., accompanied him to the federal courthouse and hovered in the corridor outside the grand jury room in case his client needed him.

Zertuche took the oath and announced anxiously that he had a statement to read to us. Wait until you tell us your name and hear your advice of rights, I told him. With those essentials taken care of, young Arturo Zertuche read stiffly from the statement his attorney had prepared for him:

"To the members of the grand jury: My name is Arturo R. Zertuche, and I am appearing before you in response to a subpoena to testify and produce certain records concerning the Zertuche

General Store. I am unable to produce the records you request because the records are not in my custody and control and were severely damaged and destroyed by Hurricane Celia sometime during the month of August 1970."

The statement went on to explain, in his attorney's words, that Zertuche was invoking his Fifth Amendment privilege against self-incrimination and intended not to answer any questions. After a bit of verbal fencing with us and two conferences with Nass in the corridor outside the grand jury room, Zertuche loosened up enough to answer questions about his background and his education.

He had earned a bachelor's degree in Spanish at North Texas State University, in Denton, in 1970, Zertuche said. He was currently working toward his permanent teaching certificate while coaching and teaching Spanish at Freer High School. He had been a full-time student at Texas A & I, in Kingsville, from 1964 until he enrolled at North Texas in 1967. He began teaching at Freer in the fall of 1971, after teaching the previous year in Harlingen. His summers, too, had been spent in school through 1971, he said. It was pretty clear his opportunity to operate the mythical general store in Duval County during those years had been severely limited.

I showed Zertuche the checks written by the water district to his store, beginning with 1967. He declined to answer questions about any of them. In preparing for his appearance before the grand jury, we had also obtained his income tax returns for 1967 through 1969. The Zertuche General Store appeared on Schedule C (Profit or Loss from Business or Profession) of his Form 1040 each year, but the data were strangely inconsistent from year to year. The information reported cast grave doubt on the legitimacy of the payments from the water district and the county, raising the possibility of state criminal law violations. Worse yet for Zertuche, because of the federal criminal law implications, the returns appeared demonstrably false.

Zertuche's 1967 return indicated the store had only two physical assets, a 1961 Scout and a 1965 Chevrolet, both of nominal value and substantially depreciated. The 1968 return reported the sale of the Scout. The 1969 return showed the aging Chevrolet as the only remaining depreciable asset. Neither vehicle was consistent with the multiple truck rental invoices paid to Zertuche by the water district and the county. Zertuche refused, on Fifth Amendment grounds, to explain how he could have rented out all those nonexistent trucks.

Zertuche had claimed widely varying deductions for store rent from year to year, a curious claim for a business that, according to his earlier statement to Filer and Culver, had been conducted in the same, decrepit building the whole time. In 1967 the rental deduction was $5,491.54. In 1968 it dropped to $1,600. In 1969, apparently a banner year for commercial landlords in Duval County, the Zertuche Store's rent deduction was $12,981.81. Zertuche refused, on Fifth Amendment grounds, to enlighten us about the changing figures.

His claimed deductions for business and property taxes fluctuated, too, from $31.24 in 1967, to $5.00 in 1968, to no deduction at all in 1969. Even more unusual for a merchandising establishment, the store had no beginning or ending inventory for any of the three years. Again, Zertuche wisely followed his attorney's advice and declined to answer any questions about the store.

Two people remained, we thought, who might be willing to shed some light on the murky relationships among the Carrillos, Arturo Zertuche, the Farm and Ranch Store, the water district, and the county. One was the county auditor, Walter Meek. As our investigation progressed and the agents returned time after time to Duval County to ask questions and pore over records at the courthouse, they had found Meek to be a knowledgeable and outspoken critic of the way government business was conducted in the county.

Walter Wilson Meek and George Berham Parr were contemporaries, both born in Duval County. They had grown up together as close companions. On that fateful Saturday morning in May 1912, when three Hispanic public officials were gunned down on a San Diego street, the two young boys had seen it happen from a block away. Although their careers took vastly different paths after boyhood, they remained friends all their lives.

Meek was graduated from Purdue University with a mechanical engineering degree. Before retiring in 1960 he had worked, mostly as a civil engineer, for construction companies in the west and southwest, railroads in the United States and Mexico, and the Texas Highway Department. He returned to San Diego in 1960, he said, because he was tired of wandering. "An engineer can't stay put," he explained, "and I just wanted to stay put."

At a little past seventy years of age, Walter Meek looked as if he could have been a retired military officer — slender and erect as a flagpole, pants crisply pressed, shoes shined, white dress shirt crisply starched and open at the collar, aviator-style sunglasses on his nose.

Meek's personal style and manner of speaking matched his appearance. He was well-read and articulate, with a keen interest in history, a perceptive, acerbic commentator on the human condition in general and his fellow Duval Countians and himself in particular. His personal and business correspondence was spiced with quotations from Machiavelli, Samuel Johnson, Shakespeare, Voltaire, and latter-day heroes and historians such as Winston Churchill and Will Durant. Unlike anyone else we encountered, Walter Meek spoke his mind about the foibles of local government in George Parr's domain. The grand jury was fascinated.

The county auditor is appointed by the district judge, Meek explained, for a two-year term, at the same salary as the county commissioners, $6,750 per year. He had held the position continuously since returning to the county in 1960, initially by appointment of Judge Woodrow Laughlin. "It was after the unpleasantness of the 1950s," Meek said, using his customary euphemism for the turbulent era of investigations and unsuccessful prosecutions of George and his cronies that kept the county in turmoil for years. "They knew I was a lifelong friend of George Parr's and they thought I had more influence on George than I actually did. They hoped I'd be able to influence him in some of his endeavors, and I think I have had some effect just by running a stricter office, but I don't have any CPA qualifications, which a good auditor really should have. I turned the job down a couple of times, but Judge Laughlin thought I could help straighten things out, so I said I'd take it for a year, and I've just stayed on."

The job of county auditor, Meek explained, is largely ceremonial, although it did give him a vantage point from which to monitor the county's financial affairs. The county commissioner's court has exclusive authority to prepare the county's budget and appprove its use of public funds, he pointed out; and even though he saw imprudence in the way the commissioners spent the county's money, he had no authority to rein them in for anything short of statutory illegalities, such as making capital expenditures of more than $1,000 without obtaining competitive bids. "I have several opinions from the attorney general," Meek said ruefully, "that the commissioners are the county's governing body and that I have no authority to investigate whether the claims they pay are valid."

Meek explained how Duval County's bills were processed, approved, and paid. Vendor invoices were received by his assistant, checked for mathematical accuracy, and placed in individual envelopes known as claim jackets. They were accumulated by the county treasurer, whose assistant, Sylvester Gonzalez, delivered them on the second Monday of each month to the commissioners for approval at their regular meeting. Gonzalez attended the meetings and returned the approved bills for payment. Checks were prepared in the auditor's office, signed by Meek and the county clerk, and countersigned by the county treasurer.

I held up for his identification one of the printed claim jackets used for sending individual invoices to the commissioners court for approval. "What we have here is essentially an envelope with the end cut off; is that right?" I asked Meek.

"That's right. We used to have a manila folder, and a plain envelope would do just as well if you put the claim number on it; but there's a local printer that we feel sorry for, and we let him make those envelopes for us. It keeps him in booze."

Many of the bills were hand-delivered to his office each month, Meek said, by the four county commissioners, each of whom could be counted on to turn in a folder of bills from suppliers in his precinct.

"We do have an ungodly number of bills," the auditor said. "I think probably more than Bexar County."

"Why is that?" I asked.

"Their priorities are kind of mixed up down there and they buy everything in sight. I mean, a lot of unnecessary purchases."

"Does the county have a large budget?"

"Well, it's not a poor county. I mean, it has pretty good oil resources, but we live pretty poorly in the midst of plenty."

"Can you give us an example of their 'mixed-up priorities,' Mr. Meek?"

"Well, yes, I can think of one that upset me quite bit. We have a small county with a population of about 11,000, 12,000, and we bought three street sweepers — one for Benavides, one for Freer, one for San Diego. I think that would clean more streets per capita than you have here for Bexar County, and I've never seen one in operation. It just makes my Scot blood boil, because it's unnecessary. Or some commissioner will buy $1,000 worth of highway signs for the dirt roads in his precinct, and then not even put them up. In fact, some years ago a fast-talking salesman sold one of our commissioners a snow blade for his maintainer. It's a fact. It's still in one of the warehouses, and of course it's never been used."

Meek described the commissioners' monthly meeting to approve bills as a "rather boring session . . . There's no discussion of the bills at all."

"How are the bills approved?"

"Well, frankly, mainly by the county judge. He just looks through the bills and okays them."

"Is a vote taken?"

"No, rarely."

"Is there ever a discussion or disagreement about bills?"

"Rarely. I can't think of ever hearing one. Each commissioner has his little pile of bills, and he wants to get those paid, but they're just not interested in the rest."

For no reason he could discern, Meek said, the county judge sometimes segregates a few invoices from the batch and says, "Hold these until further notice." Those bills are then held in the auditor's vault, Meek said, until the judge releases them — sometimes only after being reminded months later that they haven't been paid.

"By the way, Mr. Meek, when you speak of the county judge, who are you referring to?"

"Archer Parr."

"Is there no logical pattern to the withholding of certain bills?"

"No, and I never question why a bill isn't paid, simply because it's not my business," he said resignedly.

The grand jurors listened intently. Here was a witness whose integrity they trusted instinctively and whose candor was unique among all the Duval County witnesses they had heard. For his part, Meek seemed grateful for an interested audience he could vent his frustrations to, as if he had been hoping for just this kind of opportunity for a dozen years. He looked at the grand jurors and at Sessions and me, and launched into an expanded explanation of the way things were in the Dukedom.

"I feel at a very great disadvantage because I can't explain to you the relaxed atmosphere in which they do business down there. Nobody is very concerned about the price of anything, and they don't shop around for a discount for prompt payment. When a bill is held up, it's never a question of the bill. In fact when our suppliers from Dallas or Houston call us about a past-due bill, the first thing I do is tell them we aren't questioning their invoice. I can't think of a case where a bill was turned down because the commissioners thought it was too high. They never look that carefully at the bills."

Walter Meek had said as much in writing to at least one out-of-state supplier who inquired about an overdue bill. Meek's letter of October 27, 1971, typed on his official county stationery and addressed to R. J. Dyniewicz, comptroller of the George D. Barnard Company of St. Louis, must have been unlike any other response that gentleman had ever received from a delinquent public-entity customer:

Dear Sir:

We have your letter of the 19th with the enclosed statement of your account. If this statement was requested of you I am afraid there has been a misunderstanding somewhere and we have caused you unnecessary trouble — and for this I apologize.

Our books, as a matter of fact, are in complete harmony with yours and the account has been processed for some time and is awaiting the pleasure of the Commissioners' Court — which, in turn, is waiting for the new tax money, due this month, to replenish our coffers. To put it bluntly, we are completely out of money in certain of our vital funds — a state of affairs which never deviates from year to year. Like the oyster, our financial solvency is seasonal and stable only in months with an "r" in them — the rest of the time we are in the financial doldrums due to lack of restraint and scrambled priorities. Now that we are entering the period of solvency again I can assure you that your account will be paid in full within the next thirty days.

I know that it is impossible for an outsider to understand the relaxed and improvident atmosphere in which we operate so I will not attempt to explain it other than to say that we are financially sound and fiscally irresponsible — which may sound like a contradiction in terms, but it really isn't, for we have more than adequate revenue, but like some individuals we have all known, we live poorly in the midst of plenty.

In closing let me say that I do understand the complexities confronting you as Controller in this situation and regret that we are the cause of it. And although you were too polite to say so, I agree that this is a Hell of a way to run a railroad.

Yours very truly,

W. W. Meek

Walter Meek was familiar with the name of the Zertuche General Store because he had seen it on invoices regularly from 1967 until mid-1971. The account records in his office also linked Arturo Zertuche's name with an entity called Benavides General Store.

Meek didn't know Arturo, nor did he know the location of his store. "I understand, and this is merely hearsay from some of the residents of Benavides," he added, "that it has changed locations several times."

"But you have no knowledge of the store, where it was or what it looked like?"

"No. For the amount of money we paid them, I would imagine it looked about like Joske's or Neiman-Marcus. I don't know where there's a store like that in Benavides."

"In other words, the Benavides General Store or the Zertuche General Store was an entity you wrote a good many checks to?"

"Yes, indeed."

"For a considerable amount of money?"

"An appalling amount."

He had never asked any questions of the county judge or any of the commissioners about the purchases from those entities, Meek said, although the pattern of payments did arouse his curiosity.

"Well, why not ask?" I inquired.

"And get a double answer?" Meek asked in response.

"I beg your pardon?"

"I don't think that would be the proper place to ask. I don't think I'd get a straight answer there."

"You think the commissioners wouldn't level with you and tell you what it was for?"

Meek smiled a "surely, you jest" smile. "I'm pretty sure they wouldn't," he said.

I asked Meek whether he knew, directly or otherwise, why the county made so many purchases from the Zertuche General Store or its apparent predecessor, the Benavides General Store.

"Well, I'll be perfectly frank with you," he said without hesitation. "I don't think a lot of those purchases were actually made."

"What do you think happened?"

"My own conjecture," Meek replied, "is that it's merely a distribution point for money. I came to that conclusion a long time ago. I don't think Zertuche benefited from that, except maybe in a small way. I think most of the money was channeled out, and I have no idea who to. That's my theory, but I can't prove it. You'd be surprised how hard it is to get any information on the Zertuche General Store, even from citizens of Benavides who couldn't be involved or affected by it at all."

Oh, no, we wouldn't be surprised, I thought.

After many inquiries, Meek said, he was able to find one credible person who told him where the store had been until recently, and told him also that two county employees ran the store.

"Is the location you've been told about anywhere near a store called Farm and Ranch Supply?" I asked him.

"I don't know where that's located," Meek replied, "but the unofficial information I have is that they're one and the same."

Cleofas ("Buffalo") Gonzalez had told us about the hundred-ton fertilizer order he handled for George Parr at the Farm and Ranch Supply store. Now we wanted him to tell us more about the store and its owners.

Gonzalez had worked for the county for about ten years, he said, starting out as a warehouseman in the Precinct Three warehouse. Over time, the warehouse also became a farm and ranch store.

"Which is it mostly," I asked, "a store or the county warehouse?"

"It's both," he answered. "The front of the building is like a store, and they have a county shop in the back. The boys go there every morning, and Mr. Carrillo comes out and tells me what to tell them to do. He's got his office right there in the store, in the back room. The store part is called Farm and Ranch Supply."

"Is that Ramiro Carrillo's business?"

"Ramiro and O. P. Carrillo are the owners," Gonzalez said, identifying the county commissioner and his brother, the district judge.

He described his current duties as taking care of the Precinct Three warehouse and the commissioner's office, and running the Farm and Ranch Supply store. His current salary, he said, was $300 per month. In addition to tending the store, he handled the related billing and banking transactions for his bosses. "But I don't work for Farm and Ranch," he clarified. "I get paid by the county; but still, I do it because I'm there."

"Well, Ramiro Carrillo is your boss, isn't he?"

"Yes."

"And he tells you to do that and you do it?"

"I have to do it, that's right."

Sometimes another Precinct Three employee, Pat Gonzales, helped him in the store, Cleofas said. So far as he knew, Pat wasn't paid anything for working in the store either, except his regular salary from the county. He first heard of the Zertuche General Store in 1967, Cleofas said, when Ramiro Carrillo became the Precinct Three commissioner. "They told me that everything I sold to the county, or the school district, or the water district, or the city, that I had to sell it to the Zertuche General Store first, and then the Zertuche General Store would sell it to them."

"And was there really a Zertuche General Store anywhere that you could walk into and say, 'This is the Zertuche General Store'?"

"Not that I know of, sir."

"And Arturo Zertuche wasn't there to run a store; he was in college, wasn't he?"

"Yes, sir."

"So really, the Zertuche General Store was a pad of invoices on your counter, wasn't it?"

"Yes, and a license; they told me they had a tax exemption license."

Cleofas' understanding of the reason for the charade was a bit hazy, but not too far off target. "Ramiro Carrillo told me that Farm and Ranch Supply couldn't sell to the county and the water district and all of those organizations because of the nepotism law, or something like that," he said. The Carrillo brothers' real problem was not nepotism but conflict of interest, because of the many governmental positions they held. Ramiro was a Benavides city councilman in addition to being a county commissioner; O. P., as a district judge, was a state official; and their father, D. C. Chapa, was president of both the water district and the Benavides school board.

Arturo Zertuche is the Carrillos' nephew, Cleofas explained; that's why they named the store after him. Arturo visited at the Farm and Ranch store occasionally, Cleofas said, but never interfered with or even mentioned the Zertuche store operation.

Cleofas Gonzalez testified that Zertuche invoices were issued only for sales to the county, the water district, the city, and the school district. Mindful of Ramiro Carrillo's testimony about customers who requested Zertuche invoices, we asked Cleofas about his experience as the store's manager. No one ever asked for a Zertuche invoice, he said; in writing up the sales that way he was simply following the Carrillos' instructions.

The monthly invoices to the county and the water district for truck and equipment rental were issued on Ramiro Carrillo's instructions. "He would tell me, 'The water district used the truck for this,' or 'This truck worked so many days or so many hours. Charge them so much.' That's the way I went about it. I just made the invoices the way they told me."

"And Ramiro Carrillo dealt with whoever rented the equipment?"

"Yes, sir. All I was in charge of was making that ticket. I had to take his word for it."

Zertuche General Store invoices were always delivered, never mailed. Similarly, the checks issued in payment of those invoices were always delivered to him at the Farm and Ranch Store, Cleofas said, by a member or an employee of each governmental entity. Duval County checks were brought to him by the commissioners of Precincts Two, Three, and Four; City of Benavides checks were delivered by the unofficial city secretary, Santiago Garcia; Benavides Independent School District checks were dropped off by the district's tax collector, Rodolfo (Rudy) Couling; and Duval County Conservation and Reclamation District checks were usually delivered by no less a personage than the district's president (and the patriarch of the Carrillo family), D. C. Chapa.

When the Carrillos opened a bank account in the name of the Zertuche store at Barney Goldthorn's First State Bank, Cleofas took care of the daily banking chores too. He deposited the customer checks into the Zertuche General Store account, and then, with blank checks signed in advance by Arturo Zertuche, he redeposited the funds to the Farm and Ranch Supply account or obtained cash for one or both of the Carrillo brothers. He picked up bank statements, but nothing else, from the post office box rented in the name of the store, he said. No checks were ever printed for the Zertuche store account; instead, Arturo signed ten or twelve blank counter checks each month and left them with Cleofas at the Farm and Ranch store. If Cleofas ran out of checks, he simply told Ramiro or O. P., or wrote to Arturo at college, and within a few days he received a fresh supply. I showed Cleofas a check signed by Arturo Zertuche and made payable to cash. Cleofas' endorsement was on the back.

"This is a check for $2,000, payable to cash, and it appears that you cashed it. What was that for?"

"Well, Mr. Carrillo would tell me when I was going to the bank to make deposits, 'Please get me this cash,' and I would make out the check for whatever he asked for and cash it and bring the money back to the store."

"Did that happen fairly often?"

"Yes, sir, mostly every time that I took a deposit, they would tell me to bring back cash, and so I did it."

The county auditor's vendor records indicated that the Benavides General Store might have been merely a different name for the same entity, and that had been Walter Meek's surmise. I asked Cleofas if he knew of a business called the Benavides General Store. Cleofas looked puzzled. "It's not the same thing as the Zertuche General Store?" he said quizzically. He had prepared invoices in the name of Benavides General Store in early 1967, he said. He understood that its purpose, like the purpose of the Zertuche store that succeeded it, was to allow the Carrillos to deal with local governmental entities. The name of Arturo Zertuche's brother, Hector, was connected with the Benavides General Store, Cleofas explained; the Benavides name was dropped when Hector entered military service, and the Zertuche name was used until 1971.

When Arturo Zertuche finished his schooling and returned to Duval County as a teacher in 1971, the Carrillos switched store names again. They stopped using the Zertuche General Store name, Cleofas Gonzalez explained, and began invoicing the same governmental customers through Benavides Implement Hardware Company, an actual business owned by Benavides school district tax collector Rodolfo Couling. Ramiro Carrillo told him about the changed procedure, Cleofas said, and Couling brought him a supply of Benavides Implement invoices. Under the new arrangement all the payments went to Couling, and Cleofas did no banking for him. Once a month Cleofas gave Couling a statement for the sales of Farm and Ranch merchandise under the Benavides Implement name, and Couling issued his check to Farm and Ranch Supply. Farm and Ranch sales on Benavides Implement invoices amounted to approximately $2,000 a month, Cleofas Gonzalez estimated.

How did the governing bodies of the county, the water district, and the school district know from month to month which invoices to approve as a matter of courtesy, without inquiry? That was another benefit of the personal-delivery procedure. Commissioners and board members were sponsors of the bills they brought to the monthly meetings for payment, and in the power structure of Duval County there was no uncertainty about such things as rank, authority, or territory. The bills might be genuine or bogus; they might represent legitimate purchases or blatant thefts from the public treasury. It didn't matter. Presentation by the right person implied authority and ensured prompt payment.

Cleofas Gonzalez was able to shed some light on the nebulous suggestions that there had been a retail store of some kind in the Vaello building in recent years. "O. P. Carrillo tried to open a store there in about 1968 or 1969," Cleofas said. "He bought some appliances and gift types of things and tried to sell them there, but that business was only open for two or three months. The building hasn't been used for anything except the commodities for the poor people since then." Central Power and Light Company's customer account records, we discovered later, showed that Duval County had paid the electric bill on the Vaello building since April 1965.

In addition to the Zertuche General Store scam, Duval County payroll records showed that Arturo Zertuche was carried as a county employee, at a salary of $225 a month, the entire time he was away at college.

By channeling public funds into the Zertuche General Store account, and having Cleofas Gonzalez withdraw the money for them in cash, Ramiro and O. P. Carrillo hid as much as $75,000 to $80,000 a year of income that should have been taxed to them. Arturo Zertuche's income was overstated by the modest profits he reported for the fictitious Zertuche General Store, and the county received nothing for the salary it paid him while he studied. All three men had exposed themselves to prosecution for violations of the Internal Revenue Code and state law.

Savvy old Walter Meek, wise in the ways of his home county and those who ran it, had been exactly right: Most of the suspect "purchases" from the Zertuche General Store never occurred; it was merely a distribution point for money.

In November 1972, well into the grand jury's second four-month tour of duty, the question arose whether they wished to ask Chief Judge Adrian Spears to extend their tenure again. Their decision was unanimous and enthusiastic.

"Mr. Sessions, Mr. Clark, we want you to be sure and tell him that's what every member of this jury wants," foreman A. B. Jones boomed. "We've talked it over, and we *definitely* want to see this thing through."

Chapter 15

Transition

When men are pure, laws are useless; when men are corrupt,
laws are broken.

— Benjamin Disraeli

BY THE LATE FALL of 1972, we were confident the tax evasion case we were putting together on George Parr would stand up under the cold-eyed scrutiny of IRS and Justice Department reviewing attorneys. It would be what prosecutors call a "specific items" case — a case based on the potpourri of specific, unreported benefits Parr had conferred on himself from the water district's accounts, plus Carl Stautz's cash kickbacks and Harris Fender's compulsory purchase of worthless bonds that George never owned. Of the four different types of tax evasion cases — known as specific items, net worth, expenditures, and bank deposits cases — prosecutors generally prefer specific items cases because they involve direct proof of specific transactions and discrete amounts that have gone unreported, rather than the less direct, inferential proof that typifies net worth and bank deposit cases.

Bryan Taylor and Eunice Powell presented a different kind of challenge. Neither man appeared to be a direct beneficiary of the funds stolen from the water district's treasury, except for a few dips into the Reserve Fund in 1970 to make payments aggregating a little more than $2,000 on Taylor's note at the First State Bank — and those misappropriations could just as easily have been Barney Goldthorn's idea as Bryan Taylor's. The two school administrators'

278

ranch purchases, though, correlated closely with the dates and amounts of some of the cash kickbacks Carl Stautz had testified he gave them.

With a little bit of luck and an extraordinary amount of pains-taking investigative work, Special Agents Jerry Culver and Harold Freeman had developed convincing "net worth" cases against both Taylor and Powell. That the two agents were able to do so while simultaneously helping with the higher-profile efforts commanding most of the investigative attention of the grand jury is a tribute to their skill and dedication. In a "net worth" case the increase in the taxpayer's net worth for each year is compared with reported taxable income and nontaxable receipts. An unaccountable increase in net worth may represent unreported income if the government can prove a "likely source" for the difference or negate the possibility of nontaxable sources for the increase.

Between 1966 and 1968, Culver discovered, Bryan Taylor had handed his sister more than $75,000 in $50 and $100 bills to deposit in five Dallas-area bank accounts, one of which was in the maiden name of Taylor's wife. At Taylor's instruction, his sister wrote checks on those accounts for such things as the down payment on his Twenty Oak Ranch, cattle to stock it, and irrigation equipment to turn it green. Taylor's accumulation of assets during those years also included thirty-two registered quarter horses. The modestly compensated school superintendent told his trusting sister only that the cash he gave her to deposit was earned from "investments." Culver's investigation, however, had eliminated every possible source except two: kickbacks from Carl Stautz and unreported gam-bling winnings. Whatever the sources were, Taylor's income was substantially underreported for those years.

Eunice Powell's deception was less convoluted than Taylor's, but Harold Freeman's thorough investigation showed that Powell, too, had accumulated wealth during those years that couldn't be ex-plained by the modest income he reported as a school superinten-dent. Like Bryan Taylor, it appeared he had benefited substantially from unreported cash extracted from Carl Stautz.

As an investigative bonus we hadn't anticipated at the outset, we were well on the way to developing solid income tax cases against O. P. and Ramiro Carrillo and their cousin, Arturo Zertuche, too. In addition, several witnesses had become candidates for perjury pros-ecutions, and the widespread misappropriations of public funds were violations of state law that would need to be referred to the state's attorney general for prosecution. Nevertheless, because all of our recommendations for prosecution would have to survive two exacting reviews before we could ask the grand jury to indict anyone for income tax violations, it was time for our team to pause and take stock, to see what else was required to finish the course we had begun — the tax evasion investigations of George Parr, Bryan Taylor, and Eunice Powell. Like an expedition of mountain climbers preparing for the final push to the summit, we needed to be sure before pressing on that we had tied down all the loose ends and anticipated all the obstacles we might still face.

The grand jury empaneled in early May had been thrust into this investigation only a few hours after taking the oath of office, starting out as twenty-three randomly selected citizens with almost no idea, individually or collectively, what to expect or what would be expected of them. They were a cross-section of the San Antonio Division of the Western Federal Judicial District of Texas, with representatives from Medina, Wilson, Comal, Guadalupe, Atascosa, Karnes, and Bexar counties. They included ranchers, housewives, civil service employees at various levels, shopkeepers, self-employed contractors, executives, a janitor, a county agricultural agent, and a law student. In the six eventful months since that first day, they had become a unified force with a powerful sense of identity and mission, determined to learn every corrupt secret of George Parr's closely held empire and confident they would ultimately succeed.

By the end of October the grand jury had met on thirteen separate days to hear the testimony of forty different witnesses in this investigation, sometimes remaining in session until after 7:00 P.M. Some of the key witnesses — Barney Goldthorn, Karl Williams, Leo Sepulveda, and D. C. Chapa — had appeared before them four or more times. Boxes of hard-won bank records and canceled checks received as evidence had been turned over to the IRS investigators for analysis. The transcribed testimony of the witnesses filled eleven volumes comprising nearly 1,900 typewritten pages. The grand jurors were ready for a break, but they weren't ready to end the investigation. They were incensed at the corruption they had discovered and eager to do something about it.

For the IRS agents on our team, and for Bill Sessions, Ray Jahn, and me, each day of grand jury testimony represented the culmination of countless hours of investigation, analysis, planning, and preparation. The names of the criminal investigators and revenue agents — I. A. Filer, Jerry Culver, Charlie Volz, Harold Freeman, Ed Watts, Santos Galvan, and Dudley Beaven — showed up more often than any others on the daily telephone log my secretary, Audrey Pridgen, kept for me. The longer the investigation continued, the more frequently we conferred with the agents about plans, theories, and developments. Like the tip of an iceberg, the appearance of each witness before the grand jury was preceded by hours or days or even weeks of interviews, record reviews, and strategy sessions not reflected in the transcripts.

When the investigation began, we were guaranteed that the two required case reviews by the regional counsel of the IRS and the tax division of the Department of Justice would be expedited if any recommendations for prosecution resulted. The deadline for those recommendations had been extended several times, first because of our struggle with the First State Bank over the production of records and later because of unanticipated investigative leads that broadened and extended the investigation. The final deadline, from which there could be no further departure, was the end of November 1972. To support recommendations for indictment, detailed, carefully documented, formal reports were required. It was the duty of our four special agents to prepare those reports by distilling and reducing to writing the results of the investigation to date.

Filer, Volz, Culver, and Freeman completed their reports by the end of the third week of November and delivered them to their supervisor, Chief of Intelligence George Stephen, in Austin. On November 28, 1972, Stephen endorsed their recommendations for prosecutions of Parr, Taylor, and Powell and forwarded the reports to the IRS regional counsel's office in Houston. From there, any affirmative recommendations would go to Assistant Attorney General Scott Crampton, at the Department of Justice, for final approval.

No one was ready, however, to make recommendations on Ramiro and O. P. Carrillo or their cousin, Arturo Zertuche. We all believed that investigative trail would lead us straight into the heart of the Duval County Courthouse. As rotten as governance of the water district was, we felt sure the county would prove to be much worse; it also was run by the Parrs and the Carrillos, and it had far more tax revenue to steal.

When the grand jury reconvened in January 1973, we learned that the subjects of the investigation had not been idle. Our first witness was Karl Williams, who was there to produce the water district's Operating Fund bank records for November and December of 1972. He brought us photocopies instead.

"Where are the original statements and canceled checks?" I asked, mildly surprised.

"They were delivered to the office of the water district."

The bank's practice of holding the statements had been changed recently, Williams said; the water district now received its statements monthly.

I called his attention to two entries on the November bank statement: a $24,000 debit on November 22, and a $45,000 debit on November 27. Williams sifted the photocopies of the canceled checks and pulled out two.

"The $24,000 item is check number 569A, payable to George B. Parr," Williams said, examining the copy. "The legend on it says 'legal advisor's fees for 1973.'"

"And what is the $45,000 item?"

"The $45,000 item is check number 470A, payable to George B. Parr. The legend is 'purchase of helicopter.' Each item is properly endorsed by the payee."

Williams acknowledged that the bank was working to comply with a grand jury subpoena for copies of the checking account records of Arturo Zertuche and the Zertuche General Store for 1966 through 1969. "We have already turned over the 1966 and 1969 records to the IRS agents, and we're producing the rest of the records now," Williams said. "We're working on it every chance we get."

Leo Sepulveda brought the grand jury the original Operating Fund bank statements and canceled checks later that same day. "For some reason I have to go to the bank and sign a receipt for them," Sepulveda said, "but I've been getting them for about three months now." I showed Sepulveda a $100 check payable to Anacleto Valerio, the new secretary of the water district's board of directors.

"This check is dated November 22, and it says it was for a special meeting. Was there some kind of special meeting of the board?" I asked.

"Yes, sir. We had a special meeting on that date."

"What was the purpose?"

"Mr. Chapa called that special meeting for the purpose of buying a helicopter, sir." Grand jurors nudged one another and shook their heads in disbelief. I asked Sepulveda for more details.

"Mr. Chapa called the meeting, sir, and this was discussed, the feasibility of purchasing a helicopter from Mr. Parr. It was suggested, discussed, and approved."

"What kind of discussion was had? What was said about it?"

"Well, it was a discussion of the feasibility of having a helicopter for emergency crews, and actually there wasn't too much discussion. Mr. Chapa said they could buy this helicopter, and he felt that the district should own one, and that's about it."

"What reason did he give for the water district to own a helicopter?"

"Just that it could be used for emergency flights, because we don't have any hospitals, and sometimes we have floods and other disasters."

Sepulveda agreed the water district's only legitimate business was to furnish water and sewer services to San Diego, Benavides, and three smaller communities. It had no use for a helicopter in its business, he conceded.

"How did Mr. Chapa sell the directors on the idea of buying it?"

"You'll have to ask them, sir."

"You were there, weren't you, Mr. Sepulveda?"

"Well, he didn't sell me on the idea, sir."

No questions were asked when Chapa made the proposal, Sepulveda reported, and the vote to approve the purchase was unanimous.

"Did he tell the directors who was selling the helicopter?"

"Yes, sir."

"Is that one of the first things he told them?"

"It might have been, yes, sir."

Sepulveda didn't know the whereabouts of the helicopter, he told the grand jury. The water district had no place to keep it, and so far as he knew it hadn't been used since it was purchased. The board approved a $600 statement for the first month's hangaring and maintenance at the January meeting, he said, and he understood they had hired a pilot. He had not seen a certificate of title to the aircraft.

"Did Mr. Parr attend the special meeting at which this purchase was considered?"

"Yes, sir."

"And what part did he play in the meeting?"

"Not very much, sir. He was just there. I don't remember that he said anything."

"Not even 'thank you' after they voted to buy it?"

"He may have said 'thank you,' sir."

"How was the price arrived at, Mr. Sepulveda? How did the directors know what it ought to be worth?"

"I think Mr. Chapa suggested the price, sir."

No one inquired what Parr had paid for the helicopter, Sepulveda said. There was no discussion of any kind. All of the directors simply voted approval of the purchase without so much as opening their mouths.

Two other checks, each for $350, one for "truck rental" and one for "equipment rental," caught our attention. The check for truck rental was payable to L. A. Garcia.

"Do you have any idea who he is, Mr. Sepulveda?"

"Yes, sir. He's Maria Barkley's brother."

"What kind of truck did the water district rent from him?"

"A dump truck sir, for trash collection there in town."

"When did the water district get into the trash collection business?"

"When the city couldn't afford it, sir; we inherited the employees of the garbage and trash collection, and we've been doing it ever since."

The equipment rental check was payable to George Parr's older sister, Marie Parr Thompson — the same, seventy-six-year-old Marie Parr Thompson who had drawn a salary from the water district for years without performing any work in return.

"What kind of equipment does Marie Parr Thompson rent to the water district?" I asked, handing Sepulveda the canceled check.

"She has a dump truck, I believe, sir."

Many of the grand jurors must have visualized the same incongruous mental image I did, of a frail, elderly lady standing proudly beside her huge, dirty dump truck. Smiles sprouted on half the faces in the room, including mine.

"And what does the water district use it for?" I managed to ask.

"I believe it's trash collection, sir. I'm not sure."

The November and December bank statements included still more intriguing transactions. There were $510 checks each month payable to Duval Cedar Yard for "equipment rental at Benavides," endorsed by Oscar Carrillo, Sr., D. C. Chapa's third son. Sepulveda had no knowledge about those transactions, he said, but D. C. Chapa might have. Several checks were issued each month to Benavides Implement Hardware Company, in amounts from $750 to $900. He knew nothing about the purpose of those checks, either, Sepulveda said. The December checks included more than $2,000 in expenditures labeled "community Christmas project." Those, Sepulveda told us, were issued for charitable purposes in Benavides and several smaller communities in the county.

"That's something they have been practicing, sir, for a number of years. They issue grocery packs; it's a $10 or $15 box of groceries that they hand out to needy families, and they buy candy bags and distribute them out to the kids. It's been done for at least the last three years."

I handed Sepulveda the $24,000 check issued to George Parr on November 22, 1972.

"At the special meeting on November 22, apparently it was decided to pay Mr. Parr his 1973 legal fee in advance; is that right?"

"That's correct, sir."

"What discussion was had about that?"

"Just that, sir. Mr. Chapa proposed that he be paid for 1973."

"Was there any discussion?"

"Not any more than there was about the helicopter, sir."

"Has there been any repayment of the previous $12,000 advance to Mr. Parr for legal fees?"

"No, sir."

Leo Sepulveda was bright enough to realize that the grand jury saw the water district and its directors as mere instrumentalities that George Parr used for his own purposes. His embarrassment at being a pawn in Parr's game was evident. "It's not up to me to accept or reject any claim that's presented to me," he said defensively. "It's not like a business entity, actually. The board can ask my advice on accepting or rejecting something, but it's their decision. I'm more of an employee than a business manager, sir."

"Mr. Sepulveda, where do you keep your business records at this time?" I inquired.

"They're in a safe, sir, now."

Memories of the walk-in vault with a window on the back wall and the combination taped to the door were still fresh in all of our minds.

"Is that the same place you lost those records from before?"

"No, sir, but I'm using a safe that was always in the office, one that belonged to Mr. Palacios, so I still don't know who has the combination, sir. But they are in a safe."

To look more closely at the Carrillos' dealings with the county, we needed the county's bank statements and canceled checks. Charlie Volz called on the county auditor, Walter Meek, with a subpoena. "I don't have them," Meek told Volz. "The canceled checks are the treasurer's responsibility, but the bank keeps them."

I gave Volz a subpoena to serve on the bank, and extras in case he needed them. Barney Goldthorn, nervous as always, was apologetic when the agent called on him. "We used to keep the county's canceled checks for them," he told Volz, "but they picked them up a couple of months ago. I think it was Mr. Gonzalez, the assistant treasurer, who came and got them."

Volz returned to the courthouse and served a subpoena on the county treasurer, Manuel Solis. Solis was bewildered. He didn't know Sylvester Gonzalez had removed the checks from the bank. Solis was exactly as Walter Meek had described him: only a figurehead with no real authority and little knowledge of the office. It was Sylvester Gonzalez, Meek told us, who was the real power in the treasurer's office; Gonzalez was the "go-between" with the county judge, Archer Parr, Meek said.

Gonzalez played down his role, describing himself to the grand jury as a clerk in the treasurer's office. He had an insurance agency in San Diego, he said, and he worked part-time for the county. His subpoena called for him to produce the county's bank statements and canceled checks, but he had brought only deposit slips.

"Where are the bank statements and canceled checks for 1967 through 1970?" I asked him.

"That's a good question," Gonzalez replied. "I don't know."

"Well, what can you tell us about them?"

"We have the current year's statements in our vault in the office, and we keep the old records in a storage room in the basement.

But the other day I went down there with one of your agents to look for them, and they were gone."

"Had the bank statements and canceled checks been in that storage room at one time?"

"Yes, sir. I put them there myself."

The county judge sent him to the bank near the end of last year to pick up the canceled checks, Gonzalez said, because the bank called the judge and said they needed the storage space. He brought all the records back to the courthouse in boxes and put them in the storage room; there were checks dating back to 1953 or 1954. He found the storeroom locked, Gonzalez said. One of the courthouse janitors opened it for him.

"Who has keys to that storage room?"

"Well, I guess all the janitors have."

"What about county officials?"

"I couldn't say."

Gonzalez denied having a key.

"Mr. Gonzalez, what do you think happened to those canceled checks and bank statements?"

"I guess somebody stole them," he said matter-of-factly. "I don't know what happened to them."

Gonzalez was unconcerned about the missing checks. "Since we don't reconcile our accounts, we don't bother with them, anyway," he said.

Even the water district goes through the motions, I thought, *at least on the accounts that aren't secret.* "How do you keep your books in balance if you don't reconcile your bank accounts?" I asked.

"Well, through the experience we've had, being there so long, we know that if we issue a check it will be cashed in the next fifteen days, and it's just a waste of time for us to go up there and spend a day or so trying to reconcile them."

Walter Meek wasn't surprised that the checks Sylvester Gonzalez had retrieved from the bank were missing. "I know this county too well," he said. "Whenever there's trouble, you can be assured records will disappear. They'll never be found." Sylvester Gonzalez was more than a mere assistant to the treasurer, Meek said. "He runs the office," Meek elaborated. "He dominates Mr. Solis, you can be sure of that. Mr. Solis is a good man, but he's more of a political appointee that really doesn't have the final say in the office."

So far as the treasurer's function of reconciling bank accounts was concerned, Meek indicated, the treasurer's office kept a carbon copy of every check issued, and they received the monthly statements from the bank. The only thing not returned by the bank was the canceled checks. Upon learning that the checks were missing, Meek said, he made it a point to find out if the bank's microfilm was intact, and had been told that it was. "Of course, there are no endorsements on the carbon copies," he pointed out, anticipating that we would want to see who cashed certain checks. "But the bank assured me they have the microfilm. They also assured me it will take a court order to get it." The carbon copies were kept indefinitely in vaults in his office and the treasurer's office, he told us, and he would safeguard them until Charlie Volz could drop by with a subpoena and pick them up.

"How did Sylvester Gonzalez come to be employed by the county?" I asked Meek.

"I couldn't tell you, really, but he's the son of an old henchman of the Old Party, and they just gravitate to the courthouse and are taken care of with a job."

By the "Old Party," Meek explained, he meant the party dominated by George Parr. "I'm sure you're all familiar with that situation," he said. "It's a paternalistic form of government, really, and once you get on the payroll, you never get off; you're taken care of. They always find a place for the children of old henchmen."

"From your knowledge of the situation, Mr. Meek, is Sylvester Gonzalez Archer Parr's man, or George Parr's man, or both?"

"Well, let's just say he belongs to the organization. Archer probably uses him more now than George does, because George is pretty inactive, but he's someone they can depend on for any errands or any arrangement they want."

In his garrulous manner, Archer Parr told the grand jury a distinctly different tale about the removal of the county's checks from the bank.

"I was over at the bank — now, I don't recall when, sir — and Mr. Barney Goldthorn and I were in a conversation. I think it was late in the afternoon. And I asked him specifically, I said, 'Barney, all the checks and stuff over there, they are having a heck of a time balancing the books on certain funds over there. Where are they?' He said, 'We have them.' I said, 'Would you mind, so they could balance the books over there in the the county treasurer's office, if I sent over here to pick the things up?' And he said, 'Be quite all right. Just sign for them.' And I told either Sylvester Gonzalez or Armando Oliveira to go over to the bank and if they would sign for the canceled checks they could get them."

It was either Sylvester Gonzalez, Manuel Solis, or Walter Meek, Archer said, who told him the bank was retaining the canceled checks and making it difficult to keep the county's books in balance.

"We were all sitting around there talking one afternoon, and they said they couldn't balance their books at the end of the month," Archer testified. "I said, 'Why not?' They said, 'Because the bank is holding the checks.' I said, 'Who gave them authority to do that?' And they said they didn't know." Barney Goldthorn didn't explain why the bank held the checks, Archer said; he just agreed to turn over the checks if someone signed for them.

Archer's story was implausible on its face: The bank had held the county's checks for twenty years or more, and the treasurer had always had carbon copies and the bank statements to use if he chose to reconcile the accounts. Sylvester Gonzalez's version was no more believable than Archer's. Karl Williams had told us Sylvester simply showed up at the bank one day and announced that he wanted to pick up the county's checks. The bank had held them all those years purely as an accommodation to the county, Williams said, and had no reason not to turn them over at the customer's request.

Probably no one in the grand jury room believed the checks were stolen from the basement of the county courthouse, unless the thief was Sylvester Gonzalez. Archer Parr surely knew carbon copies existed, as well as photographs on bank microfilm. Apparently it was important to him, though, to keep us from getting our hands on the original checks. Was he trying to protect the Carrillos, we wondered, or George, or himself? Perhaps, as Walter Meek seemed to be suggesting, the back sides of some of the checks would be more interesting than the front sides. Meek probably was correct, we thought, in predicting the checks would never be found.

Our investigative team was convinced the county's missing checks had met with the same fate as the records taken from the water district months earlier. On the streets of San Diego, the agents had heard rumors of documents being transported to Los Horcones and burned.

Chapter 16

Indictments

Income tax returns are the most imaginative fiction being written today.

— Herman Wouk

AS MARCH BROUGHT THE South Texas countryside out of its brief winter torpor in 1973, it also brought us the word we were awaiting: Our proposed prosecutions of George Parr, Bryan Taylor, and Eunice Powell were approved. We were free to ask the grand jury to indict them.

For George there were to be eight counts, two each for 1966, 1967, 1968, and 1969. In the language of the Internal Revenue Code, the indictment would charge that in each of those years he attempted to evade income taxes, and that in each of those years he knowingly subscribed a false tax return.

Bryan Taylor and Eunice Powell were to be charged in separate indictments with attempted tax evasion and subscribing false returns for each of three years, 1967, 1968, and 1969.

The IRS used the evidence developed in the grand jury investigation to calculate that George had understated his income for 1966 through 1969 by some $287,000 and thus attempted to evade more than $129,000 in taxes. Taylor's income was determined to be understated by more than $100,000 for 1967 through 1969 Powell's by more than $45,000.

The correct tax liability of a defendant accused of income tax evasion is determined by IRS experts such as Ed Watts and Jerry

Culver, who reconstruct and recalculate the wayward taxpayer's returns as they should have been filed. Unreported income is included, and the accused is given every legitimate deduction and credit he would have been entitled to take, regardless of the source of the funds. In recalculating Parr's returns, for example, water district funds expended for irrigation equipment were included as income in the years the purchases occurred, and appropriate deductions were applied for the depreciation he could have taken as owner of the equipment.

Through its career prosecutors, the Justice Department's tax division in the early 1970s had an institutional memory of George Parr that lingered from the ill-starred proscecution initiatives of the mid-1950s. The tax evasion charges filed in 1954 and shelved while the mail fraud case wound its way through the federal court system had been dismissed by Attorney General Robert Kennedy in 1963, only nine years before our investigation began. As March 1973 unfolded and the deadline for criminal charges based on Parr's 1966 return approached, Assistant Attorney General Scott Crampton and his staff were no less determined than we that this time the United States would get it right. We traded drafts of proposed indictments with tax division lawyers until everyone was satisfied with the final product.

The Internal Revenue Service relishes the opportunity to obtain high-visibility tax fraud indictments in April, when most taxpayers are preparing to file their returns. Whether news of that kind encourages taxpayers to file honest returns is debatable, but without doubt it serves to remind anyone who might think about cheating that the IRS takes its job of tax collection seriously. So widespread was George Parr's notoriety as a result of the Box 13 episode twenty-five years earlier that his indictment for income tax evasion was destined to be a story in virtually every newspaper in the United States. At the Justice Department's public information office in Washington, Assistant Director Bob Stevenson prepared to issue a press release in the attorney general's name as soon as the indictments were made public.

On April 3, Marvin Foster drove from San Diego to San Antonio to see me on behalf of Bryan Taylor and Eunice Powell, mindful of the calendar and hoping to dissuade us at the last minute from seeking indictments against the two school administrators. I listened as Marvin made an impassioned plea, but we had his clients dead to rights.

The grand jury returned to their familiar meeting room at 9:00 A.M., April 6, 1973, anticipating a chance to vote on indictments. We explained the charges we proposed, summarized the evidence gathered since May 1972, on which the charges were based, and left the jury alone to deliberate on our recommendations. It didn't take them long to act.

Later that morning, Chief Judge Adrian Spears welcomed the grand jury and the government's attorneys to his courtroom. Reporters who had endured long days of boredom in the corridor outside the grand jury room followed us inside, knowing that indictments must be returned in open court and hoping at last for a real story to report.

The grand jury foreman stepped forward, signed indictments in hand.

"Mr. Jones, I understand the grand jury wishes to return some indictments," Spears said.

"Yes, sir," Jones replied. "We have three. We'd like to have 'em sealed until the persons are arrested."

Sealing is a precaution taken to insure that the subject of an indictment doesn't learn of his impending arrest prematurely and flee to avoid prosecution. The indictments are held by the clerk of the court until arrests are made; only then are they unsealed for inspection by the press and the public.

"Has the grand jury completed its investigation, Mr. Jones?" Spears inquired.

Alvin B. Jones and his twenty-two colleagues had anticipated this question; they wanted nothing else so much as to continue their investigation of other Duval County targets who were already in their sights. Jones, a big man with a commanding voice, raised his head high and fixed the judge with a steady gaze. Reporters looked up to catch his answer. "We have not finished our work yet, sir," Jones said pointedly.

A little before 3:00 that afternoon, all three of the indicted men arrived at the courthouse with their attorneys. Nago Alaniz of San Diego and Anthony Nicholas of San Antonio accompanied George Parr; Marvin Foster had Taylor and Powell in tow. Parr, smiling and wisecracking with press photographers, was dressed for the occasion in a dark brown suit, a white shirt with a brown tie, and a light beige Stetson. After being photographed and fingerprinted by Deputy U.S. Marshal Mario Granados, Parr appeared before Judge Adrian Spears, who ordered him to post a $50,000 personal recognizance bond as a condition of his release pending trial. Taylor's bond was set at $25,000, Powell's at $20,000.

In U.S. Magistrate John Giles' office, Parr signed his bond and received instructions restricting him to the Western and Southern federal judicial districts of Texas. Signing the bond as a personal surety for George was flamboyant Clinton Manges, riding high as majority stockholder in San Antonio's venerable Groos National Bank and owner of the biggest ranch in Duval County.

San Antonio's federal courthouse didn't have the kind of tight security system in 1973 that protects all federal courthouses today. When Nago Alaniz bent over to sign a document in the magistrate's office that afternoon, a deputy marshal told us later, it was apparent from the size and shape of a bulge in the back of the lawyer's jacket that he had a pistol in the waistband of his trousers.

Exiting the courthouse a few minutes later, Parr, though still smiling, brushed past waiting reporters and photographers and walked briskly to Nicholas' car without responding to questions.

The story of the indictment and photographs of George on the courthouse steps with his attorneys flashed over the AP and UPI wires to newspapers and television and radio newsrooms all over the country. Banner headlines screamed the news the next morning in Corpus Christi and San Antonio. That particular Saturday was election day for the San Diego Independent School District, and George Parr was a candidate for reelection to the school board. He was unopposed, of course, and drew 581 votes. Not even a write-in vote was cast against him.

On April 10, Charlie Volz and Ed Watts called on O. P. and Ramiro Carrillo to advise them officially that they were under investigation for income tax evasion. Both of the brothers declined, on Fifth Amendment grounds, to answer any questions about the Zertuche General Store and the Farm and Ranch Supply store.

The indictments of Parr, Taylor, and Powell touched off a flurry of activity. By late April, the three defendants had filed motions to dismiss the charges against them, and the First State Bank of San Diego was dueling with us again over access to bank records.

This time the bank customers whose records the grand jury wanted were the three Carrillo brothers, O. P., Ramiro, and Oscar.

All three tax cases filed April 6 were assigned to the docket of Judge Dorwin W. Suttle. All were scheduled for arraignment — the formal proceeding at which the defendant is officially advised of the charges against him and is called upon for the first time to enter a plea of guilty or not guilty — on May 2, 1973.

The defendants' motions to dismiss the charges against them were based on a technical legal theory. They argued that the local court rules of the Western District of Texas should be interpreted to mean that a grand jury drawn from the counties comprising the San Antonio division had no authority to indict them for offenses committed, if at all, in the Southern District of Texas, where their tax returns were signed, or in the Austin division of the Western District, where the returns were filed. Nonsense, we replied; the Federal Rules of Criminal Procedure allow a grand jury to indict for crimes committed anywhere in the district. If the local court rules purported to limit that authority, then they conflicted with the Federal Rules of Criminal Procedure and were simply wrong.

Dorwin Suttle was — and is still, in 1995 — a wise and careful jurist. Appointed by President Johnson at the behest of Suttle's college roommate, Senator Ralph Yarborough, Suttle was in his mid-sixties and had been on the bench nearly ten years when these cases came before him. His meticulous attention to detail often led prosecutors and defense counsel alike to complain among themselves that trials in his court were tedious and unnecessarily prolonged. Suttle was aware of the criticism, though none of his critics was so bold as to complain directly to him, but it never bothered him. "I've learned over the years that it doesn't pay to rush into things," the judge was fond of saying. "When you shoot from the hip, you make mistakes, and then you've wasted everybody's time because you're just going to have to do it over and get it right." The philosophy worked for him. Cases appealed from his court to the Court of Appeals for the Fifth Circuit, in New Orleans, were seldom reversed.

We were absolutely confident our position on the question of the grand jury's authority was correct, but it was an issue that had never been presented squarely to the Fifth Circuit for decision. It was the kind of issue that would intrigue Judge Suttle, we realized, and given his cautious nature he might opt to posture it for an appellate decision before trying any of the cases. Sessions and I charted the alternatives the government would face if Judge Suttle dismissed the indictments. Before the hearing was held on the defendants' motions, we knew what we would do if the worst happened.

Judge Suttle scheduled a hearing on the dismissal motions on the morning of Wednesday, May 2, immediately before the defendants were to be arraigned. The hearing lasted nearly all day, and then, as we had feared he might do, the judge dismissed the indictments. George Parr, Bryan Taylor, and Eunice Powell walked out of Suttle's fifth-floor courtroom free men with renewed hope. Sessions and I went downstairs, disappointed but not really surprised, to face the press.

"The government has the right to appeal today's decision and ask the appellate court to reinstate the original indictments," Sessions said in a written statement distributed a few minutes later to reporters gathered outside our offices. "In the alternative we can, without appealing, present the facts to a federal grand jury in Austin, or in the Southern District of Texas, and seek new indictments in either of those locations." Sessions answered few questions, declining to go beyond the substance of the written statement. "There could be some delay, because the government has to choose whether to appeal or seek new indictments," Sessions conceded, "but this does not put an end to the matter." Because the indictments were filed before April 15, we no longer had a statute of limitations problem. Federal law allows the government an additional six months to obtain new indictments after a dismissal under these circumstances.

George Parr had faced the same reporters on the steps of the courthouse a few minutes earlier, while we were preparing our written statement. He was pleased with the judge's ruling, he told them, but he had no illusions about what lay ahead. "This is just the beginning," George said.

In fact, Sessions and I had already made our decision. We had settled on recommending to Scott Crampton and his Justice Department staff that new indictments be sought in the Southern District of Texas, where all of the defendants could — and doubtless would — insist eventually on being tried. As much as we would relish having the Fifth Circuit resolve the local court rules issue in our favor, we were not willing to delay these cases for the additional year or so that such action would require. The San Antonio grand jury could remain empaneled to consider perjury charges against some of the witnesses who had testified before it, but the unfinished investigation of the Carrillos, and others, we felt, should be continued in Corpus Christi.

We had discussed all of the options in advance with our old friend Anthony J. P. Farris, the U.S. attorney in Houston. It was his district in which the fireworks had begun more than a year earlier with the aborted IRS summons enforcement proceeding in Corpus Christi. Tony Farris was more than merely agreeable to the prospect of moving the battle to Corpus Christi and joining forces with us; he was enthusiastic. "We can put together a helluva team," Farris barked. "I'll put the chief of my criminal division in charge. Tell Crampton I endorse the idea one hundred percent."

The tax division approved the plan. On Friday, May 4, I walked down to Chief Judge Adrian Spears' chambers and presented an *ex parte* motion to transfer all of our grand jury testimony and exhibits to a federal grand jury in Corpus Christi. Because these were grand jury matters, no one else was entitled to notice of the motion. Spears signed the order without hesitation, and the curtain was about to go up on the next act in the drama.

In Duval County, strange happenings were beginning to foreshadow trouble in George Parr's tightly controlled dukedom. On May 10, District Attorney Randall Nye asked Judge O. P. Carrillo to schedule a special session of the county's grand jury to investigate persistent reports of "somebody" displaying and firing a weapon in San Diego. Because it was common knowledge that the unidentified "somebody" was the Duke himself, there was speculation whether anyone would be sufficiently fearless — or foolhardy — to testify. Nevertheless, five people appeared before the grand jury in San Diego on May 17, presumably to tell of seeing the rumored incidents. One of the witnesses was J. S. "Checo" Garcia, an owner of Duval Motor Company, the county's only Ford dealership and one of little San Diego's biggest businesses. The grand jury took no action.

On June 1, when Garcia turned on a water faucet at his Ford dealership, nothing came out. Outside, he found his water meter missing and water service shut off. "I don't know why this has happened," Garcia told the *Corpus Christi Caller*, "unless it has something to do with my run-in with Parr."

It was a good guess. Water district office manager Leo Sepulveda told *Caller* reporter Joe Coudert, "All I know is George Parr ordered it and I passed the information on to the crews." Routine disconnections were handled by the city secretary's office, Sepulveda said. "This is the first time since I've been here it's been done this way."

In another news story in the same edition, the *Caller* reported that George Parr had resigned his commission as a Duval County deputy sheriff.

Assistant U.S. Attorneys Ed McDonough, George Kelt, and I met in Corpus Christi in late May to plan our presentation to the Southern District grand jury. We agreed on June 14 as the date. I undertook to organize the voluminous testimony and exhibits so familiar to the San Antonio grand jury, to reduce them to a manageable essence that would give the new grand jury the salient facts without requiring them to relive the San Antonio experience. After the grand jury sessions in San Antonio in January, March, and April, the transcripts of testimony had swelled to more than 2,200 pages.

Ed McDonough had learned the prosecutor's trade as an assistant district attorney in Houston before Tony Farris hired him away from Harris County and put him directly in charge of federal criminal prosecutions in one-fourth of the state of Texas. McDonough was a tall, cigar-fancying, eligible bachelor from a prominent Galveston family. He was also a seasoned, no-nonsense prosecutor and, in his spare time, a capable open-water sailor.

George Kelt had been an IRS special agent before becoming an assistant U.S. attorney, and he was already acquainted with the agents on our investigative team. Short and stocky, Kelt wore a permanent look of bulldog-like determination that was indicative of his attitude toward tax cheats. He was a solid legal scholar and a quick study, and his familiarity with the tax laws and IRS personnel and procedures would serve us well.

On June 14, 1973, Bill Sessions and I, with special credentials from the attorney general that allowed us to serve outside our own district, joined McDonough and Kelt in Corpus Christi to introduce another grand jury to the inner workings of Duval County. The first witness was our San Antonio grand jury foreman, Alvin B. Jones. By the end of the day we had presented enough evidence to support the indictments of Parr, Taylor, and Powell on the same charges as before. Arraignments were scheduled for July 30, before Judge Owen Cox.

On June 25 Archer Parr's glamorous fourth wife, ex-model Jody Martin Parr, sued him for divorce in Nueces County. Archer countered with a divorce suit of his own in Duval County a few days later, and the fight was on. Their domestic dispute quickly became an all-out, no-holds-barred war over property, position, and pride, so fierce and so sensational that it commanded news coverage all over the state. The bitter conflict raged on for a year until Jody, in despair over the prospect of having to serve a six-month sentence in the Duval County jail for contempt of court, put a bullet through her head in the couple's Corpus Christi townhouse. Early on, though, Jody pried up the lid on a Pandora's box of Duval County secrets that our investigation hadn't yet discovered.

Testifying at a hearing before Judge O. P. Carrillo in August, Jody accused Archer of receiving $5,000 or more in cash from assistant Duval County treasurer Sylvester Gonzalez after each monthly meeting of the county commissioners court, and of using county employees as ranch hands while they were being paid to work for the county. Gonzalez delivered the currency to Archer each month in a brown envelope, Jody claimed, and the county employees were used regularly as cooks, ranch hands, and laborers on Archer's cattle spread. Archer Parr, under oath on the same occasion and very much on the spot, invoked the Fifth Amendment on both issues, and the *Corpus Christi Caller* reported the whole episode. Jody's revelations were destined to have far-reaching consequences for Archer, and for others as well.

On November 6, 1973, Bill Sessions and I met again with the San Antonio grand jury to propose indicting Archer Parr and Octavio Saenz for perjury. The grand jury charged Archer with six counts of perjury arising from his testimony that the $121,500 he received from the water district was compensation for legal services. In a separate, two-count indictment the grand jury charged Mayor Saenz with lying about the $5,000 he withdrew from the Benavides Special Sinking Fund.

We were convinced Barney Goldthorn had lied, too, in portraying himself as merely an innocent order-taker in the matter of the cash withdrawals from the water district's secret accounts. After studying the evidence carefully, however, we decided that we didn't have a prosecutable case against him. Nevertheless, with the unfinished investigation of the Carrillos pending, Barney wasn't out of the woods yet.

The grand jury was discharged with warm thanks from us and from Judge Spears after completing its business that day. Its twenty-three members had labored for eighteen months in an exceptionally arduous and often frustrating investigation. The twenty dollars they received as compensation each time they met barely covered their expenses for parking and lunch, yet very few had missed even one of the many meetings.

The Parrs' rock-solid foundation of control in Duval County began to show signs of cracking in late 1973. On November 26 the county commissioners tried to assuage growing taxpayer displeasure by holding a rare public hearing on the county's budget for the coming year. More than one hundred angry property owners showed up to complain about the county's high taxes, the first time a public display of that kind had occurred in decades. Earlier that month, for the first time in twelve years, the commissioners had published the county's budget for the coming year. The figures told the story of the county's graft-burdened overhead: Duval County, with a population of 12,000 souls, adopted a budget of $4.2 million for 1974. Webb County, its neighbor on the west with a population of 80,000, budgeted $1.7 million for the same year. Armando Benavides, a Laredo resident and Duval County landowner who had helped organize an ad hoc taxpayers' protest group, asked the county judge to explain the discrepancy. "Sit down," Archer growled. "I don't want to hear any of your politics."

George Parr accused the press of "stirring up a bunch of old crap" after the *Corpus Christi Caller* reported that most of the county's highest elected officials, including the tax collector, were on the delinquent tax rolls. In a series of copyrighted articles, the *Caller* analyzed the peculiarities of the county's budget, exposed its lax procedures for paying bills, and compared its vehicle maintenance expense with that of Nueces County. With twenty times the population, the newspaper pointed out, Nueces County's vehicle expenses were less than half the amount spent by Duval County.

In a copyrighted article published November 30, 1973, *Corpus Christi Caller* reporters Joe Coudert and Spencer Pearson described in detail their discovery of twenty-six Duval County checks issued in January of that year to individual payees for labor or for goods and services, many endorsed in the same handwriting, and all bearing a second endorsement by the same Sylvester Gonzalez identified three months earlier by Jody Martin Parr as the man who delivered "illegal money" to Archer each month. Spot checks of the county's records for February and March revealed a similar pattern, the two writers indicated. In a separate article the same newspaper reported that as county judge, Archer Parr had an "unlimited" charge account at a service station owned by former Duval County sheriff Vidal Garcia, and that the county had paid an average of nearly $1,900 a month on the account for the first eight months of 1973. Moreover, the *Caller* reported, Duval County was paying $175 a month to lease a new Thunderbird for Archer.

By the time Archer Parr and Octavio Saenz were arraigned before Judge D. W. Suttle in December 1973, the big push was on to get ready for the trial of George Parr. Ed McDonough, George Kelt, and I, along with I. A. Filer, Jerry Culver, Charlie Volz, and Ed Watts, had coalesced into a smooth-running prosecution team and were devoting substantial time to preparations for the pretrial motion hearings Judge Cox had scheduled in early January. It was agreed that Ed McDonough would take the lead in trial, since we were in his district. I would assist in the second-chair position, handle D. C. Chapa as a witness, and split the final jury argument with McDonough. Kelt would be our primary "book lawyer," taking responsibility for briefing legal issues arising throughout the trial and ensuring that the all-important jury instructions to be submitted by the judge at the close of the trial were correct.

I. A. Filer would serve as our principal case agent for the trial. Charlie Volz and Jerry Culver would assist him, and Culver would also be the government's summary witness, to testify as an expert on the tax consequences of the government's evidence at the end of the trial. Ed Watts, our revenue agent, completed the courtroom team as an all-around tax code expert, witness handler, and walking encyclopedia of knowledge about the facts to which each of our witnesses could testify.

Parr's lead attorney, veteran San Antonio defense counsel Anthony Nicholas, was recruited for Parr's defense by Nago Alaniz, but Nicholas withdrew from the case in late September. "It was getting to be too much of a hassle," Nicholas told me later. "Judge Cox insisted that every motion we filed had to be signed by me as lead attorney, and by all the other defense counsel too. We had too many lawyers involved, and I could see things weren't going to work the way I wanted them to, so I wanted out."

The Duke had taken a liking to Nicholas and was sorry to lose him. "He wanted me to learn Spanish, which was his first language," Nicholas said. "George liked to tell jokes, but he said all the really good jokes he knew were in Spanish and they didn't translate well. He was going to hire a tutor for me so he could tell me jokes in Spanish." Going anywhere in public with Parr and Alaniz in Duval County was a unique experience, Nicholas said. "Two or three of George's *pistoleros* went everywhere with him, and Nago was always armed." Despite the rapport that developed between them, Parr never told Nicholas the facts of the case.

Anthony Nicholas' replacement as lead counsel was Douglas Tinker of Corpus Christi, whose substantial criminal trial experience at that time had been gained principally in the state court system. During a recess on the first day of pretrial hearings before Judge Cox, after the judge had overruled virtually all defense motions, Tinker remarked to McDonough that he would like to be in the Nueces County Courthouse "in a good 'ol state murder case with just a legal pad and a number two pencil."

McDonough grinned wickedly at Tinker. "Welcome to the NFL," he replied.

Parr's attorneys had blitzed us with more than two dozen motions before trial, some aimed at discovering the government's evidence in advance, some designed to exclude evidence harmful to Parr, some accusing the government of tapping Nago Alaniz's telephone and committing the Fourth of July burglary that resulted in the disappearance of the water district's records. One motion called for us to produce President Richard Nixon's "enemies list," apparently on the theory that there was such a list, that George Parr's name would be on it, and that the prosecution would thus be discredited as a Republican political plot. Judge Cox found no merit in most of the defense motions. Though originally scheduled to commence January 28, the trial was rescheduled for March 4. Besides responding to the defense motions, we had also prepared legal memoranda on more than forty issues that might arise in trial. We were ready, and confident.

On January 4, 1974, the second day of pretrial motion hearings,

I was handed an urgent telephone message upon returning to the courtroom after lunch: I was about to become a father for the fourth time. Judge Cox excused me from the rest of the day's proceedings, and I rushed back to the Nix Hospital in San Antonio, hoping to arrive before my wife, Carolyn, delivered. Bill Sessions met me with a broad smile and a handshake as I stepped off the elevator. "You've got another son, John," Sessions beamed. "He's a fine-looking boy, and I *know* you'll want to name him William."

Political ferment continued in Duval County. On January 21 D. C. Chapa resigned as chairman of the water district's board of directors and as a member of the Benavides school board. The vacancy on the school board was filled by Oscar Carrillo, one of Chapa's sons. Chapa's grandson, Rogelio Guajardo, was appointed to fill the vacancy on the water district's board of directors.

Archer and Jody remained in the headlines as charges and countercharges flew back and forth while Jody fought to avoid a trial in Archer's backyard. Their divorce litigation spawned nearly a dozen related lawsuits, some involving the county. By early March, Jody was facing the contempt of court charges in Duval County that would ultimately weigh heavily in her decision to commit suicide.

The entire prosecution team assembled in Corpus Christi for final trial preparations in late February. A serious snag developed on the Friday morning before the trial was scheduled to begin when Judge Cox ordered the prosecution to give Tinker all of our "Jencks Act" materials — all written statements of our witnesses, including their grand jury testimony — on Monday, at the beginning of the trial. We objected strenuously. The law requires that a witness' written statements be turned over to the defendant only after the witness testifies, we reminded the judge, for use in cross-examination. The rule is designed to prevent the defendant from manufacturing evidence or intimidating witnesses. Certainly, we argued, we had legitimate concerns on both scores in dealing with so powerful a defendant as George Parr. The judge listened patiently but stuck by his ruling.

This was a huge issue in our eyes. The trial was likely to go on for two weeks. We simply couldn't put our witnesses or our case at risk by giving George Parr two weeks to tailor a defense or to tamper with our witnesses. The law was squarely on our side. We needed to force the issue with Judge Cox, even if it meant delaying the trial. We sought and received advice from the Justice Department's chief appellate lawyer, the solicitor general.

Over the weekend we crafted a four-page letter to the judge, citing additional appellate decisions that supported our position. In diplomatic but firm language, we asked Judge Cox to put his ruling in the form of an appealable order so that we could take the issue to the Fifth Circuit immediately. In the alternative, we suggested, we would voluntarily give the defense each witness' Jencks Act materials one day before the witness was expected to testify. McDonough and I referred to the document respectfully, almost gingerly, as "The Letter." We didn't know what reaction it would evoke from the judge. Because I had known Owen Cox before he was appointed to the bench and had always had a cordial relationship with him, it was my job to present him with The Letter on Monday morning.

On the morning of March 4, Cox was still adamant. "I have ruled on it and I am not going to change my ruling at this time," he replied when I raised the issue. I urged him to read The Letter, pointing out that we were asking for an appealable order if he remained unconvinced we were correct. "Well, I'm going to recess until two o'clock this afternoon," the judge responded. "I'll defer the requirement to deliver the Jencks Act material until then, but I see no reason to delay the trial, and I see no reason not to turn over the Jencks Act material. We'll begin jury selection at two o'clock."

Judge Cox reentered the courtroom at 2:30, and seated himself at the bench, looking grim. We held our breath, not knowing whether we would be selecting a jury or preparing an appeal.

"The court is going to have to reverse its position on the question of the Jencks Act material . . ." he began.

We had won. The trial of *The United States of America vs. George B. Parr* was about to begin.

Chapter 17

Trials

*Justice is a machine that, when someone has once given it the
starting push, rolls on of itself.*

— John Galsworthy

The United States of America vs. George B. Parr
March 4, 1974 — United States Courthouse, Corpus Christi

AN OVERSIZED PANEL OF sixty-six prospective jurors filled
Judge Owen Cox's courtroom at 2:00 P.M., jury summonses in hand.
The size of the panel reflected the judge's awareness that in the
counties comprising the Corpus Christi division of the Southern
District of Texas, many prospective jurors would know George Parr
personally or by reputation, and many would have preconceived no-
tions of his guilt or innocence no matter what he was charged with.

As most federal judges do, Judge Cox conducted the *voir dire*
examination of the jury panel, drawing to a limited extent from written questions the prosecution and the defense had separately requested the judge to ask. The judge's announcement that the jury
would be sequestered during the trial drew some frowns from the
panel. By late afternoon a jury of twelve, and two alternates, had
been selected. Judge Cox recessed until 2:00 the next afternoon. The
U.S. marshal transported the jury to their temporary home, the
Holiday Inn Shoreline, on Ocean Drive just south of Corpus Christi's business district.

The trial began slowly, as trials often do. When Ed McDonough called Carl Stautz to the witness stand late Wednesday afternoon, though, the tension level rose at both counsel tables. We
couldn't be sure Stautz would remember his own name when he sat

down in the witness chair and saw his nemesis, the Duke, facing him a few feet away. We were apprehensive that Stautz might either collapse or erupt under hostile cross-examination; he was an emotional, frightened, unpredictable witness. The defense team had read all of Stautz's grand jury testimony. They were worried about the effect of his melodramatic tales of threats, and of cash bribes delivered in grocery sacks on the courthouse steps, and they were determined to discredit him with their cross-examination. Because of the lateness of the hour, we wouldn't get into the real substance of Stautz's testimony until the following day.

Stautz was back on the stand Thursday morning to tell the jury about his big payoffs to "Papacito," glancing nervously in George's direction every few seconds as he did so. Parr sat calmly, hands folded, his face expressionless. After admitting he had at first lied to the San Antonio grand jury, Stautz was allowed to explain that he lied because he was threatened and feared for his life. Judge Cox limited Stautz's testimony about the details of the threats and cautioned the jury to consider that testimony only for the purpose of evaluating Stautz's own credibility. Stautz spent all day Thursday and most of Friday on the stand. Tinker hammered away at him on cross-examination, but Stautz stuck to his story. The IRS agents assigned to watch over him when he wasn't in court or meeting with McDonough, Kelt, and me were suffering from acute overexposure to their irascible ward by the time he was finally released.

One evening during that first weekend, we watched on television a fictionalized version of the near-calamitous *Apollo 13* moon flight. The name assigned to the ground control crew striving to save the astronauts in the drama was "Tiger Team." Before the evening was over, we had adopted the name for ourselves. It was frivolous, perhaps, but indicative of the *esprit de corps* we had developed.

The pace of the trial accelerated in the second week as we began presenting the evidence that was at the heart of the government's case. The jury saw and heard the same witnesses who had testified before the grand jury about such things as Harris Fender's $40,000 payment for nonexistent bonds, and all the water district funds used for brush killer, helicopter services, fertilizer, irrigation equipment, the purchase of the Atlee Parr note, and assorted other illicit expenditures for George Parr's benefit. Leo Sepulveda's testimony provided one mild surprise: Parr's salary as the water district's legal adviser had risen to $5,000 a month.

In a little more than two weeks of trial we introduced nearly 300 exhibits through the testimony of twenty-five witnesses, giving the jury in condensed form the whole panoply of incriminating evidence developed before the San Antonio grand jury between May and November of 1972. When our summary witness, Jerry Culver, concluded his testimony on Saturday afternoon, March 16, 1974, McDonough announced that the government would rest.

On Monday morning the defense rested without calling any witnesses. After lunch the attorneys met with Judge Cox to go over the instructions the court would give to the jury.

On Tuesday, March 19, 1974, we made final arguments to the jury. I led off for the government with a forty-five-minute summation, taking the jurors back over two weeks of testimony to remind them what we had proved. James Dula had summed up the case in just four words, I told the jury in concluding, when he explained why George's wish was everyone's command: "George was the boss," Dula had said. Ed McDonough made a stemwinding closing argument for conviction after Doug Tinker and his partner, Richard Bradshaw, argued the case for George.

Only two hours and forty minutes after they retired to deliberate, the jury returned. A quick verdict is usually bad news for the defendant. They didn't look at George as they filed into the jury box, another bad sign for him. George stood, listening impassively as the verdict was announced: guilty on all eight counts.

A dozen or so of George's loyal supporters were in the courtroom to hear the verdict. Some didn't take it well; George consoled them, telling them not to worry.

Judge Cox excused the jury and announced that the defendant would be allowed to remain at liberty on his bond pending sentencing. Tinker and his colleagues congratulated us quietly with handshakes and began gathering up their files and briefcases. We retreated to the privacy of the U.S. attorney's office, closed the door, and exploded with pent-up jubilation.

That night the Tiger Team made a pilgrimage to a favorite watering hole, the Mai Tai, a Polynesian restaurant on a North Beach pier jutting into Corpus Christi Bay. We were too tired to be rowdy, but not too tired to release weeks of tension and celebrate a hard-won victory that was two years in the making and sixty years overdue.

The United States of America vs. Archer Parr
April 23, 1974 — U.S. Courthouse, San Antonio, Texas

Barely a month after the jury verdict in Corpus Christi, Bill Sessions and I were about to begin Archer Parr's perjury trial before Judge D. W. Suttle, in San Antonio. The feisty ex-Marine was optimistic about his chances of acquittal. George tried to disabuse him of that notion. "Your last name is Parr," he told Archer. "That's enough. They'll get you too."

Archer was represented by Jimmy Gillespie, an able San Antonio defense attorney with plenty of experience in federal court. I would take the lead in this case, and Sessions would sit in the second chair. It was comforting to have I. A. Filer on board as our case agent and Ed Watts to assist.

A jury was empaneled on Tuesday, April 23, and instructed to report back to begin the trial at 9:30 A.M. on Monday, April 29. Sessions, Filer, Watts, and I had begun preparing for the battle a couple of weeks earlier. This trial, we knew, would be vastly different from the one in Corpus Christi. This one would be a credibility contest, Archer versus the directors of the water district, and if our case went well the defendant would take the stand to testify in his own behalf. When we planned our division of labor in the case, Sessions made it clear that he wanted the privilege of cross-examining Archer.

George's trial had moved slowly at first; Archer's alternated for days between lurching forward and grinding to a halt. After counsel for both sides made opening statements to the jury, most of Monday was spent wrangling over the form in which the transcript of Archer's grand jury testimony would be admitted into evidence. Another delay occurred when the substitute interpreter pressed into emergency service for D. C. Chapa's testimony proved inadequate to the task. Chapa's half-day of testimony on Tuesday was stricken from the record. Offical court interpreter Louis Marquez was called in the following day for a fresh start with the same witness.

On Friday, just as I concluded my cross-examination of defense witness Harris Fender, Jimmy Gillespie rose to his feet and requested a bench conference. As we stood before Judge Suttle, Gillespie said weakly, "Your honor, I don't feel so good," and began to fold at the knees. Sessions and I caught him and eased him to the floor. The judge hustled the jury out of the courtroom while we moved Gillespie to a place where he could lie down more comfortably to await emergency medical help. After receiving a preliminary report that Gillespie's condition was not life-threatening, Judge Suttle recessed the trial until the following Tuesday.

As anticipated, Archer testified. "It's something I've wanted to do since this thing began, baby," he told reporters outside the courtroom before taking the stand. Archer adopted the philosophy that the best defense is a good offense, telling the jury that the $121,500 he received from the water district was only part of the fee that was owed him. He had made an agreement with Jose Tovar, he said, to create the water district for a fee of $150,000. The payments he had received were merely installments on the larger sum, Archer insisted; the water district still owed him $29,500. Conveniently for Archer, the late Mr. Tovar was in no position to take issue with the story. The surviving directors of the water district, however, repeated the testimony they had given before the grand jury: They knew of nothing Archer had done to earn $121,500, much less $150,000.

The second major thrust of Archer's defense was to paint the government's case as a Republican political vendetta against loyal Democrats. Gillespie, playing straight man, asked Archer's sister, Mary Elizabeth Ellis, if she had been questioned at the water district office by IRS Agent Ed Watts in 1972.

"Yes, I was," she said.

"Did you ask him who ordered this investigation?"

"Yes, I did."

"What did he say?"

Mary Elizabeth Ellis fixed the jury with a steady gaze. "By executive order of the president of the United States," she said dramatically.

Ed Watts had been present for the first week of the trial, and we hadn't expected it to last beyond that week. But Watts was needed as a witness in another trial the second week, and when Archer's sister testified, Watts was on the witness stand in Brownsville. I. A. Filer got him on the phone when court adjourned that day. "I don't care what you thought you were going to do tonight," Filer told him. "We've got to have you here as a rebuttal witness at nine o'clock tomorrow morning."

Watts returned to San Antonio that night by the only public transportation he could book — a bus — arriving with the sunrise, stiff and bleary-eyed, to refute Mary Elizabeth Ellis' testimony.

Mary Elizabeth's story had become even more surrealistic on cross-examination. Government agencies were watching her, she indicated; an FBI agent had called on her recently and advised her of her rights. She suspected she was under surveillance by government agents at the state Democratic convention in San Antonio, in 1972, she said. I asked why. There were "just too many coincidences" that made her feel she was being watched, she responded. "There are just oodles and oodles of government agencies we don't know anything about."

Gillespie closed out Archer's defense on a blatantly political theme with a parade of character witnesses brought in to testify that Archer had a good reputation for truth and veracity in his home community. The high-profile Democrats in the lineup included Frank Erwin, the Austin lawyer who was chairman of the University of Texas Board of Regents, counselor to high-level Democratic politicians, and a political power broker with few peers; retired Texas Supreme Court Justice Robert Hamilton, a distinguished former judge who admitted that he had always been supported by the Parrs and had always run well in Duval County; and Texas Agriculture Commissioner John C. White, later chairman of the Democratic National Committee, who opined that Archer had a good reputation for truth and veracity "in the political community in which he lives, breathes, and operates."

None of those three had any firsthand knowledge of Archer's reputation for truthfulness in his home community, and we could have excluded their testimony by objecting on that ground. But rather than risk having the jury think we were afraid of what they might say, Sessions and I elected to allow them to testify and then let me turn them to our advantage through carefully targeted cross-examination. Exposing their political indebtedness to the Parrs and their personal unfamiliarity with Duval County discredited their favorable opinions of Archer's reputation and showed the jury that Archer had the political clout to call on powerful friends for important favors.

Best of all, our tactic allowed me to require Judge Hamilton to explain the duties of the county judge and the importance of integrity in the person who holds that office. Because of the county judge's role as ethical watchdog over executors, guardians, and the county's finances, Judge Hamilton agreed, sterling character was essential for the holder of that office. The evidence the jury had heard previously, of secret account withdrawals for fictitious legal services and Archer's willingness to lie about them, stood out in stark, negative contrast to the high standard of honesty prescribed by his own witness.

Archer's other character witnesses included representatives of two major oil companies that had long been given preferential property tax treatment on their holdings in Duval County, which made them easy to skewer on cross-examination. A prosecutor probably shouldn't be allowed to have so much fun on cross-examination in one day, I thought; that much professional enjoyment should be spread out and savored a little at a time.

On May 9, 1974, the jury heard final arguments. Sessions led off, meticulously summing up the government's evidence, and then it was Jimmy Gillespie's turn. "This is a nit-picking prosecution," Gillespie roared, launching his Watergate argument. "This is an attempt at political assassination of a prominent Democrat in Texas to detract from the horror and corruption we have in Washington."

I made the closing argument for the government. "Watergate is 2,000 miles from here," I began. "This case is about Archie Parr's lies to the grand jury." A juror winked at me.

An hour and a half after the jury began its deliberations, Archer bantered with friends, supporters, and reporters in the corridor outside the courtroom, entertaining them with a chorus of "Please Release Me." A few minutes later, the jury returned with a verdict of guilty on all six counts.

Judge Suttle immediately raised Archer's bail. Until that moment Archer had been free on a $5,000 personal recognizance bond. His bail would now be $121,500, Suttle announced — in cash. It was the first indication, but a powerful one, of how Suttle perceived Archer after listening to the evidence. As Gillespie watched helplessly, Archer was remanded to the custody of the U.S. marshal and whisked away in handcuffs to spend the night in jail.

Maintaining our decorum until we could make our way out of the courtroom, across the elevator lobby, and into a closed stairwell was almost more than any of us could manage. Once inside, Ed Watts tackled me with a shout of exultation, and we all went whooping and stumbling down the stairs from the fifth floor to the third, and into the back entrance to our offices. Emerging a few minutes later to face reporters, Sessions said only, "We're obviously pleased with the verdict, but I think it would be inappropriate to say anything further."

Clinton Manges arrived the next day with a cashier's check for $121,500 to set Archer free pending sentencing. "I've slept in worse foxholes than that," Archer told a group of supporters who greeted him outside the Bexar County jail on his release from custody.

On May 20 Judge Suttle lowered the boom on the convicted county judge. Archer would serve two consecutive five-year sentences on the first two counts of the indictment, Suttle ordered, with five-year sentences on each of the other four counts to run concurrently with the second count. He would also pay the maximum fine of $10,000 on each of the six counts, plus $3,810 to cover the government's costs for the trial. He would be allowed to remain at liberty on his bail pending appeal, but only after depositing the amount of the fine and costs with the clerk of the court. Finally, the judge recommended that Archer serve his time in the Federal Correctional Institution at Leavenworth, Kansas — reputedly one of the toughest correctional institutions in the federal system.

A shocked Clinton Manges coughed up the additional $63,810 to set Archer free. "I never heard of a judge doing anything like that before," Manges told reporters after increasing his total cash investment in Archer's temporary freedom to nearly $185,000. Asked why he anted up the additional money, Manges replied, "Because I thought he was being deprived of his civil rights."

By the late spring of 1974, the half-century-old alliance between the Parrs and the Carrillos was turning into a bitter war for control of the county. Symptomatic of the feud was George's endorsement of John Traeger of Seguin over Oscar Carrillo for the Democratic Party's nomination for state senator. Oscar was publicly furious at George, but to no avail. Without Duval County's traditional bloc vote in his column, Oscar had no chance of winning the primary.

While awaiting trial in his perjury case that same spring, Octavio Saenz was opposed in his race for another term as mayor of Benavides. When Saenz and his opponent deadlocked at 350 votes each — an almost unimaginable result in Duval County — a recount committee looked at the ballots a second time and declared that Saenz had won by forty votes. The committee consisted of George Parr, Barney Goldthorn, and Duval County Sheriff Raul Serna.

The United States of America vs. Octavio Saenz
August 26, 1974 — United States Courthouse,
San Antonio, Texas

On August 26, 1974, Bill Sessions and I commenced the perjury trial of Octavio Saenz, the mayor of Benavides, teaming up just as we had done in trying Archer Parr and dividing responsibility for the witnesses. Sessions, we agreed, would cross-examine Saenz. The principal players in the drama were all familiar: Jimmy Gillespie was the mayor's lawyer, Charlie Volz was our case agent, and the presiding judge was D. W. Suttle. Banker Karl Williams was a key witness again, testifying this time about the draft drawn by Stewart & Stevenson on the water district and mysteriously paid from the City of Benavides Special Sinking Fund, and the $5,000 draft drawn by Octavio Saenz for himself a few days later.

Saenz stuck to his story. He didn't know how much money, if any, had been returned to the city from the Mercantile Bank in Dallas, but the City Council had authorized him to pay $5,000 to himself for his many years of service as mayor. Unfortunately for Saenz, an officer of the Dallas bank produced the mayor's letter requesting the return of the surplus funds and a copy of his own response to Saenz reflecting the precise amount of money transferred to the First State Bank of San Diego. The council members reiterated their testimony before the grand jury. All denied giving Saenz authority to pay himself anything except the traditional $50 Christmas bonus they gave themselves each year.

The trial proceeded quickly, without incident. Saenz, testifying in his own behalf, was the only witness called by the defense. Early on Wednesday afternoon, August 28, after hearing final arguments from Sessions, Gillespie, and me, the jury retired to deliberate. The jaunty mayor kept smiling, though we thought he had little cause to feel good about the case. We were disappointed when the jury deliberated until early evening on Wednesday and recessed without reaching a decision. By noon the next day we were beginning to feel a bit apprehensive, wondering if Saenz might be smiling because he knew something we didn't know. Shortly after lunch the jury dispelled our concern by returning guilty verdicts on both counts. Judge Suttle doubled Saenz's bail to $10,000 cash pending sentencing, and the U.S. marshal led him away. After Archer Parr's experience, though, Gillespie and his client had anticipated what might happen; before the afternoon was out, Saenz had posted bail and was temporarily free again.

A week later Saenz stood before Judge Suttle again and heard himself sentenced to serve five years in prison. Suttle also ordered Saenz to pay a $10,000 fine and $2,404.18 in costs of prosecution before he could be released on bail pending appeal.

George Parr's sentencing drew a crowd of reporters and wire service correspondents, a delegation of his most loyal friends and supporters, and a few of the merely curious. Offered a chance to address the court, Parr declined. "I have nothing to say, sir," he responded to Judge Owen Cox's invitation.

Not available to either the defense or the prosecution under the federal rules in 1974 was the presentence investigation report prepared by U.S. Probation Officer Calvin H. Bowden for the eyes of Judge Cox alone. It was twenty-eight single-spaced pages in length and dealt with virtually every aspect of Parr's life. Bowden appended a sort of bibliography of his sources of information, which included public records; interviews with Parr himself and with friends, adversaries, reporters, and public officials from Duval and other South Texas counties; newspaper and magazine articles from the 1950s; and the presentence investigation report prepared by another federal probation officer in 1957, after Parr's mail fraud conviction.

Bowden's report detailed Parr's entire criminal history, beginning with the 1934 income tax evasion conviction for which he served less than a year in prison, and continuing through incidents of gunshots and threats in 1973 and 1974 that were considered but not acted on by local prosecutors and the Duval County grand jury.

Bowden's interview of Parr revealed a little-known marriage that Parr entered into between his two marriages to Thelma Duckworth of Corpus Christi. Shortly after his first marriage to Thelma ended in divorce in 1933, Parr married Sandy Moss Williams of Beaumont, he told Bowden. District court records reflect the termination of that marriage by divorce on October 2, 1934, in Duval County. Before 1934 ended, Parr had remarried Thelma Duckworth in Houston. That marriage also ended in divorce fifteen years later.

Bowden's report stated that Parr "started living with another woman, Maria Luz Garcia, age 39 at the time, in 1954." Shortly thereafter, Bowden reported, Parr "began dating Evangelina Perez, his present wife, when she was thirteen years of age, as well as her sister, who was somewhat older." According to Bowden's report, which cites the volume and page of a public record in Mexico, Parr married Evangelina (Eva) Perez in Nuevo Laredo on December 10, 1955, after her father attempted to file charges against him for contributing to the delinquency of a minor. Parr's lifelong interest, Bowden commented, had been politics. "His other prime interests are his wife, of whom he is very jealous, and his daughter," he added.

The probation officer noted Parr's apparent obsession with the notion that other men liked to look at his wife. Bowden was told by unnamed local residents that in April 1973, Parr shot at a roofer working on top of a house across from his home, accusing the man of looking at his wife. "Threatening to shoot others who have looked at his wife is not a new thing with Mr. Parr," Bowden wrote. "There have been quite a few incidents where threats were made with a weapon against people he accused of looking at his wife." Parr told Bowden that he did not smoke, drink, or use drugs. "My only vice is chasing women," he told the probation officer. Parr told San Antonio lawyer Anthony Nicholas in 1974, "If I ever get to the point where I don't enjoy a woman, I won't want to live any longer."

"To Mr. Parr," Bowden wrote, "politics is a game he has played day in and day out for many years, the final outcome of which would favor those who were helpful and loyal to him. He was, in turn, very loyal to his friends and supporters, but ruthless in his dealings with the opposition. His friends portray him as a stalwart knight in white armor, but to those who oppose him, he is a ruthless, vindictive, greedy individual who will use every means at his disposal to win the game."

Although the Duke declined to speak for himself, perhaps feeling that nothing he could say would help his cause, several friends stepped forward to urge leniency for him. Father Antonio Arguelles told Judge Cox that George never refused a request to help the poor. "In my opinon," the priest said, "he has a very compassionate feeling for the poor people." Domingo Pena urged the judge to consider that "this man has done so much good for so many people." Because of George's generosity, Pena said emotionally, "there is not another county in the whole state that has more Mexican-American high school graduates who are going on to college and becoming outstanding citizens." Doug Tinker and Nago Alaniz both spoke in behalf of their client. "I am here not only as his lawyer, but also as his best friend," Alaniz said. "I know some bad things have been said about him, but there are so many, many, many, many things that this court and the government have never heard of that Mr. Parr has done for these people."

Cox's sentence was relatively light: He assessed five years in prison and a $14,000 fine. He also raised Parr's bail to $75,000 cash pending appeal. Clinton Manges, who had previously signed as a surety on George's appearance bond without having to put up any money, now stepped up with the cash. Manges appeared to be signaling a strong political commitment to the Parrs in the face of their weakening hold on the county; after putting up George's bail, Archer's bail, and Archer's fine and costs, Manges had bet more than $260,000 in real money that both Parrs would continue to show up in court whenever they were ordered to do so.

Chapter 18

Finishing Up

Unlimited power is apt to corrupt the minds of those who possess it; and this I know, my lords, that where laws end, tyranny begins.
— William Pitt

AFTER THE TRIALS OF George Parr, Archer Parr, and Octavio Saenz, we were ready to turn our attention once again to the unfinished business of suspected tax evasion by other Duval County figures. O. P. and Ramiro Carrillo and their cousin, Arturo Zertuche, were the immediate targets, but common sense and the evidence already developed told us that graft in Duval County was so widespread, so entrenched, that we must have identified only a few of its many perpetrators.

In the meantime we had learned that the county auditor, Walter Meek, could shed some light on the late Jody Martin Parr's allegation that the treasurer's assistant, Sylvester Gonzalez, delivered thousands of dollars in cash to Archer each month.

"I'm like the piano player in a whorehouse," Meek told a government agent in the early days of the investigation. "I know illegal activities occur in my employer's establishment, but not in my presence, so I can say truthfully that I have no personal knowledge of criminal wrongdoing." But in late July 1973, four months before the *Corpus Christi Caller* published Joe Coudert's copyrighted story detailing his discovery that Gonzalez had endorsed some $16,000 in county checks in a single month, Meek had made a similar discovery of his own and had seized the evidence.

What Meek stumbled upon in the summer of 1973 was the key to the Parr organization's method for stealing thousands of dollars from the Duval County treasury each month. Having found direct, irrefutable knowledge of wrongdoing, Walter Meek gave the evidence to an attorney friend for safekeeping until Meek felt the time was right to come forward and tell us about it.

On July 19, 1974, between trials, Bill Sessions and I were in Corpus Christi with George Kelt to develop Meek's story before the grand jury. Meek reminded us that Gonzalez was close to George and Archer Parr and that, as the Parrs' man, Gonzalez had the real power in the treasurer's office. Meek's testimony before the grand jury in San Antonio in March 1973 had indicated that the county's procedures for paying claims were so lacking in proper accounting controls that Gonzalez could, if he wished, cause the issuance of virtually any check merely by preparing a claim and inserting it in a stack of bills already approved and awaiting payment.

His discovery of evidence implicating Gonzalez occurred late one afternoon in July 1973, Meek said. He had spent the day in Corpus Christi and returned to the courthouse after 5:00 P.M. to sign some checks he expected his assistant, Octavio Hinojosa, to leave on his desk. "The checks I found weren't what I expected," Meek said. "They looked like some kind of payroll, and we had already finished the payroll. It wasn't unusual to get a late payroll, though, so I went ahead and signed them, but the amounts of some of the checks were unusual."

The next day Meek's assistant told him the checks were for a special payroll that Sylvester Gonzalez had brought in. "And then it suddenly occurred to me," Meek told the grand jury, "that the county judge's wife had accused him recently, in the divorce case, of receiving a certain amount of cash each month from Sylvester Gonzalez." Meek said he had been amused by Jody's allegation at the time. "We don't handle cash at all," he explained. "I laughed and said, 'Where would he get cash?'" The special payroll triggered his recollection of Jody's allegations and made him suspicious, Meek said. He went immediately to the First State Bank and asked head teller Romeo Salinas if anyone had turned in a bundle of checks to be cashed.

"He nodded his head and didn't say anything, but he started writing on a piece of paper," Meek testified. "When I said 'How many checks?' he turned around, and he had written a figure on the paper from memory. It was $12,800."

The teller retrieved the freshly cashed checks from the book-keeping department and turned them over to Meek. "I asked him if it had ever happened before, and he nodded his head again," Meek said. "And of course they were all endorsed by Sylvester." Meek commandeered the bundle of checks, took them back to his office, and conducted a limited investigation of his own. He didn't recognize the names of any of the payees, all of whom supposedly were county employees. He showed the special payroll to the county tax assessor and to an ex-sheriff, both of whom he trusted and both of whom knew, or knew of, most of the county's employees; neither man recognized the names on the list. Meek adopted procedures to "fence off" Sylvester Gonzalez from opportunities to continue the scheme, but he did not approach the commissioners or the county judge. He had assumed they wouldn't give him a straight answer about the Zertuche General Store, I recalled, and doubtless he made the same assumption about Sylvester's special payroll. In 1974 Meek gave us the opportunity to subpoena him and the checks.

I handed the checks to Meek as he sat before the grand jury. Sylvester Gonzalez's name was subscribed as a second endorsement on each one, below the endorsement of the payee's name.

"Do you recognize Sylvester Gonzalez's endorsement?" I asked.

"I'm not a handwriting expert, but I think all of those are his. After I knew he cashed the checks, I knew they were his endorsement, no question about it. The first endorsements, I think, might be made by half a dozen different people, spread out just to get different handwriting."

"Do you have any idea who those people are?"

"No, but it could be any clerk, or group of clerks, in the courthouse; I just assume that, on the assumption those payees are fictitious names."

Romeo Salinas, the First State Bank's assistant cashier and head teller, retreated behind a standard answer when pressed about cashing bundles of county checks each month, all in numerical order and all bearing the second endorsement of Sylvester Gonzalez. The only thing that interested him, Salinas insisted, was the second endorsement. If the checks were signed by county officials, he didn't care about the first endorsement; he relied exclusively on Sylvester's second endorsement.

Sylvester cashed Duval County payroll checks at his teller window after each payroll period, Salinas said.

"Sometimes a fair-sized stack of checks, is that right?" I asked.

"Right."

"Do you remember that you have cashed checks amounting to as much as $15,000 at one time for Mr. Gonzalez?"

"Oh, yes."

"That's not uncommon, is it?"

"No, sir."

"In fact, it happens at least once a month, doesn't it?"

"Yes, sir."

Gonzalez would bring in a stack of checks and endorse them at a table in the lobby, Salinas said, and then present them at the teller window with his own adding machine tape. Salinas would run a tape, too, before paying out the cash. There was no conversation between them.

"When he comes in with a number of checks, do you count out the cash for each individual check?"

"No, I total the whole amount."

Gonzalez always wanted the money in $100 bills, Salinas said.

"Well, if he's cashing checks for other persons, and he receives the total amount in hundred-dollar bills, how is he going to divide it for people who are going to get lesser amounts from him?"

"I don't know. I just went by the last endorsement."

Sylvester Gonzalez was a personal friend, Salinas said; he had known him for about forty-five years. Gonzalez's check cashing was obviously as much of a routine for Salinas as it was for his old friend. "He had done it for so many years," the teller said.

"Did he ever tell you why he brought in large numbers of checks to cash?"

"He never did, no, sir."

"Did you ever ask him why?"

"No, sir," Salinas responded. "If they are signed by the officers of the county and endorsed by him, I wouldn't want to ask him that." Salinas' lack of curiosity about this patently fraudulent cash outflow mirrored Barney Goldthorn's indifference to the huge cash withdrawals from the water district accounts.

Under further questioning Salinas revealed that Gonzalez told him each month, a day or two in advance, how much cash he would need. "He would call or drop by the bank and say he was coming over and bringing the checks, and say, 'I need this much money,'" Salinas explained. Sometimes the amount was so large Salinas would have to ask the San Diego bank's vice-president, Fletcher Brown, to order additional cash from their correspondent bank in Alice.

Salinas denied Gonzalez ever gave him anything for his role in the scheme. He denied, also, that any other bank customer followed a similar practice. To all questions about his mindless payout of as much as $15,000 in cash each month under such blatantly irregular circumstances, closing his eyes to the true nature of the transaction, Salinas' answer was the same: He simply relied on the second endorsement of the man he knew, Sylvester Gonzalez.

"Did other people in the bank know Sylvester Gonzalez was cashing thousands of dollars in checks every month?" George Kelt inquired.

"I think the whole bank knew about it."

"Did you ever have any conversation with any other bank officer about these checks being cashed?"

"They knew I was cashing them."

"How did they know?"

"My cash would go up and down, and I would have to go for more."

Manuel Solis, the county treasurer, confirmed indirectly for our investigators that Sylvester Gonzalez's loyalty was to a higher power. Hiring Sylvester as an assistant wasn't his own idea, Solis said; George Parr told him to do it.

More water would flow under the bridge before the whole story was known, but in 1977 Sylvester Gonzalez gave details of his central role in the extensive scheme designed by George Parr for systematically looting public treasuries in Duval County. In a presentencing report filed in State District Judge Darrell Hester's court, Gonzalez told all in hopes of obtaining a light sentence on his guilty plea to a state charge of felony theft.

Gonzalez described himself in the presentence report as the Duke's "bagman." It was his job to manufacture false claims and get checks issued in payment, Gonzalez said, and then to cash the checks at the First State Bank and deliver the money according to George's orders.

"I was the quarterback receiving the plays from the coach (George Parr)," Gonzalez told the probation officer. "My job was to hand off (the money) to the fullback (Archer Parr) and the halfback (Dan Tobin)." Gonzalez described Barney Goldthorn as "a scout" for the team: "He would place a certain amount of Water District funds in secret accounts and the coach would send me notes (the plays) — give so-and-so, so much."

Gonzalez's version of his relationship with Romeo Salinas differed somewhat from the teller's account. "The matter was of such a routine nature that (the cashier) would call ahead of time asking me how much money I would need that month. I would just walk up to the cashier's window in plain sight of everybody and get the falsified checks cashed. I would give (the cashier) $100 for his help, as he has an ailing wife that needs treatment for cancer every month."

By the time Walter Meek and Romeo Salinas testified before the grand jury in July 1974, Duval County was in an alarming state of political disintegration. Through the latter half of the year George Kelt continued the investigation of the Carrillos from Corpus Christi with the backing of Ed McDonough and the help of Jerry Culver, Charlie Volz, and the federal grand jury. In San Diego, Benavides, and Freer, there was speculation that the enigmatic, reputedly wealthy Clinton Manges intended to exploit the increasingly acrimonious Parr-Carrillo split to gain control of the county for himself. George Parr ridiculed the idea.

"He can't any more take over this county than I can take wings and fly to heaven," George said in early 1975.

Walter Meek concurred, dismissing the Freer mystery man as irrelevant despite his wealth. "Clinton Manges is an outsider who can't even speak Spanish," Meek scoffed.

In December 1974, Bill Sessions was appointed by President Gerald Ford to be a United States district judge for the Western District of Texas, on the recommendation of Senator John Tower. At the same time, Tower advised me that he was sending my name to the president for appointment as United States attorney to succeed Sessions.

School Superintendents Bryan Taylor and Eunice Powell threw in the towel in early 1975, each pleading guilty in January to one count of tax evasion. Both drew short prison terms from Judge Cox the following month; Taylor was assessed two years, Powell one.

In early March, the Court of Appeals for the Fifth Circuit heard oral arguments in New Orleans on Archer Parr's appeal. I stayed up all night preparing for my appearance before the three-judge panel. I was determined to have a ready answer for any question the court might ask, any issue Archer's attorney might raise. The argument went well. Afterward, I left the federal courthouse on Camp Street feeling confident the court would affirm his conviction.

On March 28, the Corpus Christi grand jury returned a sealed indictment charging O. P. Carrillo, Ramiro Carrillo, and Arturo Zertuche with filing false tax returns and conspiring to obstruct the collection of income taxes based on the Zertuche General Store scam. On April 10, nine days after George Parr's suicide at Los Horcones, the two Carrillos and Zertuche were arraigned and released on cash bonds. Asked by Judge Cox to comment on a prospective trial schedule, George Kelt didn't hesitate. "The government can be ready for trial in two weeks, your honor," he replied.

O. P. Carrillo quickly found himself engaged in a two-front legal war when an impeachment resolution was introduced in the Texas House of Representatives by Parr loyalist Terry Canales of Premont, to remove Carrillo from the 229th District Court bench. On May 20, Cleofas Gonzalez was under oath again, this time describing the operations of the ethereal Zertuche General Store to the state legislature. By the end of the month, Judge Cox had ordered the two Carrillo brothers to stand trial before him on June 30. Arturo Zertuche, the judge ruled, would be tried separately, after his two cousins.

Texas Attorney General John Hill, Crawford Martin's successor in that office, was eager for his chance, too, to play a role in cleaning up Duval County. Hill had waited with commendable patience through all of 1973, while federal grand juries heard a parade of witnesses and reporters pieced together tantalizing bits of information to describe the likely goals of our federal investigation. Hill knew we were uncovering violations of state law as well as federal, but he understood that federal rules precluded us from disclosing what the grand jury and its agents were developing. Sessions and I had assured him we would seek permission to turn over as much information as possible when our prosecutions were completed.

Hill finally got his foot in the county's door when Governor Dolph Briscoe appointed Arnulfo Guerra of Roma to serve as district attorney for the 229th Judicial District, after the resignation of Randall Nye. Guerra's invitation allowed the state's attorney general to send a task force of lawyers, accountants, and Texas Rangers to conduct the thorough investigation the county had needed desperately for decades. When we were able at last, with permission of the federal courts, to turn over to Hill the testimony and evidence developed by our federal grand juries, Hill's staff had enough information about state law violations to cut a broad swath through Duval County officialdom.

In early 1975, Hill announced the opening of a staffed office in San Diego, dedicated to looking under every rock in the county to ferret out corruption. The principal investigative thrust was provided by John Blanton and Otis Klar, both assistant attorneys general, and Ray Bravenec, an accountant for the Texas Department of Public Safety. Hill's team also included supervisory assistant Tim James and Texas Rangers Gene Powell, Ray Martinez, and Rudy Rodriguez, as well as other attorneys and law enforcement officers who shuttled in and out to assist. Martinez was the gutty lawman who, while on the Austin police force, stormed the University of Texas Tower a few years earlier to end sniper Charles Whitman's deadly day of terror.

Within months the state had obtained indictments against Barney Goldthorn, D. C. Chapa, County Judge Dan Tobin (appointed to succeed Archer Parr after Archer's removal from office), Oscar, O. P., and Ramiro Carrillo, Arturo Zertuche, County Treasurer Manuel Solis, Rodolfo Couling, Sylvester Gonzalez, and a host of lesser players, in addition to Archer Parr, Bryan Taylor, and Eunice Powell. The list kept growing, Blanton explained, because "every time we found something in the records that looked funny, we found five or six more people stealing." The county was in a state of political shock.

Judge Darrell Hester, who presided over the trials and guilty pleas of those caught up in the state's dragnet, became convinced the county's payroll was heavily burdened with fictitious employees. His solution was to require every county employee to report to him to receive a paycheck. The county's payroll shrank overnight. Hester ultimately chose Gilberto Uresti, an apolitical pharmacist from Benavides, to fill the much-vacated position of county judge after Dan Tobin's fall from grace.

The federal income tax trial of O. P. and Ramiro Carrillo was rescheduled for September 9, 1975. Almost on the eve of that trial Rodolfo Couling, then under indictment by the state, offered to cooperate with state and federal authorities, both of whom could make good use of his testimony in upcoming trials. After signing a plea bargain agreement with the state, Couling gave information that enabled Texas Rangers to recover the Benavides Independent School District records D. C. Chapa had been unable to locate for the San Antonio grand jury in 1972. Acting on Couling's information, the Rangers found more than two hundred pounds of records dating back to 1968 hidden between the ceiling and the roof of the school district office building. To protect Couling, whose cooperation had not been disclosed at that time, the Rangers told reporters they had been tipped off by an anonymous letter.

On September 9, 1975, George Kelt led the government's forces into battle against the Carrillos before Judge Owen Cox. Assistant U.S. Attorney John Smith of Corpus Christi was there to assist, along with IRS Agent Jerry Culver. Lead counsel for the defendants was renowned Houston defense attorney Richard (Racehorse) Haynes, accompanied by Arthur Mitchell of Austin and William Bonilla of Corpus Christi.

The hard-fought trial raged on until shortly before noon on October 2, when the sequestered jury found both men guilty on all counts. Kelt proved his case methodically, with hundreds of exhibits and the testimony of twenty-three witnesses, but the star of the show was Cleofas Gonzalez, the happy-go-lucky county shop employee with the pad of invoices that comprised the entire physical substance of the Zertuche General Store. On September 24, after Cleofas' testimony was reported by the press, a Corpus Christi convention hotel poked fun at the defendants by announcing on its marquee in huge block letters:

"WELCOME
ZERTUCHE GENERAL STORE
MEETING."

Judge Cox probably smiled, too, in the privacy of his chambers, at the humorous side of the brothers' preposterous fraud, but on November 24 he somberly sentenced both men to prison. Judge O. P. Carrillo was assessed five years of incarceration and fines totaling $22,000; Ramiro Carrillo drew four years in prison and $20,000 in fines.

Arturo Zertuche elected to seek a plea bargain with the government rather than go through a similar ordeal with little chance of acquittal. Ed McDonough approved a guilty plea to one count, and Judge Cox imposed five years of supervised probation and a $5,000 fine.

The state's continuing investigation solved another lingering mystery when the state charged George Parr's longtime attorney and friend Nago Alaniz with the July 4, 1972, burglary of the water district and the theft of its records. Bryan Taylor, then under indictment by the state on other charges, testified at Alaniz's trial that he helped Alaniz hide the records on A. E. Garcia's ranch.

"Nago told me it might be beneficial to Mr. Parr to have the records stored," Taylor said. "I would have done anything for Mr. Parr, within reason."

A former county shop employee testified that he burned the records later at Los Horcones, at Parr's instruction, after helping Parr transport the documents from the hiding place to the ranch in a pickup truck.

Alaniz's luck held, though, as it had twenty years earlier when he was tried as an accomplice to the murder of Buddy Floyd, and acquitted. Despite Taylor's testimony and that of an eyewitness who saw Nago carrying boxes out of the water district building in the dead of night, the jury found him not guilty.

When the Fifth Circuit affirmed Archer Parr's perjury conviction on July 24, 1975, we moved immediately to take Archer into custody and prevent any unfortunate occurrences. Minutes after the court clerk advised us by telephone that morning that the conviction was affirmed, I presented to Judge D. W. Suttle a motion to revoke Archer's bail pending any further appeal. Judge Suttle read the motion, signed an order directing Archer to show cause why his bail should not be revoked, and issued a bench warrant for Archer's arrest. Quick work by the U.S. marshal and the Texas Rangers did the rest. A few hours after I received the telephone call from the Fifth Circuit, a surprised Archer Parr was arrested by the Rangers at his home and turned over to the marshal.

Judge Suttle scheduled the bail question for a hearing on July 28, in San Antonio. Archer's attorney, Jimmy Gillespie, requested a delay, necessitating a rescheduled hearing in Midland, where Suttle had other trial commitments. Clinton Manges, no longer Archer's ally and eager to get his money back, sought to be released from his obligation as Archer's bondsman. The show-cause order and Manges' motion were scheduled for August 7 in Midland's new federal courthouse.

We had never viewed Archer as potentially suicidal, but we did fear he would flee to Mexico once his conviction was affirmed. In legal memoranda we pointed out to Judge Suttle that three factors were relevant to his decision: the risk that Archer might flee, the probability that he would pose a danger to the community, and the lack of merit in his appeal. Any one of those factors could justify revoking Archer's bail and requiring him to pursue any further appeals from inside a federal penetentiary. The burden of proof was on Archer to show that he should remain at liberty.

The judge began by allowing Clinton Manges to recover the $121,500 he had posted as Archer's bail a year earlier. Manges had to testify in support of his motion, though, which gave me a chance through cross-examination to develop some of the evidence I wanted to put in the record to support the government's argument that Archer should be denied bail. Praxides Canales, the purchaser of a $121,500 cashier's check that was in Archer's possession when he was arrested, urged Judge Suttle to accept the check as a replacement for Manges' money. Suttle denied Canales' motion and commenced the hearing on the primary question whether Archer should remain at liberty while pursuing further appeals.

The danger that Archer would flee was founded on the factors that would make the risks of flight a tempting alternative to the certainty of federal prison: his wealth, the proximity of the Mexican border, his fluency in Spanish, his legal status as a Mexican national under the Constitution of Mexico, the practical impossibility of extraditing a Mexican national from Mexico, and the extreme unlikelihood that further appellate efforts would result in a reversal of his conviction.

Evidence that Archer had the means to sustain himself in nearby Mexico was readily available. The inventory filed by the court-appointed receiver in Archer's divorce case before Jody's death reflected Archer's ownership of land, cattle, furs, and jewelry worth more than $1.5 million. Archer hadn't bought the $121,500 cashier's check in his pocket, but it was apparent he still had affluent friends willing to come to his aid.

Jimmy Gillespie argued that Mexico would consider Archer's wartime service in the U.S. Marine Corps an act of expatriation, terminating his Mexican citizenship rights. Not likely, we replied. The birth records in Mexico City would refer to him as Archer Weller, his pre-adoption name, and the American military knew him as Archer Parr. The Department of Justice provided evidence that the United States had not succeeded in obtaining extradition of any Mexican national from Mexico in this century.

To show that Archer would pose a danger of harm to the community if allowed to remain at liberty, we called on Texas Ranger Gene Powell for details of Archer's continuing misappropriation of public property and public employees for his personal benefit while his federal conviction was on appeal to the Fifth Circuit. Archer had been removed from office as county judge in 1975 on those grounds, but county employees had continued to work on Archer's ranch, Powell testified, and had even been used to build a private horse-racing track on the premises. Powell supplied a stack of affidavits of county employees who worked at Archer's ranch, and copies of their county payroll records to match. One full-time county employee had worked nowhere except at the ranch from 1967 through March 1975.

The Rangers had found part of Duval County's substantial inventory of heavy construction and earth-moving equipment on Archer's ranch, where county employees had used it for years in his farming and ranching operations and to build the racetrack. One piece of county equipment was still on the ranch a few days before the current hearing, Powell said. Walter Meek had once remarked that Duval County had enough heavy equipment to make Brown & Root envious.

The hearing stretched into the second day as we presented the government's case through the testimony of a half-dozen witnesses and nearly fifty exhibits. The Rangers' assistance in gathering the evidence was invaluable. True to form, Judge Suttle didn't rule precipitously. He gave Gillespie five days to submit his views and proposed findings, and the government five days to respond. He would hear oral arguments in Midland on August 20 before announcing his ruling, he told the lawyers.

For more than two hours in the afternoon and early evening of August 20, Gillespie argued his client's case for release on bail pending an attempted appeal to the U.S. Supreme Court. I spoke for twenty minutes in opposition. Gillespie spoke again on Archer's behalf for five minutes, and at 6:45 P.M. it was over except for the judge's ruling.

Throughout the bail hearing and the trial that preceded it, Judge Suttle was a model of judicial patience, courtesy, and fairness, treating every player in the drama with respect, maintaining a poker face, never revealing how he felt toward the attorneys, the witnesses, or the defendant. The first indication of his strong feeling about the case was the cash bond he required of Archer after the jury verdict, in the precise amount Archer had been convicted of lying about. The second indication was the sentence he imposed. By "stacking" two five-year sentences, to be served one after the other, the judge ensured that Archer would spend at least forty months in prison — a very substantial sentence for that offense. Archer contended it was the stiffest sentence ever assessed for perjury by any federal court.

The judge announced his ruling as soon as Gillespie ended his argument. The defendant would be remanded to the custody of the attorney general of the United States. No bail pending further appeal would be allowed. The court would issue written findings in support of the ruling the next day. Archer Parr left the courtroom with a deputy marshal, disappointed but probably not surprised.

The depth of Judge Suttle's revulsion and anger over Archer Parr's conduct was revealed by the written findings published over his signature the following day. The judge's own moral compass was geared to the philosophy that a public office is a public trust. He was profoundly offended that an elected official — especially one who held both a law license and a judicial title — would misappropriate public funds and then lie about it under oath; would use his position to grow rich at the expense of those who entrusted him with the powers of government; and would thumb his nose at the law by continuing to commit the same kinds of offenses after his conviction and removal from office. It was too much.

The judge's formal findings of fact, comprising eight legal pages of text, concluded with a paragraph that crystallized the essence of his cold fury over the evidence he had heard, beginning with Archer's perjury trial in the spring of 1974: "The record in this case tells the story of the power of the Defendant Archer Parr in Duval County; that such power is virtually absolute; that such absolute power has corrupted him absolutely. That the exercise of such power by the Defendant Archer Parr has prostituted the democratic and judicial process in Duval County, and constitutes a threat and danger to law and order, the citizens, the taxpayers, and public and private properties located in Duval County, Texas."

Archer and his fiancée, Syleta Hawn of Alice, had made hurried plans to be married before Archer was shipped off to prison. She arrived at the Midland County jail with a marriage license on August 21, only to learn that the wedding was off; Archer had suddenly been moved to an undisclosed location by the U.S. marshal overnight.

Archer began his incarceration in the federal penetentiary at Leavenworth, Kansas, a tough institution, but served most of it at Marion, Illinois, in what was reputed to be an even tougher institution. After serving his federal sentence he returned to Duval County to face state criminal charges growing out of John Hill's cleanup campaign. State District Judge Darrell Hester accepted the plea bargain between Archer and the state, which called for ten years of probation and no prison time. One of the conditions of probation assessed by Hester, however, was unusual if not unique. Archer was, in effect, exiled; he could not reside in Duval County until he had completed his term of probation.

In December 1988, a free man at last after successfully completing Judge Hester's requirements, Archer announced plans to move back to Duval County and revive the Old Party. "The Old Party still exists," he said. "I just don't see any individual strong enough right now to come in here and pull it all together. It's a shame, because Duval used to have a say in state politics, but nobody pays attention to us anymore."

Epilogue

The death of democracy is not likely to be an assassination from ambush. It will be a slow extinction from apathy, indifference, and undernourishment.

— Robert Maynard Hutchins

HAD CARL STAUTZ'S TAX return not been selected for audit in 1971, there can be no doubt George Parr would have reigned as the second Duke of Duval as long as he chose to do so, barring physical or mental incapacitation. That the chance income tax audit of an Austin contractor would have such profound and unexpected consequences for so many individuals, and for an entire county, can only be described as a quirk of fate.

Who, if anyone, would eventually have succeeded George as Duval County's *patrón grande* had outside forces not intervened? It is an intriguing question, and one that has been debated in South Texas political circles since his demise. Archer Parr was the natural heir to George's power and position, but many observers of the Duval scene were doubtful even before 1972 that Archer could fill George's shoes successfully. George was held in genuine affection by the populace, they point out with considerable justification; Archer, on the other hand, did not inspire such intense personal loyalty because he lacked George's common touch. So while Archer had his hands on the controls of the Parr machine — the Old Party — even before George's death, it is generally accepted that his succession to power would not have been nearly so well received as George's succession to old Senator Archie Parr's power in the mid-1930s.

330

Could the Carrillo family have produced a new Duke? Perhaps, but none of the three brothers who held positions of power in 1972 exhibited the leadership talents or the personal charisma necessary to take over the county. Collectively, they and their aged father, D. C. Chapa, held dominion over certain territory, certain public entities, and certain sources of graft, but they did so as subordinates of the the Duke, and their authority was derived from him. To rule as effectively as George did without a dominant personality as the focal point of public support would have been difficult, and they would have had to turn on Archer Parr and convert the Parr loyalists of the Old Party to their cause.

Despite speculation in some quarters that George Parr had selected Clinton Manges to be his successor, and a belief by some that Manges intended to win control on his own, the paradoxical sometimes-millionaire may have been the least likely man in the county to become its political leader with or without George Parr's help. First of all, Manges never seemed to want to control Duval County. His principal political interest at home was stability, and he was content to be a Parr loyalist until the Parrs began to slip from power. His allegiance seemed to shift thereafter as severe political storms blew the local ship of state first in one direction and then in another, but at no time did he appear to be maneuvering to gain control for himself. Whether he ever aspired to power in Duval County, however, is a moot point. George Parr was right, and so was Walter Meek. Clinton Manges would never have become the new Duke even if he had tried.

Perhaps there would have been no stable, lasting successor to George Parr in the infamous tradition of George and his father even if our investigation had never begun; certainly, it is difficult to identify anyone who could have played that role successfully. But if George's would have been an impossible act to follow, why is that so? How could a man so ruthless as to destroy the small businesses of his political enemies, so petty as to cut off the public water service of a taxpayer who deigned to question the county's tax rate, so corrupt as to treat the public treasury as his own bank account for decades, so dangerous as to shoot at a roofer he thought was looking at his wife from across the street, be so revered by most of the county's population that his wishes were treated as royal edicts?

The answer seems to lie in George Parr's extraordinary ability to relate, person to person, to his subjects. U.S. Probation Officer

Calvin Bowden said of Parr in his presentence investigation report to Judge Owen Cox, "He states that he realizes he is Number One, but he often wonders why people follow his advice, a function he inherited from his father. He states that although he is a 'gringo,' he is not thought of as such, but is thought of as a 'Mexican,' and this is one of the reasons, he believes, why he has been able to develop good will." Bowden also talked to Parr about his reputation for helping the poor in his county. "He states that he has never turned a man away who has come to him and asked for help," Bowden wrote. "He states that if he does not refer him to the county welfare office for assistance, he will give him cash out of his own pocket."

Reactions from local residents immediately after Parr's suicide reflected their affection for the Duke. Typical was Mrs. Eugenio Hinojosa. "He was a wonderful man," she told Spencer Pearson of the *Corpus Christi Caller*. "We went to him many times for money for the hospital. He would help with all his heart and he would never say to pay him back." Mrs. Fela Laurel described Parr's generosity after her husband had a stroke; Parr helped them many times with $10 for medicine, she said, or $25 for groceries. Deputy Sheriff Ramiro Perez, in tears, told Pearson he had been with Parr for thirty years. "We will never forget him. As long as I live and as long as the people of Duval County live, they will never forget him," Perez said. Perez's terminology reveals a common perspective. He hadn't actually been "with Parr" for thirty years as an employee. He probably had been employed by Duval County for thirty years, during most of which time George Parr held no official position; nevertheless, George and the county were one to him, as they were to many residents.

Objective observers discount George's reputation for generosity, pointing out that it's easy to be generous with stolen money, especially when it serves to perpetuate the thief's political machine. Parr's legitimate income in each of the tax years covered by our investigation was negligible in comparison to the huge sums he took illegally from the county and the water district. When George handed out the financial assistance for which he was so widely praised, he was actually returning to local taxpayers a few of the hard-earned tax dollars he had stolen from them in the first place. It should surprise no one that Duval County's tax rates were far higher and its budgets far larger than other Texas counties with several times more population; the overburden of graft that lined the pockets and fattened the bank accounts of the Parrs and their henchmen for so many years was a ruinously expensive habit for the public to finance.

Duval County withdrew into itself on the day of Parr's funeral. Streets were empty. The courthouse and the schools were closed. Flags hung at half staff. Life was temporarily on hold. A rosary in the courtyard of George's palatial home in San Diego the previous evening was attended by some 2,000. ("The subject states that he is of the Episcopalian faith," Probation Officer Calvin Bowden had written in his presentence report to Judge Cox, "but religion does not appear to be a factor in this case.") George's body lay in state at Hilda Parr's big ranch house. A hundred and fifty cars followed the hearse from Los Horcones to the Benavides cemetery for burial services at the family plot.

The Carrillo family, locked in a bitter political struggle with George, kept a low profile for a few days. D. C. Chapa avoided reporters. Oscar Carrillo expressed shock. "My father feels very bad about this," he told *Corpus Christi Caller* reporter Billy Newton. "He and that man were friends for a long, long time."

From his home in Telegraph, Texas, Coke Stevenson declined to say anything about the man who cheated him out of a seat in the United States Senate in 1948. "Everybody would know if I paid him a compliment that I wasn't sincere about it," the plain-spoken former governor told the Associated Press. "I haven't lived that way. I don't believe I ought to make any comment at all."

Ironically, on the day George Parr died, another acknowledged master of the stuffed ballot box, Richard J. Daley, was reelected overwhelmingly to an unprecedented sixth term as mayor of Chicago. And on that same day in Washington, D.C., jury selection began in the bribery trial of an old acquaintance of Parr's, John B. Connally.

Parr's death quickly became the subject of speculation and rumors despite abundant, straightforward evidence that he killed himself. Eva Parr was outspokenly skeptical about the cause of death. There was no autopsy, she said, because no one asked her if she wanted to have one performed. Texas Ranger Gene Powell said Archer Parr opposed an autopsy and the justice of the peace wouldn't order one. Some of the faithful suggested vaguely that George was murdered, but no one offered any credible reason to believe it.

John Blanton was an investigator with the federal Bureau of Narcotics and Dangerous Drugs (the forerunner of today's DEA) before joining John Hill's staff. His personal observations in Duval County convinced him that Parr was a user of methamphetamine, or "speed," in the weeks preceding his suicide.

"His behavior reflected the classic symptoms of methamphetamine use," Blanton said, and explained further:

> George would be hyperactive for a couple of days at a time, and he'd do strange things, like demanding food from restaurants in San Diego at three or four o'clock in the morning, when everyplace in town was closed, and then he'd sleep around the clock and start over again. He had hallucinations too. He called the sheriff's office and told them he had killed his wife. When the deputies came rushing over to his house he said, "I killed Eva. See, there's the blood, right there on the floor," but nothing was there. He fired shots at imaginary enemies and real people, and he kept floodlights burning around his house all night. His behavior was bizarre. His neighbors were really afraid of him; they didn't know what he might do next.

Commenting on the county's long tradition of bossism and corruption, Dan Tobin, Jr., then county judge but under indictment for misuse of public funds, told the *El Paso Times* in September 1975, "I was born into the system. If George said it was okay, then it was okay. Was there corruption? Not in the literal sense of the word. It was a political custom. Most people benefited from it."

Walter Meek put it more simply: "Many people in Duval County have been raised on corruption and they just don't know any better."

Donato Serna, the old Freedom Party warrior of the 1950s, was still angry about conditions in his county. "Ask the Parrs why other counties have progressed and Duval County hasn't," he told the *Houston Post*. "Ask them where all the money has gone."

Perhaps the most insightful commentary on the complex and contradictory character of the Duke of Duval came from Walter Meek, the man who was his lifelong friend but was in many ways his opposite. In a letter he wrote to Assistant U.S. Attorney George Kelt during the Carrillo trial, Meek drew on historian Will Durant's descriptions of Robert Walpole and William Pitt to paint a picture of his lifelong friend:

Robert Walpole was no saint; he was probably the most corrupt minister that England has ever had, but he was also one of the best. In that corrupt age only through corruption could wisdom rule.

When he ceased to talk politics, said Macaulay, he could talk of nothing but women, and he dilated on his favorite theme with a freedom which shocked even that plain-spoken generation.

— Will Durant (from *The Age of Voltaire*)

William Pitt used deception, calumny, intimidation, intrigue, ingratitude, perjury, treachery; these were the tools of the statesman's trade, and were to be judged not by preachers but by kings . . . and his success — which was England's — sanctified his sins and haloed his head.

— Will Durant (from *The Age of Voltaire*)

N.B.: A truer picture or more perfect evaluation of George Parr you will never find — his political side, that is — but strike "ingratitude" and "treachery" — they don't apply. And I doubt that his sins will ever be sanctified or his head haloed, but there was another and better side to him which endeared him to those who knew him best — and of which the general public was little aware.

WMM
September 20, 1975

George Parr remains a legend in Texas, and Box 13 will always be synonymous with election fraud. No one since George has been called the Duke of Duval. He seems to have retired the crown.

Appendix

OFFICE OF THE ATTORNEY GENERAL OF TEXAS
AUSTIN

GROVER SELLERS
ATTORNEY GENERAL

January 15, 1945

Honorable Franklin D. Roosevelt
The President of the United States
Washington, D. C.

Dear Mr. President:

Some years ago Mr. George B. Parr of Duval County
was convicted of evasion of income tax before
United States District Judge McMillan. He was
deprived of his citizenship and his term of conviction expired January 19, 1938. All taxes due
have long since been paid.

Mr. Parr now has pending before you an application
for restoration of his citizenship. Without reser-
vation, I endorse his application and respectfully
recommend its approval.

Sincerely yours

Grover Sellers
Attorney General

GS-s

LIEUTENANT GOVERNOR'S OFFICE
AUSTIN, TEXAS

JOHN LEE SMITH
LIEUTENANT GOVERNOR

January 15, 1945

Hon. Franklin D. Roosevelt
President of the United States of America
Washington, D. C.

My dear Mr. President:

On January 19, 1938, the sentence for income tax
evasion terminated for my friend George B. Parr of
San Diego, Duval County, Texas. It is my understanding
that Mr. Parr's citizenship, which was lost by him on
account of said conviction, has never been restored and
that he is very anxious to secure such clemency.

Mr. Parr was born and has spent practically all of his
life in South Texas. He is the son of the late Archie
Parr who served with distinction as a member of the
Texas Senate for some 20 years. During the past 7
years since the termination of Mr. Parr's sentence, he
has been very active in the business and civic affairs
of his native Duval County and generally over South
Texas. A restoration of Mr. Parr's citizenship to him
will, I am sure, meet with the universal approval of his
many friends and acquaintances in Texas.

Therefore I wish to take this opportunity to recommend
that the requested clemency be granted.

Yours very respectfully,

John Lee Smith
Lieutenant Governor of Texas

JLS:KB

General Land Office
State of Texas
Austin
14

January 16, 1945

BASCOM GILES, COMMISSIONER
[ALVIS VANDYGRIFF, CHIEF CLERK
  NOW IN ARMED FORCES]
DENNIS WALLACE, CHIEF CLERK

HIS EXCELLENCY, THE PRESIDENT OF THE UNITED STATES

Sir:

It is with no small degree of pleasure that I
join with a legion of good citizens of Texas in petition-
ing you for the restoration of citizenship to Mr. George
B. Parr, of San Diego, Duval County, Texas.

In making this appeal, I am prompted not only
by ties of a friendship extending over a decade, but by
an abiding faith in the honor and integrity of Mr. Parr,
whose conscientious efforts to demean himself as an
honorable and upright citizen, worthy of the trust that
is placed in him by his fellow men, who know him best,
have been noted and have impressed me with their
sincerity.

It is my belief that the conduct, demeanor and
habits of thought of Mr. Parr are those of an honest,
patriotic and upright citizen, who not only merits the
confidence and respect of his countrymen, but also the
honor of being their fellow citizen.

The blessing of American citizenship is not to
be lightly bestowed, nor capriciously withheld, and we who
seek its benefits for Mr. Parr do so with due appreciation
of its value, notwithstanding which, we unhesitatingly urge
its gift to him.

Respectfully submitted,

Bascom Giles
BASCOM GILES, COMMISSIONER
OF THE GENERAL LAND OFFICE

Giles:ks

Letters from Texas
officials requesting
President Roosevelt to
pardon George Parr . . .

STATE BOARD OF CONTROL
AUSTIN 11, TEXAS

January 16, 1945

Honorable Franklin D. Roosevelt
President of the United States
Washington, D. C.

My dear Mr. President:

Judge George B. Parr, of Duval County, was convicted for failure to pay income tax in the United States District Court for the Western District of Texas, and his conviction expired January 29, 1938; by reason of which he lost his citizenship, and I desire to concur in the endorsement of the application, along with many other citizens of this State, for the following reasons:

(1) Judge Parr and his distinguished Father and other members of the family, have rendered a service to the people of the Lower Rio Grande Valley, unequalled by that of any other family, and by reason of such humanitarian service, Judge Parr is entitled to a full measure of consideration that he may again render, unimpaired, his full duty as a citizen.

(2) For more than fifteen years, the writer was a prosecuting officer in this State, as District Attorney of the 112th Judicial District, and private prosecuting counsel for such organizations as the Texas Sheriff's Association, Texas Sheep and Goat Raisers' Association, and others of a similar nature and kind, and it is my deliberate judgment that as a matter of public policy, the full restoration of citizenship should be granted, after the penalty of the law has been paid.

Failure to pursue this practice often results in a breakdown of a law enforcing program, rather than a strengthening of the purposes of the law.

Therefore, I respectfully request that you grant the petition of Judge Parr for a restoration of his citizenship.

Respectfully submitted,

Weaver H. Baker

WHB/s

Comptroller of Public Accounts
State of Texas
Austin

IN YOUR REPLY PLEASE REFER
TO DIVISION NO _____
FILE NO _____

January 15, 1945

Honorable Franklin D. Roosevelt
White House
Washington, D. C.

My dear Mr. President:

It has been brought to my attention that Mr. Geo. B. Parr of Duval County, Texas, has long since served his term for an income tax evasion charge and that his citizenship has not been restored to him.

Mr. Parr is from one of the pioneer families of Texas. His father served a long and successful time in the State Senate of Texas. I do not believe that the best interests of the State can be served by withholding the restoration of his rights as a citizen.

His many friends throughout the State of Texas, especially in the broad Rio Grande Valley, would appreciate very much your extending to him this favor.

Sincerely,

Geo. H. Sheppard
Comptroller of Public Accounts

GHS:ms

RAILROAD COMMISSION OF TEXAS
AUSTIN

OLIN CULBERSON
CHAIRMAN

January 15, 1945

SIR:

It has come to my attention that Honorable George Parr of San Diego, Duval County, Texas has made application for restoration of his citizenship.

Having discharged the obligation which the Courts held he owed society and having returned to the place of his birth and continued to make an excellent citizen, I sincerely feel that Judge Parr's citizenship should have long since been restored to him.

I earnestly petition your Excellency to extend this recognition to a man who is invaluable to his community and state.

Very respectfully,

Olin Culberson, Chairman
Railroad Commission of Texas

His Excellency
The President of the United States of America
Washington, D. C.

TREASURY DEPARTMENT
STATE OF TEXAS
AUSTIN
January 15th,
1945.

JESSE JAMES
TREASURER

Honorable Franklin D. Roosevelt,
President of the United States,
Washington, D.C.,

Dear Mr. President:

My good friend George B. Parr, of San Diego,
Texas, is asking for a restoration of his citizenship which
he lost some years ago by reason of a conviction of income
tax evasion. His sentence ended on January 19th, 1938.

Mr. Parr has been a good friend of mine for many
years, as was his father, the late Senator Archie Parr,
who served in the Texas Senate for some fifteen or more years.

Since the end of his said sentence, Mr. Parr has
had no charges of any kind filed against him. He is very
popular in South Texas where he has lived all of his life.

I would therefore, like to join with Mr. Parr's
other many friends in Texas, in recommending that a favorable consideration be given his application.

Yours very respectfully,

[signature]

JJ/p.

COMMISSION
BRADY GENTRY, Chairman
REUBEN WILLIAMS
FRED E. KNETSCH

TEXAS HIGHWAY DEPARTMENT
Austin 26, Texas
January 16, 1945

STATE HIGHWAY ENGINEER
D. C. GREER
REFER TO FILE NO.

Honorable Franklin D. Roosevelt
The President of the United States
Washington, D. C.

Dear President Roosevelt:

Some years ago Mr. George B. Parr of Duval County, Texas,
was convicted in the Federal Court at San Antonio for
evasion of income tax and it is my information that
his term has long since expired and the tax liability
has been satisfied.

Mr. Parr is always cooperative with the State Highway
Department in our work in his section. He is an outstanding man in his community and as a citizen could
and would perform many worthwhile duties and obliga-
tions to our great Country.

May I join others in requesting that you extend full
citizenship to Mr. Parr.

Yours sincerely

[signature] Brady Gentry

Chairman
State Highway Commission

T. M. TRIMBLE
FIRST ASSISTANT
SUPERINTENDENT

T. F. WALKER
AUDITING AND ACCOUNTING

JOHN OLSEN
CENSUS

C. L. KUYKENDALL
CERTIFICATION

NELL TAYLOR PARMLEY
COLLEGE EXAMINER AND
PUBLIC SCHOOL MUSIC

MRS. BASCOM H. STORY
CORRESPONDENCE CLERK

J. J. BROWN
CRIPPLED CHILDREN

EDGAR ELLEN WILSON
ELEMENTARY EDUCATION

H. E. ROBINSON
EQUALIZATION

S. B. CULPEPPER
HEALTH EDUCATION

JOSEPH R. GRIGGS
HIGH SCHOOLS AND
CURRICULUM

MYRTLE L. TANNER
INFORMATION AND
STATISTICS

C. L. YARBROUGH
SAFETY EDUCATION

JOHN W. GUNSTREAM
RADIO AND VISUAL
EDUCATION

L. C. PROCTOR
SCHOOL PLANT AND
VISUAL EDUCATION

GORDON WORLEY
SPECIAL SUPERVISOR

H. A. GLASS
TEXTBOOKS

STATE
DEPARTMENT OF EDUCATION
L. A. WOODS, STATE SUPERINTENDENT

AUSTIN 11, TEXAS

January 15, 1945

The Honorable Franklin D. Roosevelt
President of the United States
White House
Washington, D. C.

My dear Mr. President:

It has been brought to my attention that my good friend,
George B. Parr of San Diego, Duval County, Texas, has not had his
citizenship restored since the termination of his sentence for
income tax evasion on January 19, 1938. This is approximately seven
years ago.

I have watched Mr. Parr during these seven years. He
is highly respected throughout South Texas where he has spent all
of his life to date. He comes from a pioneer Texas family. His
father, Senator Archie Parr, served in the Texas Senate for 20
years. To my knowledge, no criminal charge of any kind has been
filed against Mr. Parr since the termination of his sentence, and
I feel sure that it will meet with universal approval of his
friends throughout this State if and when his citizenship is
restored.

May I take this opportunity of personally recommending
such clemency.

Respectfully yours,

[signature]

State Superintendent of Education

LAW*f

The Senate of
The State of Texas
Austin

JAMES A. STANFORD
DISTRICT NO 20
AUSTIN

January 16, 1945

Honorable Franklin D. Roosevelt
President of the United States of America
Washington, D. C.

Dear Mr. President:

Mr. George B. Parr of San Diego, Duval County Texas,
does not live in my senatorial district; however, I have
known him for many years and am acquainted with his standing
not only in his section of the State but over Texas in general.

I understand that Mr. Parr has made application for
the restoration of his citizenship. Please permit me to
support Mr. Parr's application and to urge that his citizenship be restored at this time.

Sincerely yours

J. A. Stanford

James A. Stanford

JAS:vz
CC Mr. George B. Parr
San Diego, Texas

The Senate of
The State of Texas
Austin

ROGERS KELLEY
DISTRICT NO 27
EDINBURG

January 15, 1945.

Honorable Franklin D. Roosevelt,
President of the United States of America,
WASHINGTON, D. C.

Dear Mr. President:

It is my understanding that my old friend George B. Parr
of San Diego, Duval County, Texas, has filed an application for restoration of his citizenship which was lost
by him on account of a conviction for income tax evasion,
the term of the sentence for which expired on January 19th,
1938.

Mr. Parr is the son of the late Archie Parr, who served
the 27th District, the one which I now have the honor of
representing, for twenty years.

I wish to take this opportunity to recommend that the
requested clemency be granted.

Since the termination of his sentence some seven years ago
Mr. Parr has lead an exemplary life and no charge of any
kind has been filed against him. I know of no one in the
27th Senatorial District, which includes Eighteen South
Texas Counties, who would object to such clemency being
granted, and I know that Mr. Parr's many friends would
be delighted with such action.

Very respectfully yours,

Rogers Kelley

Rogers Kelley,
27th Senatorial District.

RK-vz.

The Senate of
The State of Texas
Austin

BOB BARKER
SECRETARY

January 15th,
1 9 4 5.

Honorable Franklin D. Roosevelt,
President of the United States of America,
Washington, D.C.,

Dear Franklin:

Some years ago my good friend, George
B. Parr, of Duval County, Texas, was convicted of
income tax evasion. His term expired January 19th,
1938, practically seven years ago. He is now making
application for restoration of his citizenship.

It has been my privilege and pleasure
to know George, and the other members of this pioneer
Texas family, for a great many years. He is one of
the sons of the late Senator Archie Parr, who served
with honor in the Texas Senate for twenty years.

Since the end of his sentence, George
has been very busy attending to his private business
in South Texas, but he always finds the necessary time
to devote to the best interests of his town, county,
state and nation.

A favorable consideration of my friend's
application will be very popular in Texas, and personally, I take great pleasure in recommending such
action.

With kindest personal regards, I remain,

Yours very cordially,

Bob Barker

BB/p.

The State of Texas,
County of Jim Wells

Before me, the undersigned authority, on this day personally appeared _____
Enriqueta Acero , who after being by me duly sworn did depose and say
as follows:

My name is Enriqueta Acero . I reside at 1700 So Aransas
(street)
Alice , Jim Wells , Texas. I am a quali-
(city)   (county)
fied voter of Jim Wells County, and vote in precinct number 13 .
My poll tax number is _____ . I did not vote in the August 28th primary election in Jim Wells County this year. I voted for _____
None for United States Senator from Texas. Further
deponent sayeth not.

x Enriqueta Acero

Sworn to and subscribed to before me the undersigned authority, a notary public in
and for Jim Wells County, Texas on this the 7 day of Septem-
ber, 1948.

Frank Perez Jr.
W. L. Poole Jr.
Witnesses

_____
Notary Public in and for _____
County, Texas.

*Affidavits by Duval County residents who stated that they did not vote in
the infamous 1948 "Box 13" election.*

The State of Texas,
County of Jim Wells

Before me, the undersigned authority, on this day personally appeared _____
Luis Salinas , who after being by me duly sworn did depose and say
as follows:

My name is Luis Salinas . I reside at 1129 Seabreeze
(street)
Alice , Jim Wells , Texas. I am a quali-
(city)   (county)
fied voter of Jim Wells County, and vote in precinct number 13 .
My poll tax number is _____ . I did not vote in the August 28th primary election in Jim Wells County this year. I voted for _____
None for United States Senator from Texas. Further
deponent sayeth not.

Luis Salinas

Sworn to and subscribed to before me the undersigned authority, a notary public in
and for Jim Wells County, Texas on this the 7 day of Septem-
ber, 1948.

W. L. Poole Jr.
Candelario Luis
F. Frank Perez Jr.
Witnesses

_____
Notary Public in and for _____
County, Texas.

The only check ever written to George Parr on the secret "Special Account" was this "salary advance" that wasn't on the water district's books and was never repaid. The endorsement is written in Parr's confident, flowing hand.

Index